Contents — Southern Sandstone Climbs

Introduction. 4
Other Information Sources 8
The Rockfax App 10
Acknowledgements. 12

Southern Sandstone Logistics 14
Getting Around and Map 18
Accommodation 20
Pubs 22
Climbing Walls and Gear Shops 24
Guiding and Climbing Courses. 26
Other Activities 28

Southern Sandstone Climbing 30
Code of Practice. 32
Ethics and Climbing Styles. 34
Top-roping. 38
Gear 42
Grades 46
Bolts 48
Access 50
Volunteering Groups. 54
HRMG. 56
Top50 58
Destination Planner 60

Bowles Rocks. 64
Eridge Rocks. 106
Harrison's Rocks 160
High Rocks 272
High Rocks Annexe 350
Rusthall and Tunbridge Wells Commons 360
Happy Valley 364
Bull's Hollow. 384
Toad Rocks 402
Mount Edgcumbe Rocks 418
Bassett's Farm Rocks 424
Under Rockes 436
Stone Farm 448

Route Index. 478
Map and General Index 488

Sara Ortiz climbing the fantastic *Moonlight Arete* (5a *4c*) - *page 223* - on the Sewer Wall at Harrison's Rocks.

Rob Greenwood bouldering out the starting moves on *Mick's Wall Arete* (6c+ *6a*) - *page 80* - at the Kemp's Delight area of Bowles Rocks. Photo: Rob Greenwood.

Introduction   Southern Sandstone Climbs

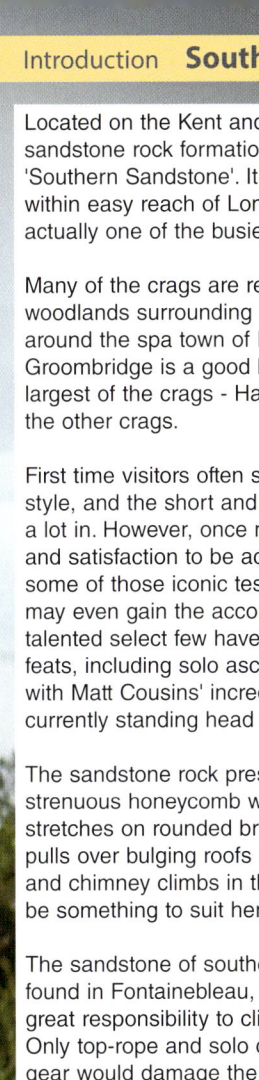

Located on the Kent and Sussex border are the mysterious sandstone rock formations of southeast England commonly known as 'Southern Sandstone'. It is an unlikely place to look for rock but, being within easy reach of London and Brighton, Southern Sandstone is actually one of the busiest climbing destinations in the UK.

Many of the crags are remarkably hidden, tucked away in valleys and woodlands surrounding by rolling hills and lush, green countryside around the spa town of Royal Tunbridge Wells. The small village of Groombridge is a good base when visiting the area, close to the largest of the crags - Harrison's Rocks - and within easy reach of all the other crags.

First time visitors often struggle with the unique and delicate climbing style, and the short and intense nature of the climbs means they pack a lot in. However, once mastered, there is a great deal of pleasure and satisfaction to be achieved by pushing your grade and tackling some of those iconic testpieces. Spend enough time here and you may even gain the accolade of being called a 'sandstoner'! A highly talented select few have honed their skills to pull off some amazing feats, including solo ascents of some of sandstone's hardest routes, with Matt Cousins' incredible solo of *Chimaera* (8a+) at High Rocks currently standing head and shoulders above the rest!

The sandstone rock presents many unique climbing features - strenuous honeycomb walls, crimpy technical masterpieces, tenuous stretches on rounded breaks, thuggy struggles up cracks, powerful pulls over bulging roofs and some of the most interesting off-width and chimney climbs in the country. Whatever your style, there should be something to suit here.

The sandstone of southeast England is a close relation to the rock found in Fontainebleau, but even softer. This delicate nature brings great responsibility to climbers to ensure it is not damaged or eroded. Only top-rope and solo climbing is allowed since any lead climbing gear would damage the rock too much. There are some simple and important rules to be followed known as the Southern Sandstone Code of Practice - see page 32 for more information. Unlike any other climbing area in the UK, the specific requirements regarding access, gear, top-rope set-up and climbing technique on Southern Sandstone are vital to help preserve the rock for present and future generations of climbers.

Southern Sandstone caters for all, and the general climbing culture is friendly and laid back, with many indulging in weekend picnics while top-roping classics at the various crags. Those who make the journey will be pleasantly surprised to find an abundance of memorable and highly-regarded climbs which sit happily amongst some of the best technical climbing the UK.

Daimon Beail, July 2017

Coverage

This book contains all the information covering the best climbing on the major crags of the Southern Sandstone area. The big five of Bowles Rocks, Eridge Rocks, Harrison's Rocks, High Rocks and Stone Farm are displayed in all their glory with big photo-topos, overview photos, detailed maps, character symbols and full text descriptions. The same treatment is given to the smaller venues; Happy Valley, Bull's Hollow, High Rocks Annexe, Bassett's Farm and Under Rockes. The bouldering at Toad Rocks and Mount Edgcumbe make their guidebook debut.

The book is more than a traditional selective guidebook since it covers the vast majority of routes on the main and minor crags in the area. It can not claim to be 'comprehensive' though since there are climbs that have been done which aren't described and crags which have been omitted. These are mainly banned crags, minor venues with difficult or unknown access, climbs that have become too overgrown to be viable or long high traverses that have been climbed but see little interest these days and have exacting set-up requirements for top-roping.

The coverage sees a switch in grading policy with the much lamented Sandstone Tech Grade being given a minor role in favour of the more versatile and well know sport grade for the top-rope routes. With the use of bouldering pads now being widespread, many of the shorter routes have been reassessed as boulder problems and given Font bouldering grades in common with the rest of the country. The bouldering coverage extends to boulder problems that have mutated from routes with overgrown top-outs or are notable problems in their own right. See page 46 for more on grades.

More information on crags and access can be found on the following web sites:
BMC - thebmc.co.uk/modules/RAD/
SSC - www.southernsandstoneclimbs.co.uk
UKClimbing - ukclimbing.com/logbook/
Rockfax - rockfax.com

Guidebook Footnote
The inclusion of a climbing area in this guidebook does not mean that you have a right of access or the right to climb upon it. The descriptions of routes within this guide are recorded for historical reasons only and no reliance should be placed on the accuracy of the description. The grades set in this guide are a fair assessment of the difficulty of the climbs. Climbers who attempt a route of a particular standard should use their own judgment as to whether they are proficient enough to tackle that route. This book is not a substitute for experience and proper judgment. The authors, publisher and distributors of this book do not recognise any liability for injury or damage caused to, or by, climbers, third parties, or property arising from such persons seeking reliance on this guidebook as an assurance for their own safety.

Emma Harrington attempting an unconventional method on the final moves on *Engagement Wall* (6c *6a*) - *page 308* - on the Advertisement Wall at High Rocks.

Southern Sandstone Climbs — Other Information Sources

Climbing on the southern sandstone outcrops has been documented since 1926. We are very grateful to everyone who has worked on previous guidebooks and to all who have documented their climbs in the area. A particular mention needs to be given to the **UKClimbing.com** crag moderators for their time and effort moderating their particular crags.

Guidebooks
Southern Sandstone and the Sea Cliffs of South-East England
Mike Vetterlein, Robin Mazinke (Climbers' Club 2008, reprint 2014)

Southern Sandstone Bouldering
James O'Neil and Ben Read (2011)

Sandstone Climbing in South East England
David Atchison-Jones (Jingo Wobbly Guide Books 2010)

Bowles Rocks - A Climbing Guide
Steve Turner and Marion Williams

Websites
ukclimbing.com - The UKC Logbook route database for all areas covered in this guidebook.

rockfax.com - Information on Rockfax publications and including an access blog.

www.southernsandstoneclimbs.co.uk - A central point of information for all things southern sandstone.

sandstonevolunteers.org.uk - Information on the sandstone volunteers group and their activities.

thebmc.co.uk/modules/RAD/ - Latest access information to the climbing areas in England and Wales.

New Routes
The paper book that use to be kept at the old Evolution Climbing Wall in Groombridge has now been retired. These days online databases like UKC logbooks are the best place to submit new route information **ukclimbing.com/logbook/**

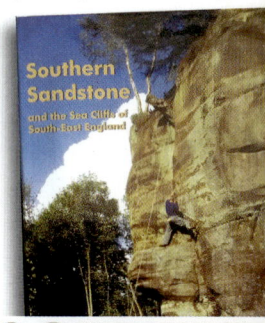

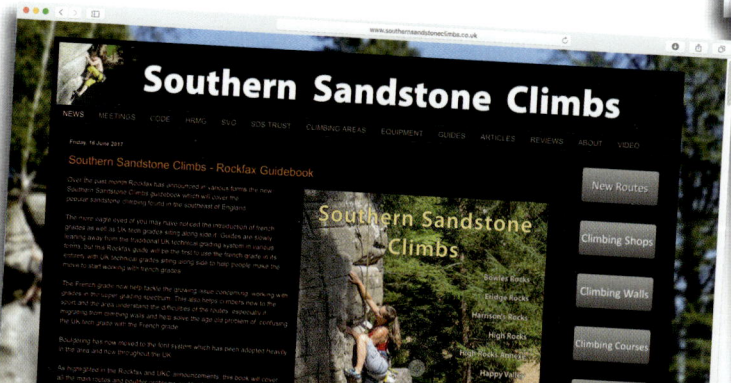

Advertising Directory — Southern Sandstone Climbs

We are grateful to the following companies who have supported this guidebook.

Alauzon - *Page 55*
alauzon.com

Awesome Walls - *Page 2*
awesomewalls.co.uk

Boulder Brighton - *Page 29*
boulderbrighton.com

Castle Climbing Centre - *Page 27*
castle-climbing.co.uk

Chimera Climbing Centre - *Page 21*
chimeraclimbing.com

Reading Climbing Centre - *Back flap*
climbingcentres.co.uk

Cold Mountain Kit
- Inside back cover and page 37
coldmountainkit.com

DMM - *Outside back cover*
dmmclimbing.com

Nuts4climbing - *Inside front cover*
nuts4climbing.com

Paramo - *Page 57*
paramo-clothing.com

Rock On - *Page 49*
rockonclimbing.co.uk

Vauxwall - *Page 25*
vauxwallclimbing.co.uk

Alex Armitage climbing *Pig's Nose* (5c *5a*) - *page 92* - at the Pig's Nose Area of Bowles Rocks.

Southern Sandstone Climbs — The Rockfax App

This Southern Sandstone Climbs guidebook is also available on the Rockfax App which brings together all the Rockfax climbing information with UKC Logbooks and presents it in a user-friendly package for use on Apple iOS devices (Android version available in 2017).

The heart of the app is the Rockfax crag and route information which is downloaded by way of paid in-app purchases for individual crags, or bundles of crags, in 'Areas' which correspond roughly to printed guidebooks. You can purchase each crag or area individually, or the whole book. The main data on the app is downloaded and stored on your device so you don't need any signal to be able to read the descriptions and see the topos and maps. There is a free sample crag for each area and some of these are quite extensive, enabling you to get a really good impression of what the app is like without shelling out any money.

The Rockfax App itself is a free download and incredibly useful in its own right. It contains a detailed crag map linked to the UKClimbing crags database. The map also displays all the 4,000+ listings from the UKClimbing Directory of climbing walls, outdoor shops, climbing clubs, outdoor-specific accommodation and instructors and guides amongst others.

To find the app, search for 'Rockfax app' in Google or in the appropriate app store.

UKC Logbooks

An incredibly popular method of logging your climbing is to use the **UKClimbing.com** logbooks system. This database lists more than 404,000 routes, over 21,400 crags worldwide and, so far, more than 33,000 users have recorded over 5.4 million ascents! To set up your own logbook, all you need to do is register at **UKClimbing.com** and click on the logbook tab. Once set up you will be able to record every ascent you make, when you did it, what style you climbed it in and who you did it with. Each entry has a place for your own notes. You can also add your vote to the grade/star system linked to a database on the Rockfax site used by the guidebook writers. The logbook can be private, public or restricted to your own climbing partners only.

The Rockfax App can be linked to your **UKClimbing.com** user account and logbook so that you can record your activity while at the crag and look at photos, comments and votes on the routes. To do this you will need a 3G/4G data connection. You can also look at the UKC logbooks to see if anyone has climbed your chosen route recently to check on conditions.

Symbol, Map and Topo Key — Southern Sandstone Climbs

Route Symbols

- **1** — A good route/problem.
- **2** — A very good route/problem, one of the best on the crag.
- **3** — A brilliant route/problem, one of the best in the area.
- **Top 50** — A route of great significance in sandstone climbing in southeast England - see page 58.
- Technical climbing requiring good balance and technique, or complex and tricky moves.
- Powerful climbing; roofs, steep rock, low lock-offs or long moves off small holds.
- Sustained climbing; either lots of hard moves or steep rock giving pumpy climbing.
- Fingery climbing with significant small holds on the hard sections.
- Fluttery climbing often associated with highball bouldering or scary top-roping.
- A long reach is helpful, or even essential, for one or more of the moves.
- Sloping holds may be encountered.
- Graunchy climbing, wide cracks or awkward thrutchy moves.
- A sit-down start for a boulder problem.
- A dynamic move ('dyno') may be required.
- Loose or friable holds or vegetated rock may be encountered.

Crag Symbols

- **14 min** — Angle of the approach walk to the crag with approximate time.
- **Lots of sun** — Approximate time that the crag is in the direct sun (when it is shining).
- **Green** — The rock is often green or prone to bad conditions.
- **Seepage** — The crag suffers from seepage and may be wet and unclimbable in winter and spring.
- **Restrictions** — Some or all of the routes are affected by an access problem. Details in the crag information.
- **Deserted** - Currently under-used and usually quiet. Fewer good routes or remote and smaller areas.
- **Quiet** - Less popular sections on major crags, or good buttresses with awkward approaches.
- **Busy** - Places you will seldom be alone, especially at weekends. Good routes and easy access.
- **Crowded** - The most popular sections of the most popular crags which are always busy.

Topo Key

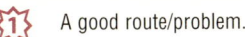

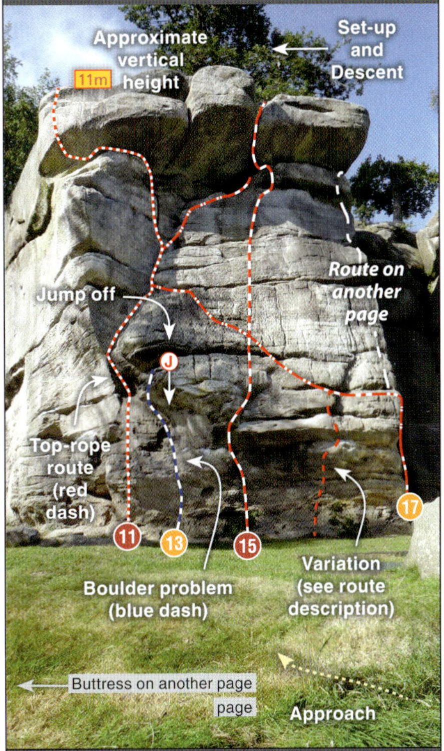

- Approximate vertical height (11m)
- Set-up and Descent
- Route on another page
- Jump off
- Top-rope route (red dash)
- Boulder problem (blue dash)
- Variation (see route description)
- Buttress on another page
- Approach

Map Key

- N
- A crag page
- Path
- GPS Coordinates of parking
- Wooded area
- Pub
- Buildings
- Campsite
- A Roads
- A crag on another page
- B Roads
- Train station
- Town/village
- QR code for smartphone navigation
- Railway
- Scale

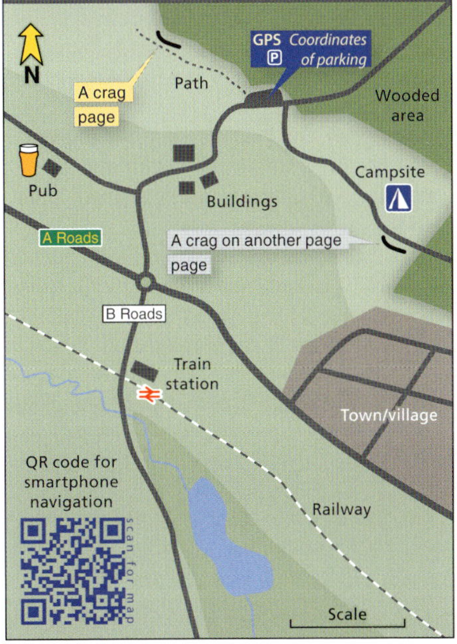

Southern Sandstone Climbs — Acknowledgements

This guide has been a labour of love spanning the past five years. The aim has been to produce a book worthy of promoting Southern Sandstone's unique climbs and the great sandstone environment while stressing the special conservation requirements. Much work has been undertaken to help move sandstone climbing forward in a new and positive direction particularly with regard to grading.

The first person I need to thank is Emma Harrington. Without her hard work, dedication, help with the project and support over the years, this guide would certainly not be what it is today. Emma was heavily involved behind the scenes at all stages. She organised photo-shoots, as well as climbing and posing for much-needed action shots herself. She assisted with the endless route testing, proofing and checking data. Emma is also a member of the HRMG (see page 56), contributed also towards the current Code of Practice (see page 32) and jointly runs www.southernsandstoneclimbs.co.uk to help promote information on all aspects of southern sandstone climbing. Jayda, the Labrador, has also been a big part of this and has patiently been with us on many a trip for photo-shoots, crag research and crag maintenance work.

Emma and Jayda

Tim Skinner, a true 'Sandstoner' and walking encyclopaedia of sandstone climbing, needs a special mention as he was my guru and guide when I first arrived on the sandstone scene back in the late 1990s. Many thanks to all those who have been out on the rock with me and those who have kindly posed for action shots over the years. Adrian Paisley deserves a special thanks for the days climbing and especially for helping with the Toad Rocks clear-up project. Zara Bloomfield has posed for photos and helped with clear-up projects and has also been out with us for many enjoyable days on the rock. Thanks to Robin Mazinke and Sarah Goodman - both keen Sandstoners, especially Robin who has climbed almost every route in the area within reason! Tom Gore has supplied me with up-to-date information on his ascents and has his ear to the ground concerning other new developments. Ben Read has offered valuable route information and Laurence Reading has helped on the new section unearthed at Bowles Rocks. Sarah Cullen for access to the now retired new routes books.

Many thanks to the Rockfax Team, especially Alan James for green lighting the project back in 2012 and being patient with me whilst it was being produced; his amazing work on the maps and for taking this book past the finishing line. Stephen Horne for his late night technical support responses and wizardry throughout the process.

Thanks to those who have supplied photos for the book - Tim Skinner, Rob Greenwood, Neal Grundy, Ben Hall, Szymon Dziukiewicz, Amy Wiggins and Richard Enticknap. I am also very grateful to Rebecca Ting for her amazing detailed proofing work.

Finally to all those people who have helped in whatever aspect however big or small, I hope you enjoy this guide.

Daimon Beail, July 2017

Acknowledgements — Southern Sandstone Climbs

Daimon Beail on *Camel* (**f6B+**) - *page 78* - on the Fandango Wall at Bowles Rocks. Photo: Emma Harrington.

About the Author

Daimon Beail has been involved with guidebook production since the late 90s and in particular with Rockfax since 2003 producing numerous guides to Deep Water Soloing on Mallorca. He became a sandstone climber in the late 90s and became mesmerised by its unique characteristics and climbing styles. Daimon is a member of the HRMG (see page 56) and contributed towards the current Code of Practice published by the BMC as well as undertaking much needed volunteering work at various crags. He jointly runs www.southernsandstoneclimbs.co.uk with Emma Harrington.

Southern Sandstone Logistics

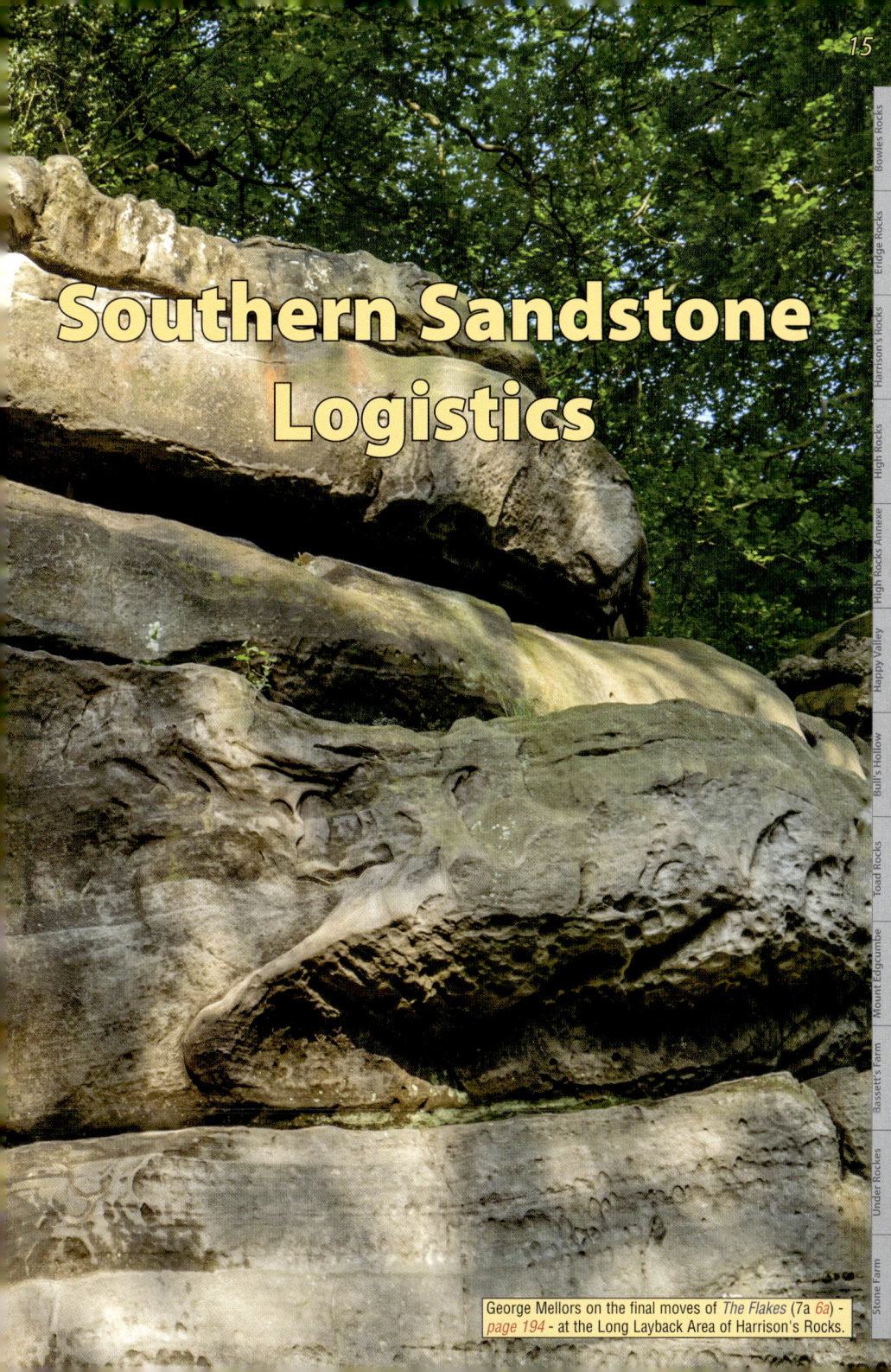

George Mellors on the final moves of *The Flakes* (7a *6a*) - *page 194* - at the Long Layback Area of Harrison's Rocks.

Southern Sandstone Logistics

Emergencies and Search and Rescue
In the event of an accident requiring assistance:
Dial 999
As the area is low-lying, standard ambulance services may well be all that is needed. For more extreme circumstances you should advise the 999 service that Search and Rescue may be required.

Search and Rescue
The two relevant local search and rescue services are charitable organisations dedicated to assisting the emergency services where the circumstances are too difficult for a straightforward ambulance rescue.
Kent Search and Rescue - ksar.co.uk
Sussex Search and Rescue - www.sussar.org

Mobile Phones
The area is well covered by mobile phone signals. Occasionally there are black spots and Harrison's carpark is sometimes bad in this respect. Please remember that even with little, or no signal on your phone, you may still be able to make an emergency call since these are channelled through all available networks.

Tourist Information Centres
If you are short of ideas about what to do on a wet day or need some accommodation, take a look at the Tourist Information Centres listed below; they contain a lot more useful information than it is possible to include in these pages.

Tunbridge Wells - Unit 2, The Corn Exchange, Royal Tunbridge Wells, TN2 5TE
Tel: 01892 515 675   visittunbridgewells.com

East Grinstead - Library Buildings, West Street, East Grinstead RH19 4SR
Tel: 01342 410121   eastgrinstead.gov.uk/tourism/

More information can be found at visitsoutheastengland.com and visitkent.co.uk

When to Go
Climbing on sandstone is possible all year round as long as it is dry, but the best season for most of the crags is between spring and late autumn. Crags like Stone Farm and Bowles Rocks do well in the winter and dry out quickly after rain, whereas many of the other crags take a lot longer to come into condition, particularly if the foliage is dense. It is important to remember that you should not climb on wet sandstone as it becomes more brittle and prone to damage when wet.

Yearly Averages	Jan	Feb	Mar	Apr	May	Jun	Jul	Aug	Sep	Oct	Nov	Dec
Average Max Temp (°C)	7.5	7.6	10.3	13.0	16.5	19.1	21.2	21.5	18.8	15.0	10.9	8.0
Average Min Temp (°C)	2.1	1.8	3.5	4.9	8.0	10.7	12.8	12.7	10.7	8.1	4.8	2.6
Average Rain Days/Month	13	10	10	9	8	7	7	8	10	12	12	13

Grant Dobson pulling through the powerful moves of *The Leaf* (**f6B+**) on the Yew Crack Buttress at Eridge Rocks. This is a sit-start to *Tortoise on a Spin Out* (7a *6b*) - *page 130* - which finishes at the first break. The top-outs at Eridge have become more difficult to negotiate in recent years, which has led to an increase in the popularity of these hybrid boulder problem starts.

Southern Sandstone Logistics — Getting Around and Map

The Southern Sandstone crags are mostly on the border of Sussex and Kent, close to London and Brighton, with Royal Tunbridge Wells being the closest town to many of the crags.

Getting Around

The approach descriptions are written assuming that you are in a car and are approaching from either Royal Tunbridge Wells, or East Grinstead for Stone Farm. The parking spots are indicated with a precise GPS location in the form of two decimal numbers as in the sample blue box. QR codes have been included with the approach maps which can be scanned with your mobile device to open direct into a navigation app.

GPS 51.106280
P 0.188631

Public Transport

It is possible to get to many of the more popular sandstone crags by public transport.

Trains and Buses - The stations in Royal Tunbridge Wells and Eridge are well located for most of the crags, with a bit of a walk. There are good bus services as well. Check - traveline.info

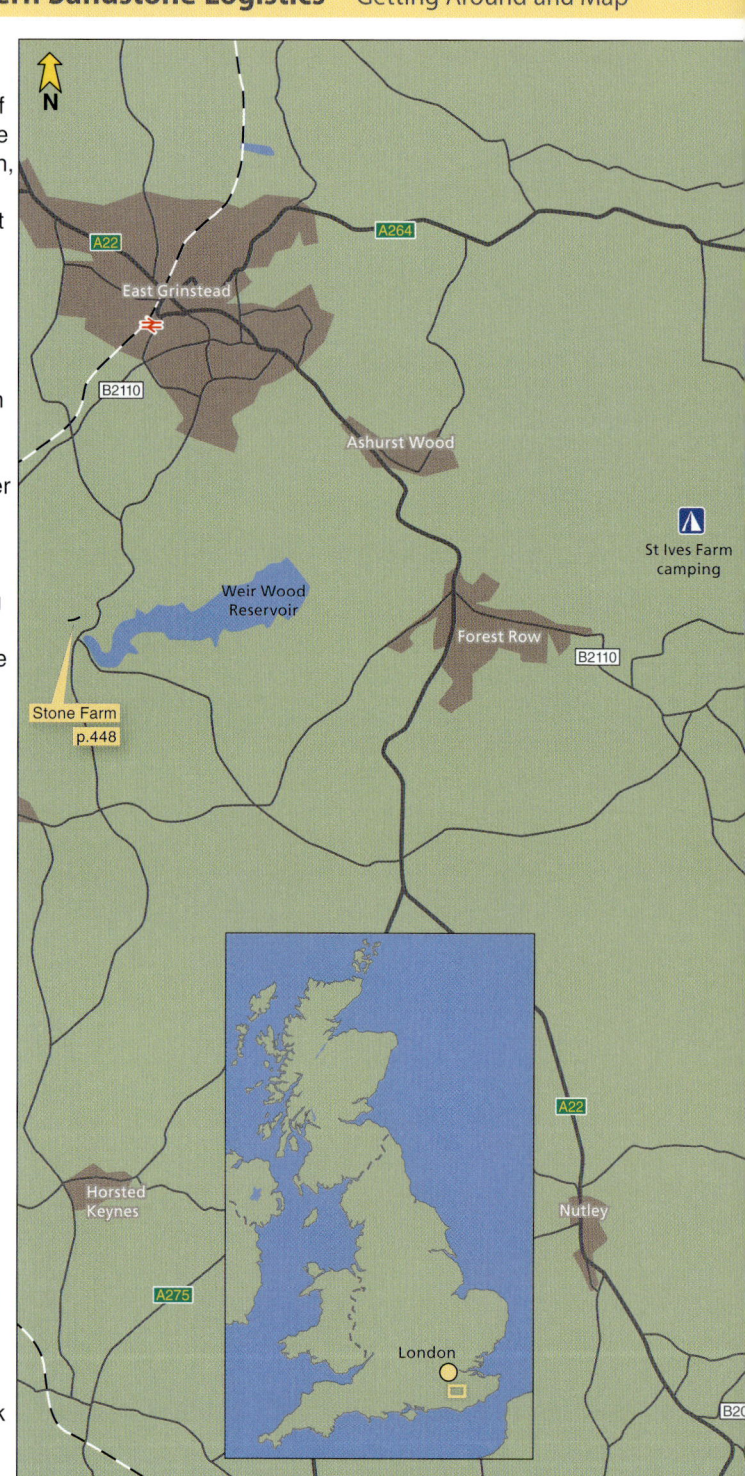

Getting Around and Map — Southern Sandstone Logistics

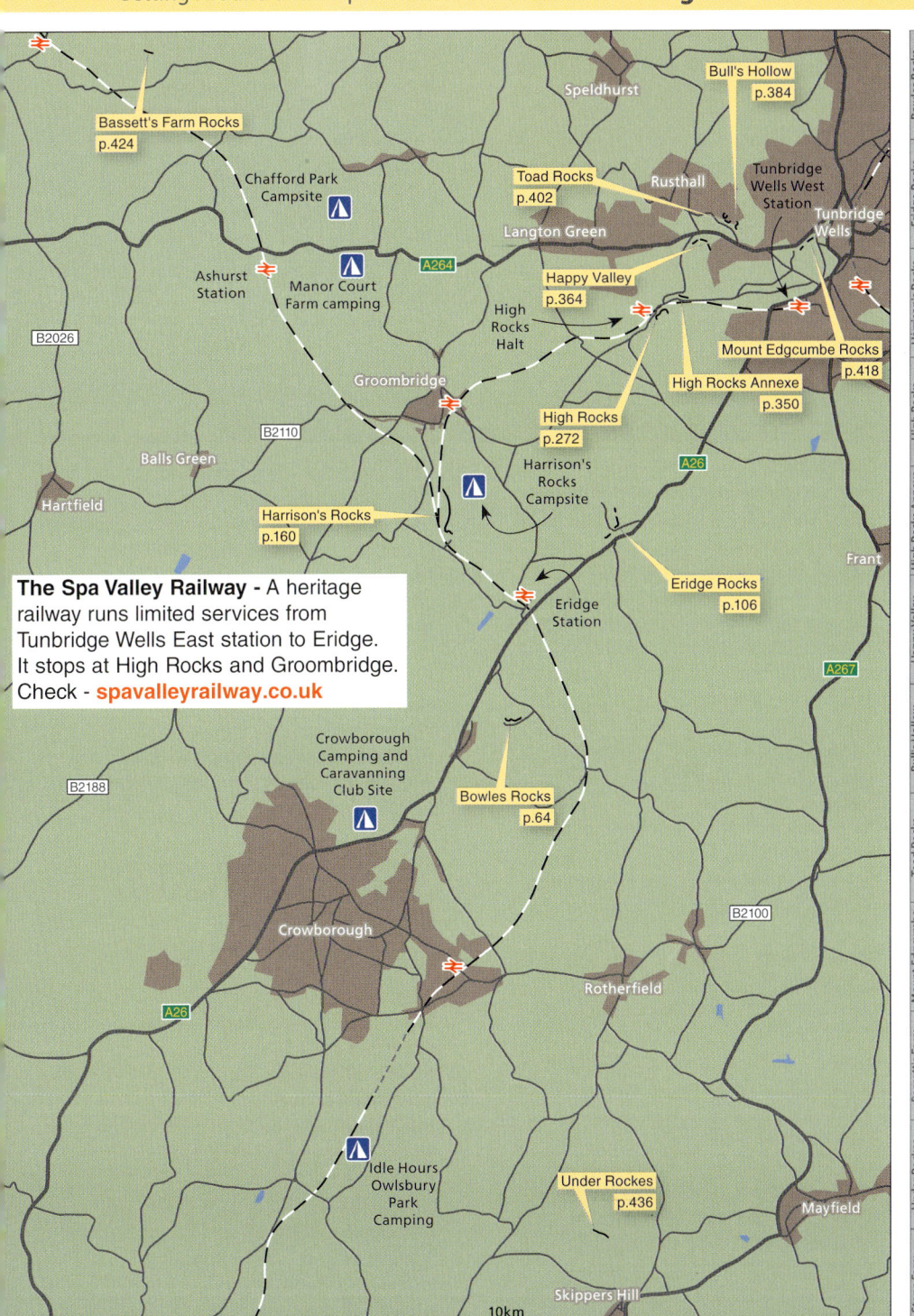

Southern Sandstone Logistics — Accommodation

Camping at Harrison's Rocks.

Campsites

Harrison's Rocks Campsite/Birchden Wood Camping – *See page 162*
forestry.gov.uk
A 16-pitch campsite allocated on a first come first served basis. Toilet and washing-up facilities available, but no showers. Purchase your ticket from the pay and display machine. Camping fees do not include car parking.

Manor Court Farm - *See page 18*
Ashurst, Tunbridge Wells. Tel: 01892 740210
manorcourtfarm.co.uk
On a working farm with views to the Ashdown Forest. Tents, campervans and caravans welcome. Shower, washing facilities and logs for the campfire sites.

St Ives Farm Campsite - *See page 18*
Butcherfield Lane, Hartfield.
Tel: 01892 770213 stivesfarm.co.uk
A secluded family site situated midway between Stone Farm and Groombridge. Tents, campervans and caravans. Minimum charge for 2 nights at weekends and 3 for Bank Holiday weekends.

Chafford Park Campsite - *See page 18*
Ashurst, Tunbridge Wells
Tel: 01892 740222 chaffordpark.co.uk
Located just off the A264, between Tunbridge Wells and East Grinstead. A small tents-only site with showers.

Crowborough Camping and Caravanning Club Site - *See page 18*
Goldsmith Recreation Ground, Eridge Road, Crowborough. Tel : 01892 664827
Near the A26 on the north of Crowborough, close to Bowles Rocks. Tents, campervans and caravans.

Idle Hours Owlsbury Park - *See page 18*
Hadlow Down Road, Crowborough
Tel: 07787945667
South of Crowborough close to Under Rockes. No groups of under 25s. Full facilities.

Self-Catering Accommodation
The websites below all advertise self-catering accommodation in and around the Royal Tunbridge Wells area.

homeaway.co.uk
kentandsussexcottages.co.uk
cottages.com
sykescottages.co.uk
ownersdirect.co.uk
mulberrycottages.com
countrycottagesonline.com
hollambys.co.uk
lovecottages.co.uk
britainsfinest.co.uk

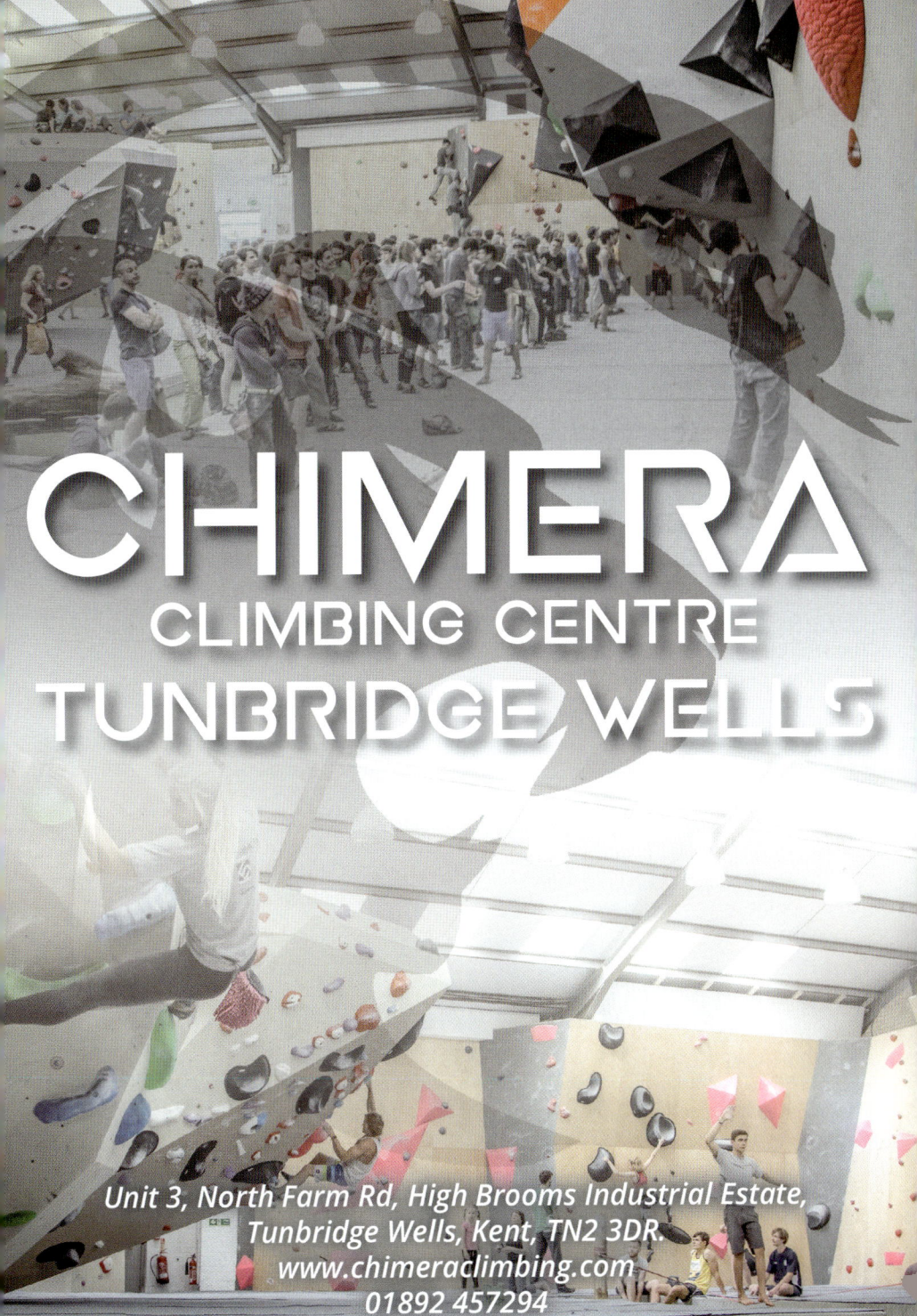

Southern Sandstone Logistics — Pubs

Harrison's, Eridge and Bowles Area

The Junction Inn - See *page 162*
Park View, Station Road, Groombridge.
Tel: 01892 864275
junctioninngroombridge.co.uk
Near Harrison's. Beer garden available.

The picturesque Crown Inn in Groombrdge.

The Crown Inn - See *page 162*
Groombridge. Tel: 01892 864742
thecrowngroombridge.com
Cosy pub near Harrison's. Has an outside space overlooking the village green.

The Huntsman - See *page 162*
Groombridge Lane, Eridge.
Tel: 01892 864258. Good for Harrison's and Eridge Rocks. Situated next to Eridge train station.

The Nevill Crest and Gun - *See page 107*
Eridge Road, Eridge. Tel: 01892 864209.
nevillcrestandgun.co.uk
Near Eridge Rocks. Historic pub with garden for those summer days.

Tunbridge Wells Area

The Hare
Langton Road, Langton Green, Tunbridge Wells. Tel: 01892 862419
hare-tunbridgewells.co.uk
Traditional English country pub with large garden. Dogs welcome.

High Rocks - See *page 274*
High Rocks. Tel: 01892 515532
highrocks.co.uk
By the crag. Weddings take place here frequently during the summer.

The Beacon - See *page 362*
Tea Garden Lane, Tunbridge Wells.
Tel: 01892 524252 the-beacon.co.uk
Good pub near Happy Valley.

Toad Rock Retreat - See *page 362*
1 Upper Street, Tunbridge Wells.
Tel: 01892 520818
toadrockretreattunbridgewells.co.uk
Situated next to the parking for Toad Rocks and Bull's Hollow. Traditional pub with beer garden available.

The Mount Edgcumbe - See *page 362*
The Common, Tunbridge Wells.
Tel: 01892 618854
themountedgcumbe.com
Situated next to Mount Edgcumbe Rocks. Pub and restaurant with secluded garden. Dogs welcome on leads.

Bassett's Farm Area

The Bottle House Inn - *See page 424*
Coldharbour Road, Penshurst.
Tel: 01892 870306.
thebottlehouseinnpenshurst.co.uk
Country pub, which serves seasonal food and has a large garden.

The Spotted Dog
Saints Hill, Penshurst. Tel: 01892 870253
spotteddogpub.com
Small 15th century pub.

Stone Farm Area

The Old Dunnings Mill
Dunning's Road, East Grinstead.
Tel: 01342 821080. olddunningsmill.co.uk
An extended 15th century pub and old mill.

The Cat Inn
North Lane, West Hoathly.
Tel: 01342 810369. catinn.co.uk
A 16th century pub with an outside terrace.

Daimon Beail re-living the traumatic birthing experience on *Sapper* (5b 5a) - *page 83* - at the Serenade Arete area of Bowles Rocks. Daimon is performing a 'clip-up' to protect those final moves - see page 40.

Climbing Walls

There is one climbing wall local to the sandstone area and lots more in London and Brighton. A few are listed below. More walls can be found at
ukclimbing.com/listings

Chimera Climbing Centre - *see page 21*
3 North Farm Road,
Tunbridge Wells
TN2 3DR.
Tel: 01892 457294   **chimeraclimbing.com**

Modern bouldering facility with competition wall, roof section, top-out boulders and a dedicated training room. The closest bouldering centre to sandstone.

The Castle Climbing Centre
- *see page 27*
Green Lanes, London N4
2HA. Tel: 020 8211 7000
castle-climbing.co.uk

A huge wall in a Victorian water pumping station. Spread over 5 floors, over 450 roped and lead routes between 8m and 13m and a range of bouldering and training rooms.

Vauxwall Climbing Centre - *see opposite*
Arch 46 - 47a, South Lambeth
Road, Vauxhall, London, SW8
1SR. Tel: 020 7160 0248
vauxwallclimbing.co.uk

A modern bouldering centre located in the arches of Vauxhall train station with good train and underground links.

Boulder Brighton Climbing Centre
- *see page 29*
Victoria Road
Trading Estate,
Portslade, Brighton,
BN41 1XQ. Tel:
01273 422408   **boulderbrighton.com**

A large modern bouldering centre with walls of a variety of angles - slabs, overhangs, a cave and a top-out boulder. Has a dedicated training room.

Gear Shops

If you are short of gear, need to top up on chalk, looking for a new pair of boots, then consider the shops listed below.
More shops can be found at
ukclimbing.com/listings

Cold Mountain Kit - *see page 37*
44 Tower Bridge Road,
London, SE1 4TR
Tel: 020 7740 3393
coldmountainkit.com

Visit store and online store available.
Specialists in big wall equipment. Stocks climbing clothing and climbing equipment.

Rock On - *see page 49*
Mile End Climbing Wall,
Haverfield Road, London,
E3 5BE
Tel: 020 898 150 66
rockonclimbing.co.uk

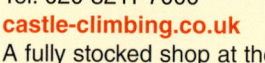

Stocks climbing equipment and clothing.

The Castle Climbing Centre
- *see page 27*
Green Lanes, London N4 2HA.
Tel: 020 8211 7000
castle-climbing.co.uk
A fully stocked shop at the
Castle Climbing Wall.

Cotswold Outdoor
95-97 Mount Pleasant Road, Royal
Tunbridge Wells
cotswoldoutdoor.com

Gearshack
Fullers Passage, 19 High Street, Lewes
gearshack.co.uk

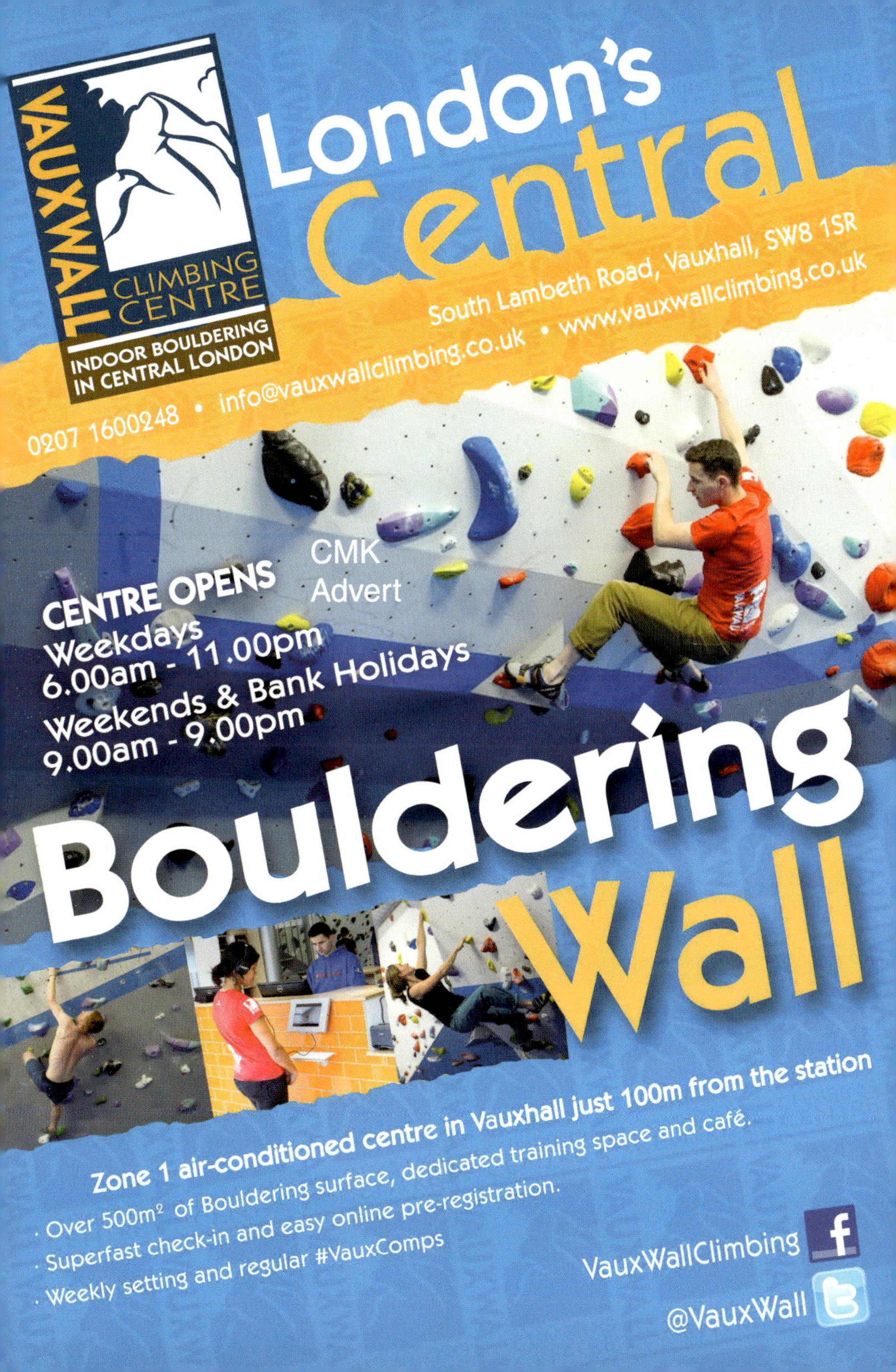

VAUXWALL CLIMBING CENTRE
INDOOR BOULDERING IN CENTRAL LONDON

0207 1600248 • info@vauxwallclimbing.co.uk

London's Central Bouldering Wall

South Lambeth Road, Vauxhall, SW8 1SR • www.vauxwallclimbing.co.uk

CMK Advert

CENTRE OPENS
Weekdays
6.00am - 11.00pm
Weekends & Bank Holidays
9.00am - 9.00pm

Zone 1 air-conditioned centre in Vauxhall just 100m from the station
- Over 500m² of Bouldering surface, dedicated training space and café.
- Superfast check-in and easy online pre-registration.
- Weekly setting and regular #VauxComps

VauxWallClimbing
@VauxWall

Southern Sandstone Logistics — Guiding and Climbing Courses

Nuts4Climbing
- See inside front cover
Merlin's Cottage, Motts Mill,
Groombridge, TN3 9PE
Tel: 01892 860670
nuts4climbing.co.uk

Climbing courses are located outside on the sandstone outcrops and include taster sessions, introduction courses, personal training, family and school courses.

Rock climbing courses and teaching is common place on sandstone. Here a class is being undertaken by one of the instructors at Bowles Rocks.

Bowles Outdoor Centre
bowles.ac
Climbing courses for all ages next to Bowles Rocks.

Extreme Ventures
extremeventures.co.uk
Climbing courses for all ages specialising in sandstone techniques

Hatt Adventures
thehatt.co.uk/adventures
Introductory and intermediate climbing courses and sandstone rope-work courses.

Kent and Sussex Climbing Ltd
ksclimbing.co.uk
Courses on sandstone. Taster sessions, private tuition and climbing tips.

Skyhook Adventure
skyhookadventure.com
Skills courses for adults at Harrison's Rocks. Beginners and intermediate courses for sandstone set-up and climbing skills.

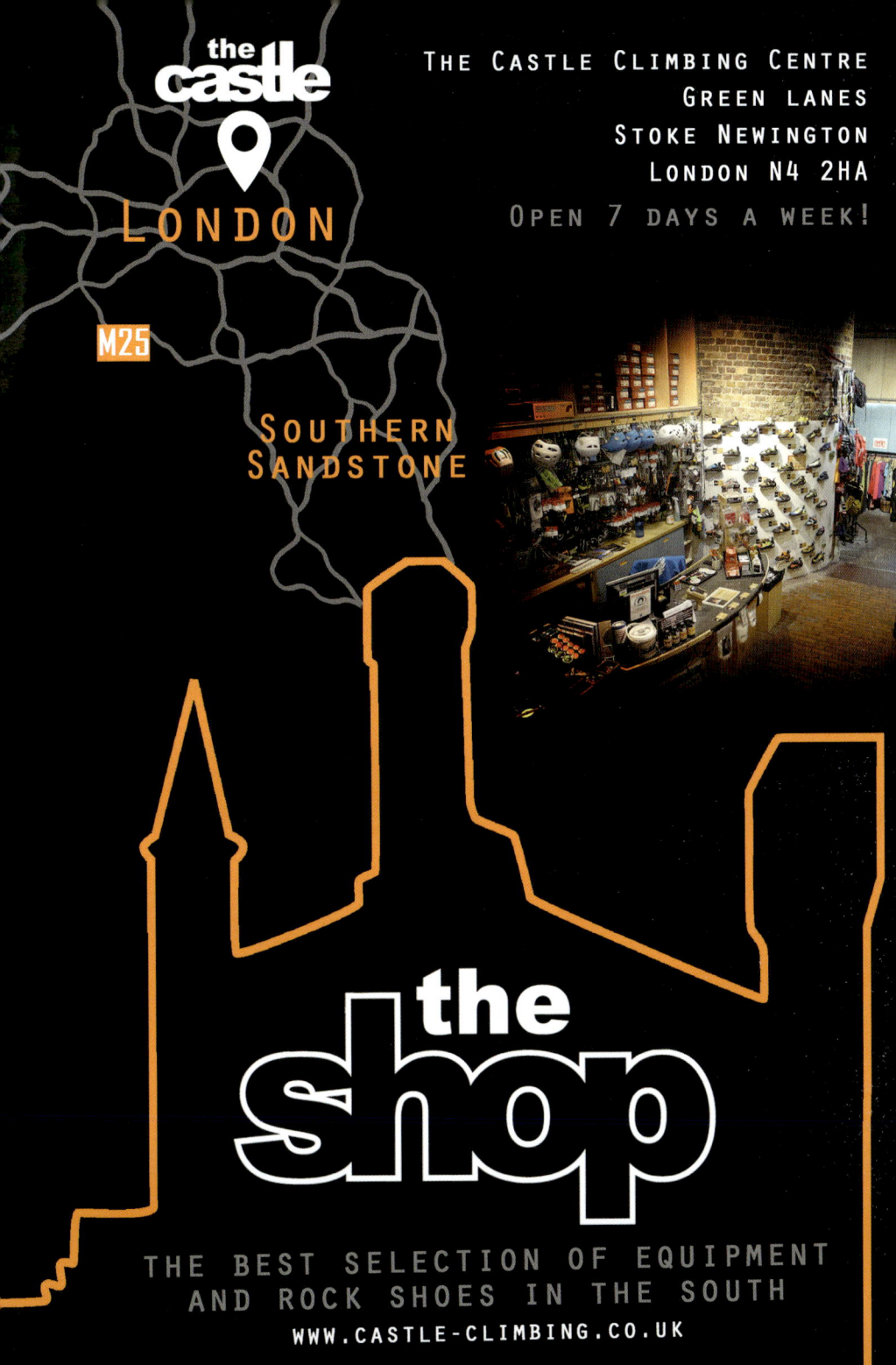

Southern Sandstone Logistics — Other Activities

A great place to look for ideas for things to do is the Tunbridge Wells Tourist Information website **visittunbridgewells.com**

Kayaking - The section of River Medway from Tonbridge to Maidstone has been developed for canoeing with some great water shoots along the river at various grades. There are various places to hire canoes or you can use your own - you will need a licence. More information at **medwaycanoetrail.co.uk**

Cycling - The roads and surrounding woodland trails make for great cycling and mountain biking territory.

Walks and Trails - There are many footpaths and trails all over the Kent and Sussex countryside and this is a good option for seeing the surrounding countryside.

There are many things to see or do in the area depending on your time here and how far you're wishing to travel. In the local area are Dunorlan Park and Groombridge Place Gardens. Another local favourite is to visit one of the hop farms in the area.

Emma and Jayda enjoying a day out on the river Medway.

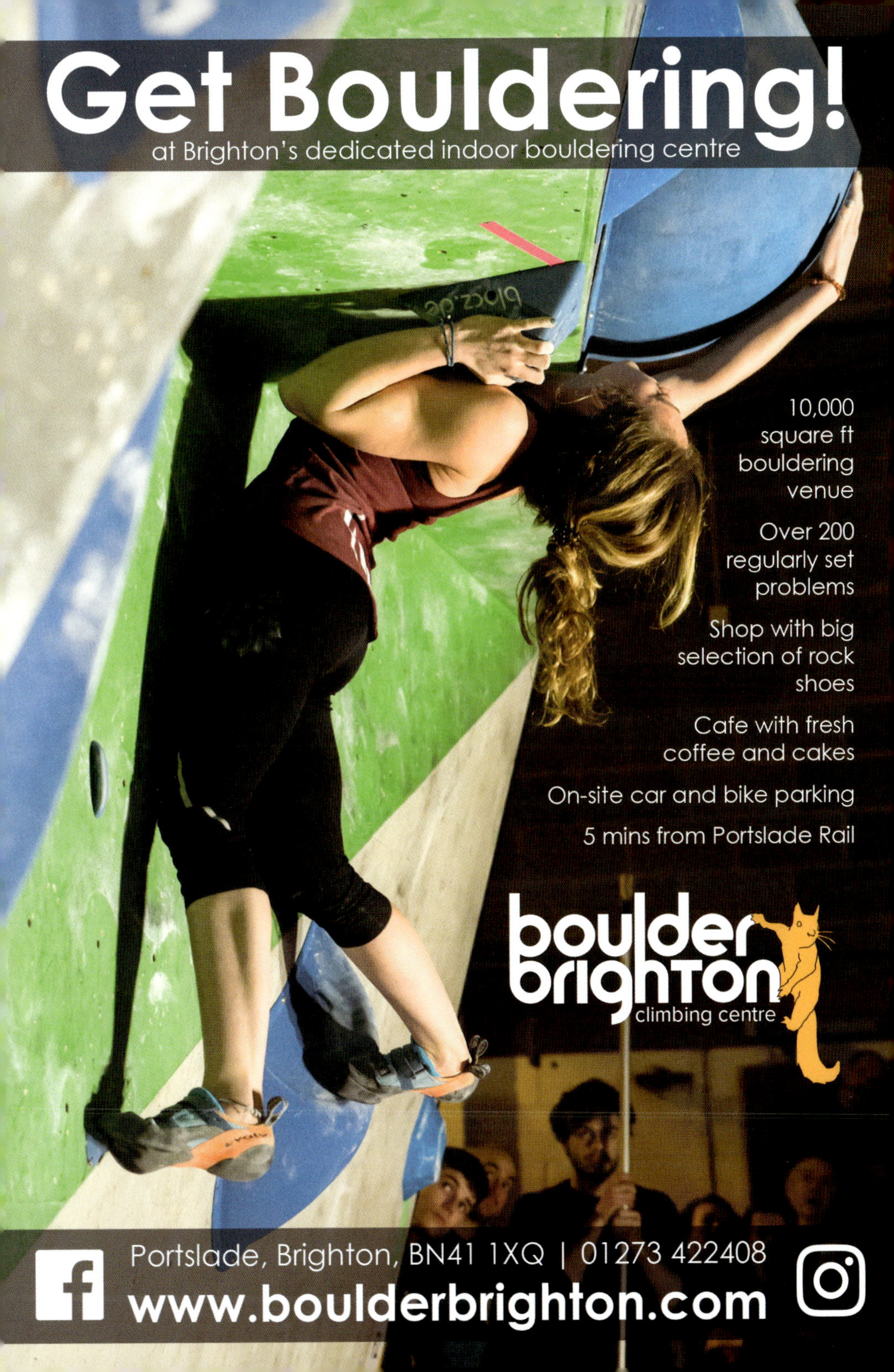

Get Bouldering!
at Brighton's dedicated indoor bouldering centre

10,000 square ft bouldering venue

Over 200 regularly set problems

Shop with big selection of rock shoes

Cafe with fresh coffee and cakes

On-site car and bike parking

5 mins from Portslade Rail

boulder brighton
climbing centre

 Portslade, Brighton, BN41 1XQ | 01273 422408
www.boulderbrighton.com

Southern Sandstone Climbing

Bobbie-Jo Bowes on *Archer's Wall* (6b *5c*) - *page 203* - at Harrison's Rocks. Harrison's is situated in some fine countryside and is one of the most popular climbing destinations in the southeast.

A broken section of sandstone at Bowles Rocks. This gives a very good impression of what sandstone is, and why it is very important to protect it.

Sandstone

Before we go any further, we need to talk about sandstone and how delicate it is. Sandstone is basically just compressed sand with a thin weather-hardened outer layer. Once the outer layer is worn through, the sand underneath will erode rapidly if rubbed or left untreated. Holds often collapse through overuse, particularly where excessive brushing has taken place. Repair work is needed using cement, resin or other coating methods.
If you see any damaged holds, please report them to access@thebmc.co.uk or call 0161 438 3309 - do not attempt to treat the damaged rock yourself.

Rope groves created by moving ropes.

A rope groove potentially created in one single climbing session, likely due to climbers being lowered down with the rope running over the edge and cutting into the rock.

Code of Practice — Southern Sandstone Climbing

Code of Practice

Climbing on Southern Sandstone requires rules to help protect the rock and ensure climbing can be enjoyed by future generations. The rocks are extremely popular, being the only outdoor venue near London, and receive heavy traffic throughout the year. A 'Code of Practice' was first developed by John Galloway in 2003 and the official document, which is now managed by the HRMG in conjunction with the BMC, is reviewed and updated when necessary in consultation with the climbing community.
A PDF version is available from **www.southernsandstoneclimbs.co.uk**

Pass on what you have learnt to others who may be new to sandstone. If you see bad practice, then politely challenge the climbers and show them this book or the Code of Practice leaflet.
If you are ever challenged, then please remember to never take it personally and to assess what you are doing and make changes where appropriate.

Code of Practice Rules

❶ Top-rope, bouldering or solo climbing only - no lead climbing is allowed.

❷ Use static (non-stretch) ropes or slings to ensure the top-rope carabiner hangs clear over the edge of the crag. When set up properly, there should be no rope moving in contact with the actual rock - see page 38 for more on setting up top-ropes.

❸ Walk off when you have finished a climb, do not lower off or abseil.

❹ Clean your climbing shoes before starting each climb.

❺ Use only soft bristle cleaning brushes or a soft rag/towel to flick away sand and chalk. No stiff-bristled wire, tooth, bouldering or climbing-specific brushes.

❻ Use as little chalk as possible and consider using chalk balls, Eco Balls or liquid chalk. Do not use resin (sometimes called 'pof').

❼ Sandstone becomes even softer when wet, and it is strongly advised not to climb when the crags are drying out after rain.

❽ Never use extreme methods to dry holds, always allow them to dry out naturally.

For organised groups please also take note of the following guidelines:

❾ Avoid popular climbing areas at weekends.

❿ If using popular areas at other times, please limit your time.

⓫ Remove ropes when climbs are not in use.

⓬ Do not choose climbs which are too hard - skidding feet contribute significantly to erosion.

⓭ Ensure that all footwear is cleaned using matting, carpets or rags before climbing. Use proper climbing shoes when possible.

Top-roping, solo climbing and bouldering are the only methods of climbing permitted on Southern Sandstone.

Lead Climbing

Lead climbing is strictly forbidden and there are no exceptions to this rule. The rock is simply too soft to take protection and this also includes soft protection like jammed knots.

Top-roping

A successful ascent is made when a route is climbed from the ground up, on a slack rope and topped out. Lowering off is not permitted and any ascent on which the climber doesn't properly top-out is not regarded as a proper ascent. See page 38 for more on setting up top-ropes.

Emma Harrington deploying a mantle move to top out properly and complete her ascent.

Solo Climbing

The line between solo climbing and bouldering can become pretty vague these days especially with bouldering pads used extensively to protect highball problems. Purists may claim that an ascent above a pad is not a true solo ascent but, in reality, solo climbing is very much an individual pursuit and as such you should be happy with your own style. With all highballs there is a point at which a pad becomes redundant anyway.

That said, solo ascents are not recorded in this guide (except one) for the reason that they are not particularly encouraged on sandstone due to the sandy and friable nature of the rock. If you do solo, please be aware that rock conditions can change; dampness and sandy rock making things more difficult than they could be with uncertain consequences. Only experienced sandstone climbers need apply!

Ethics and Climbing Styles — Southern Sandstone Climbing

The impressive night photography of Neal Grundy, here climbing *Siesta Wall* (6a+ *5b*) - *page 118* - on the Equilibrium Wall at Eridge Rocks with the aid of a head torch and a long exposure. Further works and prints can be found and purchased from **nealgrundy.co.uk**

Bouldering

Bouldering on sandstone is increasingly popular and many of the areas covered in this book have been extensively developed with bouldering in mind in recent years. Some of this is at very friendly grades and it is a great way to enjoy lots of climbing without the hassle of a top-rope set-up, usually in a relatively safe environment. Of course you can still hurt yourself and a decent bouldering mat or two, and some friends as spotters are always advised. Bouldering can have an even more intense impact on the soft rock and you should familiarise yourself with the Boulder Sense section in the Code of Practice to learn how best to boulder without damaging the rock.

Boulder problems have been given Font grades - see page 46 for more on grades. 'Highball' problems (where you end up pretty high above the ground) are given a heart flutter symbol. If you are in any doubt, then ignore the bouldering grade and feel free to set up a top-rope since it is better to be safe than sorry.

Some of the problems described are alternative starts to routes which are commonly bouldered, but can be continued on a top-rope. More independent problems to certain points are, either noted in the text, or indicated with a finishing point on the topos - a 'J' for jump icon, although don't feel you need to jump since a partial down-climb is usually safer.

Rob Greenwood on *Parisian Affair* (**f6A+**) - *page 124* - on the Parisian Affair Area at Eridge Rocks. Photo: Rob Greenwood.

CMK Reading store manager Ed gurning on Sansara f7a, Eridge Rocks.

**LONDON'S INDEPENDENT
HIGH STREET CLIMBING SPECIALISTS**

www.coldmountainkit.com

Southern Sandstone Climbing — Top-roping

The soft nature of sandstone rock is the reason that special care is needed when setting up a top-rope, and why lead climbing is strictly forbidden. In days gone by this wasn't always the case and many routes on the popular crags have deep grooves at the top caused by overuse and bad top-rope set-ups. These days, general good practice and some modern techniques can be used to ensure that the damage to the rock is minimal.

Top-rope Set-up

The majority of routes on the popular crags have either bolts or trees for top-rope set-up. By necessity these tend to be some distance back from the edge so an extension belay set-up is required to ensure that the belay carabiner hangs clear over the edge. When set up properly, the top-rope itself should pass through the belay carabiner but not really come into contact with the rock at any stage and certainly not so that it causes abrasion to the rock. Photos 1 and 2 below show a correct and incorrect method with bolt belays.

A static sling with a sheath clipped into the bolt and extended over the edge. Bolts are often placed to give an easy set-up for 120cm slings. This is not always possible so please extend your set-up where necessary.

Never just thread or clip your rope direct into the belay bolts as shown here. This will mean that the rope runs over the edge of the crag with the potential to create bad erosion grooves.

Extended Set-ups

Where there are no bolts, you need to use the crag-top trees which are often some distance back from the edge. A static rope can be used to provide an extended adjustable set-up. This can still incur some movement against the rock when loaded, so it is advised that you use sections of carpet and/or some other method of shielding the rope from the rock - photo 3.

A plastic bottle can be used as a knot protector as shown in photo 4.

Use protection for where the static rope comes into contact with the rock.

The 'Demma' system - a 19mm PVC tube which allows the rope to move freely when under load without damaging the rock - see page 43.

The carabiner hanging freely over the edge.

A plastic knot protector prevents wear and tear incurred through loading if in contact with the rock.

Southern Sandstone Climbing — Top-roping

Clip-up Technique

True sandstone climbing often involves a short section of 'lead' climbing when topping out since you pass the belay which hangs freely some way below the edge. Those who are uncomfortable with this tend to set their belays too far back which causes erosion to the rock as the rope runs over the edge. A good method to avoid this is to use the 'clip-up' technique. This is where a quickdraw (sling or rope with a crab) is in place, connected to the top anchor, for you to clip above you before you attempt the last moves.

In some cases there is a ledge a good distance below the top which creates a second edge which is vulnerable to erosion - photo 5. In these cases two clip-ups can be in place to help protect the final moves - photo 6. It is important to note that clip-ups should only be clipped when you are attempting the last move. The technique is not a substitute method of lead climbing to be used over a whole route.

A basic example of a 'clip-up' set-up. The belay is extended well over the lower edge but the climber can protect themselves by clipping into the extended quickdraws before attempting the finishing moves

6

Use extended quickdraws to protect those final moves.

5 ✗

A bad set-up with the rope cutting its way through the rock and also damaging the rope.

Southern Sandstone Climbing

Sandstone Top-rope Climbing Style
On sandstone the rope is there purely for protection and should not be used to provide assistance to a climber by giving them a 'tight rope'. It is different from top-roping at an indoor wall in this respect. Treat your top-rope only as a back-up in case of a fall and keep it reasonably slack throughout an ascent. In some cases the routes don't go in straight lines and care is needed in the set-up to ensure the rope is correctly positioned, both to offer protection for the whole length of the route, but also keeping in mind the hardest section where a fall is most likely. Certain routes in the book traverse long distances and may require special double top-rope set-ups.

Descent Method
Lowering off, or abseiling, from the top of routes is not permitted. Ensure you always top out and walk off when finished. If you 'take' at any point and are to be lowered back down, please do so as delicately as possible and do not jump in and out onto the wall as this will break holds.

Working Routes
The practice of working routes is where you rest on the rope and practice hard moves until you can do them, the idea being that you then attempt the route from the bottom in good style to complete the ascent. This practice on sandstone has long been debated since the aim when top-roping is that the rope is only weighted in the event of a fall, and it is only when rope is weighted that it causes damage to the rock. 'Working' routes is bound to increase the amount of time a rope is weighted, hence it is likely to be more damaging. However, it is often possible to have a system where the rope is completely free from contact with the rock. In this case working a route is acceptable as long as the belay is properly set up as described in this section.

Do not lower off when you have finished a climb.

Southern Sandstone Climbing Gear

The sandy nature of the rock means that climbing on sandstone can take its toll on your gear much more quickly than on other rock types. This can be mitigated by good practice when setting up your top-ropes and it is certainly true that shoddy top-rope set-ups will not just damage the rock, but they will also hit you in your pocket as your gear gets trashed remarkably quickly. Most seasoned sandstone climbers keep a special set of gear for the purpose and usually this will be fat solid ropes and slings, big sturdy carabiners, plus much of the other gear described on these pages. This is not the place to try out your brand new expensive skinny 70m or lightweight slings and carabiners.

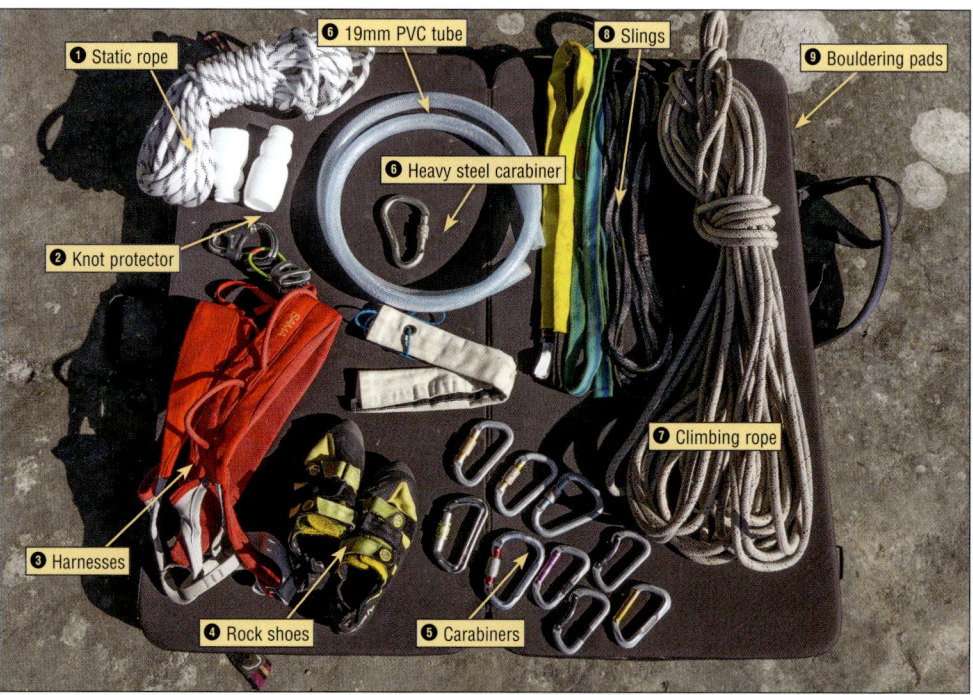

❶ Static Rope
For extended anchor set-ups, usually from trees, you must always use a static rope. 15m to 20m is long enough.

❷ Knot Protector
Where the belay knot hangs over the edge, a considerable amount of abrasion can be caused on the knot. A plastic bottle, cut off at the bottom and slid over a knot, is a good and inexpensive way to protect the belay knot where it hangs over the edge.

❸ Harness
Since you are only top-roping, a harness full of extra features isn't required. You just need something solid that you can tie into. Some traditional climbers wrap the rope around their waists instead of using a harness. The idea here is that you don't hang around too long on a rope once you have fallen off.

❹ Rock Shoes
There is no specific style of rock shoe for sandstone although most people don't tend to use their best pair if they have a choice. The only requirement is that you do use a rock shoe - no trainers or non-climbing footwear since this will cause more damage to the rock.

❺ Carabiners

Carabiners are useful for top-rope set-up and, since weight isn't an issue, decent solid screwgate carabiners are preferable. A heavy steel carabiner is recommended for the one hanging over the edge.

❻ Rope Protector

A rope protector is vital to protect both your rope and, more importantly, the rock. It should be used in conjunction with a static rope or sling. Standard canvas rope protectors tend to wear out quickly so seasoned sandstone climbers tend to use more robust solutions like inner tubes, hose pipes, rubber-based carpets or plastic sheeting.

The 'Demma' System is a cheap and simple solution for sandstone set-ups using static ropes. It consists of a 2mm section of 19mm (3/4") clear braided flexible PVC reinforced plastic tube that allows the static rope to move freely through the pipe. A heavy steel carabiner and a bottle knot protector made from two plastic bottles cut and slotted over each other and secured together by gaffer tape to stop them slipping up the rope.

❻ 'Demma' system — 19mm PVC tube / Split bottle knot protector / Static rope / Steel carabiner / Climbing rope

❼ Climbing Ropes - Static or Dynamic?

For the actual climbing (not the belay set-up) a 30m rope is adequate for any climb in this book. Some use a static rope since this minimises the movement in the system reducing the erosion caused by the moving rope. It also cuts down rope stretch which may stop you decking out if coming off low on a route. It does give a hard catch on the fall which can be a bit jarring for the climber. A dynamic rope is more pleasant to climb and fall on, since it gives a nice soft catch. It also puts less strain on any belay point, or clip-up point you might use. However, the drawback is that a dynamic rope will move more when in contact with the rock causing more erosion, and you might hit the ground on stretch if falling from low on a route.

❽ Slings

Where there are well-placed belay bolts a single 2.5cm x 120cm static sling may be all you need. For more complicated belays, longer slings and extra slings for linking together are worth bringing along. Thick robust slings are better for sandstone so any wear can easily be identified. Slings are also needed to wrap around trees as well as for more advanced set-up techniques like the clip-up method.

❾ Bouldering Pads

Bouldering pads are pretty much essential these days and come in all shapes and sizes. They also have the added advantage of protecting the ground from erosion and, because of this, they are also worth considering when top-roping routes with hard starts. Launch pads are special thinner pads that offer a small amount of protection if falling from the at the start of a problem. They also cut down on ground erosion and help keep your feet clean before setting off on a climb. If you don't have a pad of any kind then a section of rubber backed carpet is a useful replacement to clean your rock shoes on and keep them dry before setting off.

Richard Enticknap on *Ducking Fesperate* (**f5+**) - *page 474* - on the Inaccessible Boulder at Stone Farm. Photo: Richard Enticknap.

Chalk and Eco Balls

Although the use of chalk is accepted and normal on sandstone, it is strongly advised that you consider using an alternative to loose chalk in order to keep the impact to a minimum. Chalk balls are great at reducing the amount of chalk on your hands and preventing spillage. Eco Balls leave next to no residue on the rock and can give even better friction than chalk. Liquid or cream chalk substitutes leave no residue and can dramatically reduce the number of times you need to dip in your chalk bag if used in conjunction with chalk.

At some areas, like Eridge Rocks and High Rocks, access is sensitive and climbers' impact is always on show, so it is essential that chalk use is kept to a minimum at these venues.

The use of resin powder (pof) is not permitted at any of the crags in this book.

Cleaning Brushes

Sandstone does need cleaning from time to time to remove natural debris and loose sand. The best method is to use an extra-long very soft bristle hand brushes, such as those used to clean cars. Flicking holds with an old towel or rag is another option. Stiff-bristled toothbrushes, specific bouldering/climbing brushes and any form of wire brush are not to be used on sandstone. The damage that can be caused by the use of an inappropriate brush, or over-brushing, should not be underestimated.

Carpets, Towels

Clean rock shoes are essential when climbing sandstone. A dirty shoe will make the climb much more slippery and subsequently harder. Dirty shoes that skid against the rock also contribute to erosion. Use an old towel to clean your shoes and a section of carpet at the base of the climb to wipe your feet on and keep them clean before setting off.

Southern Sandstone Climbing — Grades

Grades have always been a contentious issue on sandstone. For years the standard method has been to give each route a single UK technical grade which aims to give an indication of the hardest move on a route. This works to an extent, but can give a false impression of how difficult a climb actually is overall - a route with one *6a* move has the same grade as one with six *6a* moves without a rest yet is obviously not as hard. Another problem is that historically the UK technical grade has become very limited at the top end with a huge variation in difficulty within some of the top *6a*, *6b* and *6c* grade bands. This is well illustrated in the table opposite where UK technical grade *6b* spans sport grades from 7a to 8a!

Sport Grades

To give a better indication of the difficulty of routes in this book we have adopted a dual grading system. The first grade is a sport grade which gives an overall impression of the difficulty of the whole route and is familiar to most climbers both from sport climbing and climbing walls. The second grade is the more traditional UK technical grade, which gives an indication of the hardest move on the route. These are being included in this book to help with the transition between the grading systems. They do not appear in the app version of this guidebook.

It is worth bearing in mind that sandstone grades are renowned for being incredibly stiff primarily due to the unique climbing style and the historical compression of routes into the upper technical grade ranges. Routes also tend to be technically hard because the climber doesn't need to worry about the protection since you should always be on a top-rope.

Sport Grade - Overall difficulty of the route

⓭ **Pig's Nose** .... Top 150   5c *5a*
A true sandstone classic up the nose on massive jugs. The top provides an exciting steep and exposed finale on good holds.

UK Tech Grade - Old grade for the hardest move

❻ **Devour** ....   *f6B+*
Traverse the lower break from right to left, with a difficult drop down midway. Finish at the central break on the arete.

Font Bouldering Grade - For boulder problems

Bouldering Grades

For boulder problems, Font bouldering grades have been used since this is now familiar to most climbers. The table opposite gives a very rough comparison of Font bouldering grades to the equivalent UK technical grade.

Feedback

There are bound to be some grading anomalies during the switch from the primary grade being the UK technical grade to sport and bouldering grades. Please use the UKC Logbook system to register your opinion on the grades - **ukclimbing.com/logbook/**

Colour Coding

The routes are given a colour-coded dot corresponding to a difficulty level. This gives you an impression across different climbing styles of routes you may be happy attempting. The difficulty level of boulder problems is a little higher for the equivalent colour code.

❶ **Up to 4c / Up to *f4***
Mostly these should be good for beginners and those wanting an easy life.

❷ **5a to 6a+ / *f4+* to *f5+***
General ticking routes for those with more experience.

❸ **6b to 7a / *f6A* to *f6C+***
Routes for the experienced and keen climber. A grade band which includes many of the area's great classics.

❹ **7a+ or *f7A* and above.**
The really hard stuff..

Sandstone Grade Table

Sport Grade	UK Technical Grade			Font Bouldering Grade
2a	2a			
2b		2b		f2
2c			2c	
3a	3a			
3b		3b		f2+
3c			3c	
4a	4a			f3
4b		4b		f3+
4c			4c	f4
5a				
5b	5a			f4+
5c				
6a		5b		f5
6a+				
6b			5c	
6b+				f5+
6c				
6c+	6a			f6A
7a				f6A+ / f6B
7a+				f6B+ / f6C
7b				f6C+
7b+		6b		f7A
7c				f7A+
7c+				f7B
8a			6c	f7B+
8a+				f7C
8b				f7C+
8b+	7a			f8A
8c				f8A+
8c+				f8B

There are many bolts on sandstone and all of them have been placed purely as top-rope anchors at the top of crags. There are no bolts actually on routes and they are never used to protect lead climbing.

Bolts on sandstone should not be regarded in the same way as bolts for leading climbing on limestone or other rock types. The softness of the rock means that there are special requirements when placing the bolts and they must not be used for any purpose other than setting up top-ropes. They are not designed for slacklines, zip wires or via ferrata. Excessive force placed on a bolt in the wrong direction may end up with the rock surrounding it failing and exploding in a sandy mess.

The twin bolt set-up common at Harrison's Rocks

Bolts come in all shapes and sizes with numerous types currently in use. Some are now getting old and are held in place by 30-year-old concrete, but even these are still strong enough in most cases. New bolts are sunk into holes approximately 20cm in depth and kept in place by resin. The modern set-up usually has two bolts with a wire cable connecting them as a back-up (photo). These placements are designed for a pull in line with the direction of the twin bolt set-up and not for a cross-loading sideways pull. Such a pull will eventually cause a bolt to spin and move, severely weakening it.

Using the Belay Bolts

Most new belay bolts are placed back from the edge at a position designed so that you can use a 1.2m static sling to reach the edge and get the belay carabiner clear of the rock - see page 38 for more on this. The top-rope itself should never be threaded, or clipped directly, into the belay bolts. Whether you connect your static extension sling to the bolt with a

carabiner or a knot is a matter of preference as long as there is no moving rope in the system. In some cases there are old bolts near the edge of the crag. You should still use a static extension sling in these cases since clipping direct to the bolt will not clear the edge sufficiently. Bolts in these positions are mostly being replaced.

Placing Bolts

Bolts are placed and tested by authorised personnel only and the majority are funded by the BMC. The Harrison's Rock Management Group test and inspect bolts once every 3 years. This involves weighting the bolt while closely observing it for movement. You must never attempt to place bolts yourself. If you encounter any problems with bolts on Sandstone then please email **access@thebmc.co.uk** or call 0161 438 3309

Tim Skinner (HRMG) installing new bolts at Harrison's Rocks.

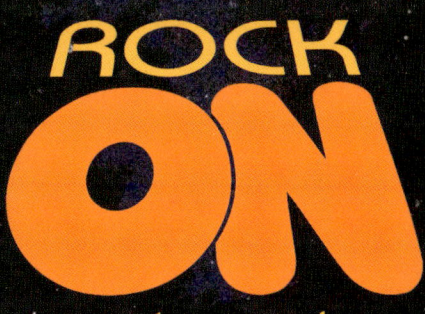

ROCK ON

Bulging with climbing gear!

Many shops claim to be climbing specialists.

At Rock On we sell climbing/mountaineering equipment and books, and absolutely NOTHING ELSE.

Now that's specialist!

Find us at:

Mile End Climbing Wall
Haverfield Road, Bow,
London, E3 5BE.
Tel: 0208 981 5066

Craggy Island
9 Cobbett Park, Slyfield Estate,
Guildford. GU1 1RU.
Tel: 01483 565 635

Redpoint Climbing Centre
77 Cecil Street, Birmingham, B19 3ST.
Tel: 0121 359 8709

www.rockonclimbing.co.uk

Jess jumping in the dark at Harrison's.

Southern Sandstone Climbing Access

There are varying requirements for access to the crags described in this book. Harrison's Rocks and Stone Farm Rocks are owned by the BMC, situated on open access land and present no problems for access. Eridge Rocks is open to climbers except for some no climbing zones which have been agreed between Sussex Wildlife Trust and the BMC. Bowles Rocks are owned by the Bowles Rock Trust and open to climbers with the proviso that you may be asked to relocate from certain areas if they are required for climbing instruction. High Rocks are on private land and have specific requirements including a fee - see page 274. The crags on Tunbridge Wells and Rusthall commons are managed by the Tunbridge Wells Commons Conservators and have no problems for access. Bassett's Farm Rocks and Under Rockes are both on private land and, although the landowners have never been identified, there are no known problems. More specific details are shown with each chapter. For up-to-date access information, check the UKC Logbook listing for the crag **ukclimbing.com/logbook/**, the BMC RAD (Regional Access Database) **thebmc.co.uk/modules/RAD/** or **www.southernsandstoneclimbs.co.uk**

SSSI
An SSSI (Sites of Special Scientific Interest) is an area protected by law to conserve the wildlife or geology and is designated by Natural England. Bull's Hollow, Toad Rocks, Eridge Rocks, High Rocks and Stone Farm are all SSSI. Climbing is allowed within an SSSI but extra care needs to be taken to ensure that no damage is done to the flora, fauna and rock. Climbing could easily be restricted at these venues if damage was attributed to climbers.

Trees
Many of the crags suffer from extensive foliage which can turn them into jungles in the summer months. Please do not take matters into your own hands by cutting down or pruning trees or using any chemical products to kill the plant life. If you think clearance work needs to be carried out, contact the BMC at **access@thebmc.co.uk** or call 0161 438 3309. Alternatively, get involved in volunteering through the HRMG (Harrison's Rocks Management Group) and the SVG (Sandstone Volunteering Group) - see page 54 for more information on volunteering.

Dogs
Dogs are welcome at all crags but must be kept under control at all times and preferably on a lead. Some people, and many other dogs, are not comfortable when dogs approach them. If your dog does not come back when called straight away, then they are not under control. Remove all dog faeces and dispose of appropriately away from site. Do not hang poo bags from tree branches for collection later.

Fire
No barbecues, fires or cooking stoves are permitted at any sandstone crags due to the obvious fire hazard within the surrounding woodland. Fire started near the rocks also has the added problem of causing serious damage to the actual rock.

Karen Gayly taking on some reachy moves on *Boonoonoonoos* (7a+ 6b) - *page 314* - at the Boonoonoonoos area of High Rocks.

Illegal Camping
Camping and bivouacking is not permitted at any crags. Please use proper campsites or the camping facilities at Harrison's/Birchden Wood next to the carpark.

Vandalism
Chipping, creating new or enlarging existing holds, making engravings, permanently marking the rock and performing other forms of graffiti are all deemed acts of vandalism which are punishable by a fine or potential prosecution. Please report any acts of vandalism to **access@thebmc.co.uk** or call 0161 438 3309

General Behaviour
Simple reasonable behaviour like not shouting and swearing loudly, taking your litter home, not using sound systems and being polite to others should be obvious. Just remember to enjoy yourself and do what you can to make sure others enjoy themselves as well.

The BMC (British Mountaineering Council)
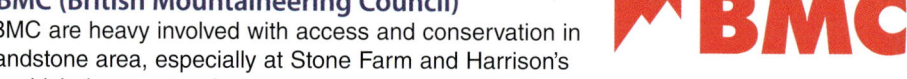
The BMC are heavy involved with access and conservation in the sandstone area, especially at Stone Farm and Harrison's Rocks which they own and manage. The bolts, fencing, signage, maintenance products and equipment are all funded by the BMC. Membership of the BMC or donations to the BMC Access and Conservation Trust (ACT) are well targeted when it comes to climbing on sandstone, so please visit **thebmc.co.uk** for information on how to join or make a donation.

The sandstone open meeting at Bowles Rocks.

Sandstone Open Meetings
Open meetings are held once or twice a year, usually in a meeting room at Bowles Rocks. They are a great place to air your views, meet other sandstone climbers and meet members of the HRMG and SVG. You can have your say, learn of any developments, feed into discussions or offer your own ideas for consideration. Meeting dates are posted on **www.southernsandstoneclimbs.co.uk/meetings**

The Steve Durkin Sandstone Trust

The Steve Durkin Sandstone Trust was set up in 2011 after an initial donation from the estate of Steve Durkin after his passing. It is to be used towards the safeguarding, maintenance and access to the sandstone outcrops of Kent and Sussex. The trust is funded 100% by donations and fundraising - **sdst.org.uk**

PROTECT THE ROCK

READ: Southern Sandstone Code of Practice
Essential good practice information for all climbers visiting southern sandstone.
www.thebmc.co.uk/southern-sandstone-code-of-practice

WATCH: Southern Sandstone Skills films
Short films about good practice techniques for climbing on southern sandstone.
www.thebmc.co.uk/southern-sandstone-skills

Southern Sandstone Climbing — Volunteering Groups

The SVG volunteers performing clearance work at Harrison's Rocks. Photo: Amy Wiggins.

Volunteering Groups

Many of the climbing environments and rock conditions you see today would not be possible were it not for the hard work of a select few volunteering groups. The first volunteering groups appeared in the late 60s, but it was the hurricane of 1987 that inspired a much needed collaborative effort to deal with what was, at the time, a huge task. This effort improved the access, environment and sustainability of many of the sandstone crags.

The Sandstone Volunteers Group (SVG)

The Sandstone Volunteers Group was founded in 2003 by Graham Adcock and has been actively involved in many projects across the area ever since. In the winter of 2003/2004 the SVG, in consultation with the Tunbridge Wells Conservators and English Nature, undertook extensive clearance work at Bull's Hollow (a similar operation was also carried out 10 years later in February 2014). Significant tree clearance at High Rocks over the winter of 2004/2005, led by both by Graham Adcock and Oliver Hill, transformed the areas around the northwest-facing walls. More recently, the SVG have been heavily involved in the Harrison's Rocks Woodland Management Plan and subsequent conservation work associated with that.

Without the help of the SVG, and its volunteers, sandstone climbing would be a very different experience and many of the areas currently enjoyed would be overgrown and forgotten. If you are interested in helping, have a look at **sandstonevolunteers.org.uk**

Sussex Wildlife Trust

Sussex Wildlife Trust, the owners of Eridge Rocks, undertake annual clearance work with the assistance of volunteers, which helps keep the rocks open for visitors. For more information have a look at **sussexwildlifetrust.org.uk**

Tunbridge Wells Commons Conservators

The Tunbridge Wells Commons Conservators concentrate their efforts on Tunbridge Wells and Rusthall Commons. They receive a grant each year to undertake work but still rely on volunteers to help out. See **twcommons.org** for further information.

BUIS-LES-BARONNIES

Accommodation in the heart of Haute Provence

- Open all year
- 2/4 person studio apartment
- 13 person bunkhouse
- 7/9 person gite
- 4 person off-grid cabin in the woods
- 12m Heated pool
- WIFI throughout
- Children's playground
- World-class, year-round climbing within 20 mins
- New via-ferrata just 20 mins away
- Great cycling - on and off-road
- Mountain bike hire on site
- Large groups and clubs welcome

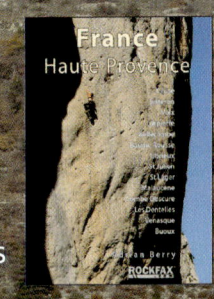

Owner Audrey Seguy hanging out at the local crag Baume Rousse, with a snow-capped Mt. Ventoux in the distance.

Our pool is open May through Sept.

La Bergerie - a 7/9 person gite

The dining room

www.alauzon.com | +33 9 87 88 65 77

Southern Sandstone Climbing — HRMG

Tim Skinner (HRMG) undertaking bolt inspections at Harrison's Rocks. This work is done once every three years by members of HRMG.

Daimon Beail (HRMG) performing repair work at Harrison's Rocks.

Harrison's Rocks Management Group (HRMG)

HRMG is a specialist sub-committee of the BMC responsible for the management of Harrison's Rocks and Stone Farm. They work with volunteers and other groups, such as the SVG, carrying out rock maintenance (resin, cement and hold repairs), bolt installation and maintenance, erosion control, conservation work, signage, fencing, woodland management programs and helping educate climbers regarding the Code of Practice. The group also works with the Forestry Commission who run and maintain Birchden Wood which includes the carpark at Harrison's and its facilities. Occasionally work is done at other sites when necessary, overseeing bolting work and maintaining good relations with landowners on behalf of the BMC.

The group meets three times a year in January, May and October. To contact the HRMG about access issues email access@thebmc.co.uk or call 0161 438 3309

EXTEND YOUR COMFORT ZONE

Visit the Páramo Brand Stores to see the whole range of award-winning Páramo. Our team can give you friendly, expert advice on choosing the best Páramo to suit your needs and activities – from high performance baselayers and water-repellent windproofs to unique moisture-moving waterproofs that can take on the worst weather and manage condensation better than any other system.

Carefully thought-out details, like innovative ventilation combined with helmet and climbing harness compatibility, leave you free to focus on your activity, whether you are tackling Southern Sandstone, Peaks Grit or Skye Gabbro.

www.paramo.co.uk

Páramo Wadhurst Shop
(in Southern Sandstone country)
1 Central Parade
WADHURST
East Sussex TN5 6AL
01892 785635

Páramo London Store
(2 mins from Baker Street)
25 Melcombe Street
MARYLEBONE
London NW1 6AG
0203 8419901

Páramo Keswick Store
13 Market Square
KESWICK
Cumbria CA12 5BJ
01768 772722

Southern Sandstone Climbing — Top50

Routes

8a+
- Chimaera — Photo 286, Page 287 — High Rocks

7b
- Krait Arete — Photo 307, Page 306 — High Rocks

7a+
- Boonoonoonoos — Photo 315, Page 314 — High Rocks
- Nemesis — Photo 317, Page 318 — High Rocks

7a
- Hangover 3 — Photo 193, Page 194 — Harrison's Rocks
- The Flakes — Photo 14, Page 194 — Harrison's Rocks
- Woolly Cub — Page 246 — Harrison's Rocks
- Infidel — Page 298 — High Rocks
- Honeycomb — Photo 330, Page 329 — High Rocks

6c+
- Fandango — Page 79 — Bowles Rocks
- Serenade Arete — Photo 1, 85, Page 82 — Bowles Rocks
- Hate — Photo 89, Page 91 — Bowles Rocks
- Craig-y-blanco — Page 329 — High Rocks

6c
- Slim Finger Crack — Photo 211, Page 204 — Harrison's Rocks
- Engagement Wall — Photo 9, 309, Page 308 — High Rocks
- The Wall — Photo 385, Page 394 — Bull's Hollow
- Belle Vue Terrace — Page 466 — Stone Farm

Top50

The Top50 list covers the 50 most iconic routes on Southern Sandstone. The list spans a good spread of grades and styles and is in a rough order of difficulty.

Bobbie-Jo Bowes on the Top50 route *Devaluation* (6a+ *5b*) - *page 90* - at Bowles Rocks.

Top50 Southern Sandstone Climbing

	Photo	Page

6b+
- Inspiration 83
  Bowles Rocks
- UN 95
  Bowles Rocks
- Henry the Ninth .... *300* ... 298
  High Rocks
- Coronation Crack .... *307* ... 306
  High Rocks
- Excavator .... *422* ... 431
  Bassett's Farm Rocks
- Uganda Wall .... *434* ... 438
  Under Rockes

6b
- Forester's Wall 228
  Harrison's Rocks
- Niblick .... *230* ... 229
  Harrison's Rocks
- Birchden Wall 248
  Harrison's Rocks
- Unclimbed Wall .... *261, 263* ... 266
  Harrison's Rocks
- Celebration 316
  High Rocks
- Odin's Wall .... *334* ... 327
  High Rocks
- Central Crack .... *445* ... 439
  Under Rockes

6a+
- Devaluation 90
  Bowles Rocks
- Hadrian's Wall 144
  Eridge Rocks
- Long Layback .... *161* ... 194
  Harrison's Rocks
- West Wall .... *258* ... 247
  Harrison's Rocks
- Simian Progress 338
  High Rocks
- Key Wall .... *468* ... 466
  Stone Farm
- SW Corner Scoop .... *446* ... 475
  Stone Farm

6a
- Zig-Zag Wall 268
  Harrison's Rocks
- Advertisement Wall .... *270* ... 308
  High Rocks

	Photo	Page

5c
- Pig's Nose .... *Cover, 9* ... 92
  Bowles Rocks

5b
- Sapper .... *62* ... 83
  Bowles Rocks

4c
- Isolated Buttress Climb ..... *244* ... 247
  Harrison's Rocks

4b
- Eyelet 178
  Harrison's Rocks

4a
- Root Route 1 181
  Harrison's Rocks
- Bow Window .... *158* ... 197
  Harrison's Rocks

Bouldering

	Photo	Page

f7A
- Nicotine Alley .... *79* ... 79
  Bowles Rocks
- Change in the Weather 353
  High Rocks Annexe

f6A
- Brenva .... *347* ... 342
  High Rocks

f5
- Red Snapper 375
  Happy Valley

f4+
- Ashdown Wall 473
  Stone Farm

Destination Planner

Routes		up to 4c / up to f4	5a to 6a+ / f4+ to f5+	6b to 7a / f6A to f6C+	7a+ upwards / f7A upwards
Bowles Rocks	247	74	56	89	28
Eridge Rocks	243	43	52	114	34
Harrison's Rocks	521	126	116	248	31
High Rocks	390	57	62	169	100
High Rocks Annexe	61	23	23	12	3
Happy Valley	92	42	19	25	6
Bull's Hollow	75	33	10	30	2
Toad Rocks	64	44	14	4	2
Mount Edgcumbe Rocks	15	2	1	7	5
Bassett's Farm Rocks	39	9	10	18	2
Under Rockes	44	9	8	24	3
Stone Farm	153	60	31	52	10
TOTALS	1944	522	402	792	226

Approach	Sun	Seepage	Green	Restrictions	Summary	Page	
1 - 4 min	Afternoon		Green		A popular year-round south-facing venue with plenty of classics. Has an entry fee. There are sometimes request from the crag owners to reserve routes for their instruction purposes.	68	Bowles Rocks
1 - 10 min	Sun and shade		Green	Restricted	A wild venue with lots of smaller buttress and some good more continuous sections. Varying rock quality and lots of vegetation. Perfect for the adventurer.	110	Eridge Rocks
7 - 17 min	Afternoon	Seepage	Green	BMC	The most popular crag in the area with hundreds of routes across the grades. Owned by the BMC and managed for climbers.	166	Harrison's Rocks
1 - 3 min	Sun and shade	Seepage	Green	Restricted	An impressive set of walls with some of the best rock and routes in the area. Not as good in the easier grades. Entry fee applies and access restrictions mean that it can be closed.	280	High Rocks
1 - 4 min	Not much sun	Seepage	Green		Short walls which give some highball bouldering. Shaded by trees and is forever green, but good climbing when dry.	352	High Rocks Annexe
3 - 5 min	Afternoon		Green		A quiet area with a good selection of micro routes which are usually done as highball boulder problems above mats. One larger 8m tower suitable for top-roping.	365	Happy Valley
1 - 4 min	Sun and shade	Seepage	Green		An esoteric old quarry with a series of vegetated walls above a swamp. One quality wall and popular with connoisseurs when in condition.	388	Bull's Hollow
1 - 2 min	Not much sun		Green		A mini Fontainebleau with lots of relatively easy bouldering on slightly soft rock. Busy with families and children on summer weekends.	406	Toad Rocks
1 min	Morning		Green		Challenging highball boulder problems within easy walking distance of Tunbridge Wells train station.	420	Mount Edgcumbe
5 - 7 min	Not much sun		Green		A small tucked away series of smaller buttresses including two excellent walls. Situated in some breathtaking countryside.	428	Bassett's Farm
15 min	Sun and shade	Seepage	Green		A small outcrop hidden in woods. One excellent wall with interesting square-cut potholes creating some unique routes.	438	Under Rocks
2 - 5 min	Sun and shade		Green	BMC	A lone crag to the west of the other areas within easy reach of south London climbers making it popular. Many good routes and problems despite the sandy nature of the rock. Owned by the BMC and managed for climbers.	452	Stone Farm

Faded symbol means that only some of the routes suffer from seepage and dampness / are green / are restricted

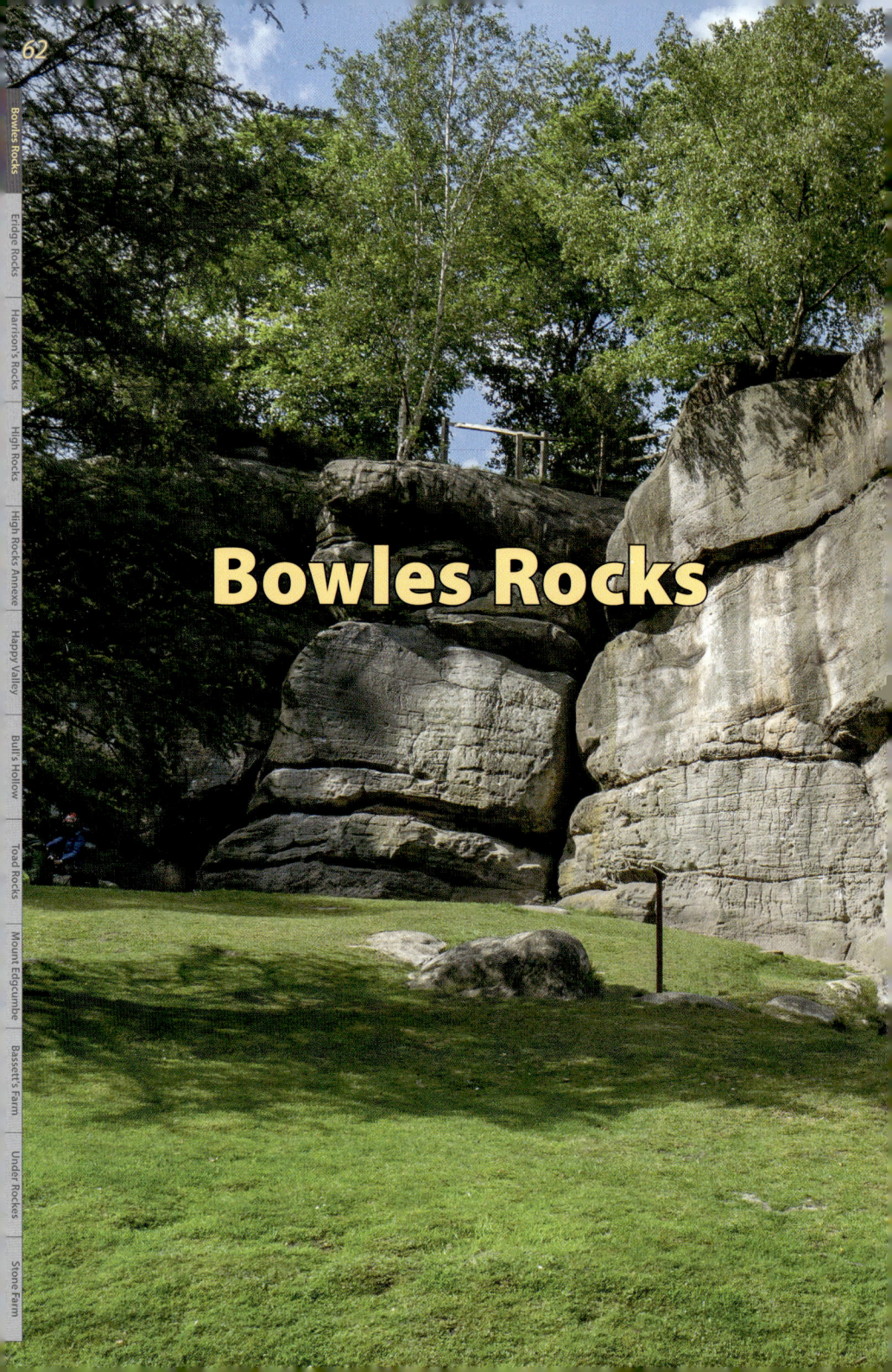

Bowles Rocks

Olga Ruebenbauer on *Sapper* (5b *5a*) - *page 83* - a fine example of the many quality sandstone climbs at Bowles.

Bowles Rocks

	No star	⭐	⭐⭐	⭐⭐⭐
2a to 4c/f2 to f4	43	23	8	-
5a to 6a+/f4+ to f5+	14	22	15	5
6b to 7a/f6A to f6C+	19	26	26	18
7a+ up/f7A up	6	14	5	3

Bowles Rocks is Southern Sandstone's premiere climbing venue; its easy access and south-facing aspect making it convenient, sunny and fast drying. The sandstone is compact and amongst the best in the area, which is well reflected in the quality of the routes and boulder problems. For the most part, Bowles is one continuous stretch of rock, reaching 11m in places. It offers everything from slabs to steep overhangs and has a picturesque amphitheatre at the highest point of the main crag. The crag name comes from a dutchman named 'Bowles' who originally owned the rocks. The walls were also used as firing ranges in World War II and famously used to house pigs (which explains the unusual route naming conventions). John Walters, a passionate rock climber, recognised Bowles' potential in 1961 and purchased the rocks, turning it into a unique climbing centre. Ownership was transferred to a charitable trust in 1964 - The Bowles Rocks Trust - which is a registered charity that 'supports children and young people to achieve their potential through outdoor education'. The site also has other facilities including a dry ski slope, a heated indoor swimming pool and, perhaps most importantly, a small and well maintained toilet block ideally situated just below the rocks.

Approach   Also see map on page 18
Follow the A26 out of Royal Tunbridge Wells for approximately 4.5 miles, passing through Eridge, until a sign to ' Bowles' directs you left onto Sandhill Lane. Follow this (keeping left) for approximately 700m until the entrance to Bowles appears on your right. From the carpark, walk up the private road a short distance beyond the electronic barrier where the rocks will appear on your right. Walking up the road all the way to the top ski slope and bearing right into the upper carpark brings you to the Ski Slope Boulders.

Access
The rocks are open to the public to use, although you may occasionally be asked to relocate along the crag if an organised session is to take place. On rare occasions the rocks are closed for special events. People under 18 years of age are only allowed to climb if supervised by a parent or guardian. Children are often resident at the site in the summer months, so please tolerate occasional noise and craziness from children and set a good example for them. Dogs should be kept on a lead.

Entrance Fee
There is an entrance fee to climb here. 2017 prices are £5 per adult (£4 after 5pm) or £3 for children (under 16s). A season ticket is available for £32 per person and can be bought from the office located by the main lower carpark. On a weekend there is normally someone checking tickets and collecting money, otherwise pay at the office. The money goes into the maintenance of the rocks and facilities. Any surplus supports the charitable work done by the trust. For more information, have alook at **bowles.ac**

Gear
Bolt anchors have been installed for setting up top-ropes, though additional equipment is also required for setting up top-rope anchors off trees (see page 38). The top of the rocks is easily reached up steps either side of the crag leading to a path that runs the full length. A small number of more awkward access points can be found along the crag, but are typically avoided by many due to rock quality, green slime or difficulty.

Bowles Rocks

Bowles with its variety of climbing styles offers something for everyone. Sarah Rossitter (centre) is on *Funnel* (4a *4a*) - *page 95* - whilst others indulge in a spot of bouldering on Larchant Wall - *page 97*.

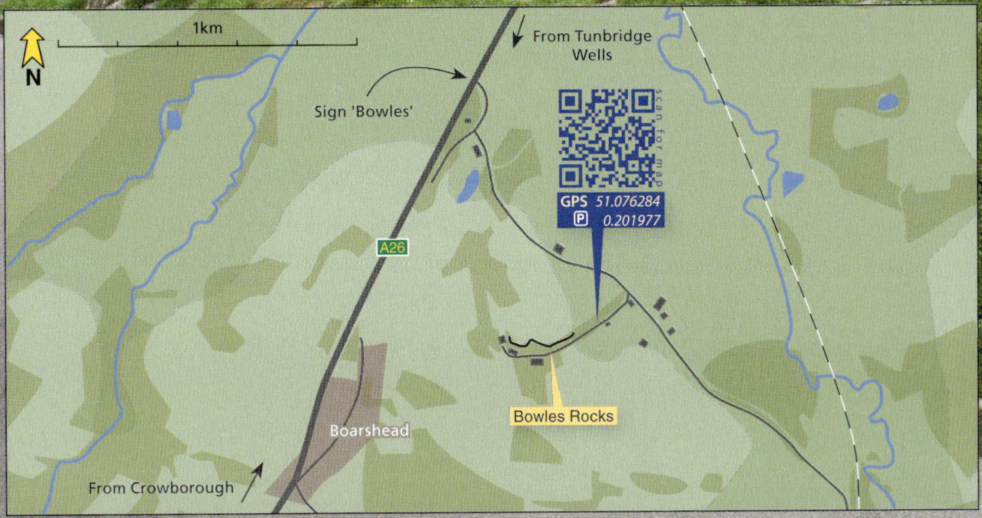

Bowles Rocks

Bowles Rocks

Bowles Rocks — Ski Slope Boulders

Ski Slope Boulders
A collection of rarely visited boulders situated around the top carpark (no general parking allowed). Many problems were originally done as routes, but they are often bouldered above mats now.

Approach (see overview on page 66) - Follow the road running past the main rocks for 350m to reach the ski slope carpark at the top.

Naughty Sporty
A small boulder situated at the top left of the carpark. Fun for the short with some good micro problems.

1 Window Smasher .... f2+
Climb the centre of the left face using both aretes.
FA. D.Beail 20.7.2014

2 Naughty Sporty f2
The left side of the main face using the arete for the left-hand.
FA. D.Beail 20.7.2014

3 Spice f2
Climb the centre of the face.
FA. D.Beail 20.7.2014

4 One in the Pink f2
Climb the arete on its right using an oddly-shaped hold.
FA. D.Beail 20.7.2014

Heidi
Situated at the top right of the carpark.

5 Heidi .... f4+
Climb the series of ledges with a mantel finish.
FA. D.Beail 2005

Bull's Nose
A short overhanging face with a few slab problems.

6 Referendum .... f4+
A tricky mantelshelf problem.

7 British Bulldog .... f4+
The centre of the roof with a rockover onto the top slab.

8 Bull's Nose .... f4+
The arete mainly on its left side with a mantelshelf finish.

9 Toreador .... f4+
An eliminate avoiding use of the arete.

10 Badger's Head .... f3+
A good problem past some distinct ironstone holds.

11 Badgering the Badger f2
The easy curving crack.

Problems 12-14

Boulder Hill

The three small boulders situated on a slope are more fun for shorties.

12 End of it All . . . . ☐ *f2*
The short slab.
FA. D.Beail 20.7.2014

13 Candyland . . . . ☐ *f4*
The short left arete.
FA. D.Beail 20.7.2014

14 Redwood . . . . ☐ *f3+*
The short right arete.
FA. D.Beail 20.7.2014

Bowles Rocks
Eridge Rocks
Harrison's Rocks
High Rocks
High Rocks Annexe
Happy Valley
Bull's Hollow
Toad Rocks
Mount Edgcumbe
Bassett's Farm
Under Rockes
Stone Farm

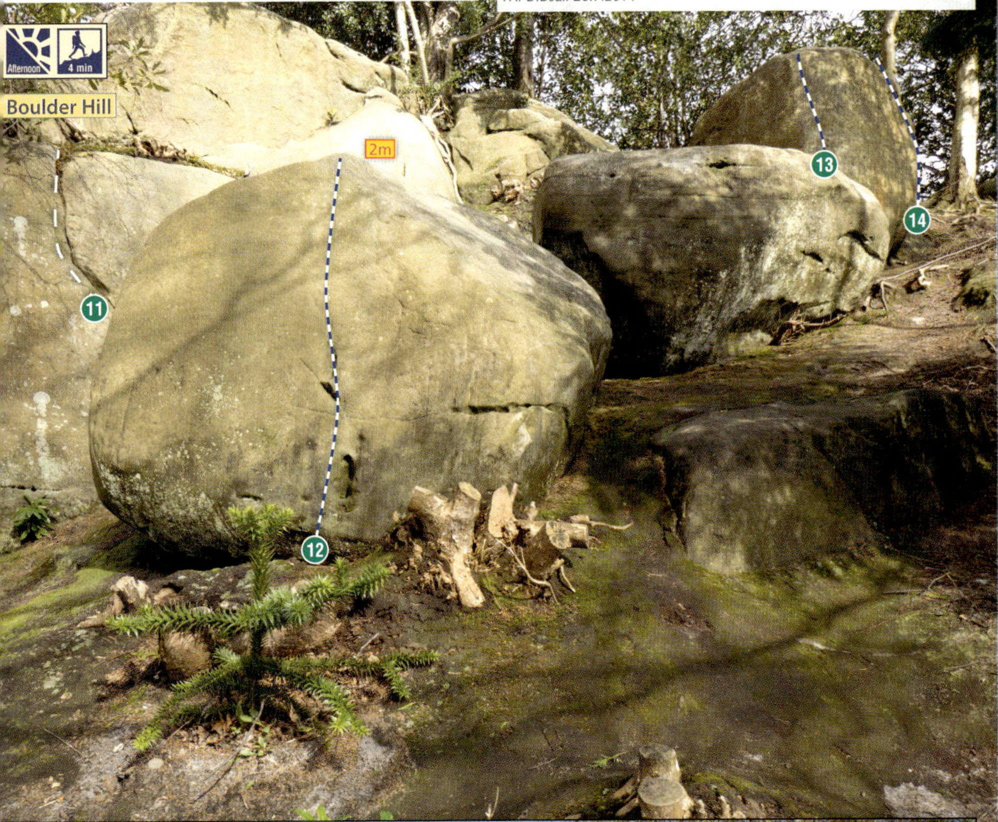

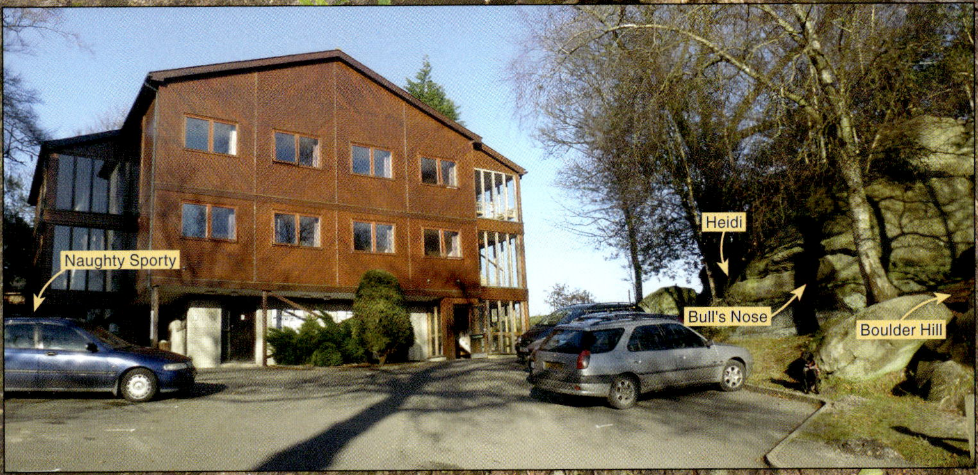

Bowles Rocks — Chalet Slab Area

Chalet Slab Area

A fantastic slab with outcrops either side of it. Further right are some less-travelled walls providing easy but dusty lines.

Approach (see overview on page 66) - Below the ski slope carpark and behind the Lower Chalet.

1 Hibiscus 5a *4c*
A challenging line up the crack to a nice slabby finish.

2 Helter Skelter 6c *5c*
A nice route with an unforgiving top-out. Graded for eliminating the rotten tree stump. Easier and less pleasant with the use of the tree stump.

3 Chalet Slab - Chimney *f3*
A short problem to gain the break and escape up the chimney.

4 Chalet Slab Left 3c *3c*
Climb past two distinct ironstone holds and exit left.

5 Chalet Slab Direct .. 6b *5c*
Climb delicately up the centre of the wall, finishing with difficulty over the top boulder. Escaping left is **4c** and much nicer.

6 Chalet Slab Right 4c *4c*
Direct up the slab and finish by squeezing through the gap.

7 Mumbo Jumbo 6b *5b*
A relatively easy wall leads to a hard mantel finish. It can be used as a right-hand start to *Chalet Slab Right* at **4c** *4c*.

8 Mohrenkop .... 6b+ *5c*
An excellent action-packed route which is difficult to flash.
FA. T.Tullis 1960s

9 Two Step 6b *5b*
Hard to start with a rounded finish.
FA. T.Tullis 1962

Chalet Slab Area — Bowles Rocks

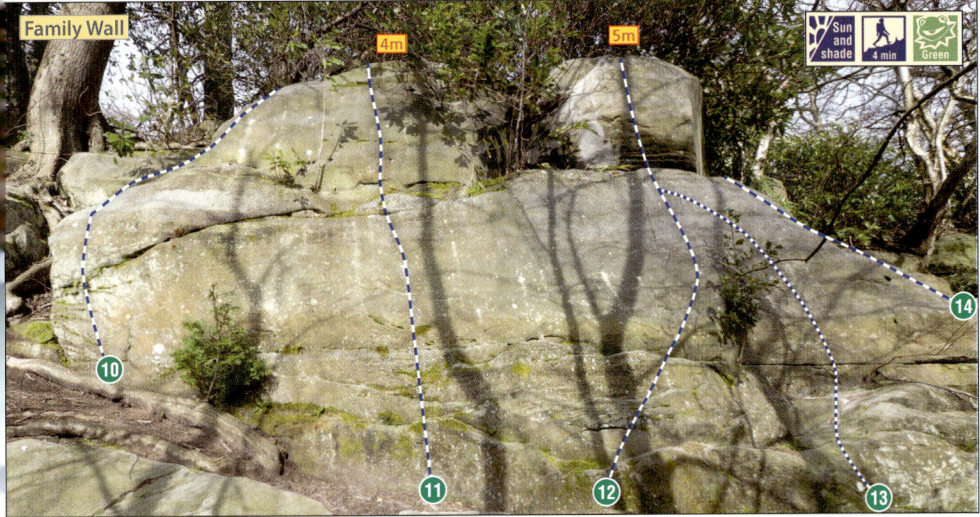

Family Wall
A neglected and dirty wall which is often overgrown at the top.

10 Vito .... ⬜ f2
The rounded left arete.

11 Michael .... ⬜ f2+
The centre of the face starting with feet on thin ledges.

12 Fredo - Left .... ⬜ f2+
A little reach for the ledge and a tricky finish.

13 Fredo - Right .... ⬜ f2+
The right-hand variation with the same tricky finish.

14 Luca .... ⬜ f2+
A long and dirty arete.

15 Sonny .... ⬜ f2
The left side of the short slab.

16 Salvatore .... ⬜ f2
The slab moving right to finish.

17 Emillio .... ⬜ f2
The small crack.

18 Tom .... ⬜ f2
The short face right of the crack.

19 Carlo .... ⬜ f4+
A precarious romp up the curving flake. Can often be green.

20 Enzo .... ⬜ f2
The small boulder below and between Family Wall and Umbilicus often done with no hands.

Bowles Rocks — Umbilicus

Umbilicus

A shady area. The rock is soft and delicate in places and the wall is overshadowed by trees which prevents it from drying out quickly.

Approach (see overview on page 66) - Head up past the upper basin and into the trees where the main crag is hidden from view.

Set-up and Descent - To the left are some steps that lead to the top path.

1 Roman Nose 5a *4c*
Climb the short wall just right of the flake. Often wet.
FA. T.Tullis 1961

2 Umbilicus 6c *6a*
The centre of the wall using a distinct small ironstone rail. Finish up the left arete of the headwall above.
FA. T.G.DeLacy 2.2.1975

3 Fallen Angels 7a *6a*
Climb *Umbilicus* and finish steeply up the undercut headwall using the odd hold round to the right.
FA. D.Beail 8.2.1997

4 Jean Genie .... 6b+ *5c*
Follow *Umbilicus* and finish round to the right on the slab.
FA. M.Fowler 1970s

5 Geoff's Route 7a *6b*
Start with difficulty and climb the wall on poor holds, past the undercut, to a difficult move to reach the slab above. Finish on the short headwall above. Often bouldered at *f6B* to the slab.
FA. G.Pearson 1970s

6 Geoffrey Moon Esquire 7a *6b*
A difficult mantel onto the top slab. Poor feet and few decent holds. Often bouldered at *f6B+*.
FA. D.Atchinson-Jones 1981

7 Blue Moon 7a *6a*
Make a difficult mantel onto the nose using the flake.
FA. G.DeLacy 1970s

8 991.8 Days 6c *6a*
From monos, slap up for the ledge and finish direct. Rarely in condition.

9 Court's Climb 4c *4c*
The side wall, starting just left of the corner. Often too green.

Iain Fuller latching the final hold on *Hidrosis* (**f6A**) - *page 87* - on the Carbide Finger roof area at Bowles Rocks.

Bowles Rocks — Scirocco Slab

Scirocco Slab
Immediately right of the Umbilicus is a fantastic slab.
Set-up and Descent - To the left of Umbilicus are some steps that lead to the top path.

1 Grotty Groove 3c *3c*
The name says it all, but it is surprisingly popular.
FA. P.Clinch 1970s

2 Grotty Slab .... *f2+*
A short problem onto the ledge.

3 Running Jump 4a *4a*
A nice route requiring a pop to the break and a mantelshelf to finish.

4 Scirocco Wall 4b *4b*
Climb direct up the face. Better holds for the feet than hands.
FA. T.Daniells 1970s

5 Scirocco Slab 5a *4c*
Follow the vague ramp-line to the break and tiptoe on shallow pockets to the top.

6 Netwall 4c *4c*
Climb the face moving rightwards at the top.

7 Knitwall *f7B*
A hard direct start to *Netwall* using poor holds and eliminating those on *Netwall*.
FA. G.McLelland 1981

8 Corner Layback .... 6a+ *5a*
A great line that can be done a number of ways. Layback, bridge and jam your way up the crack. The top moves often confuse people.

Knucklebones — Bowles Rocks

Knucklebones

Around to the right of Scirocco Slab is an easily identifiable wall with its unusual array of stuck-on holds at its centre. Most of the lines are hard with one in particular that could potentially end your climbing career!

Set-up and Descent - To the left of Umbilicus are some steps that lead to the top path; or alternatively use *Reclamation Gully* just right of *Chelsea Chimney*.

⑨ Aphrodite 6c *6a*
Climb the vague nose and traverse right to join *Zoom*.
FA. D.Atchinson-Jones 1982. The original before the direct was done.

⑩ Zoom 7a *6b*
A dyno or reach off undercuts gains the break and wall above.
FA. D.Atchinson-Jones 4.5.1983

⑪ Santa's Claws 5a *4c*
An artificial route using a series cemented in granite holds.

⑫ Maybe When You're Older... f7B
From a sit-start off the boulder, make a difficult traverse left along the break and finish at the lower uncut hold on *Aphrodite*.

⑬ Knucklebones .... 7a+ *6b*
Freezer bags at the ready! Climb the wall using artificial created bolt holds, which are just big enough to fit, and potentially lose, your fingers in!
FA. C.Murray 1992

⑭ Coast to Coast 7a *6b*
Start up *Chelsea Chimney* and reach for the slimy break. Traverse left and finish as for *Santa's Claws*.
FA. C.Murray 1992

⑮ Chelsea Chimney 3a *3a*
Climb the gully either as a layback or a tight squeeze up the gap. Step off right into the gully to finish. An alternative finish from the ledge and up the series of bulges is **The Firm**, 6c *6a*.
FA. (The Firm) R.Mazinke 18.6.2005

Bowles Rocks — Reclamation Slab

Reclamation Slab

Situated at the top left of the upper circular bowl, this wall is often used by Bowles for abseiling and teaching.

Access - Please note that this is the only wall allowed on sandstone for abseiling and has been specially equipped for this purpose. Abseiling anywhere else on sandstone is strictly forbidden.

Set-up and Descent - To the left of Umbilicus are some steps that lead to the top path; alternatively use *Reclamation Gully*.

① **Reclamation Gully** 3a *3a*
The short gully is often wet and slimy. Often used as a way up and down.

② **Reclamation Slab Left** 3c *3c*
Climb the left side of the slab using the arete if required.

③ **Reclamation Slap** ..... 6b+ *5c*
An eliminate up the centre of the wall, avoiding holds on both *Reclamation Slab Left* and *Reclamation Slab Right*.
FA. D.Turner 15.7.1987

④ **Reclamation Slab Right** 3a *3a*
The line of in-cut holds is often used as a beginners' route.

⑤ **Mental Balance** 6c *6a*
A difficult route tackling the small roof.
FA. P.Hayes 1984

⑥ **Cenotaph Corner Two** ...... 6a+ *5b*
The corner to a finish jamming your way up the top crack.
FA. B.Kavanagh 10.10.1992

Banana Bowles Rocks

Banana

A popular wall with a number of great lines including two classics, *Banana* and *Drosophila*.

Set-up and Descent - To the left of Umbilicus are some steps that lead to the top path; alternatively use *Reclamation Gully*.

7 High Traverse 5a *4c*
A difficult traverse to protect - often soloed.

8 Slyme Cryme .... 6c+ *6a*
Start as for *High Traverse* and then tackle the upper block on its right-hand side.

9 Banana Hammock *f6C*
A popular boulder problem using a series of slopers on *Banana* and finishing at the break.
FA. I.Stronghill 2003

10 Banana 6c *6a*
A great line. Follow the banana-shaped groove up and then slightly more direct to reach the break. Technical and powerful campus moves are required to exit.
FA. M.Boysen 1959

11 Proboscis .... 6c+ *6a*
An eliminate which struggles to be independent except for its final moves over the bulge.
FA. J.Mace 26.7.1983

12 Drosophila .... 6a+ *5b*
A fantastic route up the face which is quite fingery though unfortunately chipped in places. Finish by traversing the remainder of *High Traverse*.
FA. M.Boysen 1960

13 Urban Jock 7a *6b*
A fingery eliminate with a direct finish over the top bulge which can also be used to finish *Drosophila*.
FA. J.Ogilvie 1999

14 Babylon 5a *4c*
When dry, this can provide a good body jamming and laybacking exercise.

Bowles Rocks — Fandango Wall

Fandango Wall

The top-roper has become an unwanted species here, as bouldering is now the preferred activity on this wall. It provides some excellent problems and routes. There are many variations to each problem and route so play around as much as your heart desires.

Set-up and Descent - To the left of Umbilicus are some steps that lead to the top path; alternatively use *Reclamation Gully* left of Reclamation Slab.

❶ TNT 6b *5c*
A technical and precarious face climb. Often dirty.
FA. D.Mitten 10.9.1972

❷ Coathanger .... 6b+ *5c*
Starting on the front face, slap up the nose to a juggy rail and move with difficulty onto the left face. Tiptoe delicately up the slab to finish. A popular *f6C* problem goes from a sit-start to the first juggy rail.

❸ Camel .... *f6B+*
A good counter line to *Nicotine Alley* which starts from good hold on the lower break to meet and reverse *Nicotine Alley* from its midway point. *Photo on page 13*.

Fandango Wall — Bowles Rocks

④ Station to Station ... 7a+ *6b*
A route that continues over the reachy upper bulge. More common is to climb from a sit-start to the upper break to join *Tobacco Road - Extension* at *f6B*.
FA. D.Atchinson-Jones 1982

⑤ Fandango .... Top 50 ... 6c+ *6a*
A steep and powerful classic. Climb the fingery lower wall then break left on jugs to power upwards and attack the sloping rail. A difficult rockover/mantel onto the upper slab spits most contestants off.
FA. M.Boysen 1960

⑥ Fandango Central ... 7a+ *6a*
The direct link over the roof is both reachy and powerful.

⑦ Fandango Right-hand ... 6c+ *6a*
Fandango's reflected twin, moving right strenuously around the roof and back left to finish up the wall above. Not as popular as *Fandango*, but just as good.
FA. T.G.DeLacy 1974

⑧ Sonic Blue .... *f7B+*
From the lower break, reach into the side-pulls and crimps of *Nicotine Alley* before reaching up for a left-hand crimp/finger-lock. Summon everything you have got and reach for the right-hand side-pull, then pop up and left to catch a good pocket. An easier version at *f7B* can be done from a standing start.

⑨ Phasis *f7C*
Either start as for *Sonic Blue* (sit-start) or direct from a standing start (same grade). Climb the wall, eliminating the crimp/finger-lock on *Sonic Blue*. Use the holds above the right-hand side-pull on *Sonic Blue*, then move up and right to finish.

⑩ Twisted Vegas *f7B*
Use small crimps to tackle the right bulge close to the arete.

⑪ Nicotine Alley ..... Top 50 *f7A*
Perhaps the best and most sought-after traverse on Sandstone. From *Skiffle*, traverse the fingery break to the start of *Fandango* and continue leftwards using the middle line of holds, finishing up on the large jug on *Coathanger*. *Photo this page.*
Taking the lower set of holds at the end before heading up to the *Coathanger* jug is **Nicotine Alley Variation**, *f7A+*.
FA. G.McLelland 1984

⑫ Tobacco Road ..... *f6B+*
As for *Nicotine Alley*, but finish up the crimpy start of *Fandango* to the first juggy rail. Technically one should finish by climbing *Fandango Right-hand*, but that's often not the case.
FA. G.McLelland 1981

⑬ Tobacco Road - Extension
.... *f6B+*
Climb *Tobacco Road* to the juggy rail and traverse left to finish at the large jug on *Coathanger*.
FA. G.McLelland 1981

⑭ Poff Pastry .... 7a+ *6b*
Climb *Skiffle* and step left onto the face to attack the first bulge. From there, break out left to tackle the series of bulges left of the nose and finishing at the tree.
FA. G.McLelland 6.10.1983

⑮ Pastry 6c *5c*
As for *Poff Pastry* to the point just over the first bulge, then climb the right-hand set of bulges, finishing right of the nose.
FA. N.S.Head 1971

⑯ Skiffle 4a *4a*
A good crack-climb when dry, using the slab out right for feet.

⑰ Sugarplum *f6A*
Head left to finish at *Coathanger*. Usually soloed above mats.

⑱ Icarus............ 6c+ *6a*
Head left on the higher break to finish at *Coathanger*.

Lenaya Page making an impressive bare foot traverse of the fingery *Nicotine Alley* (*f7A*) - *this page*.

Bowles Rocks

Kemp's Delight

The popular climb of *Kemp's Delight* (5a *4c*) - *opposite* - at the Kemp's Delight area at Bowles is all good fun until the final few moves, which make you wish you had your rope set-up a few metres further right.

Bowles Rocks — Serenade Arete Area

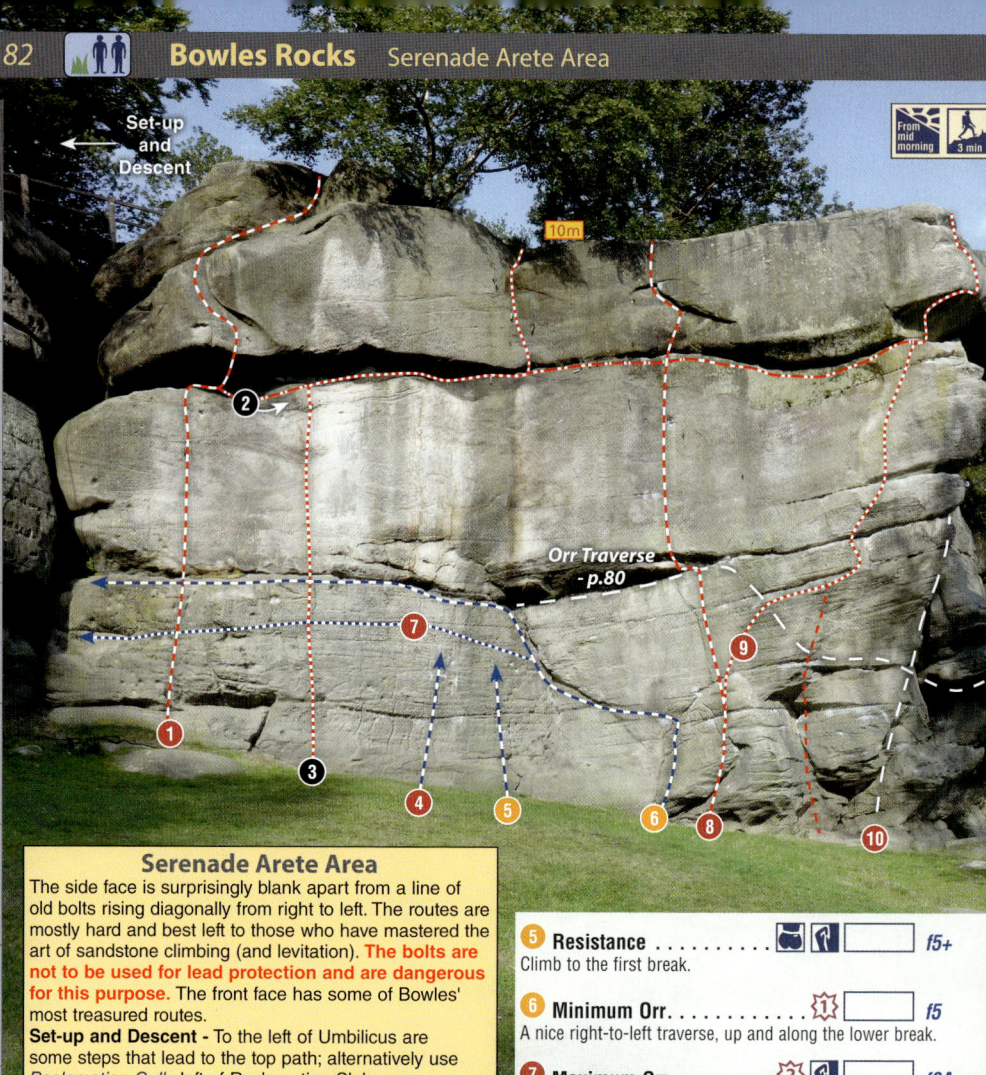

Serenade Arete Area
The side face is surprisingly blank apart from a line of old bolts rising diagonally from right to left. The routes are mostly hard and best left to those who have mastered the art of sandstone climbing (and levitation). **The bolts are not to be used for lead protection and are dangerous for this purpose.** The front face has some of Bowles' most treasured routes.

Set-up and Descent - To the left of Umbilicus are some steps that lead to the top path; alternatively use *Reclamation Gully* left of Reclamation Slab.

1 Patella 7a 6a
Balance up onto the ledge and reach for the upper break avoiding the old bolt. Continue with difficulty over the lip and layback using the large flake above.

2 Kinnard .... 7a+ 6b
A long high break traverse between *Patella* and the finish of *Digitalis*. Hard to protect and pumpy!
FA. P.Hayes 1970s

3 Nutella 7b 6b
Using very small pockets, and deploying some levitation skills, gain the upper break before yarding out right to reach the tempting (but out-of-bounds) bolts at the groove. Continue to levitate with difficulty to finish.
FA. D.Turner 4.6.1983

4 Inclination to Sin ...... f6A+
A short problem to the first break.

5 Resistance .... f5+
Climb to the first break.

6 Minimum Orr f5
A nice right-to-left traverse, up and along the lower break.

7 Maximum Orr .... f6A+
A good fingery alternative avoiding the use of the lower break.

8 Temptation 7a 6b
Precarious and fingery climbing up the face resisting the temptation to use the line of old and rusty bolts.
FA. D.Turner 4.6.1983

9 Digitalis .... 6c+ 6a
Great face climbing on slightly worn holds. From the pedestal, crimp your way up and right past a series of breaks to engage a fingery side-pull and reach for a sloping ledge above. Finish as for *Inspiration*. The direct start is graded at 7a 6a.
FA. M.Boysen 1960

10 Serenade Arete .... 6c+ 6a
The magnificent overhanging arete is both inspiring and exhilarating to climb. Starting on the left side of the arete, climb up and right using a series of breaks to tackle the right side of the arete and its distinctive crux move. From the ledge above, finish as for *Inspiration*. *Photo on page 1 and 85.*
FA. N.S.Head 1971

Serenade Arete Area — Bowles Rocks

11 Inspiration .... Top 50 — 6b+ *5c*
A popular adventure up the open flake with an easy reach to the top break just right of the crack (bit of a swing if you come off at this point). Traverse left onto the ledge on the arete and reach precariously over the lip to grab the rounded ledge. Without much for feet, commit to those final moves!
FA. M.Boysen 1959

12 The Thing 7b *6b*
A short fingery crack through the roof to some serious jamming at the lip.
FA. M.Boysen 1959

13 Jabba .... *f4+*
A short problem using a good flake to reach out and finish on a large sloper.

14 The Fridge .... *f6C+*
Slap your way up the bulging nose and finish at the break.
FA. I.Stronghill 2004

15 Juanita 6c *6a*
Difficult moves gain the slab, which is climbed up the centre of the face to the roof. Jam through the roof using the crack which leads from the hole used for *Sapper*.

16 One Nighter 7c *6c*
Climb the lower roof and slab above to reach the roof. Using pockets, stretch out to reach the lip and slap up dynamically to a sandy finish.
FA. M.Saunders 23.8.1986. Direct start added later.

17 Sapper .... Top 50 — 5b *5a*
The classic adventure not to be missed. Start up the right side of the arete and pull round onto the slab. Traverse left across the face (carefully) to reach the large open flake. Romp up the flake to a large hole in the roof and squeeze and huff your way through this to finish. *Photo on page 23 and 62.*

Bowles Rocks — Serenade Arete Area

18 Burlap — 6a+ 5b
Start as for *Sapper* (it can be done more direct at the start **6b+ 5c**) and move onto and then climb the slabby left side of the arete (it is also possible to climb the arete on its right). There are two ways to tackle the upper wall, both the same grade.
FA. T.Tullis 1960

19 Burlap Eliminate — 6c 6a
A good but tight eliminate up the centre of the side wall.

Ensure when placing a top rope on the Yoyo slab that the crab hangs sufficiently low to avoid the rope rubbing on the rock. Place an extended crab to clip up higher up.

20 Yoyo — 4c 4c
Climb/jam your way up the crack. Alternatively climb the slab only using the left arete which goes at **6b 5c**.

21 White Verdict — 7a+ 6b
The fingery left side of the face avoiding the arete.
FA. C.Arnold 4.5.1983

22 The Ly'in — 7a 6b
The right-hand side of the slab sharing some holds with *White Verdict*.
FA. C.Arnold 4.5.1983

23 Meager's Right-hand — 6b 5c
A good route laybacking the right-hand arete and finishing up the centre of the headwall as for the other routes.
FA. N.Head 16.1.1972

Anton Belodedenko climbing the powerful *Serenade Arete* (6c+ *6a*) - *page 82* - at the Serenade Arete Area. This climb usually requires work to unlock the sequence before a successful ascent can be made.

Bowles Rocks — Salamander Slab

Salamander Slab

A great set of routes above an undercut section - harder direct versions are also available. The upper wall provides great air walks if you can get to them! Further right is a big roof, home to *Carbide Finger* and other powerful roof climbs

Set-up and Descent - To the left of Umbilicus are some steps that lead to the top path; alternatively use *Reclamation Gully* left of Reclamation Slab.

1 Sing Sing 3c *3c*
Squirm or bridge your way up the chimney.

2 Manita .... 6b+ *5c*
A short but intense pocket-pulling problem up the centre of the face, with more than one way to do it. Finish on the slab around to the left.
FA. T.G.DeLacy 1970s

3 Jackie .... 6a+ *5b*
Start as for *Manita* and pull round and climb the right-hand side of the arete. Finish as for *Manita*, or try the short and footless direct finish up the wall above at **6c** *6a*.
FA. N.S.Head 1970s

4 Jackie Direct .... f4+
An alternative and more direct start to *Jackie*, often bouldered.

5 Murph's Mount .... 6a+ *5a*
A filler-in up the slab right of *Jackie*. Finish up *Jackie*. It can be started from *Sing Sing*.

6 Nero .... 6b+ *5c*
Traverse round from the start of *Manita* and climb the centre of the slab to tackle the fine headwall above.
FA. N.S.Head 22.9.1974

7 Hellbender f6A
A direct to *Murph's Mount* starting from the large flat jug.

8 Flatwoods .... f6A+
A boulder problem start to *Nero* or *Salamander Slab*, finishing at the first break. If linked into either route, this increases the grade of both routes to **6c+** *6a*.

9 Salamander Slab .... 6b+ *5c*
A great line that may require two top-rope set-ups in order to cross the wall safely. Follow *Nero* across the slab and continue to curve rightward, finally finishing steeply past the rotten tree stump which may require an escape rope since the stump is now unusable.
FA. P.Maher 1960s

10 The Twilight Zone f6B
Slap blindly through the roof and finish at the first break for the tick. For the full experience, continue through and finish as for *Salamander Slab* at **7a** *6b*.
FA. T.Nagler 8.7.2002

11 Perspiration Direct 6c *5c*
After an all powerful steep start, follow the crack to its end., Continue climbing up and right over the bulges on good holds to finish left of the top block.
FA. J.Smocker 1960s

Salamander Slab — Bowles Rocks

Abracadabra - p.88

12 Perspiration — 6c 5c
The original moves right at mid-height to climb the slab. Weave up to exit between the two top blocks.
FA. J.Smocker 1960s

13 Peter's Perseverance — 6a 5a
A grand tour of the slabs, starting from *Manita*, that requires multiple top rope set-ups in order to complete. Finish up the wide crack above *Swastika*.
FA. J.Smocker 1960s

14 Hidrosis — f6A
Come in from *Perspiration*, and finishing at 'large-but-not-that-large' jugs. Photo on page 73.

15 Boiling Point — 7a+ 6b
Climb direct to a square hole under the lip. Power over, passing the large letterbox ledge/poor jug, to reach a rail and wall above. Using the arete higher is not frowned upon unless you are a purist. Finish up *Perspiration* or *Peter's Perseverance*.
FA. J.Woodward 1970s

16 Them Monkey Things — 7c+ 6c
Gain the short vertical crack in the roof and use a small layaway to reach for the break above. Make a difficult transition onto the upper slab. Finish up *Perspiration* or *Peter's Perseverance*.
FA. R.Mazinke 2.6.1995

17 Carbide Finger — 7c 6c
Technically easier than *Them Monkey Things* but more sustained. Tackle the roof using a thin crack, undercuts and square-cut holds. Getting over the lip is another game altogether. Finish up *Perspiration* or *Peter's Perseverance*.
FA. J.Morgan 1981

18 Cardboard Box — 7a+ 6b
The most popular of all the roof climbs herabouts. Launch up to the large flake, traverse right and pop for slopers, then quickly slap for the break above. Finish up any of the lines above.
FA. D.Turner 17.8.1983

19 Thieving Gypsies — 6c+ 6a
A good but short roof climb continuing past a rounded pocket just above the lip. Finish up the corner of *Abracadabra*.
FA. J.Wade 15.5.2001

The following routes are usually started from the corner of *Abracadabra* (page 88).

20 Swastika — 6b 5b
A nice and exposed line moving left across the face and finishing up the wide crack.
FA. P.Smocker 1959

21 Bubble Wrap — 7a+ 6b
Also considered the direct (ish) finish to *Cardboard Box*.
FA. R.Mazinke 12.9.1996

22 Nightmare — 6c+ 6a
Great airy climbing up the blunt arete. Finish as for *Swastika*.
FA. J.Durrant 17.9.1972

23 Recurring Nightmare — 7b+ 6b
A crimpy direct finish to *Thieving Gypsies*.
FA. M.Saunders 198

Bowles Rocks — Range Wall

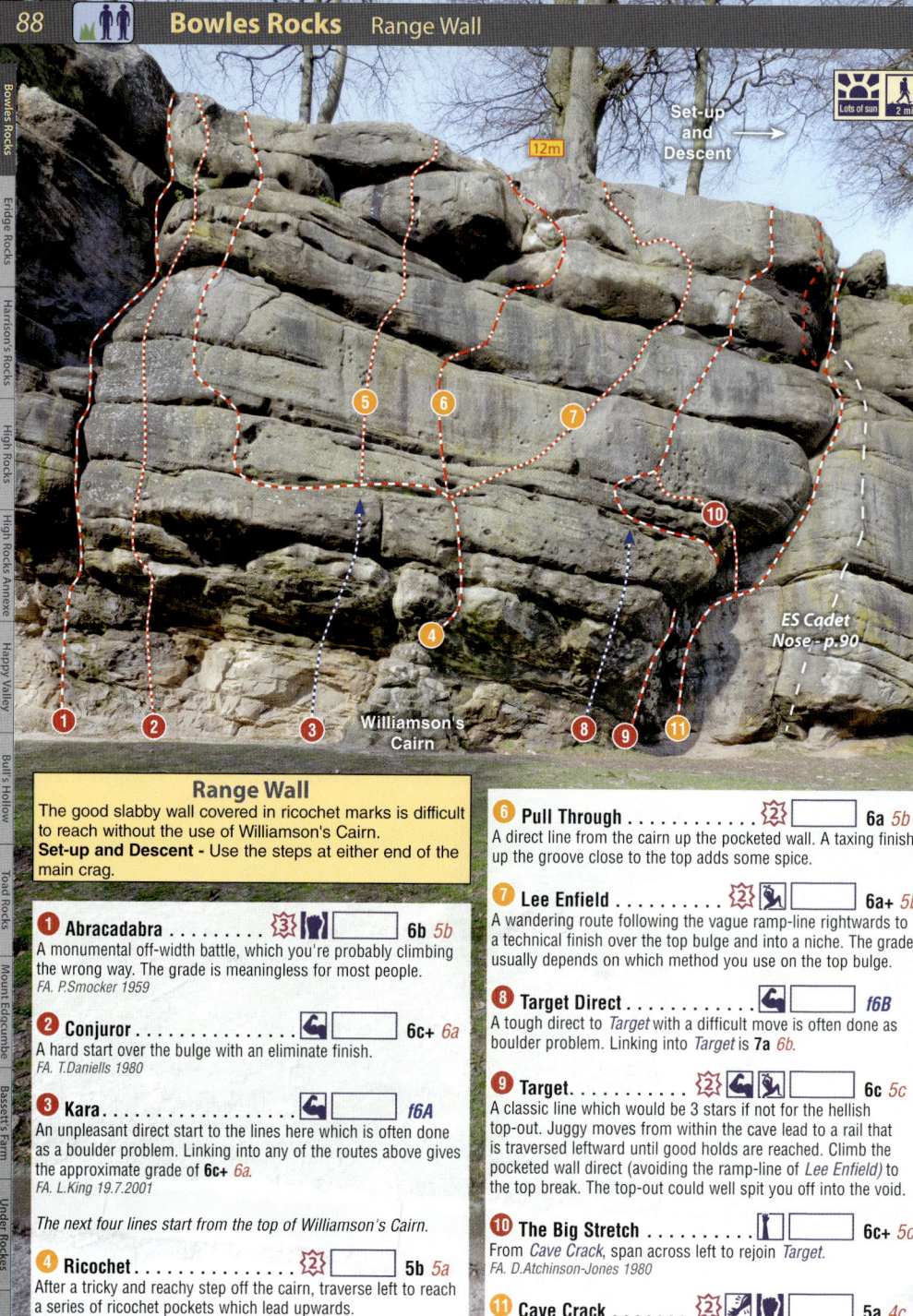

Range Wall
The good slabby wall covered in ricochet marks is difficult to reach without the use of Williamson's Cairn.
Set-up and Descent - Use the steps at either end of the main crag.

1 Abracadabra 6b 5b
A monumental off-width battle, which you're probably climbing the wrong way. The grade is meaningless for most people.
FA. P.Smocker 1959

2 Conjuror .... 6c+ 6a
A hard start over the bulge with an eliminate finish.
FA. T.Daniells 1980

3 Kara f6A
An unpleasant direct start to the lines here which is often done as a boulder problem. Linking into any of the routes above gives the approximate grade of **6c+** 6a.
FA. L.King 19.7.2001

The next four lines start from the top of Williamson's Cairn.

4 Ricochet 5b 5a
After a tricky and reachy step off the cairn, traverse left to reach a series of ricochet pockets which lead upwards.

5 Four-by-Two 5c 5a
Similar to *Ricochet*, finishing left of the roof.
FA. J.Ouseley 10.9.1972

6 Pull Through 6a 5b
A direct line from the cairn up the pocketed wall. A taxing finish up the groove close to the top adds some spice.

7 Lee Enfield .... 6a+ 5b
A wandering route following the vague ramp-line rightwards to a technical finish over the top bulge and into a niche. The grade usually depends on which method you use on the top bulge.

8 Target Direct f6B
A tough direct to *Target* with a difficult move is often done as boulder problem. Linking into *Target* is **7a** 6b.

9 Target 6c 5c
A classic line which would be 3 stars if not for the hellish top-out. Juggy moves from within the cave lead to a rail that is traversed leftward until good holds are reached. Climb the pocketed wall direct (avoiding the ramp-line of *Lee Enfield*) to the top break. The top-out could well spit you off into the void.

10 The Big Stretch .... 6c+ 5c
From *Cave Crack*, span across left to rejoin *Target*.
FA. D.Atchinson-Jones 1980

11 Cave Crack 5a 4c
Climb the back of the cave using the wall to the right and layback out from under the roof to finish up the crack above. An alternative finish can be made up the nose left of the top crack **6b+** 5c.

Emma Harrington making a late evening ascent of *Hate* (6c+ *6a*) - *page 91* - on the Pig's Nose Area of Bowles Rocks. Photo: Ben Hall

Pig's Nose Area

The jewel in the crown of Bowles Rocks, providing some of Bowles' finest and most sought-after routes.

Set-up and Descent - Use the steps at the right-hand end of the crag, just beyond Hargreaves Buttress..

① ES Cadet Nose .... 6a+ *5b*
From a tricky start, climb the arete mainly on its right-hand side, avoiding contact with *Cave Crack* at its mid-point. Adding a sit-start and finishing at the central break is *f6B*.

② Skallagrigg .... 7b+ *6c*
A difficult eliminate up the face.
FA. B.Franklin 20.8.1994

③ Devaluation .... 6a+ *5b*
A popular, eye-catching line up the centre of the face using the cut-out pockets, which are not as good as they first appear.
Photo on page 58.

④ Sandman .... 7a+ *6b*
A short power problem up the right-hand arete popping for a big thread on the upper break. The grade is height dependent.
FA. M.Boysen 1977

⑤ Stoneman 7b *6b*
A hard and reachy direct finish to *Sandman* over the upper bulge.
FA. J.Patterson 1994

⑥ Devour .... f6B+
Traverse the lower break from right to left, with a difficult drop down midway. Finish at the central break on the arete.

⑦ Charlie's Chimney 4a *4a*
An entertaining back and foot shuffle up the chimney. Finish left across the platform.

Pig's Nose Area — Bowles Rocks

⑧ Love............ 7a *6a*
Great climbing up the left arete until you reach the roof where the fight begins....
FA. B.Wyvill 1980

⑨ Hate............ 6c+ *6a*
Excellent technical face climbing on the lower section with a shoulder-wrenching finale through the bulge and crack above.
Photo on page 89.
FA. M.Boysen 1960

⑩ Upside Downies...... 7a *6b*
A squeezed in eliminate with a hard move over the bulge onto the ledge.
FA. D.Atchinson-Jones 1989

⑪ Pig's Ear......... 6b+ *5c*
Follow the shallow curving groove up the centre of the face to better holds. Power steeply over the roof to reach the upper wall stylishly, or fail miserably in a mix of heel hooks and curses.
Photo on page 93.
There is an eliminate to the right called **Watson-Watt, 7a** *6b*, but is too eliminate for its own good.
FA. (Watson-Watt) D.Potts 17.10.2004

⑫ TT.............. 6a+ *5b*
The centre of the face via a letterbox and some half decent holds up the pocketed cracks. Turn a blind eye when reaching for holds out right which are not quite part of *Pig's Nose* but feel like they should be.
FA. T.Tullis 1960

Bowles Rocks — Pig's Nose Area

⑬ Pig's Nose .... Top 50 5c *5a*
A true sandstone classic up the nose on massive jugs. The top provides an exciting steep and exposed finale on good holds.
Photo on cover and page 9.

⑭ Koffler 6c *6a*
A fierce and fingery wall climb that eases with height. Avoid contact with the rail on *Gully Wall* and, if you're feeling strong, then try the smooth footless direct finish, **6c+** *6a*, that requires one hell of a mantel and is much harder for the short.
FA. N.S.Head 1972

⑮ Gully Wall .... 6a+ *5a*
A great and often ignored adventure up the side-wall following the flake to take on the bulges above.

The ever youthful Raz Parmar demonstrating his sandstone abilities by cruising *Pig's Ear* (6b+ 5c) - *page 91* - at the Pig's Nose Area.

Bowles Rocks — Funnel

Birch Crack - Set-up and Descent
Please take note that this is generally a descent only option which should only be undertaken by experienced sandstone climbers who are familiar with it.

Set-up and Descent

Tricky descent scramble

Pig's Nose - p.92

① Birch Crack 3c *3c*
A long and fairly easy climb up the gully with a number of obstacles to overcome.

② Chris 6b *5c*
A short but worthwhile line up the face. It's all in the final moves. Most people finish at the ledge and climb down *Birch Crack*.

③ Kennard's Climb 4a *4a*
Climb the crack and tackle the nose to a difficult mantelshelf finish. *Photo on page 103.*

④ Rib 6b *5c*
Climb the nose using a series of rounded bulges to the short headwall which is easy to finish over.

⑤ Love Without Resistance f6B
A sustained left-to-right traverse on mega slopers starting up *Rib* and finishing at *Harden Gully*. Traversing the slightly higher break is **Chelsea Traverse**, *f3*.

⑥ Dib 4a *4a*
Start in the crack and wander leftwards to finish as for *Rib*. Linking the start of the route onto *The Scouter Direct* is a logical and nice **3c** *3c*.

⑦ The Scouter Direct 4c *4c*
Traditionally started up *Nelson's Column*, this line is better done direct. Start up a juggy (ish) lower wall and continue up the corner slab and crack.

Funnel — Bowles Rocks

Funnel
A good selection of technical slab climbs with often taxing starts. Ensure you have your ropes over the lower ledge, and use a clip-up to climb the final short wall above - see page 40 for more information.

Set-up and Descent - Use the steps at the right-hand end of the crag, just beyond Hargreaves Buttress.

Belay anchor for kids and groups to use

⑧ Corbett Slab 4c *4c*
Start up the face (some move more right at the start). From the upper ledge, reach up to grab juggy holds either side of the nose and smear up to gain the break above. Finish with a little mantel onto the ledge.

⑨ Nelson's Column 5b *5a*
Climb the crack and thinly pocketed wall above.

⑩ Dival's Diversion 6a *5b*
Make a tricky start - which gives this route its grade - then climb the upper face, right of the thin crack which is handy for your left-hand.

⑪ Funnel 4a *4a*
A tricky start leads quickly to the upper groove, which is a bit trickier than it looks. *Photo on page 65.*

⑫ Coolcaringer .... 6a+ *5b*
A surprisingly good eliminate which shares holds with its neighbours on the final moves.

⑬ UN .... 6b+ *5c*
A classic that follows the vague crack system to the upper slab with a tricky mantel onto the ledge. The super steep upper wall has some surprisingly welcome jugs and an exciting top-out, which is easier once you know where the good holds are.

⑭ Wells's Reach 3a *3a*
Climb the gully and take the disjointed left-hand crack to the upper ledge below the roof. Exit to the right. A good way to approach the next two lines.

⑮ The Wrecker .... 7b+ *6c*
A futuristic route at the time, and sandstone's very own *Separate Reality*. Tackle the crack running through the roof and brutally exit over the lip.
FA. J.Smocker 1960s

⑯ One of Our Buzzards is Missing . 7a+ *6b*
From the ledge, climb the rib right of the bolt to the roof. Make a long reach out left to pockets on the sidewall close to the rounded arete. Exit powerfully above.
FA. R.Mazinke 20.3.1994

⑰ Harden Gully 3a *3a*
A simple gully climb which is also used as a down-climb by the daring.

Bowles Rocks — Larchant Wall

Larchant Wall

A popular wall that feels like something from a climbing gym, with many of the routes feeling quite pumpy or impossible if done wrong!

Set-up and Descent - Use the steps at the right-hand end of the crag, just beyond Hargreaves Buttress.

1 Silvie's Slab 5a *4c*
Climb the vague arete and make an awkward move to gain the slab, which is climbed up its centre.

2 Six Foot 5a *4c*
Climb up and left to join the sloping arete using two nice holds to help launch up the remainder of the climb.
FA. N.S.Head 3.4.1972

3 Larchant .... 6a+ *5a*
A good and popular line with good juggy holds throughout.
FA. T.Tullis 1962

4 Hennessy Heights 6b *5b*
A fantastic sustained route up the centre of the wall. Despite being chipped and repaired in places, the headwall does provide a great finish. *Photo opposite.*

5 August Variation .... 6b+ *5c*
A tight eliminate - it is difficult to avoid the flake on *October*.
FA. M.McPherson 15.8.1982

6 October 5a *4c*
The nice overlapping flake that is tackled mostly on its right side.

7 Fragile Arete 5c *5a*
A good direct version of *Fragile Wall* (page 98) up the arete.
FA. N.S.Head 1974

8 Process of Elimination f6B
From a sit-start, launch up and then left, eliminating the large break and finishing almost in *Harden Gully*. A good testpiece for any aspiring climber wishing to get into the harder grades.

There are a number of boulder problems along the face, most of which are sit or crouch starts to established routes.

Larchant Wall — Bowles Rocks

Steven Nayler undertaking the final moves on *Hennessy Heights* (6b *5b*) - *opposite* - on the pumpy headwall of Larchant Wall.

Above the platform are a number of short additional exits which can be added into the mix.

⑨ Basilisk 4b *4b*
The centre if the left block.

⑩ Acromantula 4a *4a*
The central crack between the blocks.

⑪ Centaurs . . . . 6a+ *5b*
The left side of the right block.

⑫ Firenze . . . . 6b+ *5c*
The right side of the right block.

⑬ Pop's Slab 5a *4c*
A nice juggy slab with an awkward high step.

⑭ Pop's Chimney 5a *4c*
A good but awkward off-width that is best approached from *Fragile Arete*.

Bowles Rocks — Finale

Finale
A good and varied cluster of routes tucked into a gravel bay, which can become rather noisy when groups arrive!
Set-up and Descent - Use the steps at the right-hand end of the crag, just beyond Hargreaves Buttress.

1 Fragile Wall 4a *4a*
Starting around the right side of Larchant Wall, traverse left to the arete. Climb up to reach the left-trending crack and follow this to the platform above. Finish up *Pop's Slab*.

2 Escalator 6a *5a*
Climb the centre of the face on small holds to a typical sandstone finish.

3 Elevator 6a *5a*
An eliminate right of *Escalator* and avoiding *Renison Gully*.

4 Renison Gully 4b *4b*
A nice but awkward corner that is often finished by climbing *Pop's Chimney*.

5 Finale .... 7a+ *6a*
Making your way up the left wall is relatively straightforward, tackling the roof and headwall above is not. It is also possible to finish more direct.

6 Alka 5a *4c*
A good climb up the juggy nose, finishing off up the wide crack.

7 Morpheus .... 6c+ *6a*
Start independently up the centre of the face then tuck in and take on the narrow nose between *Alka* and *Seltzer*.
FA. D.Potts 3.9.2002

8 Seltzer 6b *5b*
Climb the tricky lower wall to the thin and sustained finger-crack.
FA. M.Smart 1960s

9 Encore .... 6b+ *5c*
A tricky lower wall is followed by a reach/dyno (depending on your height) to a small ledge on the upper face. A strenuous mantelshelf finish remains.

10 Zugabe 7a *6b*
Climb the short lower wall using an ironstone knob to gain the second break. Tackle the blunt arete above, mainly on its right-hand side, to a dirty ledge, and finish by making a difficult mantelshelf to exit.
FA. T.Skinner 4.6.1991

11 Otra! 6b *5c*
Climb *November* then tackle the blank face to the left using thin flakes to gain a mossy ledge.

Beginners' Buttress — Bowles Rocks

Beginners' Buttress
Almost exclusively used by beginners and groups. All the top sections of the routes are on easier ground.
Set-up and Descent - Use the steps at the right-hand end of the crag, just beyond Hargreaves Buttress.
Conditions - The rock in *Easy Gully* is soft in places so please avoid using this as a way down.
Access - Please vacate these lines when requested by any organised Bowles climbing groups.

12 November 3a *3a*
Fun climbing up the gully.

13 Baby Boulder 4c *4c*
Much harder than people first anticipate. Climb the right-hand arete of the block. Also the start to *Otra!*.

14 G Force 6b *5c*
Climb the narrow face using either arete for assistance and finish up *Otra!*
FA. G.Jones 2009

15 Easy Gully 2a *2a*
One of the easiest climbs on sandstone.

16 Ballerina 4b *4b*
A technical lower wall which often gets done as a boulder problem. Finish up the slab.

17 Red Peg 3a *3a*
The narrow and smooth crack. Finish up the gully.

18 Claire 3c *3c*
Climb the left side of the arete and finish off up the left side of the upper slab.

19 Barham Boulder 4b *4b*
The right-hand variation of *Claire*. Finish any way you like.

20 Rad's Cliff 5c *5a*
A nice curving problem using good pockets.

21 Rad's Cliff Direct 5c *5a*
A direct to *Rad's Cliff*.

Bowles Rocks — Nealon's Buttress

Nealon's Buttress

The second buttress reached from the carpark with a selection of quality lines that are more engaging than they first appear.

Set-up and Descent - Use the far right-hand steps approximately 20m to the right.

1 Bovril - Left-Hand .... 6a+ *5a*
A hard start and is awkward above on poor holds.

2 Bovril 5a *4c*
Climb the arete on its right-hand side finishing up and around the top block. A sit-start problem to the first break is *f5+*.

3 Wally 5a *4c*
Go direct up the lower wall finishing any way you like. An alternative eliminate requires making a hard mantel over the nose above - **Jack in the Box, 7a** *6b*.
FA. (Jack in the Box) D.Atchinson-Jones 2009

4 Oliver's Twist 6b *5c*
A good technical route up the face on pockets with an interesting sequence midway through. Finish direct over the top boulder.
FA. M.Smith 3.12.1989

5 Nealon's 4c *4c*
Climb the diagonally overlapping flake to the ledge, with an awkward but fun manoeuvre up the top chimney. A harder direct finish **Nealon's Direct** takes the bulging nose above the ledge at 6c *6a*.

6 A Lady in Mink .... 6c+ *6a*
Climb the lower wall to the break and use a small crack scar to pull over the bulge and onto the upper face. Proceed by making a difficult lock-off to reach the lip and a typical mantel to finish.
FA. J.Woodward 1970s

Hargreaves Buttress — Bowles Rocks

Hargreaves Buttress

The staff at Bowles have dramatically transformed this area by literally unearthing the rock to reveal a number of new routes in the lower grades aimed primarily at beginners and groups. The rock is still a little dirty in places, but it will improve with time.

Set-up and Descent - Use the steps at the right-hand end of the crag and do not tie ropes to the fence posts. Boulder problems can be exited by traversing left along the ledge and back down the gully of *AS Peck*.

Access - Please vacate these lines when requested by any organised Bowles' climbing groups.

7 Whimper 3a *3a*
Climb the face on the left side of the gully finishing left over the top block.
FA. R.Priory 5.2017

8 Hillary 2a *2a*
Climb the centre of the gully finishing up and left over the disjointed block. A harder variation can be climbed over the block to the right at 3c *3c*.
FA. R.Priory 5.2017

9 AS Peck 3a *3a*
Climb the right-hand side of the gully and move right to finish. It can also be done by climbing the lower block to the right to start making things a bit more tricky at 3c *3c*.
FA. R.Priory 5.2017

10 Hargreaves 3a *3a*
The left side of the wall, finish left around the top block.
FA. J.Frasier 5.2017

11 Mercator's Projection 4a *4a*
The right side of the wall, finish direct over the top block.

12 Simpson 2a *2a*
The gully finishing rightwards around the top block. Harder variations can be done over the top block starting at 6a+ *5a* on the right, or moving left to increase the grade to 7a *6b*.
FA. A.Finney 5.2017

13 Steck 2c *2c*
Climb the corner-crack and finish as for *Simpson*.
FA. C.Hardwick 5.2017

14 Healy .... f2+
The small slab just left of the arete.
FA. M.Vetterlein 12.3.2005

15 Ben .... f4+
Climb the centre of the face.
FA. P.Highams 12.3.2005

16 Wilson f2
Climb the shallow corner.

17 Heath f2
Climb the left side of the slab.

18 Tullis .... f2+
The centre of the slab is short but nice.
FA. E.Hardwick 5.2017

19 Lino f4
Climb the very right-hand end of the slab.
FA. P.Clarke 5.2017

Bowles Rocks — Woodland Buttress

Woodland Buttress

Hidden slightly from view is a short and often neglected buttress.
Approach - Just past the main barrier leading from the carpark, the rocks are visible up and to the right.
Conditions - Lack of sun means the rocks are a little green in places but still very much climbable. Some of the top-outs can be overgrown at times.

1 Pat's Progress 4a *4a*
A series of mantelshelves up the left side of the block.

2 Dubonnet 4b *4b*
The centre of the wall with a slight bulge and crack at the top.

3 William's Layback 3a *3a*
Climb the short flake finishing right of, the tree.

4 Free Willy 3a *3a*
The centre of the face on good holds.
FA. R.Mazinke 4.5.1995

Immediately to the right is a small protruding block.

5 Index 4b *4b*
From the small mossy ledge, reach out along the break to reach the eyelet on the arete and finish above.
FA. T.Tullis 1962

6 Index Direct *f6A*
A great problem up the arete using crimps and pockets. It is also possible to do this from a sit-start at *f6A+*.

7 Gore Brothers *f5*
Follow the vague ramp-line / pocketed flakes up to a dirty top-out.
FA. N.Gore 12.4.2017

Bowles Rocks

Charlie Pickin, carefully shunting his way up *Kennard's Climb* (4a *4a*) - *page 94*. - located at the popular Pig's Nose Area at Bowles.

Eridge Rocks

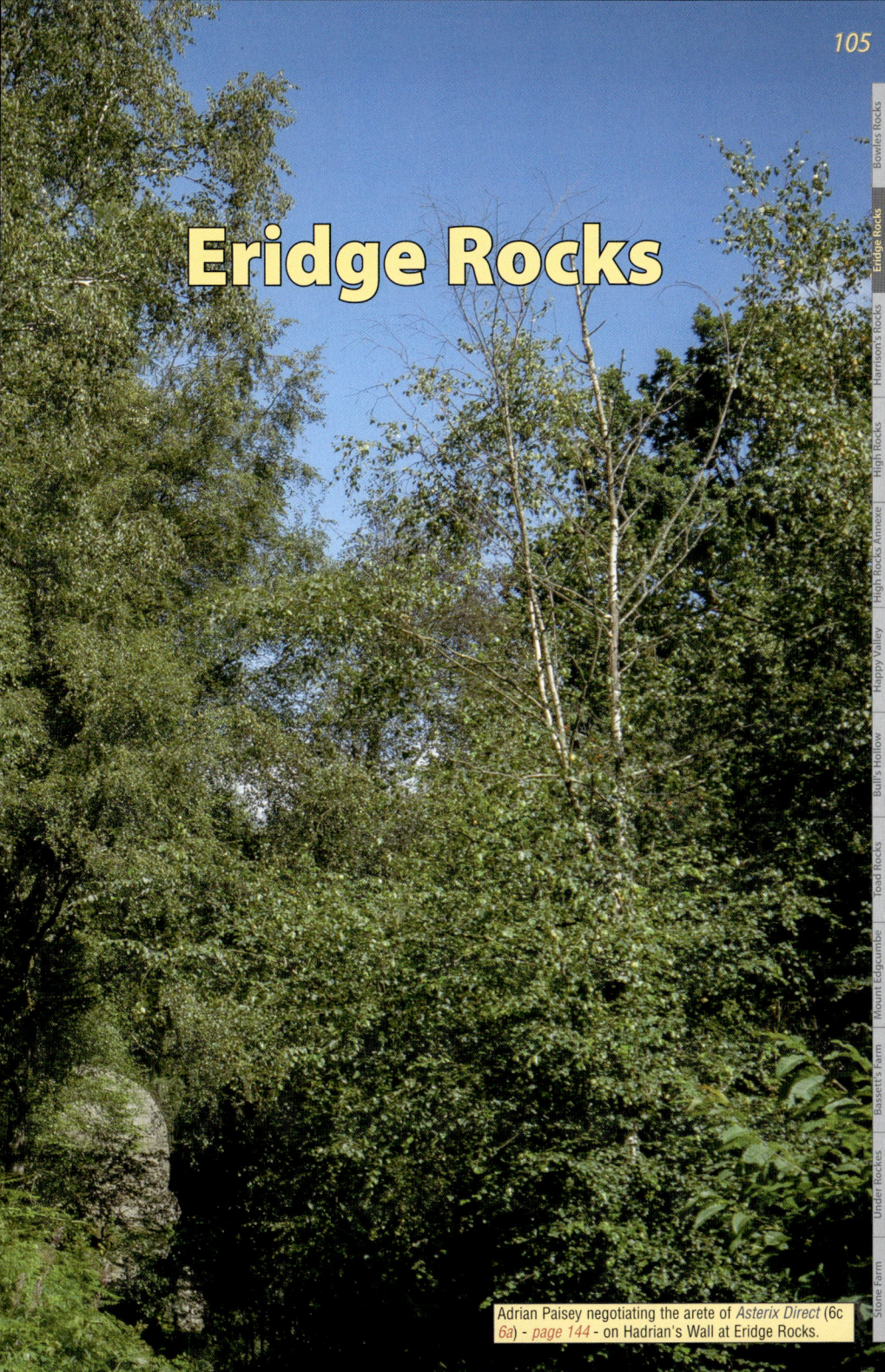

Adrian Paisey negotiating the arete of *Asterix Direct* (6c *6a*) - *page 144* - on Hadrian's Wall at Eridge Rocks.

Eridge Rocks

	No star	★	★★	★★★
2a to 4c/f2 to f4	26	13	4	-
5a to 6a+/f4+ to f5+	31	10	8	3
6b to 7a/f6A to f6C+	35	43	27	9
7a+ up/f7A up	4	10	15	5

Eridge Rocks, commonly also referred to as Eridge Green Rocks, is part of a nature reserve owned by Sussex Wildlife Trust. The environment is more rugged and wild than other crags so Eridge is not a place to bring beginners or to have as your first sandstone experience. The grades tend to be higher and sandstone technique is useful for many of the routes and problems.

Eridge Rocks is split up into four main areas: the rarely visited woodland area of Eridge South; the rocks above the carpark; the main northern stretch of outcrops where the majority of the climbing is; and the final outcrop of Eridge Tower, beyond which no climbing is permitted.

Approach Also see map on page 18

Drive south from Tunbridge Wells on the A26 for approximately 3 miles past a rather grand pub on your right called 'The Nevill Crest and Gun'. Shortly after this you will spot a Church and a wooden bus shelter - turn right here onto Warren Farm Lane. Drive for just under 300m and park on the right in the main free carpark. It is also possible to continue on the A26 for another 900m and park in a lay-by on the left, which is handy for climbing at Eridge South. Please do not park on the road outside the main carpark since access is needed for wide tractors.

Conditions

A large proportion of Eridge Rocks faces east seeing the sun from early morning to early part of the afternoon. The extensive tree cover means that the place can be dusty, damp and overgrown in places. This makes some top-outs tricky and locating the way back down is another matter altogether. Routes see fewer ascents than elsewhere and tend to be more dirty, so cleaning requires a very delicate approach, ensuring you don't cause any further damage to holds that may have already lost their harder outer layer. The area generally receives maintenance once a year from Sussex Wildlife Trust team of volunteers, who do an amazing job. Eridge is also famous for its insects and mosquitos in the summer months, especially when there is no breeze. Dog walking is popular here so be mindful of this when walking and setting down your gear.

Access

Climbing has only been officially permitted here since 1996 when Sussex Wildlife Trust purchased the rocks and surrounding woodland. In agreement with the BMC, climbing is allowed as long as certain conditions are met. There are three no climbing areas and a no chalk policy on Sandstorm Buttress. In addition, no organised climbing groups are allowed. **It is also requested that the use of chalk is kept to a minimum and the foliage and plant life should not be disturbed in any way.** Eridge Rocks is an SSSI (Site of Special Scientific Interest) - see page 50 for more information. Please abide by these reasonable requests. Failure to do so could put the future of climbing at Eridge Rocks at risk.

Gear

There are no bolts at Eridge Rocks, so a full arsenal of sandstone equipment is essential to set up a top-rope.

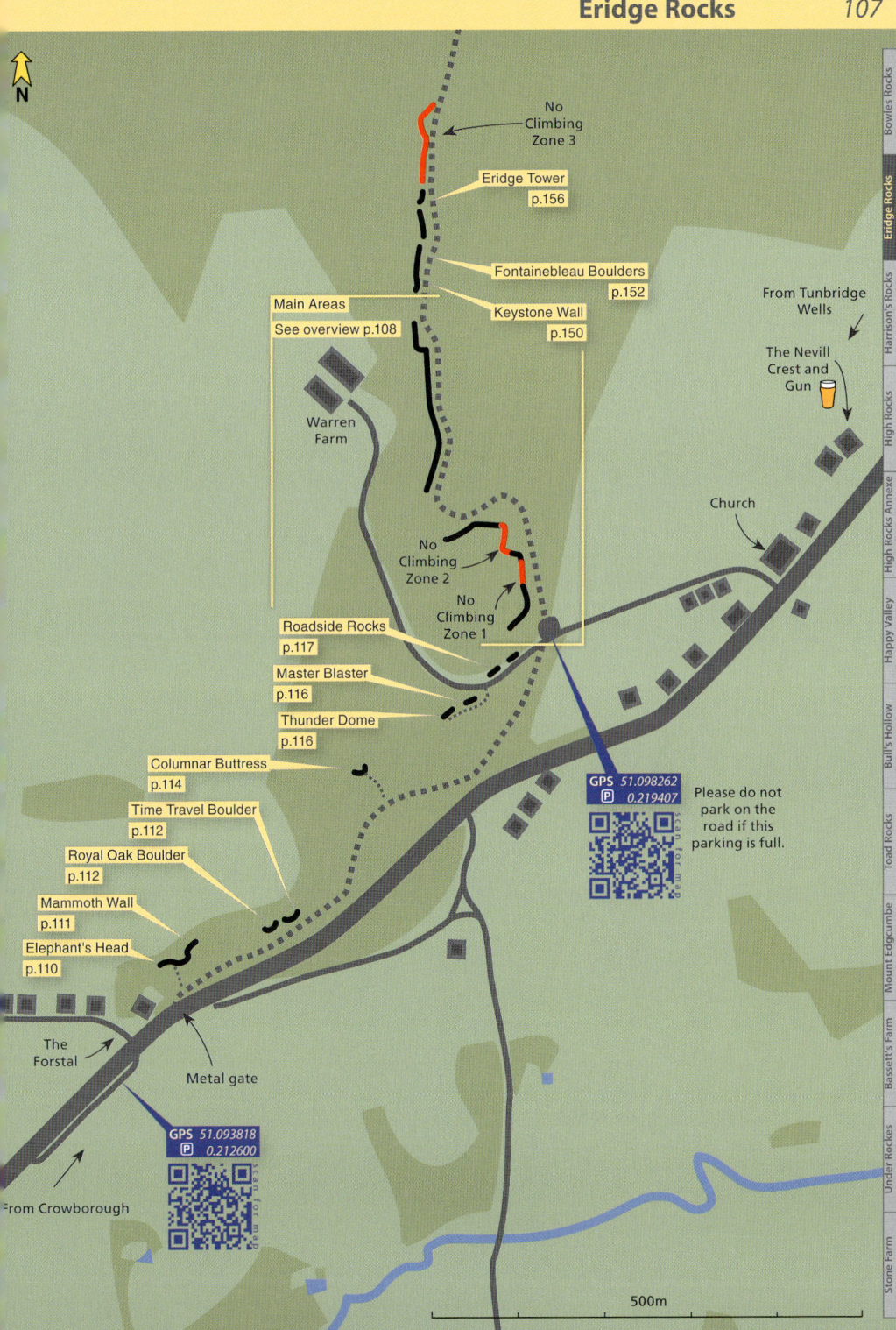

Eridge Rocks

Eridge Rocks 109

Sandstorm Buttress p.127

Judamondo p.128

Main path leading to Yew Crack Buttress and beyond

No Climbing Zone - Area Two

Hadrian's Wall p.144

Concorde Area p.148

Fandango Buttress p.149

Main path to Keystone Wall and beyond. See map on page 107.

Top approach

Top approach

Steelmill Buttress p.140

Roman Nose p.146

Eridge Rocks — Elephant's Head

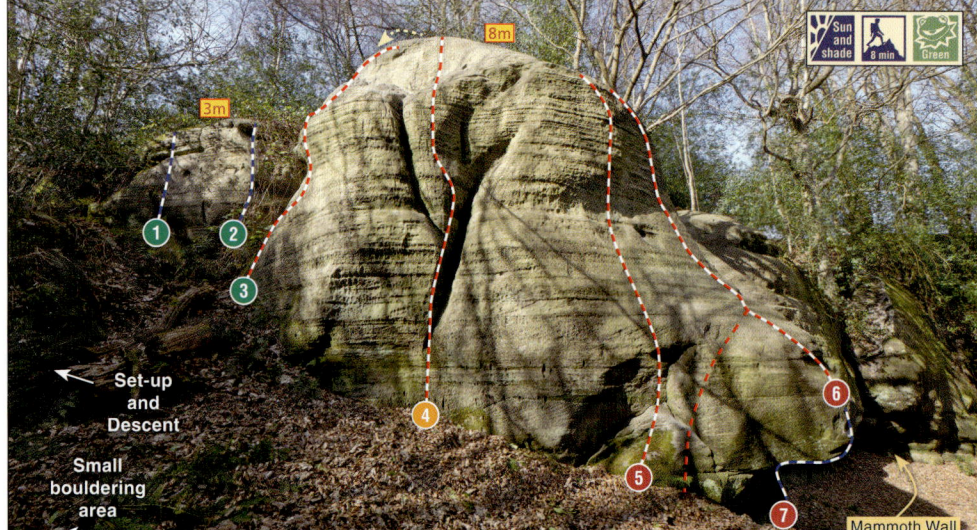

Elephant's Head

This is a neglected area and its close proximity to the road makes things more noisy than usual. For anyone wanting something away from the main areas, there are a few worthwhile routes to add to your collection. There are also some more small boulders to the left which are not documented here.

Approach - Head south along the woodland path from the main carpark to almost the most southerly point. Alternatively, approach from the south by parking in the lay-by opposite the bus stop and 'The Forstal' road turn off, and cross the road to enter the wood via a large metal gate. The rocks are up and right from here.

Set-up and Descent - Either just left of the Elephant's Head area next to a small block, or the gully to the left of Mammoth Wall.

① Heffalump .... *f2+*
A short problem up the left side of the wall.
FA. G.Prarson 1984

② Heffalump - Right .... *f3+*
The overgrown nose on sandy holds.
FA. G.Prarson 1984

③ Elephant's Tail 3b *3b*
An easy slab climb starting in the gully.

④ Y Crack 5a *4c*
Climb the short Y-crack any way you see fit.

⑤ Elephant's Arse 6c *6a*
An eliminate up the slab avoiding holds on other routes.
FA. R.Mazinke 15.4.1997

⑥ Elephant's Head .... 6b+ *5c*
Start on the nose, gain the slab with difficulty and finish awkwardly on the upper slab via the slot on the arete. Commonly started from the left at a slightly easier grade.

⑦ Elephant's Chode... *f6B*
A powerful sit-start problem over the nose, finishing up *The Elephant's Head* if you're brave enough. It can be a bit green under the nose at times though.

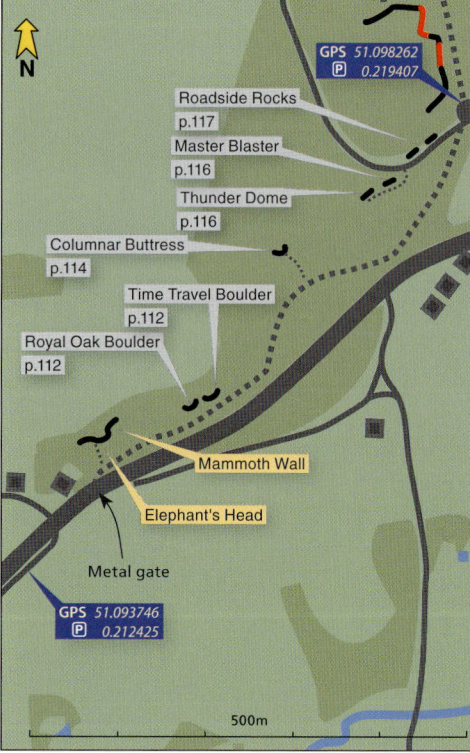

Mammoth Wall — Eridge Rocks

Mammoth Wall

Just to the right of the Elephant's Head is a rarely climbed wall with some very green routes.

Approach - Head south along the woodland path from the main carpark to almost the most southerly point. Alternatively, approach from the south by parking in the lay-by opposite the bus stop and Forstal Road turn off, and cross the road to enter the wood via a large gate. The rocks are up and to the right from here.

Set-up and Descent - Either just left of the Elephant's Head area next to a small block, or the gully to the left of Mammoth Wall.

8 Diagonal 7b 6b
A 'nails' line leading diagonally leftwards up the shallow overlap.
FA. G.McLelland 1984

9 Mammoth Wall 6b 5b
Climb the crack moving leftwards to finish.
FA. N.S.Head 18.4.1971

10 Wall E Mammoth .... 6b+ 5c
A harder direct finish to *Mammoth Wall*.
FA. T.Skinner 20.4.1991

11 Tusk .... 6a+ 5b
Traverse in from the base of *Mammoth Wall* and climb the dirty right side of the wall.
FA. T.Skinner 20.4.1991

12 Tusk Direct 6b 5c
A slimy direct start to *Tusk*.
FA. R.Mazinke 6.6.1996

13 Joshua f7B
A slappy problem up the left side of the wall. Start from two good pockets and finish up the sloping rail and arete above.
FA. T.Gore 5.8.2016

14 Lord of the Light .... f6B+
Right of *Joshua*, up a slight banking and hidden by trees. Use the rail on the right side of the wall to mantel and reach for the top via an intermediate. Avoid use of the tree.
FA. T.Gore 5.8.2016

Eridge Rocks — Royal Oak and Time Travel Boulders

Royal Oak Boulder

A small boulder situated close to the lower path. The rock is sandy in places and chipped up its centre.

Approach (see map on page 107) - Follow the path southwest from the carpark passing the basin below Columnar Buttress where the path rises steeply onto a plateau. The boulder is 20m past the Time Travel Boulder on the right.

1 Royal Oak f3
The left arete to a stonking jug on the lip. *Photo opposite.*
FA. D.Beail 16.3.2014

2 Beaten to It .... f2+
The centre of the face on chipped holds.
FA. R.Mazinke 9.1.2005

3 Nipple Rash .... f6B+
A frustrating problem to unlock. Establish yourself on a high starter foothold and pop for the top.
FA. S.Hills 13.7.2013

4 It's Pub o'Clock f4
Using the arete and tree, bridge onto the sandy ledge and reach for the top. Mantel to finish.
FA. R.Mazinke 19.9.2005

Time Travel Boulder

A small and delicate disjointed boulder dominated by a big tree in its centre. The landings are not ideal and holds are a bit fragile.

Approach - Follow the path southwest from the carpark passing the basin below Columnar Buttress where the path rises steeply onto a plateau.

5 Forward in Time f4
A short line onto the mound with a mantel finish.

6 Backwards in Time .... f2+
Use the tree to avoid pulling too hard on the fragile flake.

The mossy wall to the right could yield a problem, but it's pretty blank and on fairly soft and dirty rock.

There are a few hidden boulders dotted around the south side of Eridge Rocks. Here Daimon Beail is sneaking in one of those author first ascents on the Royal Oak Boulder. *Royal Oak* (**f3**) - *opposite*. Photo: Emma Harrington.

Eridge Rocks — Columnar Buttress

Columnar Buttress

An isolated buttress in a good position high up on the hillside. Its mesmerising honeycombed wall and huge central crack system make it look like a prized find. Sadly the thin protective layer has worn very thin in places making this a much harder and sandier buttress to climb than would first appear. It can get rather overgrown here, so it is best to visit in early spring or late autumn to avoid the worst.

Approach (see map on page 107) - From the main carpark, follow the path for about 4 minutes southwest until the path curves and dips down into a semi basin-like area. At the centre of this, turn right and make your way through the trees and up a steep banking to the buttress.

① Well Left! 7a *6a*
Climb the sandy flake and make difficult moves to establish yourself on the blank-looking slab.
FA. B.Kavanagh 8.10.2006

② Columnar Buttress 4c *4c*
A nice central crack with some massive jugs to aid your ascent, though the soft nature of the rock ruins things somewhat.

③ Primrose. 5a *4c*
After a tricky start to gain the rail, climb diagonally leftwards to finish as for *Columnar Buttress*. *Photo opposite.*

④ Fenchurch. .... 6c+ *5c*
A difficult outing up the steep face with a hard top-out.
FA. J.Patterson 28.3.2006

Emma Harrington on the final sandy moves of *Primrose* (5a 4c) - *opposite* - on the Columnar Buttress at Eridge Rocks. It is rarely visited by the average climber due to its isolated location, and general sandy feel makes most routes much harder than they should. Nevertheless, there is something rather special about climbing this piece of rock.

Eridge Rocks — Thunder Dome and Master Blaster

Thunder Dome
A set of lonely mounds hidden deep in the woods.
Approach - Head up the road past the Roadside Rocks and head left into the trees for a few metres to reach Master Blaster. *The Improbable Mantle* and *Thunder Dome* are 20m to the left of Master Blaster.

1 Thunder Dome........... f3
Slightly technical moves via a large side-pull.
FA. D.Beail 16.3.2014

2 The Improbable Mantle..... f7B
A one-move-wonder mantle, on the right side of the boulder.
FA. T.Gore 1.6.2017

Master Blaster
A nice little boulder with top-outs made awkward by the large branch.
Approach (see map on page 107) - Head up the road past the Roadside Rocks and head left into the trees for a few metres.

3 Ironbar................. f4+
The centre of the face finishing on the large tree branch.
FA. D.Beail 16.3.2014

4 Master.............. f3+
The crack using the large jugs.
FA. D.Beail 16.3.2014

5 Blaster.............. f4+
A thin snappy wall just right of the arete.
FA. D.Beail 16.3.2014

Roadside Rocks - The Titanic Boulder — Eridge Rocks

Roadside Rocks
Two blocks situated next to the road that runs up the hill from the main carpark. The rock is sandy and delicate.
Approach - *Inland Empire* is on the right, approximately 80m up the road from the carpark. *Ashes and Dust* is 10m further on.

6 Ashes and Dust f6B
A short and rounded problem up the side face.
FA. Tom Gore 3.2016

7 Step of Faith f6A
Climb the bulge via the large vertical slot.
FA. Tom Gore 10.2016

8 Inland Empire .... 6a+ 5b
A snappy but good micro route which could be bouldered if it was not for the bad landing. Climb the right face (no feet on the boulder to the right) and traverse over to the crack on the left. Proceed to make a tricky exit over the nose. Low in the grade if you know how.
FA. E.Harrington 17.4.2016

The Titanic Boulder
A rather sandy boulder meaning the problems can be hard, though the top-outs are surprisingly good.
Approach - From the carpark, follow the short path up the banking for 20m.

9 Master Exploder f4
A difficult sandy outing which is a tiny bit explosive!
FA. D.Beail 10.4.2016

10 Chocolate Nibbles f4
The arete on its left side using a jug in the break which is shared with the next line *Caramel Nibbles*.
FA. D.Beail 10.4.2016

11 Caramel Nibbles .... f2+
Short and pleasant. Exit to the left of the nose.
FA. E.Harrington 10.4.2016

12 Hot Stepper .... f3+
Climb the flake to the break and awkwardly reach for the top and exit.
FA. E.Harrington 10.4.2016

13 Analord f3
The best line on the block with a mantel finish.
FA. E.Harrington 10.4.2016

14 Crouching Badger .... f3+
Climb the flake and hop up to a mantel finish.
FA. E.Harrington 10.4.2016

Eridge Rocks — Equilibrium Wall

Equilibrium Wall

These rocks above the carpark have some routes that are enjoyable in their lower halves, but are slightly spoilt by the sandy and rounded top-outs making them rather more challenging than they first appear. The wall faces southeast and the wall dries quickly after rain, except on the far left where the trees are close to the rock.

Approach - The wall is directly above the carpark.

Set-up and Descent - Use the path to the left of the buttress. Alternatively, squeeze up the gap between Equilibrium Wall and The Watchtower. The top section is very damaged here so please make sure you take special care setting up your top-rope and use carpets or other rock protectors - see page 38.

❶ Close to You .... 6c+ *6a*
Starting from two ironstone holds, battle the encroaching trees to climb the wall. Finish on a large flake at the top.
FA. M.Vetterlein 16.7.1994

❷ Siesta Wall .... 6a+ *5b*
Jam and cram your way up the steep overhanging crack, moving slightly right to finish more easily (except for the sandy top-out of course). *Photo on page 35.*
FA. J.R.Lees 1950

❸ Innominate Buttress . 7a *6b*
An eliminate up the blunt arete, originally done as a boulder problem, but more commonly top-roped nowadays.

❹ Innominate Crack 6a *5b*
Climb the crack finishing up the gully. A harder finish goes direct through the lip above at **6a+** *5b*. *Photo opposite.*
FA. JMCS 1942

❺ Last of the Summer Wine 6b+ *5c*
Climb the series of breaks up the face and onto the slab. Finish in the gully.
FA. S.Durkin 19.9.1993

Equilibrium Wall — Eridge Rocks

6 Big Fat Tart 6b *5c*
A nice line up the left side of the right face. Finish up the slab, keeping left of the pocket near the top, and make some slappy moves on the rounded top-out to finish.
FA. A.Hughes 31.5.1992

7 Equilibrium Wall 6b *5b*
Make a fantastic technical move to start and finish more easily across the slab. A popular link-up is to finish as for *Big Fat Tart*, 6b *5c*. *Photo on page 123.*

8 Hottie 7a *6a*
A difficult excursion up the blunt arete with a hard top-out via an undercut flake and large pocket.

9 Hottie Arete .... 7b+ *6b*
An often forgotten hard line up the arete. Move left at the undercuts to finish as for *Hottie*.

10 Boulder Chimney 5a *4c*
A difficult-to-grade line requiring good bridging technique.

Innominate Crack at Eridge Rocks climbed at night and self-photographed by Neal Grundy, (6a *5b*) - *opposite.*
nealgrundy.co.uk

Eridge Rocks — The Watchtower

The Watchtower

Immediately right of *Equilibrium Wall* are some nice short lines, that are sometimes done as highball boulder problems.

Approach - The wall is directly above the carpark.
Conditions - South facing, the rocks dry quickly after rain. The rock is quite soft and the holds can be a bit sandy.

❶ Nuthin' Fancy .... 6b+ *5c*
Climb the face eliminating the arete out right.
FA. T.Skinner 5.9.1992

❷ Libra 6b *5c*
A good route moving onto the right side of the arete, with an interesting top-out thrown in.

❸ Two Short .... 6b+ *5c*
The clue is in the name. A reachy move to start gains the bulging arete which is climbed mainly on its left side.
FA. R.Mazinke

❹ Trainer Drainer .... 6b+ *5c*
Tackle the bulge to easier climbing above - except the last moves.
FA. A.Hughes 8.8.1990

❺ Enigma 7a *6a*
A difficult (but short) battle over the bulge leads to easier climbing above. Avoid using holds in the crack area.

❻ Hanging Crack 5b *5a*
A fun and popular line which has a strenuous and awkward start leading to an enjoyable and easier crack-climb above.
Photo opposite.
FA. JMCS 1942

❼ The Watchtower. .... 7c+ *6c*
Originally done as a *f7B* boulder problem. Climb the juggy lower wall to a poor horizontal rail. Mount this and finish by tackling the upper face on slopers and pockets, moving left to reach a large flake near the top. Due to the soft nature of the rock, many choose to attempt this on a top-rope.
FA. I.Stronghill 27.9.2003. Done as a boulder problem.

❽ The Watchmen . ... 7c+ *6c*
An alternative start to *The Watchtower*. Climb the first half of *Prowess* (page 122) and move left to gain the rail. *f7B* again if bouldered in its entirety or *f6A* if finishing at the rail.

The Watchtower **Eridge Rocks**

Sarah Goodman enjoying *Hanging Crack* (5b *5a*) - *opposite* - on The Watchtower at Eridge Rocks. Note the sandstone belay by Robin Mazinke below which is a traditional belaying method undertaken by many old school sandstone climbers.

Eridge Rocks — The Watchtower

Around the corner is a shady north-facing wall.

9 Prowess .... 7a+ *6b*
A classic sandstone route which is taxing in its upper half. Climb the right side of the prow and make a difficult transition onto and the nose to finish up this.
FA. M.Vetterlein 10.7.1991

10 Nonpareil 7c *6c*
Not as blank as it would first appear, but nevertheless extremely thin and technical.
FA. P.Widdowson 11.6.1992

Eridge Rocks

Zara Bloomfield high up on *Equilibrium Wall* (6b *5b*) - *page 119*. This section of rock is one of the most popular areas at Eridge Rocks due to its proximity to the carpark and sunny position.

124 Eridge Rocks — Parisian Affair Area

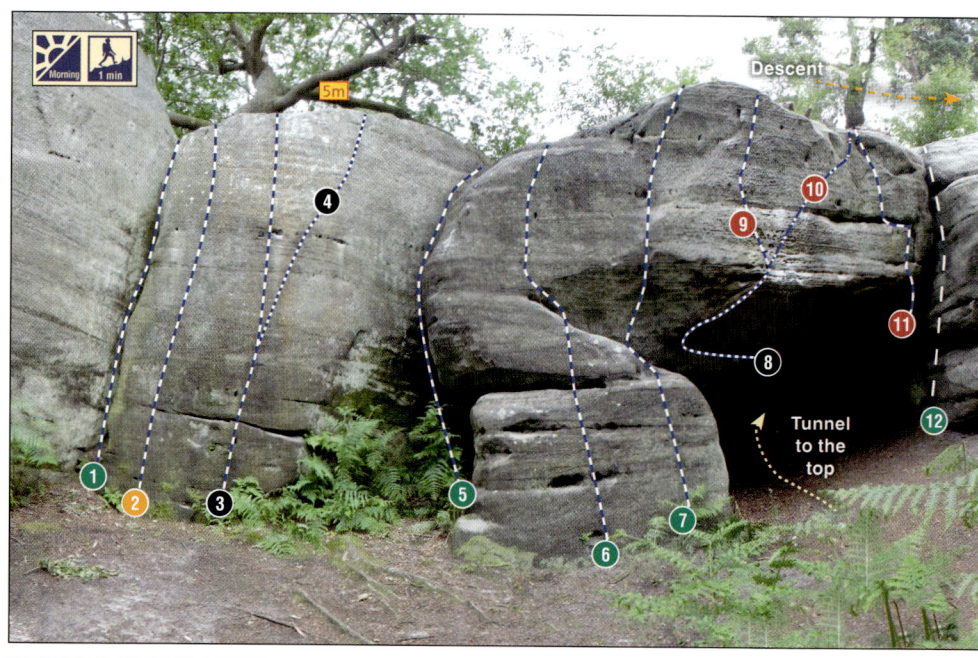

Parisian Affair Area

A great little area which is popular amongst boulderers. The routes on the left don't see much sun so can take a while to clean up and dry out.

Approach - The wall is directly above the carpark.

Descent - Us the path right of this area can be used to get to the top. Alternatively you can scramble down under *Parisian Affair* or as for The Watchtower area.

Boulderers - Hold cleaning is a delicate art so please use extra soft brushes only - toothbrushes and bouldering brushes are forbidden. Do not remove any lichens from the rock. Try to use minimal chalk and if possible use Eco Balls or liquid chalk - see page 45.

1 Flake Crack f3
The short corner crack.

2 Cracking Up f5
A variation on the previous line. Climb the face using the arete out left to aid you.

3 Sansara .... f7A+
Climb the centre of the face, without using the arete at the start, to latch the pocket at mid-height. Finish with either a massive reach or a dyno to grab the top. Hard for the grade.
FA. I.Stronghill 2003

4 Sansara Right-Hand f7A
The right-hand finish moves further towards the rounded arete.
FA. I.Stronghill 2003

The next section is the most popular bouldering area at Eridge.

5 Bivouac Chimney f3
The short and awkward crack.

6 Geronimo f3
Climb the ramp-line on good holds.
FA. R.Mazinke 1.6.1993

7 Truncate f3
A bit more taxing than *Geronimo* and slightly more entertaining. A dirty top-out.
FA. T.Daniells 1970s

8 Yankee Affair f7A
A difficult and powerful sit-start to *Parisian Affair*. Start on the rail and dyno out to grab the lip (avoiding use of lower left wall). Finish as for *Parisian Affair*.
FA. P.Zeigenfuss 2003

9 Parisian Affair .... f6A+
Reach or jump to grab the lip and campus until your feet can join the fun. Finish up left avoiding holds on both adjacent problems. *Photo on page 36*.
FA. G.McLelland 1984

10 Too Short to Mention .... f6A+
A good right-hand variation of *Parisian Affair* moving rightwards to good holds.
FA. C.Arnold 1985

11 Even Shorter Mention f6A
Starting in the corner, climb up and left (various methods used) to finish as for *Too Short to Mention*.
FA. P.Stone 1991

Eridge Rocks — No Climbing Zones

 ## No Climbing Zone - Area One
Climbing is not allowed beyond *Dr. Kemp's Cure* at the far right-hand end of the Parisian Affair Area until you reach the Sandstorm Buttress. Please abide by this restriction (no matter how good the rock looks) to ensure climbing can continue here at Eridge. See page 106.

No Climbing Zone - Area Two
The second no climbing zone extends from beyond *The Crunch - Original Start* on Sandstorm Buttress until you reach *Dusk Crack* on the opposite side of the Amphitheatre. Please abide by this to ensure climbing can continue here at Eridge.

Sandstorm Buttress — Eridge Rocks — 127

Sandstorm Buttress

Sandstorm Buttress is a small section between the two banned areas where climbing is allowed. It is north facing with a seemingly impregnatable green colour, but climbable when conditions allow.

Access - In agreement with the BMC and Sussex Wildlife Trust, climbing is permitted on these lines only, but chalk must NOT be used.

Approach (see map on page 107 and overview on page 108) - Continue along the lower path for 80m, past the first banned area. The buttress is just above the path.

Set-up and Descent - Use the path just right of the Parisian Affair Area.

① Prelude .... f6A+
A short and powerful problem up the steep overhang.

② Sandstorm .... 6c+ 6a
A fantastic line up the front of the face. Start steeply then move left to reach a large pocket. Move back right to tackle the scoop and take five at the ledge. Topping out is no easy matter - any variation is allowed.
FA. M.Fowler 2.7.1978

Not much sun — 2 min — Green

9m

No Climbing Zone - left of here

Set-up and Descent right of Parisian Affair Area

No Climbing Zone - right of here

③ The Crunch Direct 7b 6b
The proud arete provides a fierce challenge. Climb the lower wall to gain the arete, which is climbed on spaced holds. Traverse left to finish as for *Sandstorm*. Any attempt to finish direct will end in tears.
FA. M.Fowler 30.9.1979

④ The Composition f6B
The shorter version of *Encore*. The no chalk restriction makes this even more of a challenge.

⑤ More Cake for Me 7a 6a
A classic sandstone route. Climb the face using a series of distinctive flakes and pockets to finish left of the scoop. It is conditions dependent and green, but certainly delivers when dry.
FA. P.Hayes 11.1989

⑥ Encore .... f6B+
The full outing across the lower rail making your way to the finish of *The Composition*. Much harder without chalk.

⑦ The Crunch - Original Start .... 7a+ 6b
The right-hand and slightly easier start to *The Crunch*.
FA. M.Fowler 30.9.1979

Eridge Rocks — Judamondo

Judamondo

Beyond the second of the restricted areas is a rarely visited section of Eridge, but the addition of *Judamondo* has changed all that... kind of. This wall faces north seeing no sun and stays green for much of the year. The walls to the right of *5.11 Crack* are never in condition and as such have not been included.

Access - No climbing to the left of *Dusk Crack*. See previous page for details.

Approach (see map on page 107 and overview on page 108) - Continue along the path to the opposite side of the amphitheatre, just before the path heads around to the left.

Set-up and Descent - Go up a narrow gully 10m to the right of *5.11 Crack*.

❸ **The Beguiled** . . . . 7a+ *6b*
A crimpy technician's delight to the right of the arete.
FA. G.McLelland 9.9.1984

❹ **Judamondo** . . . . 8a+ *6c*
This spectacular testpiece up the centre of the green face is one of Eridge's most sought after prizes. It is often done as a shorter *f7C* boulder problem via reachy moves on pockets and side-pulls to the large pocket at 2/3 height. Continue up and right with difficulty to claim the true prize!
FA. B.Read 12.3.2010

❺ **Hour Glass** 6a *5b*
Negotiate your way out of the niche to finish up a jamming crack, past a tree.
FA. M.Boysen 1969

❻ **Snail Bail** *f6B*
From a sit-start, work your way up to good undercuts and using the pocket out right, make a dynamic move to latch the large pocket.

❶ **Dusk Crack** 4c *4c*
The crack with a mossy start.
FA. J.R.Lees 1950

❷ **Meaty Thighs** . . . . 7a+ *6b*
Climb the arete mainly on its left side.
FA. A.Grigg 1.9.1992

Judamondo Eridge Rocks

⑦ Snail Trail 7a *6b*
From the good undercuts under the lip, dyno as for *Snail Bail* to the large pocket. Head rightwards using a series of pocketed undercuts and side-pulls to reach the large undercut above. Attempt to top out elegantly from here.

⑧ Zugzwang .... 7b+ *6c*
The greasy crack to a difficult top-out.
FA. P.Widdowson 11.6.1992

⑨ Emerald .... 6c+ *6a*
Follow the dirty ramp to finish delicately up the face above.
FA. M.Vetterlein 30.7.1990

⑩ Easy Gully 3a *3a*
An unpleasant gully climb.

⑪ Sandstone Hell 6b *5c*
Climb (or don't) the short wall to the left of the lip and finish up the series of flakes above. Take the hint in the name and avoid.
FA. M.Vetterlein 30.7.1990

⑫ Nododendron 6c *6a*
Similar territory to *Sandstone Hell*, but going up and past the right side of the lip.
FA. M.Eden 16.5.1999

⑬ Splendeedo 6b *5c*
Climb the short face and arete above.
FA. B.Ventham 16.8.2009

⑭ 5.11 Crack 6c *6a*
If ever presented with dry conditions, climb the crack and use side-pulls left of the chimney.
FA. W.O.R.Hill 21.1.1990

Eridge Rocks — Yew Crack Buttress

Yew Crack Buttress

Just right again from Velcro Boulder is a rather nice buttress. Regrettably it is obscured by a Yew Tree which makes many of the lines much more challenging. Velcro Boulder is very green and elsewhere the rock can be a little bit soft in its lower half - treat with care.

Approach (see map on page 107) - Follow the path below and beyond the green walls right of *Judamondo* to the point where it curves back right and heads north.

Set-up and Descent - Either battle your way behind Velcro Boulder or, better, go rightwards and head up to the left of Stem Son Buttress - p.138

Velcro Boulder

A small lone boulder up on a steep banking. This boulder gets overgrown so can be damp and mossy.

1 Velcro Wall .... f7B+
Reachy moves to a difficult mantel over the top.

2 Krafty Undercutz ...... f6C+
A short and bunched traverse to finish up *Velcro Arete*.

3 Velcro Arete f6C
A great little problem when dry. Climb the arete using holds either side to a tricky finish.
FA. I.Hufton 2003

4 Middleclass Ponce 5a *4c*
Climb just right of the arete on pockets and the occasional handful of moss.
FA. D.Reid 6.12.1992

5 Spot the Dog and the Breath of Death .... 6a+ *5b*
The centre of the slab above a difficult start leads to a mossy and prickly finish. Easier if using pads at the start.
FA. D.Reid 6.12.1992

6 Yew Crack 3b *3b*
Wedge your way up the crack and do battle with the tree above.

7 Tortoise on a Spin Out .. 7a *6b*
Avoiding the crack, climb up the face to finish with some short but memorable tree climbing. A shorter more popular variation to the first break. **The Leaf** at *f6B+*, from a sit-start.
Photo on page 17.
FA. P.Stone 1990

Yew Crack Buttress Eridge Rocks

Boulderers - This area has suffered badly from erosion so please take extra care here. Hold cleaning is a delicate art so please use extra soft brushes only - toothbrushes and bouldering brushes are forbidden. Try to use minimal chalk and if possible use Eco Balls or liquid chalk - see page 45.

⑧ More Funkey than Monkey .. 7a+ *6a*
Climbing the lower bulge from a sit-start and finishing at the base of the groove gives you **Jack Strong**, *f7B+*. If started conventionally (standing) then continue up the groove to claim the original line.
FA. W.O.R.Hill 28.1.1990

⑨ Thrutch............. 6c *6a*
A clean line with a good finish. Climb the difficult lower bulge to better holds above. Finish more easily up and to the left.
FA. L.E.Holliwell and Co. 8.11.1964

⑩ Turning the Leaf .  *f7A+*
A powerful and sustained traverse along the lower set of holds, finishing left of *Yew Crack*. Diverting up *More Funkey than Monkey* to finish below the groove gives **Jack Strong Extension**, *f7C*.
FA. P.Zeigenfuss 2005. Also claimed by Ian Stronghill.

⑪ Earthrise Suprise *f6A*
The arete finishing at the first break.

⑫ Earthrise............ 6c+ *6a*
Climb the face right of the arete to a rounded finish.
FA. M.Vetterlein 23.7.1994

⑬ Cosmo Irrazionale ..... 7a+ *6b*
The centre of the wall with a difficult snatch to finish.
FA. C.Gibson 12.6.2005

Eridge Rocks — The Pillar

1 Empty Vee 6c *6a*
The corner-crack gets pretty greasy and wet.
FA. M.Vetterlein 27.1.1990

2 Hypersonic f7B
An impressive line up the centre of the face to a large hole. Continue up and left to better holds and top out with immense difficulty unless using a pre-placed rope.
FA. I.Stronghill 5.10.2003

3 Patience .... f7A+
A short problem finishing at a good pocket. It could well be extended in the future.
FA. T.Gore 2.7.2016

4 Triceratops .... 6c+ *6a*
Make difficult moves midway to establish yourself on the main face. Topping out is harder still!

5 Impacted Stool .... 6b+ *5c*
A grotty and overgrown line which needs a dyno to grab the holly tree. Only the truly dedicated sandstoner will climb this.
FA. P.Widdowson 15.3.1992

6 Brian's Corner 6b *5c*
Bridge and jam your way up this 'delightful' corner.
FA. B.Kavanagh 20.1.1990

7 Kinetix 7a *6b*
Climb the centre of the face, avoiding the arete and corner.

8 The Pillar .... 6b+ *5c*
An eye-catching Eridge classic on good rock. Start on the right of the pillar and migrate over to the left, finishing awkwardly on the sloping top-out. *Photo opposite.*
FA. M.Boysen 1960

The Pillar   Eridge Rocks

The Pillar

The routes on the face are rarely climbed owing to their difficult top-outs. Next is *The Pillar* which is more popular and has amenable exits. The wall of *Hypersonic* suffers from compost from the years of overgrowth at the top. If bouldering, use a knotted rope to grab onto to exit. *The Pillar* is easier to exit but the overshadowing holly tree gets in the way.

Approach (see map on page 107) - Follow the path below and beyond the green walls right of *Judamondo* to the point where it curves back right and heads north.

Set-up and Descent - Go rightwards and head up to the left of Stem Son Buttress - p.138

Edwin Jenkins on *The Pillar* (6b+ *5c*) - *opposite* - which is one of the stand-out climbs at Eridge.

Eridge Rocks — Scooped Slab

Scooped Slab

A good area with two fine walls one of which is often overlooked in favour of the other more slabby and appealing looking wall. The east-facing wall of *Obelisk* is shadowed by the north-facing wall of The Pillar meaning things take a bit longer to dry out than usual and it tends to be a bit green in places. The main Scooped Slab is also relatively shady, but does dry a little more quickly and sees more traffic.

Approach (see map on page 107) - Continue along the main path below the crag until you reach The Pillar. The first routes are tucked around to the right of this, followed by Scooped Slab.

Set-up and Descent - Go rightwards and head up to the left of Stem Son Buttress - p.138

❶ The Exit Cracks 4c *4c*
A poor line with two alternative exits around the tree.
FA. M.Vetterlein 24.12.2004

❷ Waffer Thin 7a *6b*
Climb the centre of the wall to the break which requires a difficult rockover to gain good holds above. Make one more reachy move to finish.

❸ Obelisk 6c *6a*
An excellent line up the arete using holds on either side.
FA. M.Fowler 9.6.1979

❹ Mein Herr .... 6c+ *6a*
The centre of the north-facing wall avoiding contact with the lines either side.

❺ Slanting Crack 4a *4a*
The slabby corner crack which increases in difficulty the higher you go.

❻ Nigel Mantel 7a *6a*
A good piece of thin, technical slab climbing. The last move gives the route its name.
FA. M.Smith 1990

❼ Stirling Moss 6c *6a*
A great technical testpiece up the slab. Try to avoid contact with the central groove to the right if at all possible.

❽ Scooped Slab Direct 6b *5b*
A difficult direct start to *Scooped Slab*.

Scooped Slab — Eridge Rocks

9. Scooped Slab 6a 5b
A fun route up the slab. Follow the vague ramp-line until it meets the central groove. Finish direct from here.

10. Snap, Crackle…POP!…Splat . 6c+ 6a
Start as for *Scooped Slab* and climb the face direct via undercuts and pockets.

11. Afterburner .... 6c+ 6a
The right-hand arete, with a less than pleasing top half. Needs dry and breezy conditions to make things just right.
FA. M.Smith 1991

12. The Nail 7a 6b
A rarely climbed crack-line up the sidewall.
FA. A.Grigg 19.9.1992

Eridge Rocks — Dilemma Buttress

Dilemma Buttress

An isolated pinnacle with plenty of hard lines sprawled across it. A few taxing hybrid boulder problems can be found to keep hungry boulderers happy. It stays in relatively good condition although some of the routes can be a bit sandy in places.

Approach (see map on page 107) - Continue along the main path below the crag past Scooped Slab.
Set-up and Descent - Go rightwards and head up to the left of Stem Son Buttress - p.138.

1 Mellow Toot .... 6c+ *6a*
Climb the crack and overlap to the break. Negotiate the upper face and make a long reach for the finish.
FA. A.Hughes 19.5.1991

2 Big Boss 7a *6b*
An good eliminate up the face to an action-packed finale.
FA. D.Atchinson-Jones 1999

3 Yellow Soot 7a *6a*
Head for the small overlap on softish rock. At the break, move left to finish up the wall with difficulty.
FA. G.McLelland 1984

4 Dilemma 6c *6a*
Step off a boulder and climb the left side of the nose to a rounded break. Head over the bulge any way you can to finish.
FA. S.R.Durkin 4.10.1964

5 Ken Clean Air System ... 7a *6b*
Climb the front face past a hole and up to the break. Finish as for *Dilemma*.
FA. M.Eden 21.1.1990

Dilemma Buttress — Eridge Rocks

6 Tusky — f7B+
Starting from the base of *Dilemma*, head right - poor holds for both hands and feet - to head up the arete and finish at the shallow pocket ... with both hands!
FA. P.Zeigenfuss 2003

7 Nightfall — 7b+ 6c
Often done as a f7C boulder problem. From a sit-start, climb the arete with difficulty to the shallow pocket on the arete to finish (as for *Tusky*). For the standing start version, continue to the break and head left to finish as for *Dilemma*.
FA. I.Stronghill 5.10.2003

8 Iron Man Tyson — 6c+ 6a
A good climb up the centre of the face, although a little green in places.
FA. M.Lewis 1987

9 Communist — 6b 5c
Follow the shallow flake rightwards. Move left to reach the break and follow the overhanging roof into the finishing moves on *Iron Man Tyson*.
FA. W.O.R.Hill 14.1.1990

10 Polly Ticks — 6b 5c
Climb the often overgrown arete and mossy face above.
FA. W.O.R.Hill 1.1.1990

Set-up and Descent →

Eridge Rocks — Stem Son Buttress

Stem Son Buttress

A good wall when dry. The left-hand side of the buttress is often green so needs a good dry spell to get into condition. The right-hand side, beyond *Stem Son* gives cleaner rock.

Approach (see map on page 107) - Follow the crag base path to just right of the gully beyond Dilemma Buttress.

Set-up and Descent - The gully to the left, which is also the main descent for the surrounding walls.

1 Mamba's Come Home to Roost 4b *4b*
Traverse in from the left and climb the short wall on flakes. The top is blocked by a fallen tree.

2 The Pink Pengster . . . . 6a+ *5b*
From the undercut niche, climb the wall above on flakes and crimps. Exit right of the tree stump.
FA. D.Reid 1994

3 Tweedle Dee 6a *5b*
Climb the wall direct around the right side of the small nose on flakes.
FA. W.O.R.Hill 4.1.1990

4 Tweedle Dum 6b *5c*
Climb the lower blunt nose and finish up the slab right of the arete.
FA. W.O.R.Hill 4.1.1990

5 Stem Son . . . . 6c+ *6a*
Climb the corner groove with difficulty, especially in its upper half which is tackled mainly on the left wall. It can be a bit green.
FA. W.O.R.Hill 30.12.1989

6 Evolution 7b *6b*
Crimp over the overlap using two small ironstone holds and, using a layaway, reach for a shallow ramp-line. Continue up the centre of the face using a small pocket to top out.
Photo opposite.
FA. D.Beail 10.6.1997

7 Lou 7a *6b*
Climb the arete, starting (and mainly staying) on the right-hand side, using a thin crack.
FA. P.Widdowson 31.5.1990

Robin Mazinke on *Evolution* (7b *6b*) - *opposite* - at the Stem Son Buttress. This is one of a number of routes that were put up in a new wave of first ascents back in the late 1990s, just after climbing was officially permitted following Sussex Wildlife Trust's purchase of Eridge Rocks.

140 Eridge Rocks — Just Wall

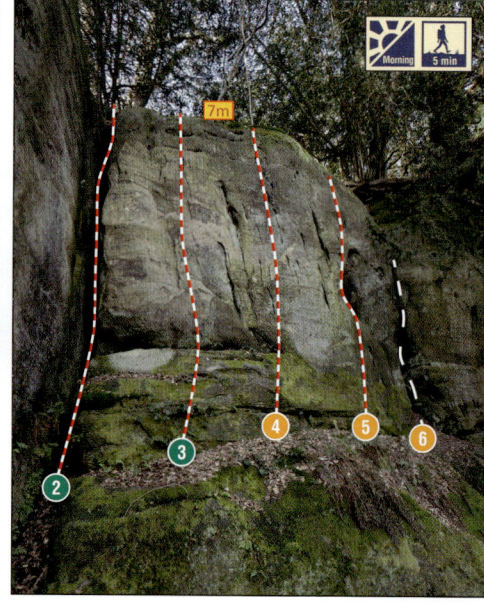

Just Wall
Around the right side of Stem Son Buttress are a few routes. They are rarely climbed but worth seeking out when dry, although *Jude's Wall* takes a long time to be in condition.
Approach (see map on page 107) - Continue around the corner from Stem Son Buttress.
Set-up and Descent - Go up the gully to the left of Stem Son Buttress - p.138

❶ **Jude's Wall** . . . . 　　　　　　　　　**7c** *6c*
Climb the centre of the wall with difficulty.
FA. B.Read 2009

❷ **Toadstool Crack** . . . . 　　　**4a** *4a*
The corner-crack. It is also possible to climb the right face laying back the arete at a slightly harder grade.

❸ **Just Cause** . . . . 　　　　**4b** *4b*
The left side of the wall up the slight depression.
FA. W.O.R.Hill 14.1.1990

❹ **Just CIA** . . . . 　　**6a** *5b*
The centre of the wall on flakes.
FA. W.O.R.Hill 14.1.1990

❺ **Just Ice** . . . . 　　　**6a** *5b*
The right side of the wall is slightly green.
FA. W.O.R.Hill 14.1.1990

Steelmill Buttress
The continuation of Just Wall becomes the impressive Steelmill Buttress. A fine wall with some good long outings. The wall has also become popular with boulderers with some of Eridge's classic problems situated in its centre. The wall generally stays in good condition, although the left wing can suffer a bit.
Set-up and Descent - To the left of Stem Son Buttress - p.138 - or to the right of the Concorde Area - p.148.
Boulderers - Hold cleaning is a delicate art so please use extra soft brushes only - toothbrushes and bouldering brushes are forbidden. Try to use minimal chalk and if possible use Eco Balls or liquid chalk - see page 45.

❻ **Backyard** . . . . 　　**5a** *4c*
The short grovelly crack to the left of the buttress.
FA. W.O.R.Hill 14.1.1990

❼ **Jihad** . . . . 　　　　　　　**7a** *6a*
The narrow left face between *Backyard* and *Genesis*, moving left to finish with the aid of the arete.
FA. C.Gibson 10.7.2005

❽ **In the Beginning** . . . 　　　　　　**7a+** *6a*
A direct on *Jihad*, without the use of the arete.
FA. B.Ventham 2009

❾ **Genesis** . . . . 　　　　　**6c** *6a*
Climb the crack and flake-line above to finish on (just about adequate!) small holds and the tree root at the top.
FA. G.Hill 12.11.1989

❿ **Steelmill** . . . . 　　　　**6c+** *6a*
A super line which can be started in a number of ways, (commonly from the left with a tiptoe to grab the break). Climb the upper wall on a series of flakes and finish by moving right into the recess or, harder, go direct.
FA. M.Fowler 10.6.1979

Eridge Rocks — Steelmill Buttress

11 Touch Down 7a *6a*
Climb the lower wall past the bulge to take on the mighty twin flakes. Move left into the groove to finish.
FA. M.Fowler 1982

12 Goat Rage ..... f7C+
Start on a large flat hold, and power your way along the line of pockets and finish up *Azazel*. Starting from the starting slot on *Azazel* and reversing the fist half of *Goat Rage*, gives you **I Don't Want to be a Goat, f7B**.
FA. (I Don't Want to be a Goat) T.Gore 6.8.2012

13 Scorpion 7a *6a*
A good steep line that tackles the main nose via pockets and a flake on its right side.
FA. G.Hill 4.1.1990

14 Indian Traverse . f7A
From the start of *Azazel*, traverse left on good crimps above the line of *Goat Rage*, to join it back at its starting hold. Finish by taking the start of *Touch Down* to the break.
FA. P.Wycislik 2008

Steelmill Buttress — Eridge Rocks 143

Boulderers - Hold cleaning is a delicate art, and toothbrushes and bouldering brushes are forbidden due to their abrasive nature on the holds. Try to use minimal chalk and if possible use Eco Balls or liquid chalk - see page 45.

Set-up and Descent →

Green Bollard Chimney - p.144

⓯ Azazel **f7A**
Start at the large slot and power up the wall on crimps. Using the feature out right for feet reduces the grade to *f6C*.
Photo on page 145.
FA. I.Hufton 2003

⓰ Goat Rage Extension **f7B+**
A slightly easier but longer variation to the original. Start as for *Goat Rage* but continue right and finish up the first half of *Lazy Chive*, stopping at the first break.
FA. T.Gore 17.8.2015

⓱ Lazy Chive .... **7a+ 6b**
Climb to the right side of the upper alcove. Finish with difficulty on the thin wall above, using cracks, to a reachy last move.
FA. P.Widdowson 31.5.1990

⓲ Vapour Trails **f6A**
Start from a thin line of holds and finish at the break.

⓳ The Read Line **f7C**
Follow the shallow break-line across the wall and finish at the first break on *Touch Down*.
FA. B.Read 2009

⓴ Revelations .... **6c+ 6a**
Reach the break and follow finger-cracks and flakes to another reachy last move.
FA. W.O.R.Hill 17.11.1989

㉑ Poofy Finger's Revenge . **6c+ 6a**
Climb the blunt nose (which edges into the green at times) using the shallow flake out right.
FA. G.Hill 19.11.1989

㉒ Daylight Throbbery . . **f6B**
A long right-to-left traverse of the break on sloppy holds. Start whereever possible on the right.

Eridge Rocks — Hadrian's Wall

Hadrian's Wall

Immediately right of Steelmill Buttress is a fine wall with a number of impressive lines to indulge in. Facing south, the wall gets sun from mid-morning and generally dries quickly, though can seep a little.

Approach (see map on page 107) - The prominent arete of *Asterix* is just beyond Steelmill Buttress.

Set-up and Descent - To the right of the Concorde Area - p.148

1 Green Bollard Chimney........ 4a *4a*
A dirty, slimy chimney climb. It is also possible to walk through to reach the top, but you will probably regret it.

2 Antoninus............ 6b *5c*
Climb the curving flake and wall above.
FA. M.Vetterlein 18.2.1990

3 Hadrian's Wall .... Top 50 6a+ *5b*
Eridge's very own *Braille Trail* (kind of). Make a rising traverse across the face - big rope swing potential if you fall depending on where you situate the rope. The top holds can be a little 'Sahara-fied' from the loose sand that occasionally trickles from the top. A great line nevertheless.
FA. F.K.Elliot 1950s

4 The Great Bald Turkey Meets a Dwarf with a Problem .... 6b+ *5c*
An early departure from *Hadrian's Wall*, up the crack and past undercuts, to a difficult top-out.
FA. P.Stone 1990

5 Hadrian's Wall Direct ... 6c *6a*
A much harder and less popular direct start with a difficult mid-section past the break.
FA. I.Bull 18.8.2009. Also known as 'Claudius Drops a Clanger' and 'Stephanie'.

6 Asterix............... 6b *5c*
Gain the break (it does not matter where from), traverse right onto the arete and finish direct.
FA. M.Fowler 2.1.1978

7 Asterix Direct 6c *6a*
The direct start to *Asterix* which makes a good but slightly harder version to the original. *Photo on page 104.*
A short problem can be done from a sit-start to the break and goes by the name, **Alex the Kidd**, *f6A*

Phil Walker blasting his way through *Azazel* (**f7A**) - *page 143* - at the Steelmill Buttress at Eridge Rocks. Bouldering at Eridge has become a popular pastime especially because of the jungle bashing required to access the tops of many of the routes. If you do boulder, please keep chalk to a minimum and only use recommended cleaning equipment.

Eridge Rocks — Roman Nose

Asterix Direct - p.144

Roman Nose
The continuation right around the corner from Hadrian's Wall is a popular section with good lines that reduce in quality the further right you go. The right side of the wall is often green.

Approach (see map on page 107) - Around the corner from Hadrian's Wall.
Set-up and Descent - To the right of the Concorde Area - p.148

❶ Fly by Knight . . . . . . 6c+ *6a*
A good technical face climb with some fingery moves.
FA. G.McLelland 1984

❷ Achilles' Last Stand 7a *6b*
A packed in eliminate up the face, avoiding contact with the lines either side.
FA. P.Stone 19.5.1991

❸ Remus 4c *4c*
A nice corner-crack. Thin in places.
FA. F.K.Elliot 1943

❹ Roman Nose 6a *5a*
A delicate excursion stepping out onto the nose and finishing up on layaways to the top.
FA. F.K.Elliot 1950s

❺ Roman Nose Direct 7a *6b*
The hard direct version of *Roman Nose* which is often done as a *f6B* boulder problem to holds just over the roof.
FA. M.Fowler 1982

Roman Nose Eridge Rocks

Set-up and Descent →

6 Romulus .... 6a+ 5b
An awkward crack with a difficult start
FA. F.K.Elliot 1943

7 Good Route ... Poor Line ... 6c 6a
A slightly wandering line up the face.
FA. P.Hayes 1984

8 Good Route ... Good Line ... 6b 5c
Head for the flake and reach for the holds above.
FA. T.Daniells 1984

9 Layaway 6a 5b
A poor route up the damp recess to the tree.

10 Scrimps 6c 6a
Climb delicately up the slab, eliminating adjacent cracks.
FA. A.Hughes 23.8.2009

18 Hipposuction 6a 5b
Greasy and a bit dirty but if you're prepared to put up with it, this is not a bad line.
FA. D.Reid 22.12.1991

12 Appetite for Destruction ... 6c 6a
Climb the arete without contact with the crack. A bit green but good when in condition.
FA. R.Mazinke 25.5.1996

Eridge Rocks — Concorde Area

Concorde Area

A good clean buttress with an elegant arete which is the main attraction of this wall.

Approach (see map on page 107) - This is the last buttress in this section before a gap in the edge.

Set-up and Descent - Use the narrow gully 5m to the right past another short wall.

❶ Capstan Wall 4a *4a*
Climb the flake up the centre of the wall.
FA. JMCS 1942

❷ Concorde .... 6a+ *5b*
A super line up the arete on good holds.
FA. M.Fowler 1975

❸ Viking Line 6b *5c*
Climb the face and crack to finish in the niche above.
FA. R.Mazinke 17.3.1996

❹ Misty Wall 6a *5b*
A short and green wall using cracks and flakes.
FA. R.Mazinke 17.3.1996

❺ Shanty Wall 5b *5a*
A short and thoroughly unpleasant traverse across the wall. You could prolong the agony and start from *Capstan Wall*, or better still, not start in the first place.

Fandango Buttress — Eridge Rocks 149

Fandango Buttress
A mossy slab - the best line is behind it on the north-facing wall. This wall never sees the sun, but seems to combat the encroaching green quite well. To the left is a block with a couple of boulder problems on it.
Approach (see map on page 107) - 50m right of Concorde Area is a cobra-shaped block next to the path.
Set-up and Descent - Back behind the right side of the buttress or either side of *I.B's Arete*.

6 Cobra Kai . . . . *f4+*
The flake, trending left at the break to a dirty top-out.

7 I.B's Arete *f6B*
Tricky climbing up the arete and nose above, which is climbed mainly on its left side.
FA. I.Bull 19.4.2011

8 Fruits 6b *5c*
The stepped left side of the face and wall above.
FA. R.Mazinke 11.7.1991

9 Eric 6a *5a*
A sustained mossy lower wall with a cleaner upper face.
FA. F.K.Elliot 1950s

10 Life in the Old Dog Yet 6c *6a*
A good line up the left side of the arete above an awkward start.
FA. C.Arnold 17.8.1993

11 Jakku . . . . *f5+*
A fun little problem up the right side of the arete.

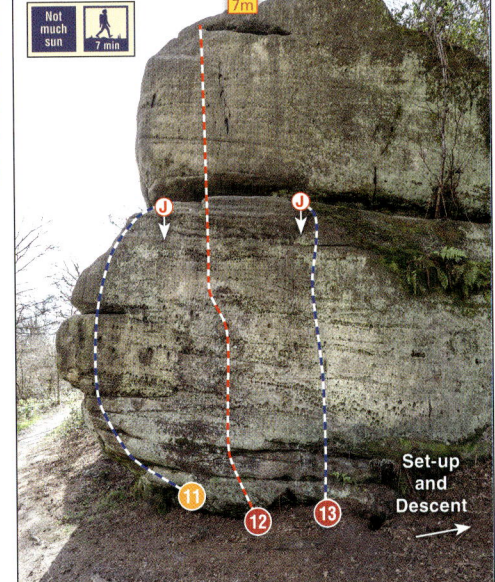

12 Fandango . . . . 6b+ *5c*
The best line in this sector. Climb the pocketed lower wall to the break and finish above with difficulty.
FA. R.Harper 1964

13 Blenjeel *f6A*
A short pocketed problem from a standing start. Often dirty and green.

Eridge Rocks — Keystone Wall

Keystone Wall

The Keystone Wall is under the cover of trees and receives little sunlight so can be dirty and green. It is rarely climbed on. If you do climb here, please don't remove any lichen with brushing.

Approach (see map on page 107) - 70m further right is a small mound of rocks, one of which is balancing on top of another.

1 Keystone Cop f5
Climb the crack to reach a large undercut. Use this to gain the mossy top-out.
FA. R.Mazinke 7.4.1996

2 Keystone Face f4
Relatively easy climbing to an often damp top-out.
FA. R.G.Folkard 1950s

3 Keystone Crack .... f2+
More of a chimney adventure than a crack.

4 Keystone Wall f3
A mossy wall that never sees the light of day - esoteric.
FA. R.G.Folkard 1950s

Adrian Paisey lining up for the final moves of *Steamroller* (6c *6a*) - *page 156*. This route which is situated on the Eridge Tower, is also the final section of climbable rock at Eridge. The area beyond is classified as a no climbing zone.

Eridge Rocks — Fontainebleau Boulders

Fontainebleau Boulders

This area gives some good bouldering. There plenty of heart-pounding highballs to contend with. Some of the boulders are a bit mossy in places.

Approach (see map on page 107) - This area is 15m beyond Keystone Wall.

Descent - Either to the left or right of the boulders.

Boulderers - Hold cleaning is a delicate art so please use extra soft brushes only - toothbrushes and bouldering brushes are forbidden. Try to use minimal chalk and if possible use Eco Balls or liquid chalk - see page 45.

1 Paisley f5
The left side of the wall on pockets.
FA. C.Murray 13.5.1993

2 Hartleys f4
A short jamming exercise up the crack.
FA. N.S.Head 1.10.1970

3 Flutings .... f5+
The good problem up the arete, finishing on the left face.
FA. J.E.Q.Barford 1940s

4 Fluted Fancy f6A
The face eliminating the use of the left arete.

5 Boulancourt .... f5+
Climb the rounded arete on its right-hand side.
FA. B.Russell 2007

6 Milly-la-Foret f6A
Tricky to start, but easier thereafter.
FA. B.Russell 2007

7 Fontainebleau .... f6A+
Gain the flake with difficulty and layback this to finish.

8 Black Cadilac f6C
A powerful blast up the blunt arete. Hard to start!

9 Oliver and His Amazing Underpants .... f6B+
Climb the thin crack with some good holds either side of it.
FA. M.Smith 1991

10 White Lincoln f6C
A hybrid problem using the face as well as the right arete and the crack used on Oliver and His Amazing Underpants.

11 Fernkop Crack .... f5+
An unpleasant squeeze up the wide crack with a hard start.

12 More Ticks for Tim .... f4+
A chimney climb between the boulders.
FA. R.Mazinke 19.9.2005

Fontainebleau Boulders — Eridge Rocks

13 Hyphenated Jones — f6B
Powerful moves up the front nose. Finish carefully up the slab.
FA. M.Vetterlein 23.7.1994

14 Short Work — f5+
Climb the flake and finish on the slab above.
FA. T.Skinner 13.5.1993

15 Sonny Dribble Chops — f5
Use the series of cracks and finish on the arete.
FA. P.Stone 1989

16 Brighton Rock — f6B
A short eliminate up the face avoiding the holds on *Sonny Dribble Chops*.
FA. P.Stone 1989

17 Wobble — f5
The mossy slab and flake above.
FA. T.Skinner 13.5.1993

18 Pedestal Wall — f3
From the platform, climb the thin flake with a tricky last move.
FA. JMCS 1942

19 Elastic Headbands — f5
The right side of the mossy shelf.
FA. A.Hughes 1990

20 Hazel — f5+
The arete with a tricky top-out.
FA. G.West 21.6.2003

21 Another Wet Bank Holiday — f5+
A damp and dirty mossy crack.
FA. R.Mazinke 3.4.1994

22 Hurricane — f6C+
A short dyno up the mossy wall via a sloping rail for the left-hand.
FA. Ian Stronghill 24.4.2011

Eridge Rocks — Fontainebleau Boulders

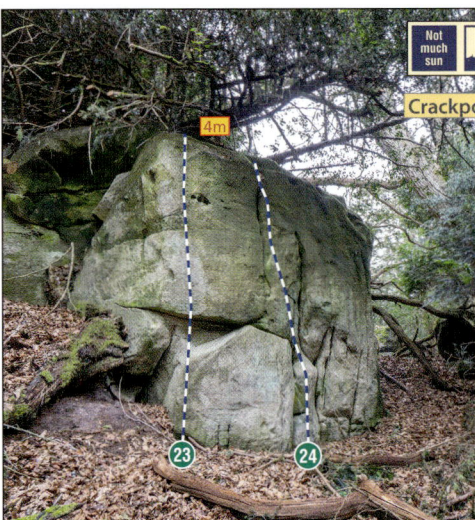

Crackpot Boulder
10m to the right of Pedestal Wall is a soft lump of rock. Only attempt these problems in the summer, if ever!

23 Crackpot Nose f4
The short left arete is very soft and best left alone.

24 Crackpot .... f3+
The centre of the face via two vertical cracks.
FA. N.S.Head 22.11.1970

25 Crackpot Arete .... f4+
The sandy arete with a tricky mossy mantel to finish.

26 Crackpot Crack .... f2+
The mossy wide crack.

Cameo Boulder
10m further right from the Crackpot Boulder.

27 Cameo .... f3+
The left set of flakes.
FA. R.Mazinke 26.3.1996

28 I Bet He Drinks at Kensington Palace
.... f5
Climb the face using the large flake out left and the flake to the right.
FA. R.Mazinke 26.3.1996

Eridge Rocks

Fontainebleau Boulders — 155

Tree Root

A green and unappealing rock 10m right past the Cameo Boulder. Probably something to do only when you have run out of routes to climb at Eridge.

29 Still, It Could Be Worse ...... f4+
Climb the short flake.
FA. R.Mazinke 26.3.1996

30 Ooh-er Missus f5
The corner has a taxing finish.
FA. R.Mazinke 22.6.1996

31 Local Vigilantes f6A
The right side of the green arete - awkward.
FA. R.Mazinke 26.3.1996

32 Tree Route f4
A mossy, green and terrible line up to the tree.
FA. R.Mazinke 26.3.1996

33 Pretentious ... Moi? f6C
A difficult start and impossibly mossy finish.
FA. J.Patterson 22.6.1996

34 I'm not Worried, I'm a Tractor .. f5+
Exit the cave and climb the short flake.
FA. R.Mazinke 26.3.1996

Eridge Rocks — Eridge Tower

Eridge Tower
A splendid tower situated at the far end of the climbable area at Eridge.
Approach (see map on page 107) - Continue along the main path and this is the prominent tower just beyond the Fontainebleau Boulders.
Conditions - The south face is surprisingly clean, but the rock makes things a little bit more difficult.

1 Broken Path .... f6B+
A small boulder up on the banking with a eye-catching the arete. It has delicate moves and some major barn door potential.
FA. T.Gore 12.4.2017

2 Optical Racer 6a *5b*
Climb the centre of the face (eliminating the corner) and finish with a tricky section up the left side of the slab.
FA. M.Smith 1989

3 Barbican Buttress 4c *4c*
The proper corner climb and slab above to a bad top-out.
FA. F.K.Elliot 1942

4 Steamroller 6c *6a*
A good but difficult line up the centre of the wall on delicate holds. *Photo on page 151.*
FA. M.Morrison 2.4.1978

5 Battlements Crack .. 6a+ *5a*
A great line up a series of off-width cracks which increases in difficulty with height.
FA. F.K.Elliot 1943

6 Portcullis .... 6b+ *5c*
Climb the crack and line yourself up for a short but powerful exit over the overlap. A harder alternative takes the left face at the harder grade of **6c+** *6a*.
FA. JMCS 1942. FA. (Left-hand exit) M.Fowler 1979

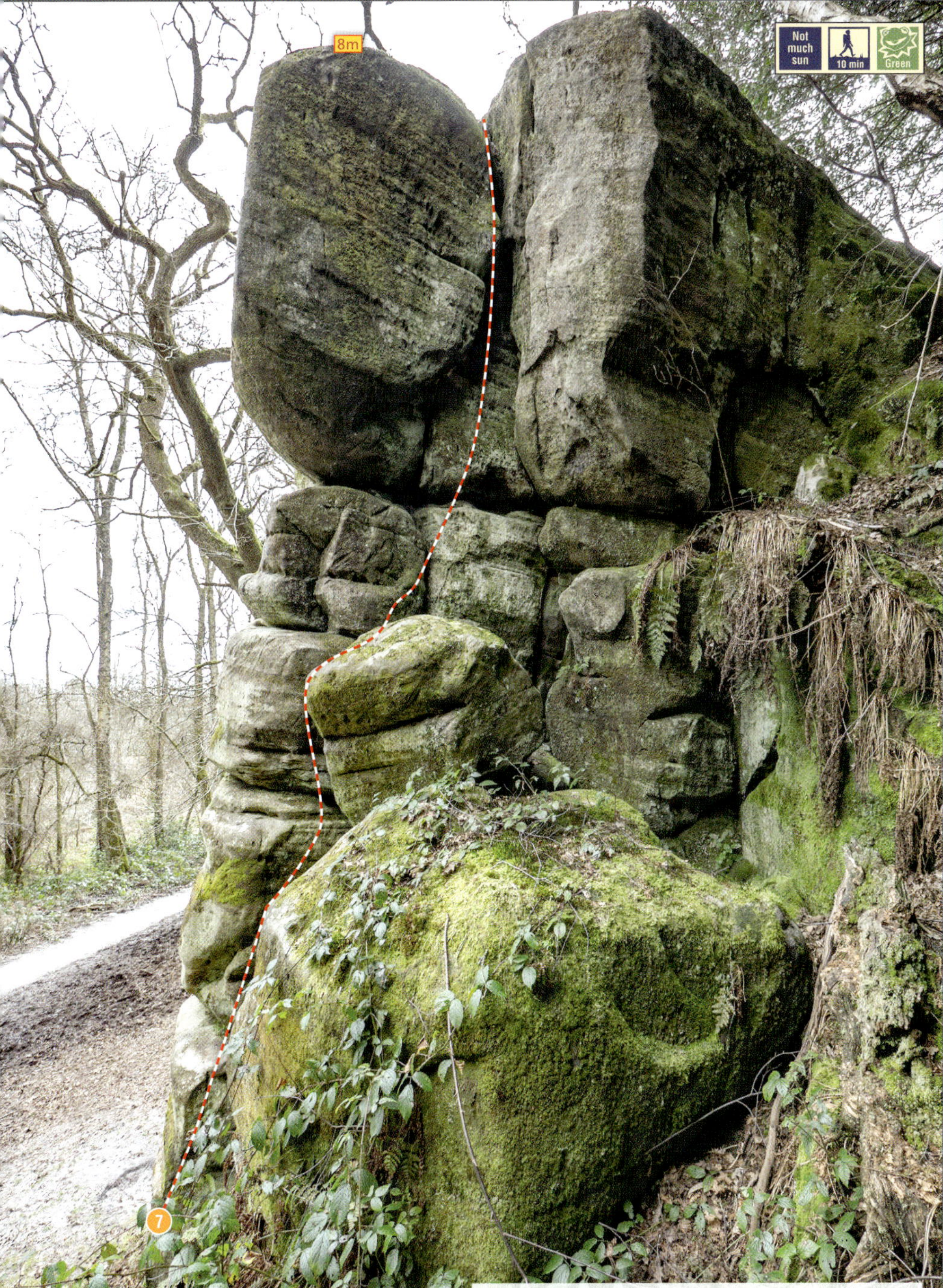

Eridge Tower **Eridge Rocks** 157

7 Eridge Tower Route 5b *5a*
Nowhere near as good as the previous lines. Climb the disjointed rocks and dirty sandy corner above.
FA. F.K.Elliot 1943

No Climbing Zone - Area Three
No climbing is allowed on any rocks beyond Eridge Tower. Please abide by this to ensure climbing can continue here at Eridge.

Harrison's Rocks

The Long Layback Area at Harrison's Rocks is one of the most popular climbing areas on southern sandstone, and justifiably so. Here a climber is undertaking the classic *Bow Window* (4a *4a*) - *page 197*.

Harrison's Rocks

	No star	★	★★	★★★
2a to 4c/f2 to f4	77	33	8	8
5a to 6a+/f4+ to f5+	52	32	27	5
6b to 7a/f6A to f6C+	104	81	49	14
7a+ up/f7A up	9	12	8	2

A place very much in the hearts of the sandstone community, Harrison's Rocks is the Southeast's longest stretch of climbable sandstone and is one of the busiest crags in England. For this reason, the climbing code of practice is heavily enforced to ensure the sandstone and environment are preserved for future generations to enjoy. The crag primarily caters for top-rope climbs, but there is plenty of bouldering available, in particular on the North Boulder which greets you as you enter from the north end. The range and style of routes on offer is extensive with many routes in the lower-to-mid grades and a lot of classics dotted along the length of the crag. No matter what your ability or preferred style of climbing, you will certainly find plenty at Harrison's Rocks to keep you entertained.

Access

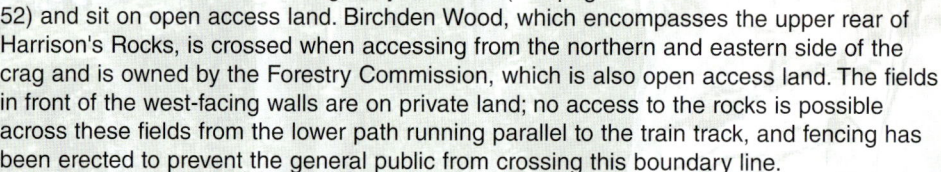

The rocks are owned and managed by the BMC (see page 52) and sit on open access land. Birchden Wood, which encompasses the upper rear of Harrison's Rocks, is crossed when accessing from the northern and eastern side of the crag and is owned by the Forestry Commission, which is also open access land. The fields in front of the west-facing walls are on private land; no access to the rocks is possible across these fields from the lower path running parallel to the train track, and fencing has been erected to prevent the general public from crossing this boundary line.

Conditions

Much of the rock comprises of solid sandstone, but years of traffic have contributed to significant erosion. However, the popularity does mean that the rock is often in better condition than the less visited crags in the area. Much of the crag faces west, seeing the sun from midday onwards. The southern end is south facing and consequently more sunny. There is currently a 13-year plan, which started in 2012 and is due to finish in 2025, to help reduce the number of trees at the crag base that block sunlight from the rocks. This will help create better climbing conditions as well as allowing native flora and fauna to grow on the woodland floor. Those areas not yet cleared can become greasy in damper conditions and eventually become green. The crag is sheltered in a valley which can make it slow to dry out but, on the whole, the general condition of the crag is good at most times of year.

Equipment

Bolt anchors have been installed at Harrison's Rocks to assist with setting up top-ropes. Additional set-up equipment may be required for anchors off trees (see page 38).

Costs and Facilities

Climbing at Harrison's Rocks is free but the carpark, which is owned and managed by the Forestry Commission, is a compulsory pay and display carpark. Visit www.southernsandstoneclimbs.co.uk for up-to-date fees and ensure to bring change with you. The fees primarily fund the upkeep of the carpark, toilet and washing facilities. There is a camping area with around 16 pitches which use the same facilities and payment for this is also done by the pay and display machine. If visiting Harrison's Rocks frequently, then consider getting a yearly Discovery Pass for the parking.

The famous toilet block at Harrison's Rocks.

Jack Gareth undertaking the final moves on *Long Layback* (6a+ *5a*) - *page 194* - at the Long Layback Area, Harrison's Rocks. The finish takes many by surprise as the last moves are much more technical than one would expect.

Harrison's Rocks

Approach   Also see map on page 18

From Tunbridge Wells, follow the A264 then turn onto the B2110 towards Groombridge. Pass the Crown Inn pub and continue to a roundabout. Branch left along Station Road passing the humped railway bridge and station on your left. After 200m branch right down Eridge Road. Follow this for 200m until you reach a turning on your right with a big sign saying 'Birchden Wood' and 'Harrison's Rocks'. Follow this narrow road down (keeping an eye out for the hidden speed bumps) to the main carpark.

Lower Path Approach (north entrance) - From the carpark, locate the track running along the south side and follow this west out of the woods and into a field. The path will begin to curve south, eventually running parallel to the railway line. After a short distance is a large gate on your left, which is the entrance to Harrison's Rocks. Turning right will lead you to the North Boulder.

Top Path Approach (central areas) - From the main carpark, follow the open hard surface track and head south. Keep right for approximately 740m to which point you will encounter the 'A vision of hell' signed area with an information board and some wooden cannonballs and a cannon. At this crossroad of paths, turn right to the area above the Long Layback Area on page 194. Following the path left leads south along the top of the rocks. See desired area for specific approach details.

Forge Farm Approach on foot - It is possible to approach from the south side of the rocks, but not by car (please) as there is not much parking and local residents have objected. This approach method is best made on foot if coming from Eridge Train Station. From the station, head southwest for a short distance and turn right onto Forge Road. Follow this for just under a mile to where the road runs parallel to the railway. On your right is a small road (signed 'private road') which crosses a river and then a rail crossing. Cross this carefully and continue straight (low profile and noise to a minimum please) to a T-junction by the converted oast houses - turn left. Follow the track past a gate and continue with the fence on your right-hand side to where a narrow purpose-built squeeze is found. This leads up to the Isolated Buttress - page 244. Alternatively, continue and use the right-hand gate (also used for emergency service access) which leads uphill to Squat Tower - page 234. Continuing straight along the footpath across the fields leads to the north entrance.

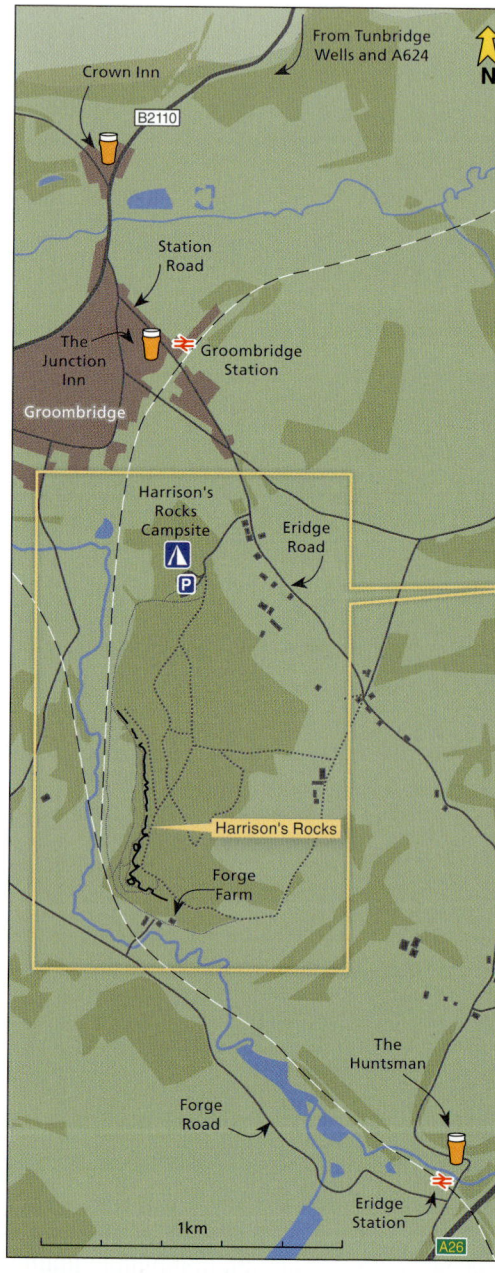

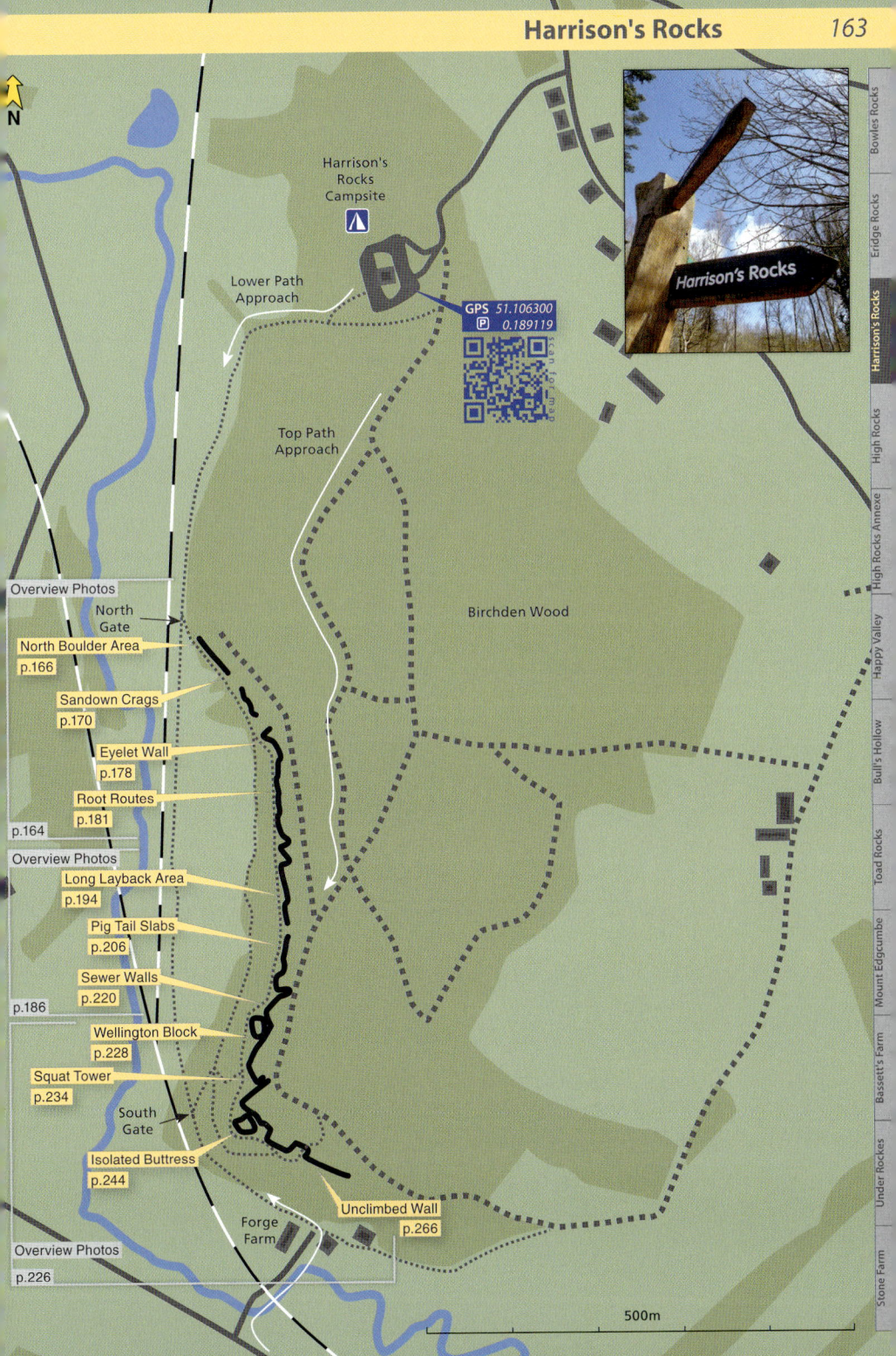

Harrison's Rocks

Harrison's Rocks

Harrison's Rocks — North Boulder Area

Passage Wall

① Wooden Stump .... *f3+*
The short slab opposite North Boulder, finishing on tree roots. It can be overgrown at times.

② Passage Direct *f3*
Mount awkwardly onto the rounded shelf, finishing more easily.

③ Ziggy *f6A*
Climb the arete, mostly on the left side, depending on your preferred technique.

North Boulder Area — Harrison's Rocks

North Boulder Area

A popular boulder that greets you as you enter from the north entrance to the rocks. A good number of problems are dotted around. The passage side tends to stay green and needs dry conditions to climb.

Approach (see overview on page 164) - Use the Lower path approach.

Descent - Either down-climb *OK Corral* or jump the gap across the passage.

Boulderers - Hold cleaning is a delicate art, and toothbrushes and bouldering brushes are forbidden due to their abrasive nature on the holds. Try to use minimal chalk and if possible use Eco Balls or liquid chalk - see page 45.

5 Piano f6B
The face between *Red River* and the arete of *Alligator Snatch*.

6 Alligator Snatch f6B
The arete - sit-down or standing start at the same grade.

7 Groovy Graeme .... f4+
A popular problem using good undercuts in the corner. Fingery moves above lead to a delicate top-out manoeuvre.

8 Letterbox f5
A nice problem on undercuts in the break followed by a pull over the bulge to good holds above.

9 Sunset Wall f5
A slightly harder version of *Letterbox*.

10 Layaway Cure .... f5+
The arete with the occasional flake for aid.

4 Red River f6B
Climb just right of centre using side-pulls and crimps. Either elegantly latch the top flat hold, or just dyno for it.

Descent jump or reverse route 23 - p.169

Harrison's Rocks — North Boulder Area

Boulderers - Hold cleaning is a delicate art, and toothbrushes and bouldering brushes are forbidden due to their abrasive nature on the holds. Try to use minimal chalk and if possible use Eco Balls or liquid chalk - see page 45.

11 Torque Wrench Left .... f6A+
The left-hand variation moving up and left of the finger slot.

12 Torque Wrench .... f6A+
Climb the nose by the original method which uses the upper slot for the left-hand.

13 Finger Flow f7A
An eliminate using the small layaway holds between *Torque Wrench* and *West Face Route*.

14 West Face Route .... f5+
Great climbing on big holds that is not as straight forward as first appears. *Photo opposite*.

15 Strong Struggle f6C
A demanding little problem up the centre of the face.

16 Papillon f6B
Slap out for the hold over the break and reach up to use the short flakes above.

17 Reve f6B
An alternative finish to *Papillon*.

18 Back Breaker .... f6B+
A steep problem over the lip past a poor thin pocket to finish via a rounded top-out.

19 Full on Fling f6B
A squeezed in eliminate.

North Boulder Area — Harrison's Rocks

Descent jump or reverse route 23

20 The Sheriff *f6C*
A popular and powerful problem over the nose. The arete is allowed as well as the hold in the left break to start. This lines you up for powerful manoeuvres over the lip. Good luck!

21 Silver Star *f6A*
An easier version of *The Sheriff* that shares some holds but exits on the right side of the nose.

22 Trigger *f5*
A good problem heading up from the holds on the left side of the break.

23 OK Corral .... *f2+*
An easy one up the corner groove with big holds just where you need them. Also used as a way down.

24 Ragtime .... *f5+*
Climb the centre of the face and negotiate the final moves over the top block.

Jun Taoka climbing *West Face Route* (*f5+*) - *opposite* - on the North Boulder at Harrison's Rocks.

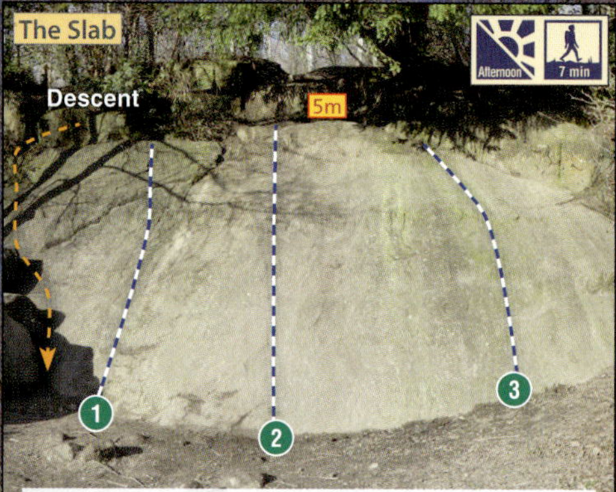

Harrison's Rocks — Sandown Crags

The Slab
An easy slab, popular with younger children.

1 Slab Left f2
The left side of the slab. Try without hands.

2 Slab Centre f2
Fun and popular.

3 Slab Right f2
The shorter right side of the slab.

Bridge Corner
Often green, often ignored.

4 Bridge Corner Left .... f2+
The short left arete.

5 Bridge Corner .... f2+
An often dirty climb up the corner.

6 Bridge Corner Right f3
The very short right face.

Central Route
The routes on this little wall are better than they first appear.

7 The Ramp 3a *3a*
A poor and dirty line.

8 DJ Face the Music .... 6a+ *5b*
A short-lived and rarely climbed route with a poor top-out.
FA. I.Mailer 19.1.1983

9 Central Route 3a *3a*
The best on this wall and fairly enjoyable.

10 Rampette Direct 4a *4a*
The direct which comes in from the right at the same grade.

Sandown Crags — Harrison's Rocks

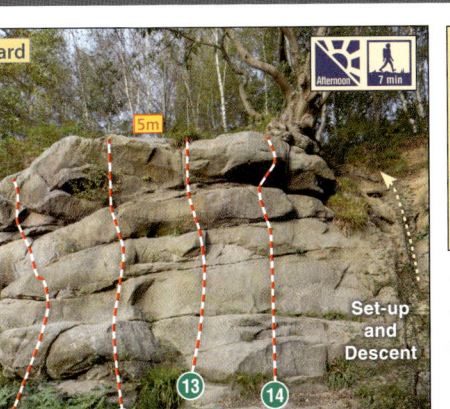

Sandown Crags
This section on the crag is only climbable when foliage is at its lowest, as some of the top-outs can be impossible. It mainly appeals to beginners apart from the odd challenging route or problem here and there.
Approach (see overview on page 164) - Use the Lower path approach.
Set-up and Descent - For the left-hand crags, head down the left side of The Slab. For all remaining crags, see descents marked on the page.

Wizard
A decent buttress with a few short micro routes.

⑪ Wizard's Little Apprentice . . . . . ☐ 3a *3a*
Pretty much a staircase up the left side of the buttress.

⑫ Wizard . . . . ⭐ ☐ 4a *4a*
Climb the staircase up to and then over a small roof.

⑬ Graham . . . . ⭐ ☐ 4a *4a*
A straightforward climb up the centre of the buttress.

⑭ Golden Graham's . . . . ☐ 4b *4b*
A tricky last move over the roof.

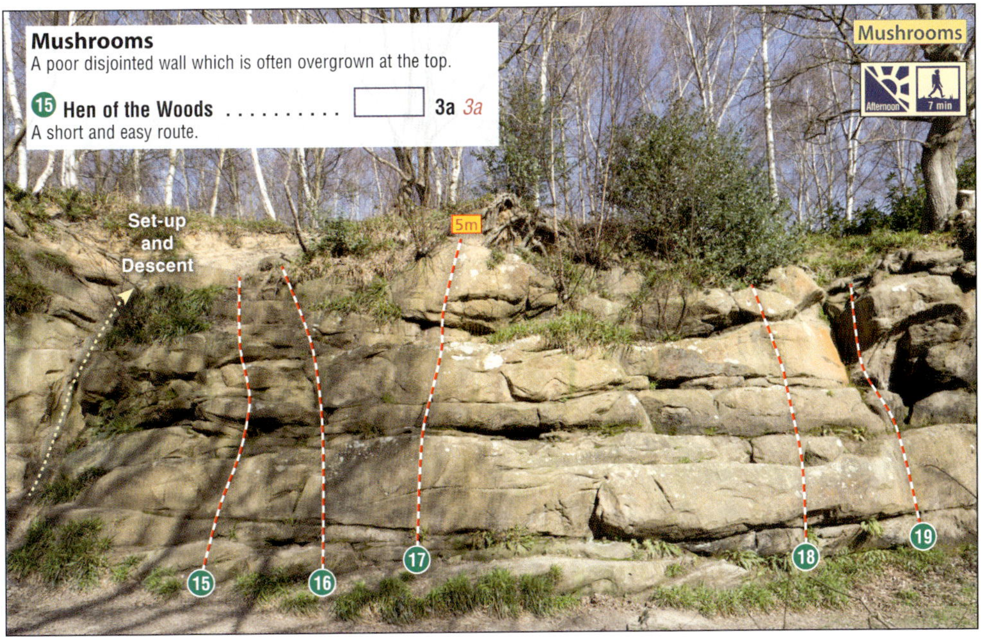

Mushrooms
A poor disjointed wall which is often overgrown at the top.

⑮ Hen of the Woods . . . . ☐ 3a *3a*
A short and easy route.

⑯ Artist's Conk . . . . ☐ 3a *3a*
Another short and easy route.

⑰ Trembling Merulius . . . . ☐ 3a *3a*
Easy again, but with a mucky top-out.

⑱ Jack O'Lantern . . . . ☐ 3a *3a*
Disjointed climbing into a holly tree. Nice.

⑲ Mushrooms . . . . ☐ 3a *3a*
Climb the groove.

Harrison's Rocks — Sandown Crags

Mushrooms - Right

The continuation of Mushrooms and equally more difficult to top-out especially after the foliage explosion in spring.

20 Isobel f3
A short problem up the crack.

21 Shrooms f3
Another short one finishing over a small lip.

22 Liberty Cap f2
A slabby problem topping out into the overgrowth.

23 Sub-space Mushroom ..... f3+
The slab is smooth and interesting. The top-out is the same as the others.

Urban Slab

A decent sized slab which is often sandy.

24 Stepped Slab 3b *3b*
Step up onto the ledge and finish easily above.

25 Mezzanine 3a *3a*
Move left to finish.

26 Urban Slab 3c *3c*
The slab with a holly tree exit.

27 Usurer 4a *4a*
Climb the slab and finish through the overlap to the right.

Sandown Crags — Harrison's Rocks 173

Panda

Panda
Perhaps the best of the Sandown Crags with a good selection of boulder problems.

28 Bamboo .... f4+
A short problem with a mantel midway.

29 Giant Panda .... f6A+
Powerful moves and a bit confusing for the feet but the top-out proves to be the crux.

30 Panda Car. f3
Climb the right side of the corner-crack.

31 Panda Pop f5
A nice and delicate problem starting on a good side-pull and finishing with a mantel onto the narrow shelf above.

32 Panda Style. f5
Similar in style to *Panda Pop* - use the small side-pull for the left-hand to gain the ledge. Perform a mantel to stand up on the ledge and exit.

33 Chinese Panda f5
More of that slabby *Panda Style*.

34 Panda Cub f4
Often mossy and green, but climbable when dry.

Harrison's Rocks — Green Wall

Green Wall

What started as a good idea soon became a mild disaster. This section of the wall was excavated in an attempt to create longer routes, but unfortunately the uncovered lower sections were almost blank making the routes much harder to start than they were originally. The wall can suffer with seepage and the top-outs are rather dirty.

Approach (see overview on page 164) - Use the Lower path approach. Continue about 10m further right of the last of the Sandown Crags.

Set-up and Descent - Go to the left of the wall, next to the Panda problems, or to the right following the vague path left of Kukri Wall - p.176.

1 Green Wall Girdle f6C
A fingertip traverse of the break, finishing up *Usurper*.
FA. R.Mazinke 18.11.1995

2 Trees are Green 4a *4a*
Climb the face right of the ledge, finishing on tree roots.
FA. T. Hill 30.5.1993

3 Photinia .... 6c+ *6a*
After a blank start, gain the slanting crack, finishing on tree roots.
FA. R.Mazinke 30.5.1993

4 Teddy Bear's Picnic 7a *6b*
Try to imagine some holds and use them to reach the break. Powerfully reach for the vague vertical cracks above and finish up the much better upper half.
FA. T.G.DeLacy 28.3.1976

5 Special Invitation 7a *6b*
Start as for *New Hat*, and break left to climb the blank wall. Finish with a difficult and dirty mantel at the top.
FA. C.Gibson 15.11.2003

6 New Hat .... 6c+ *6a*
After a blank start - which more often than not requires a little jump to the break - continue up the groove, which can suffer from seepage from the soil above.
FA. R.Mazinke 5.6.1993

7 Central Groove 6b *5c*
Climb the upper groove above another blank start.
FA. N.S.Head 28.3.1976

Green Wall — Harrison's Rocks

8. Dynamo — 6b+ *5c*
Either a long reach, or a dyno, is used to reach the break. The upper half is more enjoyable.
FA. N.S.Head 28.3.1976

9. Usurper — 6a *5b*
A more amicable lower section is climbed to reach the upper groove.
FA. J.Reevely 28.3.1976

10. The Violent Sprat — 7a *6b*
Climb the wall avoiding all contact with the arete.
FA. A.Hughes 2006

Harrison's Rocks — Kukri Wall

Kukri Wall

After a little TLC in 2014 this area became much more climbable. It will continue to improve once further tree clearance work is undertaken, bringing more light to the rock. It still suffers from seepage in places and is a little bit dirty due to lack of traffic.

Approach (see overview on page 164) - Use the Lower path approach. Continue past Green Wall.

Set-up and Descent - Follow the vague path to the left.

1 Penknife 5b *5a*
A difficult mantel onto the shelf at half-height. Finish easily above.
FA. R.Mazinke 17.4.1995

2 Breadknife Buttress 4b *4b*
The best climbing on the wall, but not entirely independent until you move left higher up. Finish with a rounded and slightly awkward top-out.
FA. J.R.Lees 1949

3 Kukri Wall 3c *3c*
The central groove on some good but dirty holds. It will improve over time.
FA. J.R.Lees 1949

4 Kukri Wall Direct 5a *4c*
Climb the wall on small holds. Often green.
FA. J.R.Lees 1949

5 Kukri Wall Tree 5a *4c*
The right-hand line is very similar to *Kukri Wall Direct*. Despite the name, avoid use of the tree.

Harrison's Rocks

Kirby's Adventures

A small reclaimed bouldering area that is not popular due to the tricky top-outs. These may clean up in future.
Approach (see overview on page 164) - Use the Lower path approach and continue approximately 15m further right of Kukri Wall.

6 Kirby's Adventures f4
A straightforward problem up the face to the left.

7 King Dedede f6A
With less than positive side-pulls to start, pop for the break. Tree roots are 'in' at the top.

8 Meta Knight f6B
Using the large pocket and side-pull on *King Dedede*, slap for the break and finish via the stump.

9 Magolor f6B
Climb the arete using holds on the main face to the left.

10 Yin-Yarn .... f6A+
A short problem with a hard start.

11 Dyna Blade .... f5+
Locate the jug high up in the crack and heave up to finish.

12 Animal Friends .... f6B+
With poor feet low down, use the side-pull to start. Finish over the large tree root.

Harrison's Rocks — Eyelet Wall

Eyelet Wall

The first of the more appealing areas at Harrison's, with some good micro routes and boulder problems.

Approach (see overview on page 164) - Use the Lower path approach. Continue along the lower path for approximately 40m beyond Kirby's Adventures. It is situated up a slight banking on your left.

Set-up and Descent - To the left of the wall.

The first routes are normally top roped because of their top-outs and poor landings, but they can be bouldered.

1 Laraletme 6b *5b*
Climb the short crack and wall left of the arete.
FA. C.Picken 11.5.2006

2 Ringlet 6b *5b*
Tackle the lower bulge and finish up the left arete.

3 Twiglet 7a *6b*
Head up to the roof and locate that left-hand undercut before a desperate finish over the bulging roof.
FA. R.Mazinke 8.5.1994

4 Eyelet 4b *4b*
A mini classic. Climb steeply over the bulge, which is far more technical that it first appears.

5 Singlet 6c *5c*
A steep leaning wall with a hard finish.

Eyelet Wall — Harrison's Rocks 179

6 Dave .... f2+
A short problem with a distinct mantel.

7 Deep Thought .... f5+
Without much for the feet, either make a long reach from the break to the top, or perform a mini dyno.
FA. D.Beail 1998

8 Don .... f2+
Layback and bridge up the short diagonal corner-crack.

9 Toad .... f5+
Climb the arete using holds on either side.

10 Patient Parmer .... f5+
It is tricky to unlock the sequence between the crimpy slots. The lack of footholds doesn't help much either.
FA. C.Murray 1998

11 Elastic f5
Fingery face climbing starting from a crimpy slot.
FA. J.Smoker 1950s

12 Bioplastic .... f6A+
An eliminate between *Elastic* and *Tight Chimney*. So tight that it is almost impossible to do without using holds on other problems.

13 Tight Chimney f3
A fairly straightforward problem up the chimney which can be done in a number of ways.

Harrison's Rocks — Eyelet Wall

The following routes / problems are graded as boulder problems here but are commonly done on top-ropes as some have delicate top-outs and are a little on the high side for some.

14 Projectile **f6B**
Mantel onto the shelf and finish up the scoop.

15 Tight Chimney Direct ...... **f5+**
The direct of the original route **Tight Chimney Slab**, *f3+*. The original traverses in from halfway up *Tight Chimney* and finishes the same. The direct is also known as 'Grasshopper'.

16 Sullivan's Travels ..... **f6A+**
Climb the bulge past the break and delicately onto the slab.

17 Sullivan's Stake .... **f6A+**
A technical undertaking passing the bulge.

18 Gillbert's Gamble .... **f4+**
A fine piece of technical slab climbing. Start from the arete and make your way delicately upwards.

19 Ejector **f4**
A pleasant little problem up the curving groove. This can be extended slightly by climbing the block above if desired.

20 Sand Piper .... **f5+**
The thin flake with nothing much for the feet.

21 Shytte .... **f5+**
The short rounded nose is not that great.
FA. C.Murray 1994

Root Routes — Harrison's Rocks

3 Carrera 6b *5c*
Start on the bottom left of the slab and zig-zag your way up. It can also be done by starting up the crack around to the left.
FA. T.Daniells 1970s

4 Open Chimney 4b *4b*
A nice chimney climb that can be done in a number of ways.

5 Cottonsocks Traverse ... 6a *5a*
Start from the base of *Open Chimney* and work your way round onto the main face, finishing up *Root Route 2*.

6 Root Route 3 .... 6b+ *5c*
Campus the overhanging nose on good holds and finish awkwardly at the top.

7 Root Route 2.5 .... 6a+ *5b*
Rounded holds along the breaks with a number of hidden holds along the way.
FA. G.Newton 6.6.1996

8 Root Route 2 .... 6c *6a*
A hard start via the circular hole.

9 Root Route 1.5 .... 6a+ *5a*
Technical climbing after a poor start.

10 Root Route 1 Direct 4b *4b*
A simple direct line to *Root Route 1*.

11 Root Route 1 .... Top 50 ... 4a *4a*
A great excursion across the face finishing up *Root Route 2*.

Root Routes

A fine and popular wall with a rather elaborate tree sprawled across it.

Approach (see overview on page 164) - Use the Lower path approach. Just along from Eyelet Wall and up a short stepped path.

Set-up and Descent - The rooted gully to the right or use the top access path to the left.

1 The Land of Green Ginger ... 6c *6a*
The short wall above a boulder, to a poor mantel to finish.

2 Trip of the Psychedelic Tortoise
.... 6c *6a*
Follow the crack to a sloping top-out.
FA. P.Stone 1985

Harrison's Rocks — Blackeye Wall

Blackeye Wall
Short but challenging climbs that take many climbers by surprise - some requiring unique climbing styles to ascend them.
Approach (see overview on page 164) - Use the Lower path approach. This wall is right of Root Routes.
Set-up and Descent - The rooted gully just to the left.

1 Soft Rock 7b *6c*
Technical face climbing on tiny holds. No use of the arete or crack.
FA. M.Smith

2 Blackeye Wall 6b *5c*
Layback, finger jam or use your own magical techniques to ascend the crack. Head left at the break and finish with a hefty mantel to reach the top. *Photo opposite*.
FA. M.P.Ward, Late 1940s

3 Blackeye Wall Direct ... 6b+ *5c*
A direct finish to *Blackeye Wall*.

4 Slanting Crack 6c *5c*
Climb the series of flakes to the break and finish more easily. Much more challenging than it first appears.
FA. M.P.Ward, Late 1940s

5 Fugazi 7a *6b*
A poor eliminate route up the face to the slot and beyond. Avoid contact with both adjacent routes if at all possible.
FA. A.Hughes 2013

6 Counterfeit 6c *5c*
Crimpy and powerful face climbing avoiding the crack altogether.
FA. T.G.DeLacy 4.4.1976

7 Right-hand Crack 5b *5a*
A super short off-width climb which is appealing to those who know how it's done.

8 Serendipity 6b *5c*
A short face climb eliminating the cracks either side.
FA. M.Smith 1989

9 A Small Bit of Black 3a *3a*
A short and easy crack heading past the tree.

Blackeye Wall Harrison's Rocks

Ho-Yin Lam on the tricky starting moves of *Blackeye Wall* (6b 5c) - *opposite* - on the Blackeye Wall at Harrison's Rocks.

Harrison's Rocks — Fang Wall

Fang Wall

Fang Wall is prone to being overgrown and can become almost unrecognisable. This neglect means that, even when open and climbable, the routes remain dirty and sandy in places. The wall was part of the unsuccessful ground-lowering program which unfortunately made some of the starts rather hard.

Approach (see overview on page 164) - Use the Lower path approach. This is the next wall along from Blackeye Wall.
Set-up and Descent - Go up the slope on the right.

1 Cucumber Madness 6b *5b*
The short arete on soft rock with a poor top-out.
FA. B.Kavanagh 30.8.2004

2 Smear Campaign 6b *5c*
A dirty start to a finish up the shallow crack.
FA. C.Tullis 1.8.1990

3 Wisdom 6c *6a*
Climb the smooth lower wall to the break and finish up the crack. The grade all depends on your height.

4 Fang 6c *6a*
Unless you're tall, you may need to pile up some pads to reach for the break (reduces the grade) or pop for the break so you can attempt the bulge above.

5 Incisor .... 6b+ *5c*
Pop for the break and clamber up the crack above. Will improve over time.

6 Stranger than Friction 6b *5b*
Gain the break then tackle the tricky finish.
FA. C.Tullis 26.7.1990

7 Steph 4a *4a*
Short and dirty up the disjointed crack.
FA. M.Smith 16.7.1990

Just up and right is Weeping Slab with two routes on it.

8 Weeping Slab 5b *5a*
The left side of the slab which is often wet.

9 Gollum 4b *4b*
The right side which is often green.
FA. D.Beall 1998

Rotten Stump Wall — Harrison's Rocks

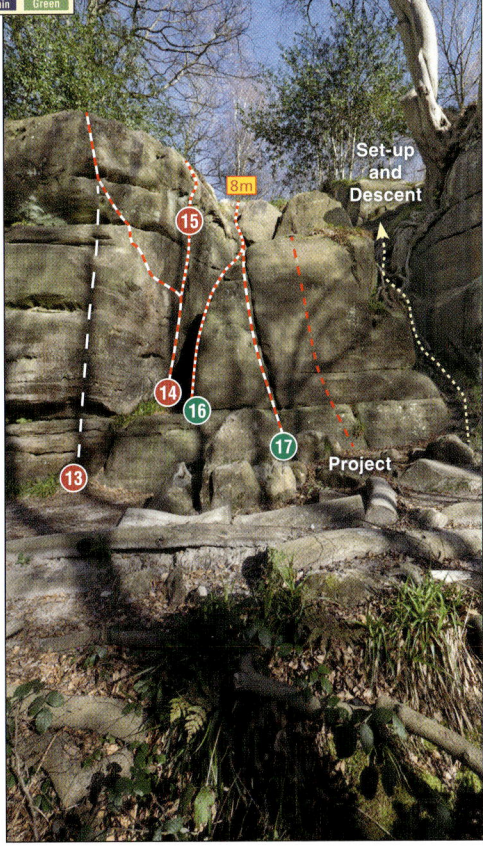

Rotten Stump Wall

The first part of a more consistent series of walls along the upper path moving closer to the popular Long Layback Area. Regrettably this wall sees little traffic and is often an unappealing green colour and greasy for much of the time. This may change with the woodland management plan, which should help the breeze reach the rock.

Approach (see overview on page 107) - This area can also be accessed from the top path from the carpark and down the gully left of this wall.

Set-up and Descent - Use the ramp to the left or the tree root gully to the right.

⑩ Corridor of Uncertainty 7a *6b*
Blank with some seriously small holds to contend with.
FA. M.Vetterlein 14.8.1990

⑪ Sticky Wicket 6b *5c*
Manoeuvre up the crack to a greasy finish. Holds either side of the crack are 'in'.

⑫ Rotten Stump Wall . . . . . 6b+ *5c*
Long moves between holds and slopers which are often greasy and unpleasant.
FA. M.P.Ward 8.6.1947

⑬ Rotten Stump Arete 6c *6a*
Climb the arete to join *Sliding Corner*.
FA. M.P.Ward 8.6.1947

⑭ Sliding Corner 6b *5b*
On the sidewall, edge up leftwards from the chimney to reach the arete. Finish up this.

⑮ Awkward Crack 6c *6a*
Continue direct from the start of *Sliding Corner* and finish up the thin crack.

⑯ Easy Chimney 3a *3a*
An easy chimney popular with children. Please note that children still need to walk off and not be lowered down.

⑰ Fingernail Crack 3a *3a*
A little crack, adjacent to the chimney, which is fun as a laybacking problem and eventually becomes one and the same with *Easy Chimney*.

The blank face to the right has a long-standing project up its centre.

Harrison's Rocks

Harrison's Rocks

Harrison's Rocks — Panther's Wall Area

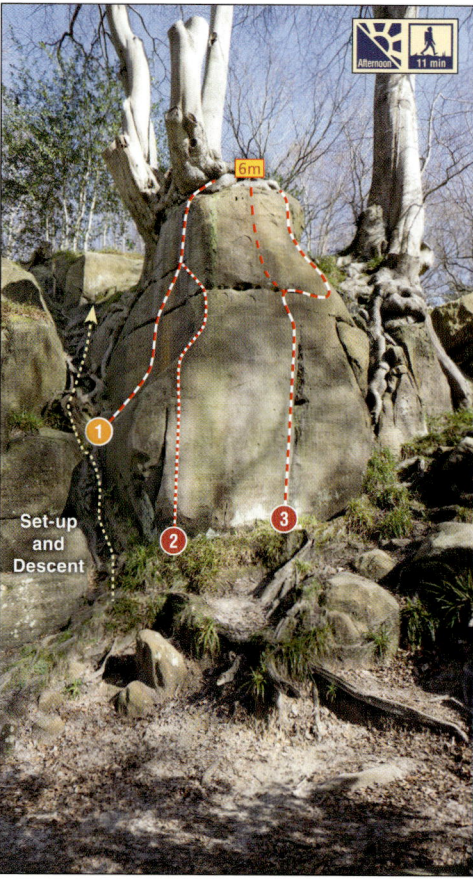

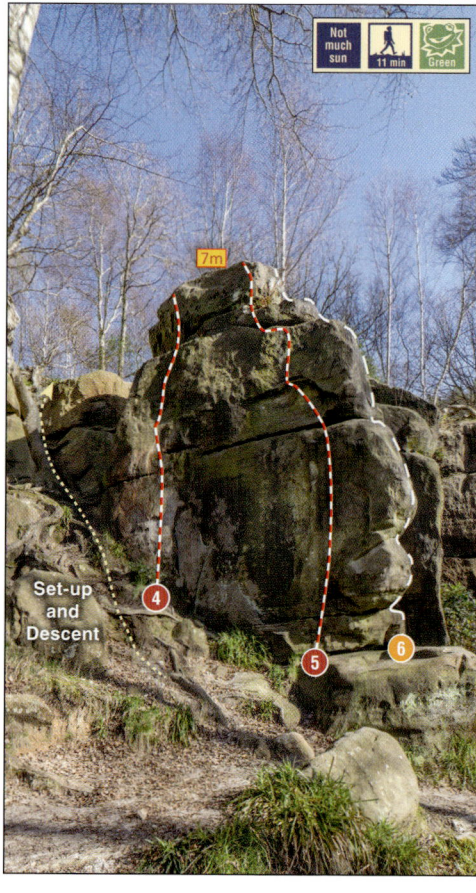

Panther's Wall Area

A number of small buttresses with a few good routes worthy of your attention.

Approach (see overview on page 186) - Use either the Lower or Top Path Approach. This area is just past Rotten Stump Wall.

Set-up and Descent - To the left of *Dinosaurus* or *Panther's Wall* (this page).

❶ Dinosaurus 6a *5b*
Gain the break from the gully and finish up the centre of the wall.
FA. M.P.Ward 1950s

❷ Dinosaurus Direct 6c *6a*
Climb direct up the arete and merge with *Dinosaurus*.

❸ Smiliodon .... 6b+ *5c*
Climb the crack and break right to finish up the arete. Continuing direct eliminating the aretes is **6c** *6a*.
FA. G.McLelland 1980s

❹ Tomcat / Simon's Wall .. 6b *5c*
Can be a bit mossy and green and the holds are thin in places.
FA. T.G.DeLacy 24.6.1973

❺ Panther's Wall 6c *6a*
Climb to the break using thin flakes and make good use of an undercut on the upper wall.
FA. T.Panther 1950s

❻ Snout .... 6a+ *5b*
A delicate start up the right side of the rounded arete which becomes easier and less reliant on the arete thereafter.
Photo on page 190.

❼ Snout Crack 3c *3c*
A good short crack climb.

❽ Guy's Problem 6c *6a*
A short arete problem to the break with an awkward finish.
FA. G.McLelland 1980s

Panther's Wall Area — Harrison's Rocks

⑨ Mantelpiece 6b *5c*
Climb directly into and through the shallow recess.
FA. G.McLelland 26.3.1983

⑩ Inimitability 6c *6a*
A technical route left of the corner.
FA. S.Quinton 14.3.1992

⑪ Beech Corner 3a *3a*
A poor corner route that is seldom climbed.
FA. R.G.Folkard 31.8.1941

⑫ Beech Crack 5b *5a*
A relation of *Beech Corner* which requires you to climb what is left of the rotten tree stump (partially removed in 2016). Alternatively, finish to the right on cleaner rock.

⑬ Out Of The Blue .... 6b+ *5c*
The left-hand side of the wall, just right of the *Beech Crack*, has a very bouldery start.
FA. C.Gibson 10.12.2016

⑭ Blue Peter .... 6b+ *5c*
Climb the arete starting on its left side and finishing up the groove at the top.

Chris Searle solos *Snout* (6a+ *5b*) - *page 188* - at the Panther's Wall Area of Harrison's Rocks.

Slab Area — Harrison's Rocks 191

Slab Area

A small alcove with a popular slab at its centre. The wall to the right is often damp and green but improves as you reach the Long Layback Area.

Approach (see overview on page 186) - Use either the Lower or Top Path Approach. Just beyond Panther's Wall Area.

Set-up and Descent - To the left of *Panther's Wall*.

Blue Peter - p.189

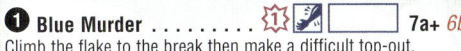

❶ **Blue Murder** . . . . 7a+ *6b*
Climb the flake to the break then make a difficult top-out.

❷ **Slab** 5c *5a*
A popular climb which is more of a chimney climb than a slab.

❸ **Slab Direct** . . . . 6a+ *5b*
Climb the centre of the clean-cut slab on crimps and less than perfect edges.
FA. R.A.Hodgkin 11.11.1934

❹ **Slab Crack** 6a *5b*
An often wet and vague jamming / laybacking exercise. Some choose to bridge across onto the right wall when its not covered in ooze. There are variations of this climb but they are not really independent of *Slab Direct*.

Harrison's Rocks — Slab Area

The overhanging wall to the right is north facing and often green and wet.

❺ Larger Frenzy 7c *6c*
Climb the cracks to the upper break, moving left to make better use of it. Finish above with a mantel on good holds. Sounds simple!
FA. D.Turner 22.9.1987

❻ Lager Shandy .... 7a+ *6b*
Climb the right crack to the break and make a dyno to a jug. Finish up the arete.
FA. S.Quinton 7.6.1993

❼ Celestial's Reach 6c *6a*
A fingery lower section leads to the mossy and damp break. Move left to finish up the crack.
FA. B.Wintringham 5.9.1965

❽ Stardust 6c *6a*
An alternative right-hand finish to *Celestial's Reach* up the open and often-dusty groove.
FA. G.Somerville

❾ Hangover 1 .... 6c+ *6a*
A left-hand and longer version of *Hangover 2* which traverses the break rightwards from *Celestial's Reach* before mantling onto the so-called 'Luncheon Shelf'. Finish as you like, but the most obvious is to climb *The Centre Finish*.

❿ Hangover 2 .... 6c *6a*
A steep and powerful roof climb between breaks. Traverse slightly right on the second break to the centre of the overhang to the perform a mantelshelf onto the ledge. Best finish via the *The Centre Finish*.
FA. L.E.Holliwell 1960s

⓫ The Centre Finish 6c *6a*
The best finish to the *Hangover* routes with an awkward footless start off the shelf to establish yourself onto the left side of the nose.
FA. L.E.Holliwell 1960s

Ernesto Silva mid-flow on the powerful moves on *Hangover 3* (7a 6a) - *page 194* - at the Long Layback Area, of Harrison's Rocks.

Harrison's Rocks — Long Layback Area

Long Layback Area
One of the more popular areas with an array of classic routes.
Approach (see overview on page 186) - The first major area when reaching the crag from the top path approach running from the carpark. Can also be a reached from the lower path.
Set-up and Descent - There is an easy climb to the right of *Sashcord Crack* - p.198 - which leads to and from the top.

❶ Hangover 3 .... Top 50 — 7a *6a*
A true sandstone classic. Latch the first juggy break and reach for the second one. Swing out and traverse left to reach up and eventually mantel onto the 'Luncheon Shelf'. Finish up the right side of the nose, known as *Nose Finish*. *Photo on page 193.*
Big Air, f7C or **8a+** if top-roping. Dyno from the first to second break.
FA. 1960s. FA. (Big Air) Matt Tullis on top-rope and Seb Powerham as a boulder problem 2013.

❷ Hangover Right-hand ... — 7a+ *6b*
A reachy direct to *Hangover 3*.
FA. D.Atchinson-Jones 1982

❸ Luncheon Shelf .... — 6c *6a*
Depart *Long Layback* at 1/3 height and reach for the ledge. Finish up the bulging headwall.
FA. A.J.J.Moulam 27.5.1951

❹ Long Layback ..... Top 50 — 6a+ *5a*
A popular route with some grand laybacking and a testing finish.
Photo on page 161.
FA. N.Barnard 1926

❺ Flakes Direct ...... — 7a+ *6a*
Climb the groove/crack, avoiding *Long Layback*, to the roof. Finish with a dirty mantel over this.
FA. M.Randall 1976

❻ The Flakes .... Top 50 — 7a *6a*
After a fingery start, head up and right slightly to the break under the roof. Traverse right and gain the slanting crack/rail. Overcome this powerfully to top out. There is a variation finish just to the left at the same grade. *Photo on page 14.*
FA. B.Wintringham 1965

❼ Coronation Crack ... — 7a *6a*
Climb direct up the thin fingery crack and finish as for *The Flakes*.
FA. M.Boysen 1960s

Long Layback Area — **Harrison's Rocks** — 195

8 Supernatural — 7b+ 6b
A fingery and technical masterpiece up the centre of the face. A close relation to *The Limpet* but independent enough if you keep away from the right-hand arete. The top section takes the final bulge at its centre and over the top block.
Photo on this page.
FA. D.Beail 3.1999

9 Supraspinatus — f6B
A long and fingery traverse along the lower wall that finishes at the far left side of the lower break under the 'Luncheon Shelf'.

10 The Limpet — 7b 6b
A classic climb up the arete, mainly on its left side and eliminating the use of the wall behind you at the start. Holds have broken so it has got harder over the years.
FA. B.Wintringham 1965

Adam Brown preparing to despatch the complex technical moves on *Supernatural* (7b+ 6b) - *this page* - at the Long Layback Area of Harrison's Rocks.

Harrison's Rocks — Long Layback Area

11 Dark Chimney 3b *3b*
The fun, easy climb up the chimney popular with beginners.

12 Dark Chimney Buttress ..... 6a+ *5a*
One of those, that always begs the question of what's in and what's not. Well it's all in and in all good.

13 Icarus .... f6B+
A huge dyno to a jug.
FA. S.Quinton 3.6.1993

14 Nut Tree .... 7a+ *6b*
Climb the blunt arete using a scary one-finger pocket (if desired) and other rather poor holds to slap up to the break. Often bouldered to the break at *f6B* (or harder if shorter).
FA. D.Lewis 1985

15 Spout Buttress .. 6b+ *5c*
A good route with a rather frustrating start if you're short. The top section can get dirty.
FA. M.P.Ward 1950s

16 Spout Crossing 6b *5b*
After a technical start, layback the groove to the break and a pumpy finish.

Long Layback Area — Harrison's Rocks

17 Windowside Spout 3c *3c*
A straightforward chimney climb with a hard start.

18 Casement Wall . . . . 6a+ *5b*
An eliminate that shares too many holds for comfort. Best described as 'Pelmet Direct'.
FA. J.R.Lees 1949

19 Pelmet . . . . 6a+ *5b*
A great little route with a reachy move for the short on the upper face moving left. *Photo on page 209.*

20 Bow Window . . . . Top 50 4a *4a*
The original and most popular line on this section. Climb the cracks and easy top section to finish up the gully above. *Photo on page 158.*
Two alternative finishes have been done. **Bow Window Left-hand, 6b** *5c*, finish left up the vague corner on the top block.
Bow Window Right-hand, 6b+ *5c* finishes over the roof.

21 Bow Window Flake 4a *4a*
An alternative start/variation to *Bow Window*, laybacking the juggy flake.

Mireille Le Bourg jamming up *Sashcord Crack* (4a *4a*) - *opposite* - at the Long Layback Area of Harrison's Rocks.

Simona Koplin making easy work of *Finger Stain* (6b+ *5c*) - *page 198* - at the Long Layback Area of Harrison's Rocks.

Giant's Staircase — Harrison's Rocks

Giant's Staircase
A short corner-shaped wall which is often in use by climbing groups under instruction.
Approach (see overview on page 186) - Use the Top Path Approach. Continue past the Long Layback Area.
Set-up and Descent - To the left of the wall.

1 Quarterdome 6a *5b*
Up the overlap and face above, which is rather enjoyable.
FA. C.Tullis 1998

2 Yosemite Big Wall Climb ... 6c *6a*
After a hard start, climb the face eliminating the arete. Short and not very sweet.
FA. R.Mazinke 14.5.1994

3 Giant's Staircase 3a *3a*
The slab and face above. Incredibly popular with beginners.

4 Arrow Crack 3a *3a*
The corner-crack.

5 Gardeners' Question Time ... 6c *6a*
A mini route up the centre of the face.
FA. B.Bevan-Pritchard 23.9.1987

6 Longbow Chimney 3a *3a*
A dark and murky chimney climb.

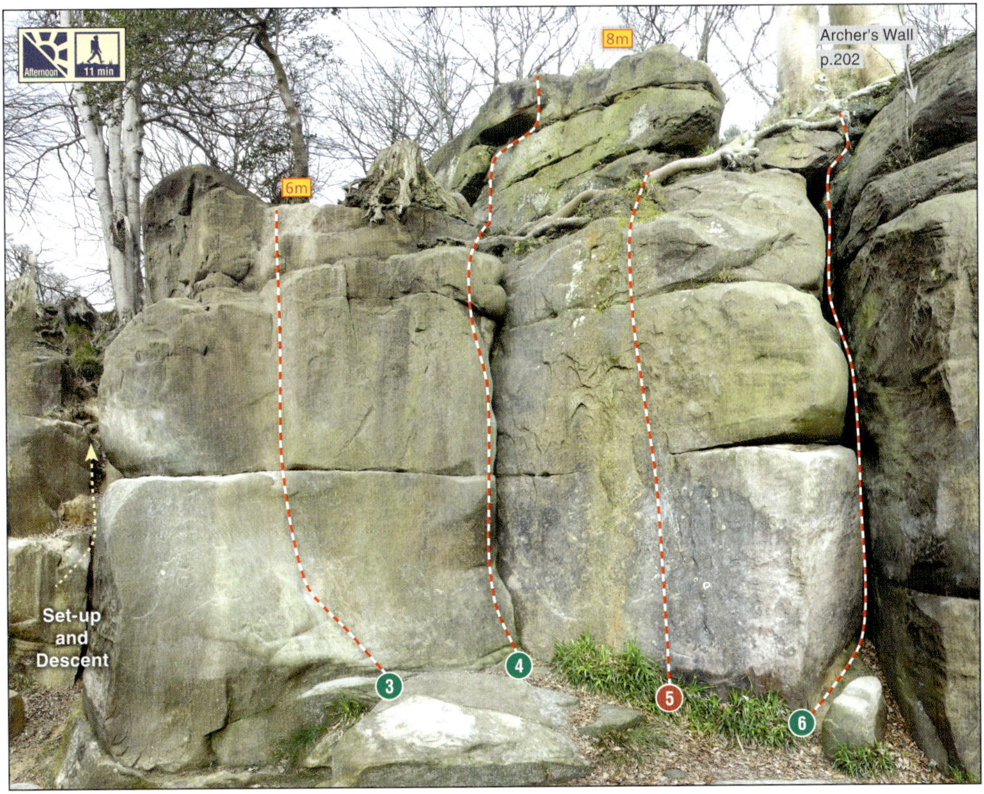

Harrison's Rocks — Archer's Wall

Archer's Wall

The wall continuing on from Giant's Staircase has some challenging and technical routes, which are regrettably often damp along the lower break.

Approach (see overview on page 186) - Use the Top Path Approach. Continue past the popular Long Layback Area and Giant's Staircase.

Set-up and Descent - To the left of Giant's Staircase. The far right-hand of the wall close to, and over the path requires an extended rope set-up to avoid ropes cutting into the rock. See page 38 for more information.

1 Grist 6c *6a*
The left side of the wall using the arete.
FA. M.Randall 1976

2 Quiver 6c *5c*
The flakes above a hard and often damp start.
FA. A.J.J.Moulam 19.8.1949

3 That Man's an Animal 7a *6b*
A squeezed in eliminate.
FA. P.Widdowson 1990

4 Toxophilite 6c *5c*
Climb the flakes with a couple of hard moves to throw you off and get you pumped.
FA. L.E.Holliwell 1965

5 Little Sagittarius .... 6b+ *5c*
Thin and fingery climbing. Start with a hard mantel onto the first ledge and then delicately manoeuvre up to finish right of the tree stump.

6 Sagittarius 5b *5a*
Climb the short slabby scoop and finish easily once you reach the top ledge. It has various starts; the best (and often the driest) being under the nose and moving left to establish yourself onto the ledge.

7 Archer's Wall 6b *5c*
Starting as for *Sagittarius*, but quickly head up the steeper face right of the scooped slab. *Photo opposite and page 30.*

Emma Harrington making an ascent of *Archer's Wall* (6b 5c) - *opposite* - on Archer's Wall at Harrison's Rocks.

Harrison's Rocks — What Crisis?

What Crisis?

This wall unfortunately sits right above the path which means you will be constantly moving for people passing by. It does have a number of excellent routes though.

Approach (see overview on page 186) - Use the Top Path Approach. The continuation from Archer's Wall.

Set-up and Descent - To the right, just left of Pig Tail Slabs - p.206.

1 Archer's Wall Direct 6c *5c*
Climb the overhanging nose with powerful moves throughout and a mantel to finish.

2 Stupid Effort 6b *5b*
Head up to attack the scoop, which requires a powerful and tricky mantel to get onto it.
FA. A.J.J.Moulam 26.6.1947

3 Long Crack 4c *4c*
A golden oldie with a hard middle section. Not to be underestimated.
FA. N.Barnard 1926

4 Riverdance 6b *6a*
A variation trending right up the smooth bulging nose.
FA. B.Franklin 26.5.1996

5 What Crisis? .... 7b+ *6c*
Follow the series of deep pockets up the centre of the face. There are a number of ways of progressing between them.
FA. A.Baker (aid) 1954. FFA. G.McLelland 1985. An impressive and daring solo ascent made by C.Murray in 1993.

6 In Crisis 7c *6c*
An alternative harder finish to *What Crisis?*
FA. B.Ventham 2009

7 Slim Finger Crack .. 6c *5c*
A much-loved crack climb which is hard to start, but delivers once established. *Photo on page 211.*
FA. C.A.Fenner 1940s

What Crisis? Harrison's Rocks 205

8 Vulture Crack 6b *5c*
Steep crack climbing, great for jamming experts. **Missing Link**, 6c *6a*, traverses the top break to finish up *Long Crack*.
FA. (Missing Link) T.Panther 1975

9 The Sting 6c *6a*
Climb the bulge and wall above. Take care with the holds as they are a bit fragile in places.
FA. M.Randall 1976

10 Marcus's Arete 6c *6a*
Use a distinct undercut at the far right side of the roof to start and power up the rest eliminating *Horizontal Birch*.
FA. P.Church 13.7.1996

11 Horizontal Birch 3c *3c*
With no birch tree to support the name any more, climb the often dirty crack in the corner.

12 Jumping Jack Flash ...... 7a+ *6b*
A squeezed in number which requires some dynamic moves between holds.
FA. P.Widdowson 14.8.1990

13 Downfall 4b *4b*
Start by climbing the unappealing crack to the right of the block and move left to finish. Can sometimes be a little overgrown.

Harrison's Rocks — Pig Tail Slabs

Pig Tail Slabs

The slabs are popular with groups and younger climbers. To the right of the ledge are three extensions which make for better and longer outings.

Approach (see overview on page 186) - Use the Top Path Approach. This section is beyond the prominent section of What Crisis?

Set-up and Descent - To the left of the slab.

Lowering off - Please note, just like all sandstone routes, you must not lower off once you have completed a climb. And please extend all belay set-ups over the edge to avoid causing any erosion to the rock.

Kids Slab
Below and to the left of the Pig Tail Slabs is a short slab favoured by young children.

❶ Kids Slab .... ☐ *f2*
A short and easy slab climb.

Pig Tail Slabs

❷ Left Edge .... ☐ 3c *3c*
The easy left side of the face.

❸ Original Route .... ☐ 3c *3c*
An easy slab without any really decent holds. Also referred to as 'Pig Tail Slab'.

❹ Big Toe Wall .... ☐ 4c *4c*
The short crack system has a committing last move.
FA. J.R.Lees 1949

Pig Tail Slabs Harrison's Rocks

5 Greasy Eliminate Left........ ⬜ 6c *6a*
From the ledge, attempt to climb the slab above, avoiding contact with the routes either side of it.

6 Greasy Crack.............. ⬜ 4c *4c*
As the name suggests, the crack can often be greasy and damp.

7 Greasy Eliminate Right....... ⬜ 7a *6b*
A squeezed in eliminate up the slab via a vertical slot.

8 Directors................. ⬜ 6b *5c*
Often a little mossy. Climb the nose and slab above.
FA. R.Mazinke 16.5.1999

9 Giant's Ear .... ⬜ 5b *5a*
The flake is greasy for most of the year.
FA. E.R.Zenthon 1940

10 Giant's Face .... ⬜ 6c+ *6a*
A committing route, first done as a *f6A* boulder problem above a bad landing. Choose your method of ascent wisely.

The next three routes start on the upper ledge and act as extended finishes to the lower routes, though can be done independently.

11 The Fonz.................. ⬜ 3a *3a*
The left side of the wall.

12 Happy Days............... ⬜ 3b *3b*
The centre of the wall.

13 Junend Arete.............. ⬜ 3a *3a*
The arete, which is traditionally started from the floor by climbing the right-hand edge of the buttress and finishing up the top arete.

Harrison's Rocks — Fallen Block

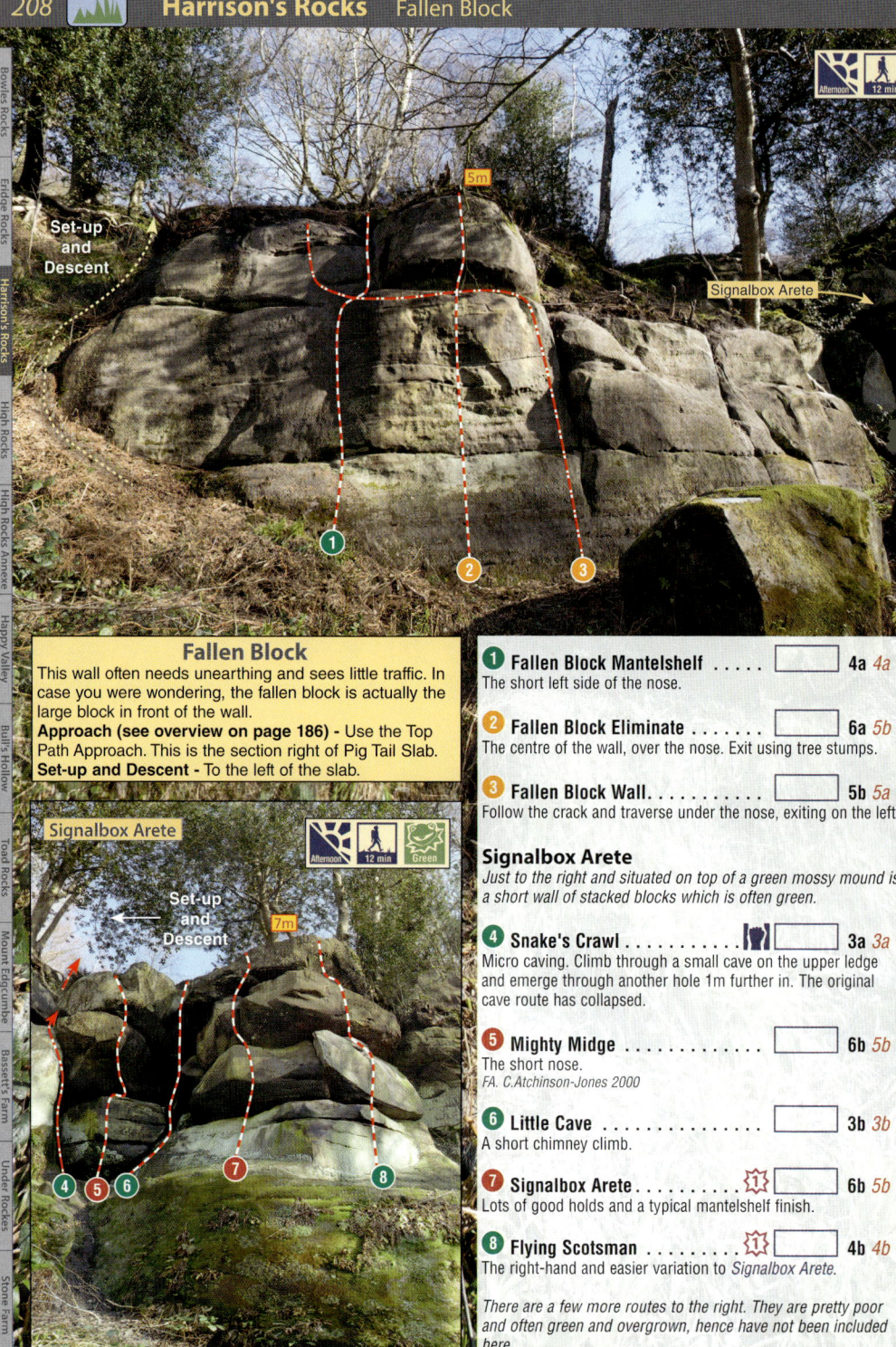

Fallen Block
This wall often needs unearthing and sees little traffic. In case you were wondering, the fallen block is actually the large block in front of the wall.
Approach (see overview on page 186) - Use the Top Path Approach. This is the section right of Pig Tail Slab.
Set-up and Descent - To the left of the slab.

❶ Fallen Block Mantelshelf 4a *4a*
The short left side of the nose.

❷ Fallen Block Eliminate 6a *5b*
The centre of the wall, over the nose. Exit using tree stumps.

❸ Fallen Block Wall 5b *5a*
Follow the crack and traverse under the nose, exiting on the left.

Signalbox Arete
Just to the right and situated on top of a green mossy mound is a short wall of stacked blocks which is often green.

❹ Snake's Crawl 3a *3a*
Micro caving. Climb through a small cave on the upper ledge and emerge through another hole 1m further in. The original cave route has collapsed.

❺ Mighty Midge 6b *5b*
The short nose.
FA. C.Atchinson-Jones 2000

❻ Little Cave 3b *3b*
A short chimney climb.

❼ Signalbox Arete 6b *5b*
Lots of good holds and a typical mantelshelf finish.

❽ Flying Scotsman 4b *4b*
The right-hand and easier variation to *Signalbox Arete*.

There are a few more routes to the right. They are pretty poor and often green and overgrown, hence have not been included here.

Emma Harrington making the reachy move on *Pelmet* (6a+ *5b*) - *page 197* - at the Long Layback Area at Harrison's Rocks. This photo was taken before the woodland in front of the rocks was cleared to bring more light to the rocks in this area. This clearance work is part of the Harrison's woodland management plan which is undertaken each year and relies on volunteers to make the clearance work possible.

Harrison's Rocks — Saint's Wall

Saint's Wall

Almost a continuation of the area adjacent to *Signalbox Arete*. This wall gains height and increases in quality and becomes less green the further right you go.

Approach (see overview on page 186) - Use the Top Path Approach. This wall is to the right of right of *Signalbox Arete*.

Set-up and Descent - Either head up the gully to the right of the Circle Area - p.212 - or head up St. Gotthard Tunnel - p.220.

1 Sinners Slimebag .... 6a+ *5b*
A grotty route that is seldom in condition.

2 In Limbo .... 6c+ *6a*
Take the left fork over the bulge and finish up a flake at the top.
FA. M.Vetterlein 13.6.1990

3 Saint's Wall 6b *5c*
The hard lower wall is best bouldered to avoid damage to the upper block where ropes may cut in under tension. The upper half is much easier using the cracks above. A harder alternative start comes in from the right at **6c** *6a*.
FA. C.A.Fenner 18.10.1942

4 Gretta 7a *6b*
An alternative finish to *Glendale Crack* which tackles a thin crack and the breaks above.
FA. P.Widdowson 26.9.1989

5 Glendale Crack 7a *6b*
Follow in the footsteps of the early aiders by climbing the network of cracks to the green breaks and ledges above.
FA. T.Panther (aid) 1952. FFA. B.Wintringham 1970s

Harrison's Rocks

Sebastian Gnaedig laybacking *Slim Finger Crack* (6c *5c*) - *page 204* - at the What Crisis? area of Harrison's Rocks

Harrison's Rocks — Circle Area

Circle Area
A better selection of short routes which are pretty popular.
Approach (see overview on page 186) - Use the Top Path Approach. This is the continuation of Saint's Wall into an alcove.
Set-up and Descent - There are two options; take the gully to the right of *Reserved* with a little scramble required at the end, or head up St. Gotthard Tunnel - p.220.

1 A Killiing Joke .... 7b+ *6c*
Thin moves up the blunt arete.
Supply and Demand, *f7B+*, a desperate sit-start which is usually finished at the first break.
FA. D.Wajzner 1980s

2 Left Circle 6c *6a*
Used to be easier in the old days - the ground has eroded making the start much harder. The rest is much easier.

3 Take That 'effing Chalk Bag Off, or I'll Nick Your Rope and Give It to Terry 'The Chainsaw' Tullis and He'll Keep it for Ever and Ever
.... 6c+ *6a*
A horrifically long name for such a short eliminate route.
FA. C.Arnold 6.8.1983. Also know as Healey Peelys.

4 Right Circle 4a *4a*
After an awkward start, the rest is much easier (and also rather pleasant).

5 Bloody Sunday 6b *5c*
A typical sandstone eliminate to the routes either side of it, though not bad for an eliminate.

6 Good Friday 6c *5c*
The rounded arete on frustratingly poor holds. It can also be done slightly further right.

7 Small Chimney 3c *3c*
A classic sandstone chimney with plenty of good holds.
Photo on page 214.

8 Small Wall 6b *5b*
A short climb that should be easier than it actually is.

Circle Area — Harrison's Rocks 213

⑨ Reserved 6a *5b*
The right-hand arete has a tricky top-out.
FA. M.Vetterlein 30.8.1998

The next routes are to the right of the gully.

⑩ Long Stretch 6a *5b*
The pillar with a reachy move to the top.

⑪ Coffin Corner 4c *4c*
A short problem up the face.
FA. J.R.Lees 1950

⑫ The Bolts 7a *6b*
Campus between the sandy breaks and mantel to finish. Regrettably, not as good as it looks.

St. Gotthard Tunnel

Javan Baker approaching the top-out on *Small Chimney* (3c *3c*) - *page 212* - at the Circle Area of Harrison's Rocks.

St. Gotthard Boulders

Situated above the Circle Area and through St. Gotthard Tunnel are a selection of lesser-known boulders which are worth a look. Potentially needing more light, some of the problems remain a little soft, but climbable nevertheless.

Approach (see overview on page 186) - Head through St. Gotthard Tunnel from the lower path or reach it easily from the top path approach.

Jelly Baby
Up and left of the passageway when exiting St. Gotthard Tunnel.

1 Jelly Baby. f2
Short, easy and good for little people.

2 Jelly Bean. f2
The side of the boulder from a sit-start.

Goats Do Roam
Opposite Jelly Baby.

3 Goats Do Roam f6A
An obscure problem. Sit-start and pull over.

Haribo
Right of Goats Do Roam.

4 Haribo f2
Short and sweet, and more suitable for kids.

5 Lolly Pop f2
The right-hand version of *Haribo*.

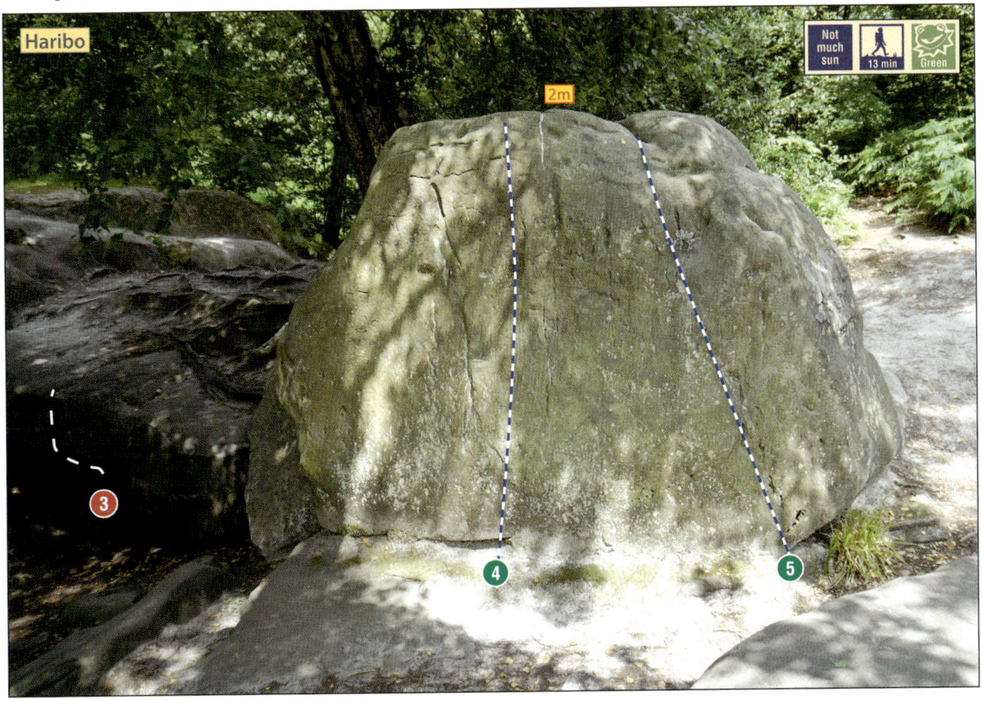

Green Goblin
Up and right of the passageway when exiting St. Gotthard Tunnel.

6 Green Goblin f6B
Start from a good side-pull.

7 Pumpkins f6A
The arete.

8 Venom f3
A short mantel problem.

St. Gotthard Boulders — Harrison's Rocks

Grimey Grimsel
Opposite the Green Goblin.

9 Monch .... f2+
The left side of the arete from a standing start.

10 Hard Furka f4
The arete on its right side.

11 Grimey Grimsel Left f5
Layback the left crack.

12 Grimey Grimsel Right f5
Layback the right crack.

13 Eigerrrr .... f4+
The vertical crack.

14 Young Frau f5
Start with hands in the vertical slot and head up.

15 Verbier f3
A direct up the face.

16 Montana .... f2+
The ramp-line heading right.

17 Leukwarm .... f4+
Mantel onto the ledge.

Harrison's Rocks — St. Gotthard Wall

St. Gotthard Wall

Above and right of St. Gotthard Tunnel is a short wall that makes up the top left side of The Sewer. The wall faces north making it green. The routes are very short so have mostly been graded as boulder problems. These problems are often done with the safety of a top-rope as the landings are poor.

Approach (see overview on page 186) - Head through St. Gotthard Tunnel from the lower path or reach it easily from the top path approach.

Set-up and Descent - Make your way almost up onto the top path from St. Gotthard Tunnel - p.220 - and circumnavigate right across the top of the Green Goblin and Grimey Grimsel boulders.

1 Long Reach f5
The left side of the wall has a long reach.
FA. H.Longley-Cook 23.4.1949

2 Domodossola .... f5+
Another one with a long reach.

3 Lugano f4
The blunt arete.

4 Simplon Route .... f3+
A short clamber up the block. No bridging if you can avoid it.
FA. M.W.Erlebach 31.8.1941

5 Lecco f4
A slightly harder variation of Simplon Route.

6 Arco f6A
A one-move wonder.

7 Billy Bong 5a 4c
The right arete.

8 St. Gotthard 4b 4b
Perhaps the best little adventure on this wall - a little contrived but still fun. Climb up the front narrow chimney above the entrance of St. Gotthard Tunnel to the platform above. Traverse right onto the main face of The Sewer and follow a line of good holds up and left leading round into a recess and the final exit.

Starlight (5a *4c*) - *page 223* - on the Sewer Walls. This route and its romantically named cousin *Moonlight Arete*, (which runs parallel to the left), are both popular with Harrison's Rocks visitors, which is surprising considering its location and the name given to the wall.

Harrison's Rocks — Sewer Walls

Sewer Walls

An impressive buttress which is hampered by its wetter and mossy lower half especially on the left-hand side. The further right you go the better things become and when things totally dry out, those mossier routes are very worthwhile. The far right does perhaps have the most popular routes on this wall and understandably so, especially in moonlight! The walls continuing right of *Starlight* are poor, wet and rarely climbed.

Approach (see overview on page 186) - Use the Top Path Approach. This is above the lower path and easily recognisable by the fallen tree leaning onto the damp left-hand side of the wall.

Set-up and Descent - Use St. Gotthard Tunnel - p.220.

❶ The Nuts — 6c+ 6a
A difficult thin crack climb which usually has a wet start.
FA. T.Panther 23.5.1965

❷ Pascale — 6c+ 6a
Branch out right from *The Nuts* and climb the face between the two cracks to finish up the overhanging nose.
FA. J.Patterson 28.8.1994

❸ Rowan Tree Wall — 6c+ 6a
Best left alone as this line is constantly wet at the start - the hardest section of the route. Better to climb *Sewer-Rowan Connection*.

Sewer Walls — Harrison's Rocks

The next set of routes start up the often wet and rather unpleasant gully. It's worth noting that when things do occasionally dry out, it does become popular.

4 Sewer-Rowan Connection . . . . 6a+ *5b*
If the lower gully is dry, traverse in from the right into the crack of *Rowan Tree Wall* and finish up this.
FA. F.K.Elliot 1943

5 Pipe Cleaner . . . . 6a+ *5b*
Branch left to climb the lower set of stalactites and head up the crack just left of the arete. Very rarely done due to the state of the lower wall.
FA. Tim Skinner 23.12.1990

6 The Sandpipe 6a *5a*
The left side of the central block with the typically unpleasant and often wet start.
FA. F.K.Elliot 1943

7 The Sewer . . . . 6a+ *5a*
An appropriate name though it proves popular when dry. Climb the right-hand (and more strenuous) side of the block up a flared open crack. Requires some awkward back and forth technique.

Harrison's Rocks — Sewer Walls

8 Cannibals 7a 6b
Climb the arete right of the gully after a wet start up *The Sewer*.
FA. A.Powell 21.9.1991

9 Sewer Wall 6b 5c
The first crack right of the gully after a wet start up *The Sewer*.

10 Monkey's Necklace .... 6a+ 5b
A long and worthwhile outing, (after a wet start up *The Sewer*), requiring multiple belay set-ups from the top. Traverse the break and finish up the wide crack a few metres right of the arete.
FA. C.A.Fenner 1940s

11 Powder Monkey .... 7a+ 6b
It is really infrequent to find this in condition and the initial mossy moves off the deck are the hardest. The upper half is much better with a tricky last move over the bulge.
FA. P.Widdowson 30.6.1990

12 Psycho 7a 6b
Eliminate in its lower half and very mossy. The upper half is better and can be used as an alternative finish to *Orangutang*.
FA. D.Atchinson-Jones 23.7.2000

13 Orangutang .... 6b+ 5c
A hidden classic on good holds - when dry. Save a bit for the final moves before hitting the slab.
FA. M.Braines 1967

Sewer Walls Harrison's Rocks

14 Primate Shot .... 7a+ 6b
A hard direct start to and finishing up the final crack of *Monkey Necklace*.
FA. P.Stone 1987

15 Oliver James ...... 7a+ 6b
A hard direct line up the face, which is often in better condition than the routes out left.
FA. T.Gerard 14.9.1989

16 Monkey's Bow 7a 6a
Traverse the lower break to the crack and finish up this. Traversing left on the break above from the arete and finishing as for *Monkey's Bow* is **Baboon, 6a** *5a*.
FA. M.Ball 1949. FA. (Baboon) J.R.Lees 1950's

17 Brookslight 7a 6a
The blunt nose gives a good and variation of *Moonlight Arete*.
FA. R.Brooks 16.5.1965

18 Moonlight Arete 5a 4c
A straightforward and thoroughly enjoyable climb in a beautiful setting, with plenty of big holds to pull on. *Photo on page 3.*
FA. R.G.Folkard 31.8.1941

19 Starlight 5a 4c
The right-hand variation to *Moonlight Arete*. There are two ways to finish, the right one being slightly harder. *Photo on page 219.*

20 Matt's Fingertip 6a 5a
A poor route on the left side of the gully.

21 Candlestick 5a 4c
Another poor route. Bridge up the front of the gully itself finishing right of the block.

Heading up the hole at the back of the gully is also fun but primarily used as a way down. Only do this when it's bone dry otherwise it's a death trap!

Harrison's Rocks — Sewer Walls

Tempestivity
The best of three poor continuation walls.

22 The Green Cleft **3c** *3c*
Grotty, green and usually overgrown.
FA. M.Vetterlein 26.3.2005

23 Tempestivity **7c** *6c*
Requires a long reach and is somewhat powerful!
FA. J.Patterson 29.7.1995

24 Bostic **6c** *6a*
The arete, which was probably last dry when the first ascent was made!
FA. P.Sorrell 19.9.1965

25 Noisome Cleft No.1 .... **3a** *3a*
Climbing the crack is a bit like dumping a bag of wet compost on your head.

Noisome Wall
An extremely dirty and wet wall right of the crack.

26 Noisome Wall .... **6a+** *5b*
Start as for *Noisome Cleft No.1* and make a damp and dirty rising traverse.

27 Noisome Wall Direct ...... **6c+** *6a*
Climb direct through the breaks.
FA. R.Mazinke 3.4.1995

28 Plagiarism .... **6c+** *6a*
Climb direct with extreme difficulty. Use vegetation at the top to aid your exit.
FA. R.Mazinke 4.5.1992

29 Noisome Cleft No 2 .... **3a** *3a*
A horrific crack climb.
FA. R.G.Folkard 20.7.1941

The Sod
The last buttress is pretty much lost to the moss and vegetation. The routes are not worth doing in their current state.

30 The Sod **6c** *6a*
A nasty overgrown crack climb.
FA. R.Brooks 16.5.1965

31 Sharp Dressed Man **6c** *6a*
The centre of the face between the two cracks.
FA. D.Reid 12.1.1992

The following short routes continue rightwards from the previous one and are not marked on the topo.

32 Squank **6a** *5b*
The crack at the centre of the short wall.
FA. T.Skinner 25.4.1992

33 Tubesnake Boogie **6a** *5b*
The face a metre right of *Squank*.
FA. C.Murray 25.4.1992

34 El Loco **6b** *5c*
The right side of the wall trending leftwards into a niche.
FA. T.Skinner 11.11.1990

35 Ten Foot Pole **6b** *5c*
The direct version of *El Loco* avoiding the niche.
FA. T.Skinner 1991

Republic (7a+ *6b*) - *page 229* - at the Wellington Block, Harrison's Rocks. Despite its seeping first hold, it is a strikingly good hard route with many coming unstuck at the reachy upper half.

Harrison's Rocks

Harrison's Rocks 227

Harrison's Rocks — Wellington Block

5 Forester's Wall 6b *5b*
The original and best of all its incarnations. Start awkwardly right of the arete and make some strenuous moves leftwards. Continue above on good pockets to the third break. Traverse left and finish up the crack to a wondrous mantel top-out - enjoy the view! Traversing right at the top drops the grade to **6a+** *5b*. Finishing right and up from the third break is also **6b** *5c*.
FA. C.A.Fenner 1945

6 Bonanza 6b *5c*
Start up *Forester's Wall* and break right up to a ledge. Traverse right for a few metres and finish over the bulge above.

7 Bonanza Direct .... 7a+ *6b*
A significantly hard direct to *Bonanza*, heading over the lower roof using the crack out left.
FA. M.Smith 1990. Also known as 'Bulging Bloody Bonanza'.

8 Sossblitz 7a *6a*
A powerful and fingery number with a tricky and frustrating crux move midway up the wall.
FA. T.Panther (aid) 4.4.1965

1 Passage Chimney 3a *3a*
The edge of the narrow passageway, or further in if you wish.

2 Forester's Wall Direct ... 6c *6a*
Climb the thin poor crack on the left side of the wall to the third break. Avoid contact with the crack on *Forester's Wall* higher up.
FA. D.Ball 1977

3 Forester's Wall Super Direct ... 6c+ *6a*
Climb the centre of the wall to join the final top crack used on *Forester's Wall*.

4 Indian Summer 6c *6a*
Climb the arete and finish as for *Forester's Wall Direct*.
FA. D.Atchinson-Jones 1987

Wellington Block — Harrison's Rocks 229

Wellington Block

This block is one of the iconic features of Harrison's. With many starred routes, it is justifiably popular. The north-facing side remains fairly green, but usually dries out in summer when it is a good shady spot. Conditions get better further right around the block with the south-facing wall being the best.

Approach (see overview on page 226) - The block is located right of the Sewer Walls, and can be approached either using the lower paths (the path running through the lower fields can also be used to approach through the south gate up towards the Squat Tower Area), or better still, use the top path approach and descend to the side of Squat Tower - page 231.

Set-up and Descent - Use the path to the right of Squat Tower - page 232.

⑨ What the Butler Saw . . . . ⬜ 7a+ *6b*
An eliminate that crosses *Sossblitz* . Make it up as you go along.
FA. I.Butler 12.6.2000

⑩ Republic . . . . ⬜ 7a+ *6b*
A classic even though the first move is often wet. Make reachy moves between breaks up the arete, which is predominantly climbed on its right-hand side. Shorties be warned - there is a stopper move waiting for you! *Photos on page 225.*
FA. D.Lewis 6.9.1983

⑪ Banana Republic . . . . ⬜ 7b+ *6c*
The smooth and hard right-hand variation to *Republic*.
FA. J.Dawes 2004

⑫ Niblick . . . . ⬜ 6b *5b*
A golden and varied route and perhaps the best of its grade on sandstone. From the top of the boulder, follow the vague crack system to a legendary move at mid-height. Delicately manoeuvre up the slab above and choose your exit wisely - one is more elegant than the other. **Niblick Direct, 6b+** *5c* - start just left of the boulder, behind the block. *Photo on page 230.*
FA. C.A.Fenner 1945

⑬ Pincenib . . . . ⬜ 7a *6b*
A good route up a distinct curving flake. It is an eliminate but only because you can't use the upper right-hand arete.
FA. D.Atchinson-Jones 1982

⑭ Pincenib Arete . . . . ⬜ 6b+ *5c*
The route *Pincenib* with use of the upper right-hand arete.

⑮ Wellington's Nose . . . . . ⬜ 4a *4a*
Chimney up onto the top of the opposite and smaller 'Wellington Boot' block. Move back onto the Wellington Block and finish by heading up a steeper section, then traversing off right and up a short crack at the top.

Phil Newman on the classic *Niblick* (6b *5b*) - *page 229* - at the Wellington Block at Harrison's Rocks. This route boasts some of the finest climbing of its grade on the block and sits proudly amongst some of the best routes on southern sandstone.

Wellington Block — Harrison's Rocks 231

Wellington Passage
Between Wellington Block and Wellington Boot is a narrow passageway.

16 Hitchcock's Horror .... 6b+ *5c*
The first crack on the left-hand side of the passage, keeping left of the final groove of *Wellington's Nose* at the top.
FA. R.Hitchcock 27.9.1997

17 Lady Jane 6b *5c*
The second and third cracks to a ledge, then the wall above.
FA. T.Daniells 1977

18 Sabre Crack 5a *4c*
Climb the wide crack below the letter 'M', step left an continue up the upper crack.

19 Caroline 6a *5b*
From the start of *Sabre Crack*, continue straight up the wall.
FA. T.Daniells 1977

20 Pete's Reach 6b *5c*
Where the passage opens out but it may have lost key holds.
FA. P.Atkinson 12.8.1990

21 Flower Power Jules .... 6a+ *5b*
Tackle the end wall then step left onto the left-hand side of the passage and follow this to the top.
FA. J.Money 12.8.1990

The right-hand wall of the passage is almost never in condition. The elaborately-named **It May Be Green but It's Not a Teenage Mutant Ninja Turtle**, 6c *6a* is up the centre, and **It Came from Beneath the Slime**, 6c *6a* is back under the slime.

Wellington Boot
The short buttress to the right of Wellington Block has a few notable routes on it.

22 Wellington Boot 7a *6b*
A short and intense route up the side face using a thin crack at the top.
FA. G.Somerville 28.6.1970

23 Kicks 7a *6b*
The arete on its left-hand side.
FA. A.Grigg 14.10.1992

24 Belts and Braces 6a *5b*
A popular one up the centre of the face and eliminating the left arete. Much harder than people often think.
FA. G.McLelland 1980

25 Jetsam 3b *3b*
The grotty chimney has an otherworldly feel.

26 Flotsam 3a *3a*
A mildly better chimney climb than *Jetsam*, but not by much.

To the right is a very overgrown wall with three routes. **Soft Cock**, 6b *5c*, is at the centre of the slab. The arete and finishing right of the nose is **Bootless Buzzard**, 6b *5c*, and the crack to the right again is **Boxing Day Cracker**, 3a *3a*.

Harrison's Rocks — Squat Tower Area

Squat Tower Area

A couple of nice blocky buttresses. The left is popular with groups and beginners whilst the right buttress, Squat Tower, has only one easier route up its front face, but it is a good one. Squat Tower curves round to the right and up a path where more routes are found.

Approach (see overview on page 226) - This area can be approached either using the lower paths (the path running through the lower fields can also be used to then approach thought the south gate up towards this area), or use the top path approach and descend to the side of Squat Tower.

Set-up and Descent - The Squat Tower is detached from the mainland and is tricky to get to the top of. Either jump across from the back left side, or solo up or down around the back. The routes around *Deadwood Crack* are easier to reach.

Lowering Off - As with all sandstone routes, lowering off and/or abseiling is not permitted; if you are unable to get to and from the top of Squat Tower then please avoid.

① **Wildcat Wall** — f5
A short problem past an oblong pocket to the ledge with a tricky mantel to finish.
FA. F.K.Elliot 1945

② **Woodside Blossom** — 7a *6a*
Attempt to reach the break using a slanting crack and make a hard mantel to finish more easily.
FA. M.Fowler 1978

③ **Deadwood Pocket** — f4
A short problem past a pocket - avoid use of holds on *Deadwood Crack*. Either jump back down or finish up the remainder of *Deadwood Crack* to the right.

④ **Deadwood Crack** — 5a *4c*
Use a poor, thin and sandy crack to reach the break with easier climbing above. Either finish off rightwards or attempt the roof at 6b+ *5c*.
FA. J.R.Lees 1949

⑤ **Toeing the Line** — 5a *4c*
A nice little extended problem that is best done on a top-rope.
FA. J.Cholawo 1999

⑥ **Tame Variant** — 3a *3a*
Popular and often in use by groups, this short slab is actually good fun. Exit right.

⑦ **Tame Corner** — 2a *2a*
The corner. Climb to the left or right of the jammed boulder.

Squat Tower Area — Harrison's Rocks

10 The Vice 4c *4c*
The best and most popular on this block is slightly more challenging that it first appears, especially for beginners. Climb on good holds to the crack and unravel its mysterious secret, which is easier once you know how. Finish up and right.
FA. R.G.Folkard 31.8.1941

11 Toevice 6c *6a*
A tricky cousin of *The Vice*. Negotiating the crack often sees climbers saying what is to some, a forbidden sandstone word, i.e "take!".
FA. M.Fowler 7.7.1974

12 Handvice .... 6c+ *6a*
Similar territory to *Toevice*, using the next short crack along. It can often be green low down.
FA. D.Jones 1966

8 Stag .... 6b+ *5c*
A difficult and poor route up the arete with a typical sandstone mantel finish.
FA. N.S.Head 3.3.1974

9 Venison Burger .... 6b+ *5c*
A poor eliminate between *Stag* and *The Vice* which (unavoidably) uses holds on both routes.
FA. I.Bull 6.9.2009

234 Harrison's Rocks — Squat Tower Area

Squat Tower - Side Wall
The right and back sides of the Squat Tower can be a bit green and mossy.

13 Birch Nose 6a *5b*
The arete on its right side.
FA. A.J.J.Moulam 27.4.1947

14 Victoria 6b *5c*
Fight your way through the bulging wall finishing at the small tree.
FA. T.Skinner 1989

Squat Tower - Back Wall

15 The Clamp 6b *5c*
The centre of the wall.
FA. T.Daniells 1970s

16 Corridor Route 4a *4a*
The shorter right-hand side of the wall.

17 Rhapsody Inside a Satsuma . . . 6a+ *5b*
The arete on the right side.
FA. D.Atchison-Jones 1982

18 Pickled Pogo Stick 3c *3c*
A short problem left of the crack. Use what you can, although it is usually very mossy.
FA. D.Atchison-Jones 1982

19 Cracking Up 3c *3c*
The right side of the green wall between the two short cracks.

Knight's Boulder **Harrison's Rocks** 235

Bouldering is popular at Harrison's Rocks, which boasts a good number of problems on actual boulders. *Imperial Knight* (**f5+**) - *page 236* - on the Knight's Boulder.

Harrison's Rocks — Knight's Boulder

Knight's Boulder

A small boulder with some 'one-move wonder' problems. The break running horizontally along the main face helps a little with those top-outs.

Approach (see overview on page 226) - Use any of the three approaches. This is the block opposite Knight's Wall.

Descent - Down the back side of the boulder.

Boulderers - Hold cleaning is a delicate art, and toothbrushes and bouldering brushes are forbidden due to their abrasive nature on the holds. Try to use minimal chalk and if possible use Eco Balls or liquid chalk - see page 45.

1 William Marshal's Sloppiness f5
The left sloping side of the boulder finishing up the arete. The start is tricky and can be a little green at times.

2 El Cid f4
The centre of the face from a crouching start.

3 Godfrey's Arete . . . . f6A+
The arete; whack a heel on for good measure and finish up the rounded nose.

4 Hawkwood Side-pulls . . . f5+
The left side of the wall on side-pulls.

5 Philippe f5
Not straightforward. Expect a 'barn door' move at some point.

6 Black Knight f3
The easiest problem up the block past a vertical pocket.

7 War Horse . . . . f3+
Climb the slightly protruding rib.

8 Imperial Knight . . . . f5+
The right-hand side of the wall eliminating the arete.
Photo on page 235.

9 Jousting Arete . . . . f4+
The arete on either its left or right-hand side, using holds on the problems either side of it.

10 Good Man Friday f5
Climb the face on good pockets, eliminating the arete out left.

11 Knighthood f5
The right side of the block, slapping your way along the lip to the arete. The longer you can make the traverse last, the better.

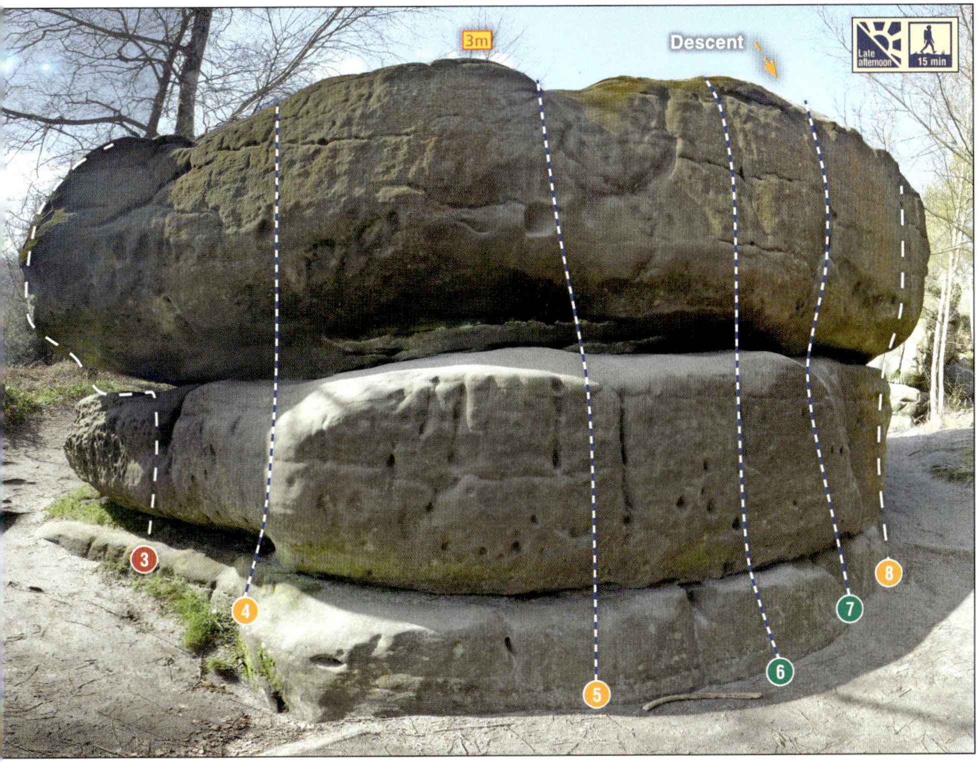

Knight's Boulder **Harrison's Rocks** 237

Harrison's Rocks — Knight's Wall

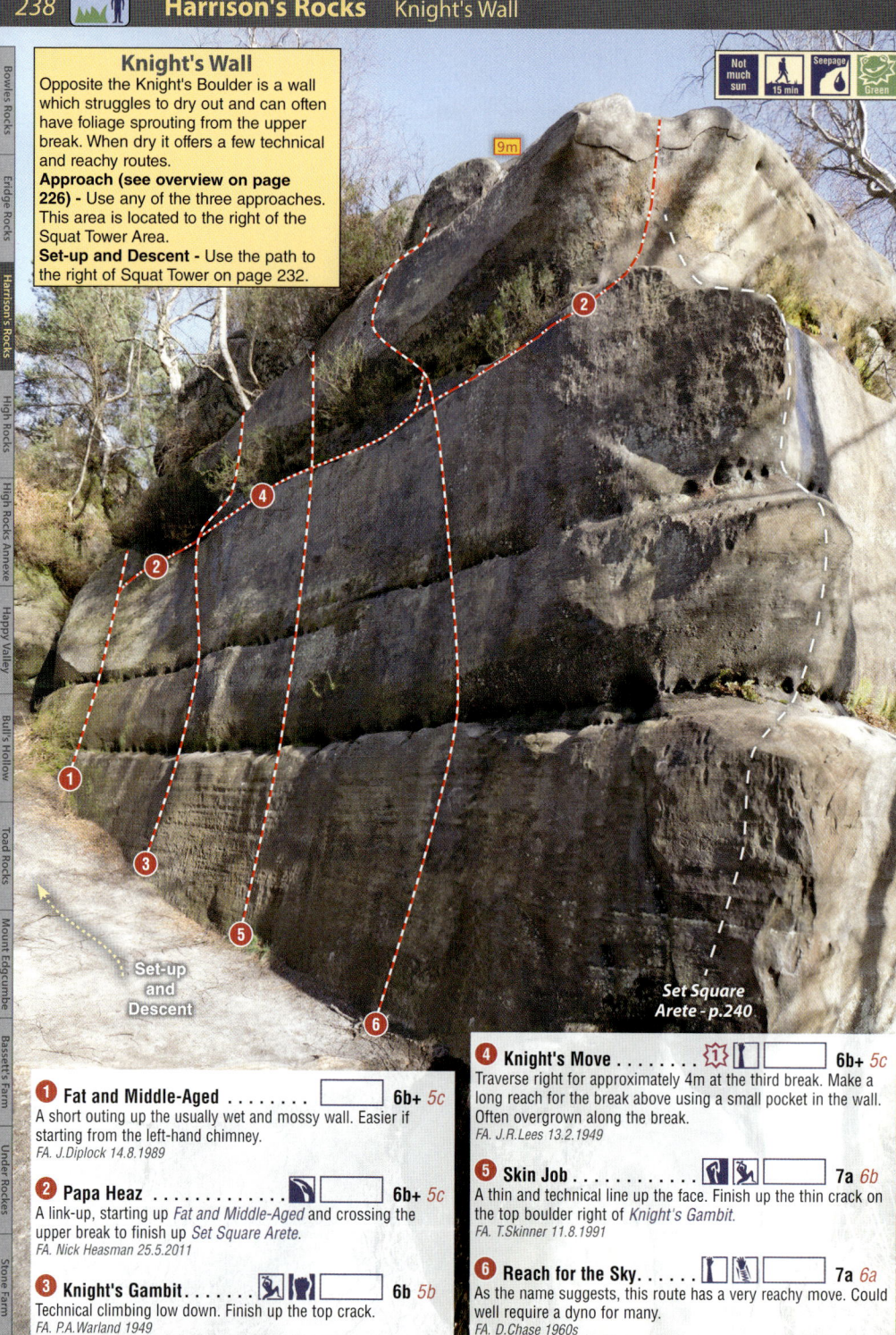

Knight's Wall

Opposite the Knight's Boulder is a wall which struggles to dry out and can often have foliage sprouting from the upper break. When dry it offers a few technical and reachy routes.

Approach (see overview on page 226) - Use any of the three approaches. This area is located to the right of the Squat Tower Area.

Set-up and Descent - Use the path to the right of Squat Tower on page 232.

❶ **Fat and Middle-Aged** .... 6b+ *5c*
A short outing up the usually wet and mossy wall. Easier if starting from the left-hand chimney.
FA. J.Diplock 14.8.1989

❷ **Papa Heaz** .... 6b+ *5c*
A link-up, starting up *Fat and Middle-Aged* and crossing the upper break to finish up *Set Square Arete*.
FA. Nick Heasman 25.5.2011

❸ **Knight's Gambit** 6b *5b*
Technical climbing low down. Finish up the top crack.
FA. P.A.Warland 1949

❹ **Knight's Move** .... 6b+ *5c*
Traverse right for approximately 4m at the third break. Make a long reach for the break above using a small pocket in the wall. Often overgrown along the break.
FA. J.R.Lees 13.2.1949

❺ **Skin Job** 7a *6b*
A thin and technical line up the face. Finish up the thin crack on the top boulder right of *Knight's Gambit*.
FA. T.Skinner 11.8.1991

❻ **Reach for the Sky** 7a *6a*
As the name suggests, this route has a very reachy move. Could well require a dyno for many.
FA. D.Chase 1960s

Dawn Regan on *The Chimney* (4a *4a*) - *page 242* - on the Isolated Walls of Harrison's Rocks.

Harrison's Rocks — Isolated Walls

Isolated Walls

This is the set of south-facing walls to the right of Knight's Wall that stretches to Isolated Buttress. It offers some good routes that are generally clean and in condition.

Approach (see overview on page 226) - Use any of the three approaches. The walls are to the right of Knight's Wall.

Set-up and Descent - Use the path to the right of Squat Tower on page 232.

Knight's Wall p.238

Set-up and Descent

① **Set Square Arete** **6b** *5b*
The best on this wall, although it is difficult to rig a top-rope over the edge, so consider setting up a clip-up rig for exiting. The climb itself is challenging but good fun.

② **Sandbag** **6c** *5c*
The centre of the face - variable grade depending upon your ability and reach. As per usual there are a few hideous mantelshelf moves above. Good luck!
FA. F.Shannon 1980s

Isolated Walls — Harrison's Rocks

③ Sunshine Crack 5a *4c*
The crack using jams and body wedges where appropriate.
FA. F.K.Elliot 1943

④ The Knam .... 6c+ *6a*
Hard bouldery moves between breaks and a reachy move above.
FA. T.Panther 7.4.1968

⑤ The Mank 6c *6a*
After a tricky start to good holds, head up to get a distinct undercut scoop. Pull hard past this, finishing up the groove.
FA. T.Panther 2.5.1965

Harrison's Rocks — Isolated Walls

6 Dr Pepper .... 7a+ *6b*
A misunderstood route up the blank-looking rounded nose.
FA. S.Quinton 21.4.1992

7 Piecemeal Wall ...... 6b+ *5c*
Climb the flared crack in the lower bulge quickly to the break. Pull over the second bulge before heading left to finish up the remainder of *Dr Pepper*.
FA. M.P.Ward 1.6.1947

8 Karen's Kondom 7a *6b*
A hard route with some hidden holds.
FA. M.Lewis 1980s

9 The Chimney 4a *4a*
A stiff undertaking up the smooth chimney. The route can also be finished up the top crack of *Reverse Traverse* at the same grade, and is known as **Chimney and Traverse**.
Photo on page 239.

10 Reverse Traverse ... 6b *5c*
Climb direct up the bulging wall to the top crack using a series of grooves and in-cut holds.
FA. F.K.Elliot 1943

Isolated Walls — Harrison's Rocks 243

⑪ Eric 7a *6a*
Feel the power of the Boysen by climbing this challenging route which has an even more challenging finish!
FA. M.Boysen 1963

⑫ Two-Toed Sloth 5b *5a*
A nice route which is often climbed as a hybrid line from the start of *Soft Rock'er*, to make things easier for beginners. More direct is better. Finish either on the ledge on the left, or direct up the groove.
FA. J.Robinsson 1947

⑬ Soft Rock'er 6b *5c*
Climb the arete and slab above. Finish more strenuously over the top bulge.
FA. P.Atkinson 12.8.1990

⑭ Tab Chimney 3a *3a*
A grotty excursion up the front of the gully.
FA. R.Mazinke 17.1.1998

The wall to the right is usually pouring with water and slime. If you are ever visiting when it has a.) dried out and b.) you have completely run out of things to do, then you may be interested.

⑮ Arustu .... 6b+ *5c*
The slab and bulge to the right of the gully finishing on the right-hand side of the block.

⑯ Agent Orange .... 6a+ *5a*
Climb up and over the bulge and finish up the short open slab at the top.

Harrison's Rocks — Isolated Buttress

A typical weekend crowd at the popular Isolated Buttress. The classic climb *Isolated Buttress Climb* (4c *4c*) - *page 247* - pictured here will usually have a top rope in place before yours.

Isolated Buttress — Harrison's Rocks

Isolated Buttress

The Isolated Buttress is one of the best known isolated blocks on southern sandstone. This rectangular block has great routes on all sides, which makes it one of the most popular spots at Harrison's. At the back of the block is a narrow passage which is worth a look on hot days, or if the front walls are busy. The buttress is open to the elements and the main wall faces south, so it generally stays in good condition year round.

Approach (see overview on page 226) - Use any of the three approaches. The buttress is located to the right of the Isolated Walls and can be approached from either of the lower paths (one of which runs through the lower fields and joins at the south gate entrance of which a path then runs up towards Squat Tower. Head right from here for a short distance to reach the buttress). The top path approach is the simplest method and descends to the right of Grant's Wall - page 256.

Set-up - In days gone by the top of Isolated Buttress was easily reached using a block to step across to the rear side of the buttress. Unfortunately this has had to be removed for safety reasons and it is now more awkward to get to the top of the Isolated Buttress for set-up. It is likely that a bridge will be added to enable easy access in the future. Until that is done, a tricky approach is required which should only be attempted by experienced and confident climbers.
Use the wooden stairs to the right of Grant's Wall (page 256) to get to and from the top adjacent to the buttress. It is also possible to do a more tricky ascent to the right of Jagger Wall (page 250). Once in position, drop down to a jammed block and carefully solo onto the top of the Isolated Buttress. To protect other climbers, you can set up a safety rope across this gap for use in getting to and from the summit for the rest of the day - see photos. Please do not use the top-roping bolts for this safety rope and please remove the safety rope when you have finished with it.

Lowering off - Please note, just like all sandstone routes, you must not lower off once you have completed a climb and should extend all belay set-ups over the edge to avoid causing any erosion to the rock.

A climber using the safety rope to exit from the buttress.

Solo across
Isolated Slab

Isolated Slab

A short slab below the Isolated Buttress which is popular with children and adults trying the problems with no hands.

❶ **Isolated Slab Left.** f2
The left-hand set of in-cut holds.

❷ **Isolated Slab Centre.** . . . . 🔺 f2
The longest and best problem up the centre of the slab.

❸ **Isolated Slab Right** f2
The right-hand set of in-cut holds.

Isolated Slab

Harrison's Rocks — Isolated Buttress

West and Southwest Faces

The west face has a set of thin and fingery routes. Around on the southwest wall under the large roof are two of Harrison's most classic routes.

① Northwest Corner . . . 6c *5c*
Climb the arete moving slightly right near the top.
FA. J.R.Lees 26.6.1949

② Storming Up the Cuvier Remparts
. . . . 7a *6b*
An eliminate up the face. No use of the arete is allowed!
FA. D.Atchison Jones 1982

③ Woolly Bear . . . 7b+ *6b*
A brutally fingery start leads to the rail in the centre of the wall. Once there, make a horrifically long reach to grab the juggy upper ledge. Finish easily above. It is possible to dyno between breaks (known as 'Woolly Jumper') but you come close to that boulder below if you fail.
FA. B.Wintringham 1967. With more holds than it has now.

④ Woolly Cub 7a *6b*
A better and more popular variation of the original. Loop right around the main crux and then using a small crimp to reach the upper break. Traverse back left and finish as for *Woolly Bear*.

Isolated Buttress — Harrison's Rocks

Southwest Face

5 West Wall .... 6a+ *5b*
A classic route to the right of the arete which finishes by traversing left and exiting up the juggy centre of the wall as for *Woolly Bear*. The start can be a bit hair raising depending where you place your top-rope. *Photo on page 251.*

6 Southwest Corner ...... 6c+ *6a*
A more direct and bolder alternative finish to *West Wall* which can be damp and green at times.

7 Pollet Virtus .... 8a+ *7a*
A wicked little number in an awesome position. Climb *West Wall* to below the roof. From here, trend outwards into space and up through the vague groove. A high heel toe followed by a knee-wrenching move will see you tackling the wall above, with long reaches, small crimps, a cut loose, and a do or die finish.
FA. Rhys Whitehouse 29.6.2017

8 Isolated Buttress Climb .. 4c *4c*
A historical route which is one of the earliest recorded routes on sandstone. Quickly move up and right from the centre of the wall and climb the rounded arete. The upper final crack is problematic, but not too bad once you know how.
Photo on page 244.
FA. N.Barnard 1926

9 Apple Crumble .... 6a+ *5b*
Climb direct up the centre of the wall from the original start to the roof, then traverse back right to finish as per the original.

10 Isolated Buttress Direct . 6a+ *5b*
A hard direct start to the arete on *Isolated Buttress Climb*.

Harrison's Rocks — Isolated Buttress

248

South Face

Set-up and Descent - see page 245

11m

Jagger W. p.2

South Face
The popular south-facing wall with plenty of classic routes.

⑪ Edwards Wall 6b 5c
A tight eliminate requiring a lot of self-discipline in order to avoid using holds on adjacent routes.
FA. L.E.Holliwell 1960s

⑫ Edwards Effort 6c 6a
A meaty climb up the flared crack with an uncomfortable finger-jam midway. Move right to finish up *Diversion* or try the *Direct*.
FA. J.M.Edwards 28.9.1946

⑬ Edwards Effort Direct 6c+ 6a
The direct finish above the lower crack.

⑭ Alexander Beetle 7a 6b
A direct version of *Diversion*, using the right edge of the crack on *Edwards Effort* for the left hand. Finish up *Edwards Effort Direct* for the full effect, although you can traverse off right.
FA. D.Atchinson-Jones 1988

⑮ Diversion 6c 5c
Climb to the right of the niche and traverse right for a couple of metres before heading straight up to a good slanting hold. Finish directly above.

⑯ Birchden Wall 6b 5b
Perhaps the best on this wall with many sequential moves on good holds.

⑰ Halibut Giblets 6c 5c
An eliminate up the narrow gap between the two *Birchden* routes. Finish up the overhangs above.
FA. C.Arnold 7.9.1982

⑱ Birchden Corner 6b 5c
Start by climbing the arete and pull left just above the second break to continue up the face.
FA. M.P.Ward 20.2.1949

⑲ Frank's Arete .... 6c+ 6a
A short link up, into *Crowbrough Corner* that continues up the arete at the point *Birchden Corner* moves left onto the face.
FA. F.Shannon 1980s

Isolated Buttress **Harrison's Rocks** 249

East Face
This face is sheltered by trees and adjacent walls and tends to keep a tinge of green to it year round. Extend all your belays and install clip-ups for the top - see page 38.

⑳ Crowborough Corner .... 6b+ *5c*
Climb the crack strenuously and make a tricky move left onto the arete. Finish direct.

㉑ Mr Spaceman 7a *6b*
Another eliminate which is generally started by climbing *Crowborough Corner* to the first break and then moving slightly right to then climb the fingery face above. Don't use the cracks on adjacent routes.
FA. G.Pearson 1984

㉒ Wailing Wall 6c *5c*
A super route up the juggy flake to a stopper move. There is more than one way to pull this off but a little extra reach comes in handy for most.
FA. M.P.Ward 1960s

㉓ Wailing Wall Eliminate .. 7a *6b*
A eliminate which is becoming increasingly more difficult as holds slowly wear out. Long arms help to reach the upper break.
FA. B.Wintringham 1965

㉔ Boysen's Arete 6c *6a*
Climb the short right-hand arete, moving left of the jammed boulder to gain the ledge. Finish up the wall above, hopefully using the clip-up technique to avoid your moving rope cutting into the rock!
FA. M.Boysen 1963

North Passage
The less popular north passage has a few good routes on offer and remarkably stays in condition. No bridging is allowed, except on *Boulder Bridge Route*.

㉕ Boulder Bridge Route ... 3a *3a*
A hidden and popular route despite its location, especially with groups and beginners. Chimney up the face just past the jammed boulder and finish on the landward side by the tree.

㉖ Power Finger 7a *6b*
The face approximately a metre from the arete, often with a greasy top section.
FA. G.Pearson 1984

㉗ Bloody Staircase 7a *6b*
Start on the left side of the large in-cut hold on the lower face and climb direct finishing slightly rightwards at the top.
FA. P.Widdowson 1992

㉘ Bloody Fingers .... 6c+ *6a*
Start just right of the large in-cut hold, and climb the face as direct as you can.
FA. M.Randall 1976

㉙ Krypton Factor .... 7a+ *6b*
Climb the face 1m right of *Bloody Fingers* to a hard finish.
FA. P.Widdowson 8.9.1992

㉚ Green Fingers 6c *5c*
Climb up a crimpy face, a metre or so left of *Northwest Corner*. Finish left of the block.
FA. T.G.DeLacy 1971

A few dirty routes on the opposite face are usually out of condition. **Bad Finger**, 6b+ *5c*, *is opposite* **Bloody Fingers**. *Climbing directly to the old stepping platform is* **Plumb Line**, 6b+ *5c*. *The wall opposite* Powder Finger *is* **Bolder Route**, 6a+ *5b*.

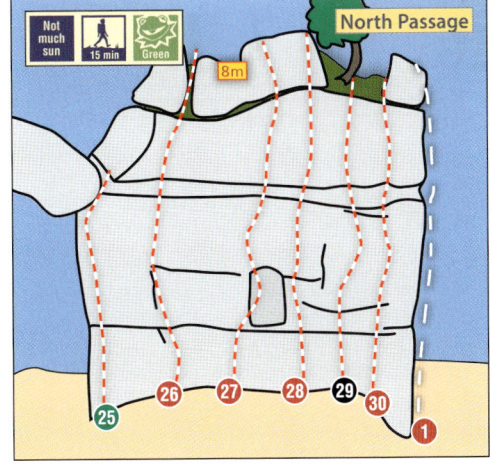

Harrison's Rocks — Jagger Wall

Jagger Wall

The continuation right of the back wall behind Isolated Buttress. It is rarely climbed and is not always in the best of condition. Wait for a dry summer!

Approach (see overview on page 226) - Use any of the three approaches. The wall is located immediately to the right of Isolated Buttress.

Set-up and Descent - The right side of the wall by the tree has a tricky and sandy problem that can be used to get to and from the top of the crag. If uncomfortable with this, use the wooden stairs to the right of Grant's Wall - page 256.

① **Gall Stone** **7a** *6a*
A powerful battle over the middle of the fallen block. Avoid all contact with the Isolated Buttress and the sidewall.
FA. P.Widdowson 22.10.1989

② **Bile Duct** **5b** *5a*
Start as for *Gall Stone* but finish more easily up the right side of the fallen block.
FA. M.Vetterlein 17.1.1998

③ **Battle of the Bulge** .... **6c+** *6a*
Technical climbing up the left side of the face.
FA. P.Atkinson 17.8.1990

④ **Jagger** .... **6a+** *5b*
Climb the centre of the wall using a poor flared crack to finish past the tree.
FA. T.Daniells 1976

⑤ **Ear-ring** **6b** *5c*
A short technical problem up the face.
FA. P.Atkinson 21.6.1992

⑥ **Scraping the Barrel** **6a** *5a*
Climb the wall, starting from a large stalactite.

West Wall (6a+ *5b*) - *page 247* - on the Isolated Buttress. This route shares its final moves with the harder *Woolly Bear* (7b+ *6b*) and perhaps its better variation, *Woolly Cub* (7a *6b*).

Harrison's Rocks — The Cave

The Cave

Hidden from view is a place seldom seen by many climbers heading to Harrison's. Those that venture inside are usually pleasantly surprised even though the routes may not be to their liking. Despite being hidden away, conditions are not too bad, though inevitably you will encounter some green or slime in those dark places. There is some bouldering on the boulder and walls around the cave entrance.

Approach (see overview on page 226) - Use any of the three approaches. To the right of Isolated Buttress is a large tree with a boulder to its right. Right of this is the entrance to the cave.

Set-up and Descent - Either head up the short bulge right of Jagger Wall by the tree (page 250) or use the wooden stairs to the right of Grant's Wall (page 256).

The face of the leaning boulder has a number of short problems.

1 Cave Boulder Front *f3*
A sandy awkward slab.

2 Cave Boulder Flake . . . . *f4+*
Difficult to get established then it's pretty much over.

3 Cave Boulder Crack . . . . *f6A+*
Awkward and slopey moves across the crack.

4 Cave Boulder Roof *f6A*
Climb the series of breaks to a rounded top-out.

Through the passage and on the reverse side of the boulder are two more problems.

5 Micro Second *f6C*
Starting as low as possible and keeping a spotter to hand, climb the arete and finish up on the right side of the face.

6 Deniability *f5*
From ironstone holds, head up the fingery wall above.

The Cave Harrison's Rocks

Through the small opening to the right of the boulder.

⑦ Pain Killers 6b *5b*
Head for a positive flat hold on the right side of the wall and traverse left into the scoops and undercuts. Delicately tiptoe up to reach for the flat ledge and make a difficult mantel to finish. There is an additional slab above this that can also be done (clip-up method only). Pushing off the right-hand block to mount it reduces the difficulty of the slab finish.
FA. D.Beail 11.3.2017

⑧ Big Cave Route 2 ...... 4a *4a*
An awkward crack/chimney climb that requires a bit of wedging technique. The left wall offers some assistance.

⑨ Right Under Your Nose .. 6b *5b*
A good route up the arete that looks a bit like *Meshuga* at Black Rocks in the Peak District. Certainly not as hard and much safer.
FA. G.West 19.5.2002

⑩ Big Cave Route 1 ...... 3b *3b*
A bit of a caving experience which can be climbed a number of different ways. Squeeze through the hole at the top to finish. For a bit more adventure, try starting on the left side of the boulder and traversing right to cross *Big Cave Route 2* and *Right Under Your Nose* into the chimney. Alternatively, approach from on top of the right side of the boulder and crawl left along the shelf into the chimney.

⑪ Rough Boy 6b *5b*
The left side of the right-hand wall when entering the cave. No bridging allowed. Finish left of the tree.
FA. G.Lulham 15.3.1992

⑫ The Wallow .... 6c+ *6a*
Crimpy climbing to the first break and sustained thereafter, with an often gunky break to deal with near the top.
FA. D.Lewis 1980s

Harrison's Rocks — Spider Wall

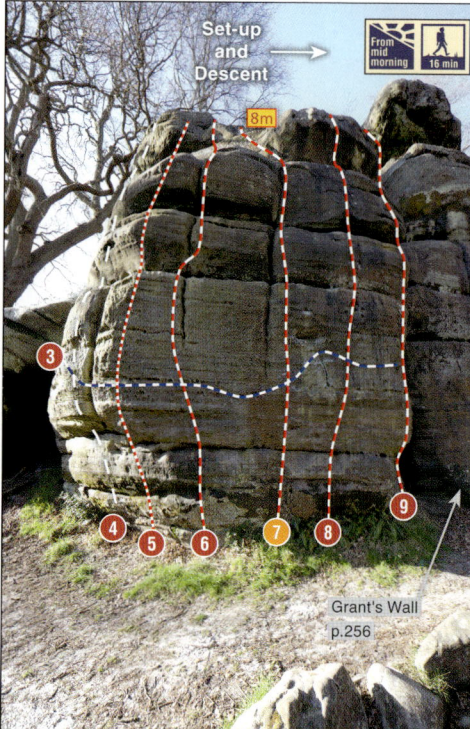

Grant's Wall p.256

Spider Wall

A great wall with challenging routes which most people hugely underestimate first time round. Rope set-ups need to incorporate the clip-up system as the top half of the walls slope back to where the bolt anchors are situated. The wall is very crimpy in places and also quite delicate, so please climb with care.

Approach (see overview on page 226) - Use any of the three approaches. This area is just right of The Cave.

Set-up and Descent - Use the wooden stairs to the right of Grant's Wall page 256.

1 Baldrick's Balderdash . . . 6a *5b*
Climb the left side of the wall bridging where necessary. A good one for dry summers.
FA. M.Smith 1980s

2 Forget-me-Knot 6c *6a*
Climb the series of small cracks up the wall after a difficult start. Finish up the crack in the top overhang.
FA. G.McLelland 1982

3 Spider Wall Traverse *f6B+*
A good fingery and sustained traverse across the face finishing at *Cave Wall*. Can also be done in reverse.

4 Second Chance 6c *6a*
A challenging first set of moves up the flared crack to the break. Things ease thereafter. *Photo opposite.*
FA. J.R.Lees 17.7.1949

5 No Chance . . . . 6c+ *6a*
A fingery eliminate up the rounded nose that is a little too close to neighbouring routes.
FA. L.King 6.4.2002

6 Last Chance . . . . . . 6b+ *5c*
A short painful start to reach the crack takes most by surprise. Continue up the crack to the top and finish with a rounded top-out.
FA. J.R.Lees 10.4.1949

7 Spider Wall . . . . 6a+ *5b*
Great fingery climbing up the central crack, making good use of the large rounded pocket on the lower wall. Finish left at the top before the final roof.
FA. M.P.Ward 10.4.1949

8 Arachnophobia 6c *6a*
Climb the central face avoiding use of both the arete out right and the crack on *Spider Wall*. Despite being an eliminate it is a good route that is both fingery and powerful, especially at the start.

9 Cave Wall . . . . . 6b+ *5c*
Climb the arete direct to a difficult rounded finish.
FA. M.P.Ward 27.4.1947

Lily Marcel on *Second Chance* (6c *6a*) - *opposite* - at Spider Wall, Harrison's Rocks.

Harrison's Rocks — Grant's Wall

Grant's Wall

A popular wall when conditions improve in mid-to-late summer. The routes are more challenging than they first appear. Despite its popularity, the wall does suffer from green and orange mosses and can seep quite a bit in places after rainfall.

Approach (see overview on page 226) - Use any of the three approaches. This area is directly right of Spider Wall.

Set-up and Descent - There is a wooden set of steps to the right of the wall which can be boggy and damp as seepage from above often saturates them, so tread with care.

① Crack and Cave 4a *4a*
A popular corner-crack requiring jamming and bridging techniques. You will undoubtedly come into contact with *Cave Wall* at times, but in the nicest possible way.
FA. J.Morin 1926

② Grant's Wall .... 6c+ *6a*
Climb the vertical slots in the lower wall which unfortunately tend to seep. Move left to climb the arete on its right side and exit over the top block.
FA. T.Panther 25.7.1965

③ Tiptoe through the Lichen 7a *6b*
A difficult line up the face between shallow rounded breaks. Harder when the conditions are poor, which they usually are.
FA. P.Atkinson 22.7.1990

④ Grant's Groove 6c *6a*
A good route up the groove just past the first shallow break. Much harder for the short and dependent on dry conditions.
FA. T.Panther 25.10.1970

⑤ Grant's Crack. .... 6a+ *5a*
The crack-line on this wall, with various methods employed to climb it. The initial few moves are the hardest for most.
Photo opposite.
FA. G.Ingles

⑥ Thingamywobs . 6a+ *5b*
A tricky start low down, making good use of the vague vertical groove where possible. Manteling skills come in handy thereafter.
FA. T.Panther 1960s

⑦ Whatsaname .... 6a+ *5b*
The last crack before the end, with everything happening within the first few metres.
FA. G.Pearson 16.9.1982

⑧ Thingy 4b *4b*
The short rounded right-hand arete.

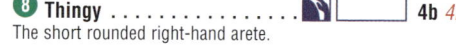

The incredibly wet, green, overgrown and slimy wall to the right of the steps does have a number of routes on it. Due to the constant poor state of the wall and the immense rarity they are actually climbed, they are best avoided and have not been included here.

Sophia Sandison unravelling the moves on *Grant's Crack* (6a+ *5a*) - *opposite* - on Grant's Wall, Harrison's Rocks.

Harrison's Rocks — Garden Slab

Garden Slab

Another wall that is rarely in good condition, but which has some good climbing if dry. Even then you will usually come into contact with some form of slime or moss.

Approach (see overview on page 226) - Use any of the three approaches. This wall is reached by crossing the bridge below Grant's Wall and on the right side of the in-cut bay.

Set-up and Descent - The narrow channel to the left provides an easy access to and from the top.

1 Araldite Wall .... 6b+ *5c*
Short, slimy and almost impossible to climb.
FA. P.Sorrell 7.11.1965

2 Garden Slab Left 6a *5a*
Climb the centre of the wall, trending left on the top slab via some balancy moves on smooth and mossy holds. A direct start is also possible (or impossible in the normal damp conditions).

3 Tiptoe through the Tulips 6a *5b*
A direct finish to *Garden Slab Left* up the centre of the slab.
FA. M.Barrett 1982

4 Garden Slab Right 5b *5a*
The right-hand finish is the easiest version.

5 Biceps Mantel .... f5+
A short mantelshelf problem up the nose and onto the shelf.

6 Biceps Buttress .... 6b+ *5c*
The arete on the left side of the Crucifix Wall has a hard move at the top.
FA. R.G.Folkard 1940

Crucifix Wall — Harrison's Rocks

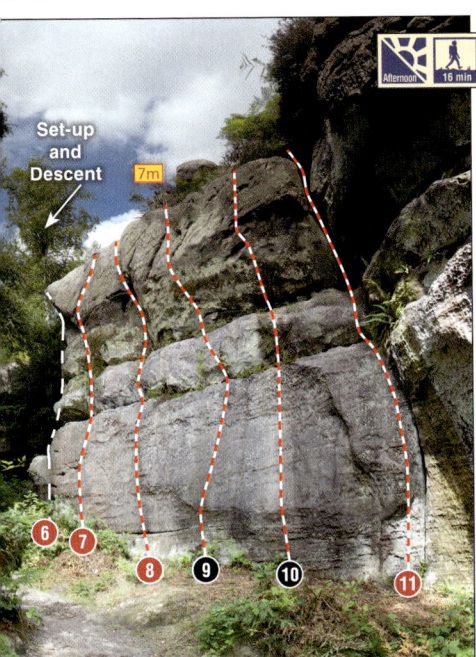

Crucifix Wall

A wall with some difficult routes. It doesn't see too much traffic, so suffers from moss and sprouting plant life from the first break onwards.

Approach (see overview on page 226) - Use any of the three approaches. Around the corner and to the right of Garden Slab.

Set-up and Descent - Use the narrow channel to the left of Garden Slab (opposite).

7 Finger Popper 7a *6b*
Climb the face right of the arete to a crux over the top bulge.
FA. I.Mailer 1985

8 Muscle Crack ..... 6c+ *6a*
It's all in the final thrutchy moves up the top crack after a fingery low start.

9 Crucifix ..... 7a+ *6a*
Climb the face right of *Muscle Crack*. An interesting top-out to say the least.
FA. T.Panther 1968

10 Hector's House ..... 7a+ *6b*
A hard finish. It can suffer from seepage.
FA. B.Knight 1982

11 Corner 6b *5c*
The crack in the corner is unclimbable when wet.

12 Mischivas ..... 7a+ *6b*
A hard fingery eliminate squeezed in between *Corner* and *Philippa*.
FA. G.McLelland 1983

13 Philippa ..... 6c+ *6a*
Climb the lower honeycomb wall to the break on good positive holds. The upper bulging wall takes most people by surprise and can cause problems if this is not your strong point or you're pumped out from the antics below you. A little condition dependent higher up.
FA. G.McLelland 1982

14 Shodan ..... 6b+ *5c*
Climb *Philippa* to the first break and finish up the arete.

Harrison's Rocks — Wanderfall

Wanderfall

The first in a series of vertical walls that are amongst the most popular and perhaps best at Harrison's.

Approach (see overview on page 226) - Take the Top Path Approach and cut down past Garden Slab. You can also use the Forge Farm Approach.

Set-up and Descent - Use the steps to the left of Garden Slab - page 258.

❶ Half Crown Corner . . . . 6a+ 5b
Begin by climbing the lower left side of the arete and move round quickly to the right side of the main wall.
FA. N.Barnard 1926

❷ Don Juander 6b 5b
The first of a trio of routes that were originally seen as variations of the same route, but in reality are pretty much independent of each other. Climb the series of slopers, pockets and side-pulls above an awkward start.

❸ Wanderfall 5a 4c
Perhaps the best route up the centre of the face with plenty of good holds.

❹ Wander at Leisure . . . . . . 6a+ 5a
Quite challenging from the word go.

❺ Birch Tree Crack 4c 4c
A nice little crack when dry.

Nelson Taj, lining himself up for the crux move on *Unclimbed Wall* (6b *5b*) - *page 266* - on the Unclimbed Wall at Harrison's Rock.

Harrison's Rocks — Birch Tree Wall

Birch Tree Wall
This section of rock mainly comprises of short routes which are often attempted as boulder problems.

Approach (see overview on page 226) - Take the Top Path Approach and cut down past Garden Slab. You can also use the Forge Farm Approach.

Set-up and Descent - Use the steps to the left of Garden Slab - page 258.

① Birch Tree Variations 6c *5c*
The left side of the wall using a small stalactite.

② Mister Splodge 6c *6a*
A technical problem up the centre of the wall.

③ Birch Tree Wall 4c *4c*
A nice steady climb just right of centre on good holds.

④ Birch Tree Wall Variation 4b *4b*
A slightly easier line to *Birch Tree Wall*.

Lidia Cordon Mayoral, mid-flow on the crux of *Unclimbed Wall* (6b *5b*) - *page 266* - on the Unclimbed Wall at Harrison's Rocks.

Harrison's Rocks — The Scoop Area

The Scoop Area

The lines on the left wall are more suitable for bouldering, although they are often climbed on a top-rope. The bulging wall to the right is a powerful playground for power-hungry apes to flex their muscles. Most people forget that there are actual routes on this wall and not just a few short moves to the first break.

Approach (see overview on page 226) - Take the Top Path Approach and cut down past Garden Slab. You can also use the Forge Farm Approach.

Set-up and Descent - Either use the steps to the left of Garden Slab page 258, or, further right, make an easy climb up or down *Isometric Chimney* - page 267.

❶ Stalactite *f6A*
The left side of the wall past a large stalactite and requires some high foot work.

❷ Skid Marx . . . . *f6B+*
An eliminate up the centre of the face. Avoid contact with anything considered a hold, such as those on *The Scoop* and the stalactite pocketed rail on *Stalactite*.
FA. A.Naylor 10.8.2003

❸ The Scoop . . . . *f5+*
Manoeuvre through the scoop using the flake and move right to finish. For an alternative and slightly easier finish, head left into *Skid Marx* at around *f5*.

❹ Scoop Arete . . . . *f5+*
The right-hand arete is awkward.

❺ Easy Cleft Left 3c *3c*
A chimney route with some big ledges for your feet.

❻ Jumper . . . . *f4+*
A short problem improved by making a hand-traverse along the break to finish at *Easy Cleft Right*.

❼ Pullover 6c *6a*
The centre of the bulging wall. Snatch for the break and make a difficult mantel off this to finish above with a sting in the tail. Joining this line from the right, as per the original sit-start of *Demons of Death* is *f6A*.

❽ Demons of Death 7a *6b*
Powerful climbing up the right side of the wall, eliminating the arete and holds on *Pullover*. A sit-start variation from the back of the small cave and pulling on edges into the original via a side-pull is *f6B+*. Starting further left under the original, and also from a sit-start, is *f6A*.

Hell Wall — Harrison's Rocks

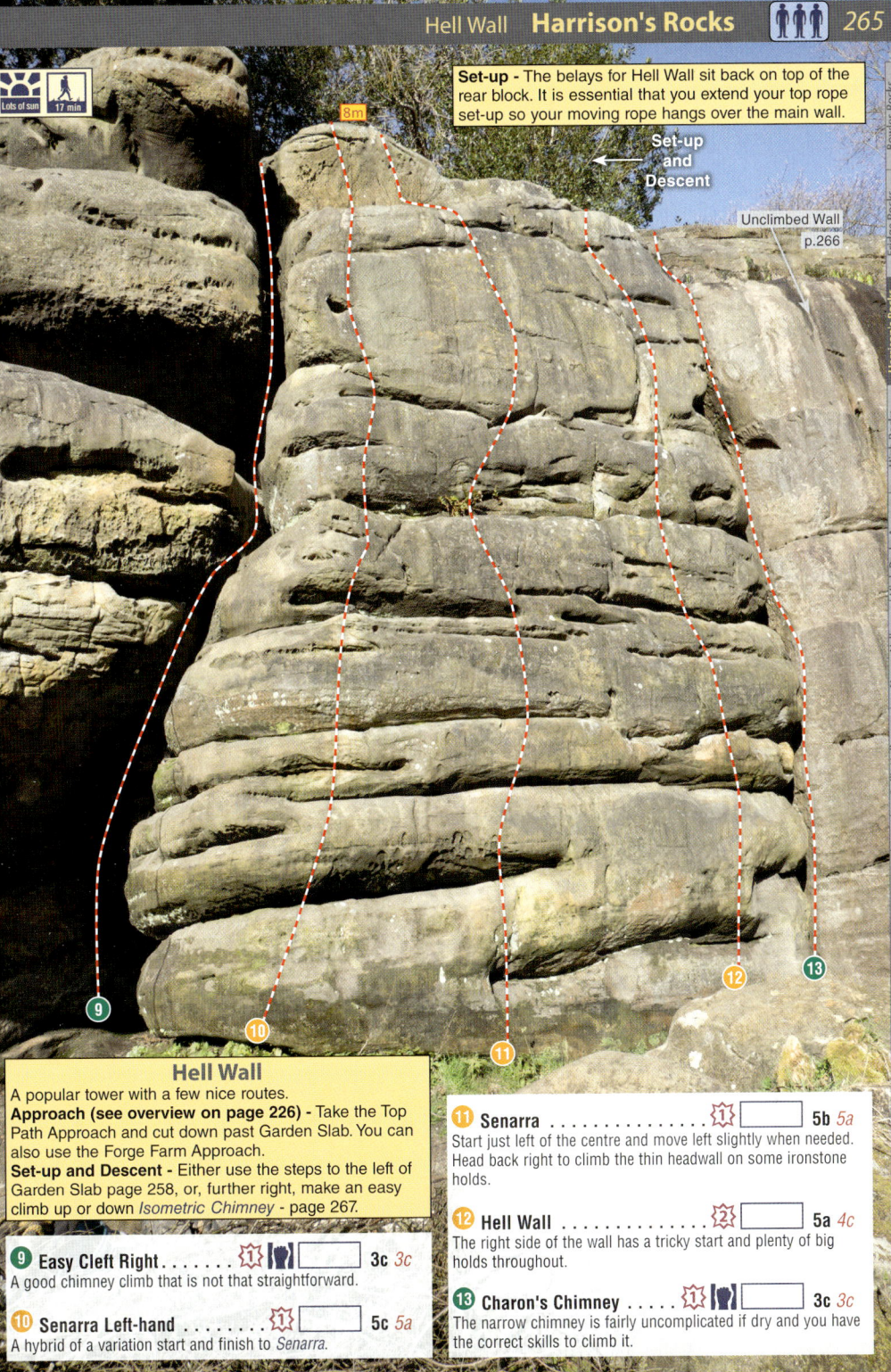

Set-up - The belays for Hell Wall sit back on top of the rear block. It is essential that you extend your top rope set-up so your moving rope hangs over the main wall.

← Set-up and Descent

Unclimbed Wall p.266

Hell Wall
A popular tower with a few nice routes.

Approach (see overview on page 226) - Take the Top Path Approach and cut down past Garden Slab. You can also use the Forge Farm Approach.

Set-up and Descent - Either use the steps to the left of Garden Slab page 258, or, further right, make an easy climb up or down *Isometric Chimney* - page 267.

9 Easy Cleft Right 3c *3c*
A good chimney climb that is not that straightforward.

10 Senarra Left-hand 5c *5a*
A hybrid of a variation start and finish to *Senarra*.

11 Senarra 5b *5a*
Start just left of the centre and move left slightly when needed. Head back right to climb the thin headwall on some ironstone holds.

12 Hell Wall 5a *4c*
The right side of the wall has a tricky start and plenty of big holds throughout.

13 Charon's Chimney 3c *3c*
The narrow chimney is fairly uncomplicated if dry and you have the correct skills to climb it.

Harrison's Rocks — Unclimbed Wall

1 Unclimbed Traverse . f6B
A long traverse along the lower break.

2 Baskerville 6c 6a
The left side of the wall with a pretty taxing crux at the top. Use of the left chimney is not allowed. The route suffers from seepage, so make the most of it when it's dry!
FA. I.Asplend 1960

3 Far Left . . . . 6b+ 5c
A nice route up the face. Climb past the breaks and move slightly right to gain the two pockets before a thin finish.
FA. M.Smart 1963

4 My Dear Watson 6c 6a
An eliminate which mixes the left side of the lower crack on *Elementary* and the right side of the right pocket on the final moves of *Far Left*. Despite this, it's actually rather good.
FA. M.McPherson 1994

5 Elementary . . . . 6b+ 5c
Climb the awkwardly-shaped crack system from left to right. Finish on the left side of the final crack at the top. Finishing direct is **6c** *6a*.
FA. M.Smart 1963

6 Dennis the Menace 7c 6c
Desperate face climbing on very small holds, eliminating all holds on *Elementary* and *Desperate Dan*.

7 Desperate Dan. . 6c+ 6a
Climb the first few moves on *Unclimbed Wall* and continue direct to the second break. Tackle the headwall using an undercut and small pocket.
FA. D.Lewis 1982

8 Unclimbed Wall . Top 50 6b 5b
One of the best sandstone climbs in the area. A super outing following a series of breaks across the face, past two distinct potholes. One hard move near the top notches up the difficulty.
Photo on page 261 and 263.
FA. N.Barnard 1926

9 Unclimbed Wall Variation 6b 5c
A direct approach to *Unclimbed Wall* joining the original at the potholes. A more challenging finish can be done to the left of the original - **Unclimbed Wall Direct Finish, 6c** *6a*.
FA. N.Barnard 1926. FA. (Direct Finish) M.Mansfield 2.5.1965

10 Unclimbed Wall Direct . . 6b+ 5c
A sustained and taxing bit of climbing direct to the second break and finishing up the final moves on *Unclimbed Wall*.

11 Jingowobbly . . . . 6b+ 5c
A poor eliminate that borrows holds from adjacent routes.

12 Right Unclimbed . 6c+ 6a
A super-technical testpiece starting from the top of the ramp and moving left onto the wall (or, harder still, starting from below). Using the crack and pockets on the face you quickly reach a stopper move - there are several methods, but only one usually works.
FA. L.E.Holliwell 1966

Harrison's Rocks

Unclimbed Wall

The creme de la creme of face climbing at Harrison's featuring one of the finest climbs on sandstone. The wall faces approximately southwest like the others along this section, so gets a lot of sun. It also tends to dry quickly, with only the odd bit of seepage on the left after persistent rain.

Approach (see overview on page 226) - Take the Top Path Approach and cut down past Garden Slab. You can also use the Forge Farm Approach.

Set-up and Descent - Either use the steps to the left of Garden Slab page 258, or, further right, make an easy climb up or down *Isometric Chimney*.

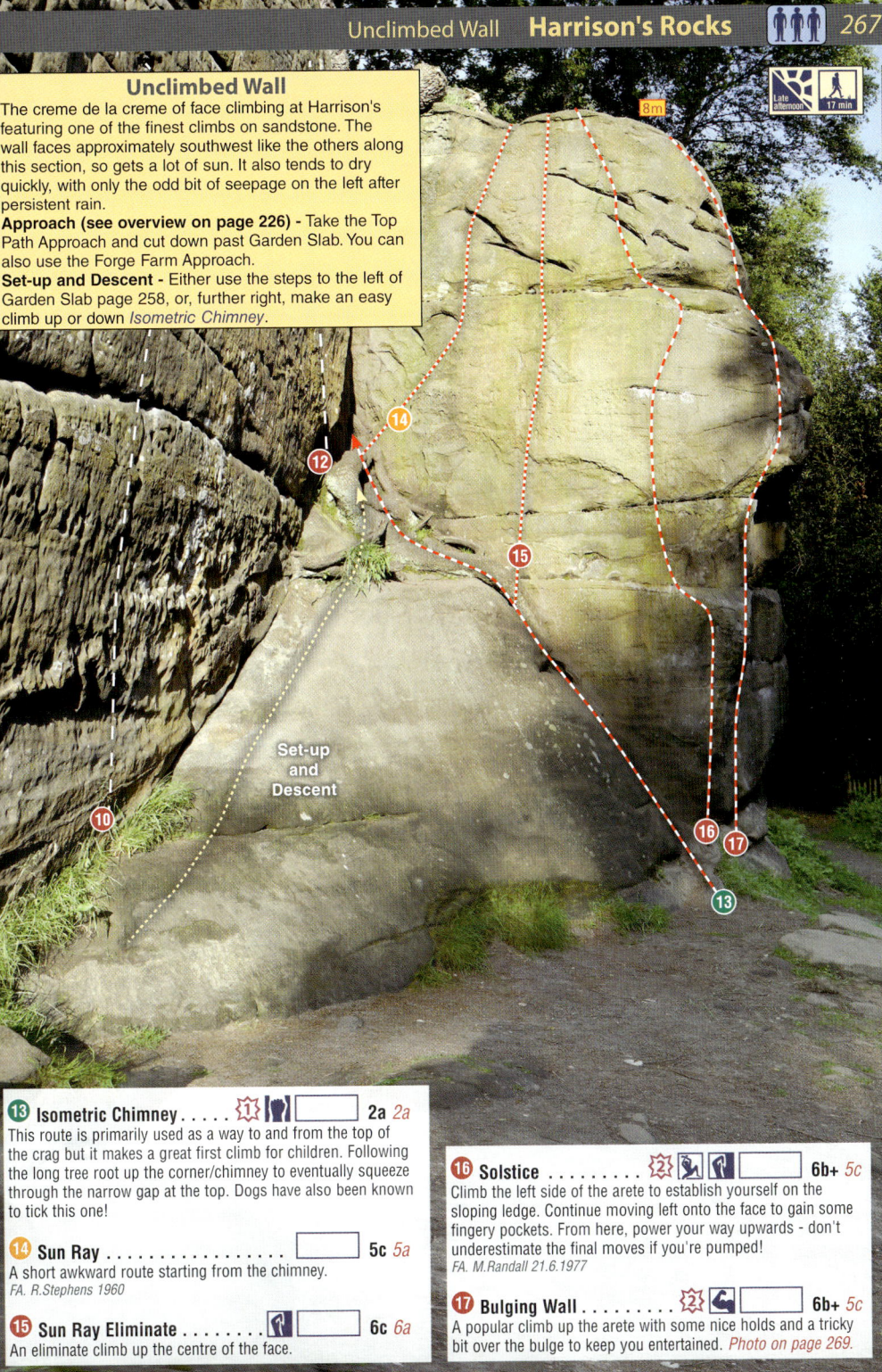

13 Isometric Chimney 2a *2a*
This route is primarily used as a way to and from the top of the crag but it makes a great first climb for children. Following the long tree root up the corner/chimney to eventually squeeze through the narrow gap at the top. Dogs have also been known to tick this one!

14 Sun Ray 5c *5a*
A short awkward route starting from the chimney.
FA. R.Stephens 1960

15 Sun Ray Eliminate 6c *6a*
An eliminate climb up the centre of the face.

16 Solstice .... 6b+ *5c*
Climb the left side of the arete to establish yourself on the sloping ledge. Continue moving left onto the face to gain some fingery pockets. From here, power your way upwards - don't underestimate the final moves if you're pumped!
FA. M.Randall 21.6.1977

17 Bulging Wall .... 6b+ *5c*
A popular climb up the arete with some nice holds and a tricky bit over the bulge to keep you entertained. *Photo on page 269*.

Harrison's Rocks — Zig-zag Wall

Zig-zag Wall

The final wall at Harrison's suffers from seepage, but has a couple of classic routes on its left-hand side. To get the best out of it, wait for it to dry out before attempting any of the routes.

Approach (see overview on page 226) - Take the Top Path Approach and cut down past Garden Slab. You can also use the Forge Farm Approach.

Set-up and Descent - Either use the steps to the left of Garden Slab page 258, or, further right, make an easy climb up or down *Isometric Chimney* - page 267.

1 Zig-Zag Wall 6a *5a*
An excellent route. The right-hand cracks can be greasy. Climb the lower groove and traverse right to move up the cracks, then finish back left and over the nose on the arete in line with *Bulging Wall*. An alternative direct finish can also be done at 6a+ *5b*.

2 Zig-Zag Wall Direct .... 6a+ *5a*
An excellent direct version which is more attractive to many and is slowly becoming easier over time. From the top of the groove, climb direct over the bulge to rejoin the original.

3 Rift .... 6b+ *5c*
Dispatch the tough crux move at the start and make sneaky use of some chipped holds thereafter to establish yourself on the face. Straightforward climbing leads to a rounded top-out.

4 Smart 6b *5c*
Climb the wall between *Rift* and the crack of *Witches Broomstick* - a bit eliminate.

5 Witches Broomstick .... 6b+ *5c*
The crack has a hard start and is often wet.

6 Max .... 6c+ *6a*
A hard move over the bulge which is almost always very green. If you made it this far then climb the face between the two cracks and avoid them at all cost.

7 Neutral 7a *6a*
The thin crack on the upper face after a hard and greasy start.

8 The Powerband ..... f6C+
Long and sustained climbing along the greasy lower break. Finish on the slab under *Isometric Chimney*.
FA. I.Stronghill 2002

9 Stubble .... 7a+ *6b*
A hard, greasy and practically impossible start. Luckily, the face climb above is much easier.
FA. S.Quinton 21.3.1992

10 Meat Cleaver .... 6c+ *6a*
A gruesome crack climb right next to the large border fence.
FA. D.Lewis 18.9.1982

Harrison's Rocks

269

Nelson Taj, climbing on *Bulging Wall* (6b+ *5c*) - *page 267* - on the Unclimbed Wall at Harrison's Rock.

High Rocks

Emma Harrington digging deep into the pockets on *Advertisement Wall* (6a *5b*) - *page 308* - on the Advertisement Wall at High Rocks.

High Rocks

	No star	★	★★	★★★
2a to 4c/*f2 to f4*	34	23	2	-
5a to 6a+/*f4+ to f5+*	28	23	6	4
6b to 7a/*f6A to f6C+*	70	51	36	14
7a+ up/*f7A up*	29	34	25	12

The High Rocks National Monument (as described by historians and the current owners) is one of the three best crags in the southeast, along with Harrison's and Bowles Rocks. It boasts the highest outcrops in the area, which are popular with those seeking out the longer and pumpier challenges.

High Rocks is also famous for its maze of passageways which are worth exploring to find hidden delights, including plenty for both the boulderer and the climber. For those into jamming, there is a delightful array of clean-cut cracks of varying difficulty to try. The walls also have some unique honeycombed featured rock, some of which needs treating with care to ensure no further holds are broken.

High Rocks has many classic routes across the grade range, although many of the better routes are in the higher grades. The inspirational line of *Chimaera* is testament to the level of hard climbing found here - it remains one of the most sought-after routes on sandstone.

High Rocks is designated as a Site of Special Scientific Interest; the area above *Infidel* is of particular interest for its unusually shaped rock formations, as well as the many honeycombed featured walls elsewhere along the rocks.

High Rocks

Equipment
The majority of High Rocks has no bolts, so top-rope anchors need to be set up using long static ropes to trees - bring a good selection of gear to do this along with protection for the rope/rock. It is awkward to get to the top of the Hut Boulder, but it does have bolts for anchors. High Rocks has many bridges in place over the numerous passageways and these bridges are not to be used for setting up top-ropes.

Conditions
The rocks generally face north and west with some of the main faces suffering from shady north-facing conditions. The west-facing walls offer cleaner quick-drying rock for the most part, although the tree cover can mean that they retain dampness and can feel muggy in hot weather. The passages and hidden gullies at High Rocks only come into condition after extended dry periods but, in a heat wave, this is the place to come since you will almost always find something to climb. The rock is typical sandstone i.e can get a bit sandy! On the north-facing section of the crag, some of the lower walls seep noticeably which causes problems with the steep starts.

The vegetation does get a hold from time to time but this has been alleviated by the clearance work that was undertaken in 2004/2005 by the SVG (see page 54 for more on the SVG).

The rocks at High Rocks are some of the most picturesque on Southern Sandstone. The garden environment brings a laid back feel to the climbing here, but it's important to remember that this area (pictured) is often the back drop for many a wedding photo, so please keep chalk to a minimum, consider using eco balls where possible and vacate when required.

High Rocks

Access and Costs

High Rocks is on private land and climbing is only permitted at the discretion of the land owner. An entrance fee (comparable to most climbing wall entrance fees) must be paid at the bar and your climbing ticket must be kept on you at all times and produced if requested. If asked to vacate any area by staff, please do so without hesitation.

High Rocks is primarily a wedding venue and this is the main business of the land owner with climbers and their entrance fees coming a very distant second. It is imperative that climbers do not interfere in any way when weddings are taking place. The areas around Nemesis and the Hut Boulder have climbing bans when weddings are taking place since they are used by photographers. Check the High Rocks website **highrocks.co.uk** for the latest information as access and rules change frequently. To reduce the visual impact of climbers, chalk use should be kept to a minimum. Dogs are allowed if kept on a lead.

Approach   Also see map on page 18

High Rocks is relatively easy to find with plenty of brown tourist signs showing you the way. If leaving Tunbridge Wells on the A26, High Rocks is signed to the right across Tunbridge Wells Common, with a left turn onto High Rocks Lane. If on the A264, turn left down Tea Garden Lane just after leaving the town. Both ways lead you to High Rocks Lane by the railway. Continue over a railway bridge, and past the main High Rocks building to park in the large main carpark.

It is also possible to take the Spa Valley Railway steam train from either Tunbridge Wells or Eridge station which stops at the rocks, though trains are infrequent.

To purchase tickets, go to the lower bar which is found in the main building complex. Enter through the front and turn left down the stairs. Alternatively, reach it from the garden and side entrance, depending if there is a wedding taking place or not. The entrance to the rocks is opposite the main entrance to the High Rocks complex. The bar has toilet facilities.

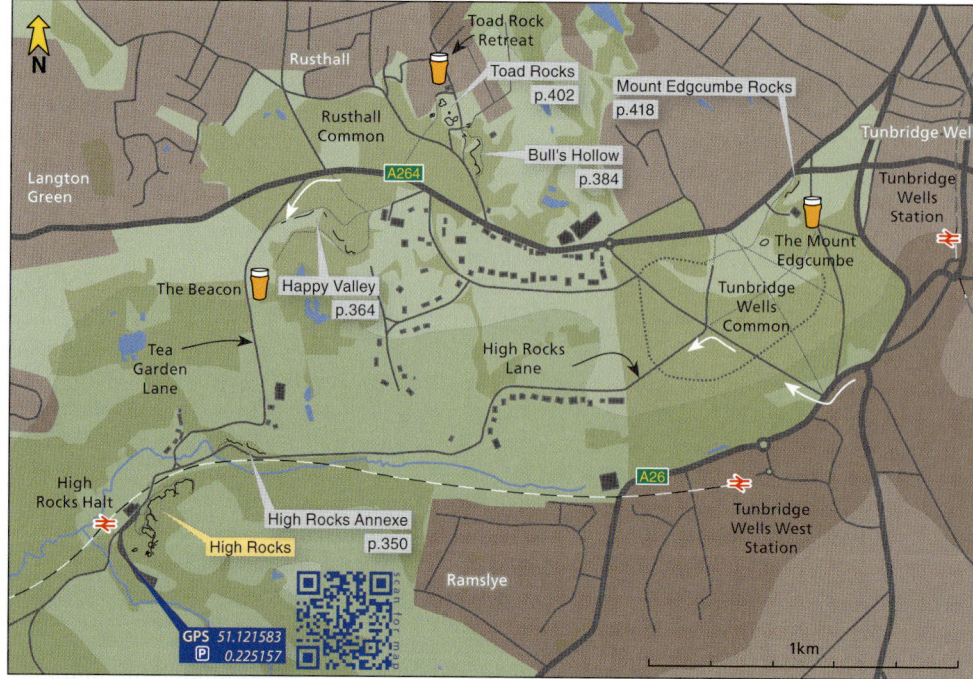

Emma Harrington laybacking her way up *Viper Crack* (6a+ *5b*) - *page 319* - at the Nemesis area of High Rocks.

High Rocks

Bouldering

High Rocks is a popular destination for boulderers with some excellent problems dotted along the main walls. It also has the renowned Slab Boulder with one of Sandstone's hardest problems - *Don't Pierdol, f8A+*.

Please take specific note of any restrictions placed upon bouldering at the time of your visit. If bouldering is not allowed, please refrain from entering the rocks with a crash pad unless specific permission has been granted from the owner. See **highrocks.co.uk** for up-to-date access information.

Ben Conibear dispatching *Magnetic* (*f7A*) - page 298 - at the Infidel Area of High Rocks. This is also the start of *The Prang* (7a+ 6a) when done from a standing start.

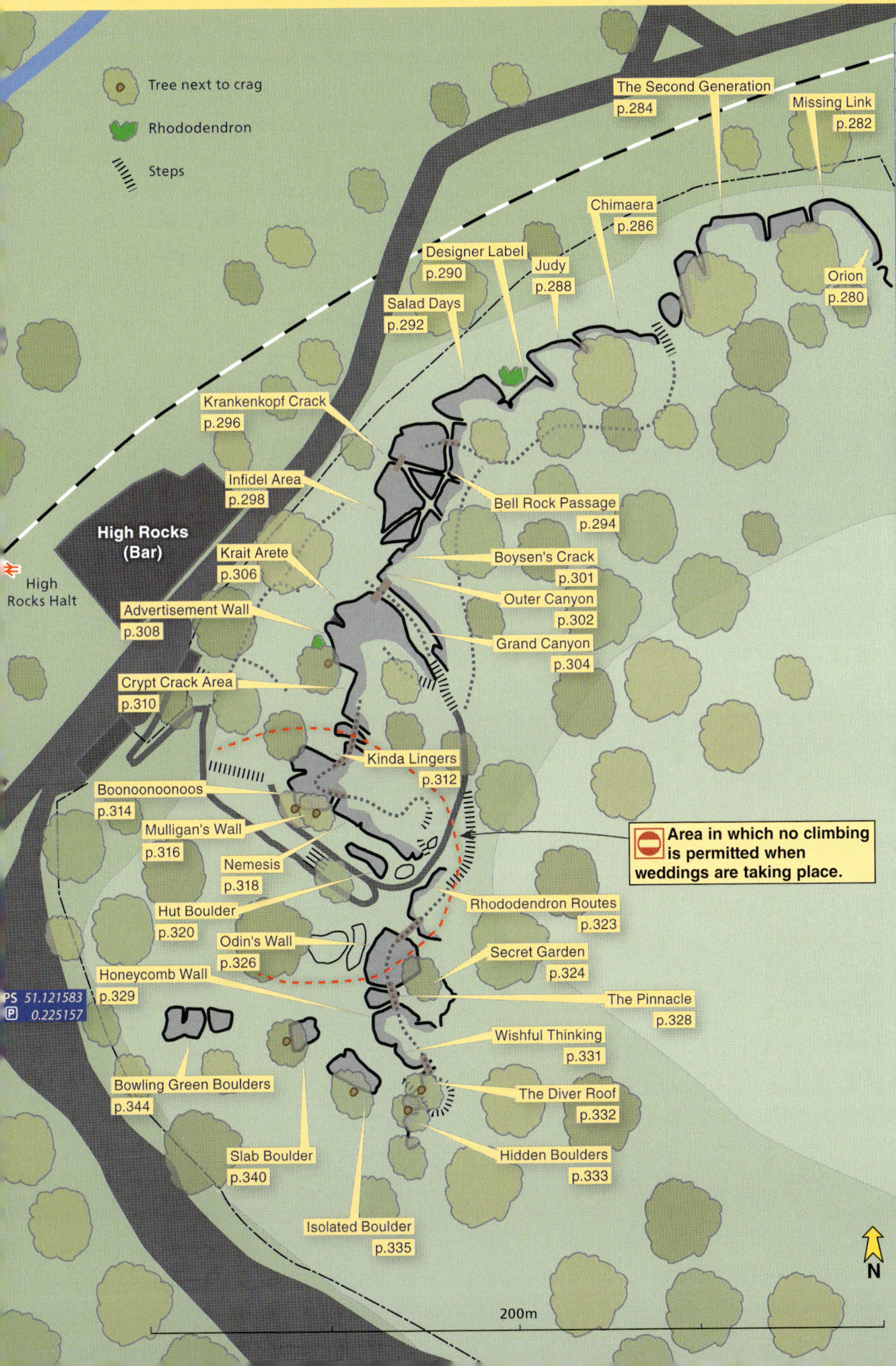

High Rocks

277

Legend:
- Tree next to crag
- Rhododendron
- Steps

- The Second Generation p.284
- Missing Link p.282
- Chimaera p.286
- Designer Label p.290
- Judy p.288
- Orion p.280
- Salad Days p.292
- Krankenkopf Crack p.296
- Infidel Area p.298
- Bell Rock Passage p.294
- High Rocks (Bar)
- High Rocks Halt
- Krait Arete p.306
- Boysen's Crack p.301
- Outer Canyon p.302
- Advertisement Wall p.308
- Grand Canyon p.304
- Crypt Crack Area p.310
- Kinda Lingers p.312
- Boonoonoonoos p.314
- Mulligan's Wall p.316
- Nemesis p.318
- Hut Boulder p.320
- Rhododendron Routes p.323
- Odin's Wall p.326
- Secret Garden p.324
- Honeycomb Wall p.329
- The Pinnacle p.328
- Wishful Thinking p.331
- Bowling Green Boulders p.344
- The Diver Roof p.332
- Slab Boulder p.340
- Hidden Boulders p.333
- Isolated Boulder p.335

PS 51.121583
P 0.225157

Area in which no climbing is permitted when weddings are taking place.

Side tabs: Bowles Rocks, Eridge Rocks, Harrison's Rocks, High Rocks, High Rocks Annexe, Happy Valley, Bull's Hollow, Toad Rocks, Mount Edgcumbe, Bassett's Farm, Under Rockes, Stone Farm

200m

N

High Rocks

High Rocks

High Rocks — Orion

Orion

Hiding in the shadows and under the canopy of trees, the first walls of High Rocks are forever green and often forgotten.

Approach (see map page 277 and overview page 278) - From the main entrance, make your way left for approximately 240m until you reach the northeast boundary fence at the end of the crag.

1 Pure Arete .... 6a+ *5b*
The left arete has a mucky top-out.
FA. R.Cole 31.5.1958

2 Peace on Earth 6b *5c*
Hand traverse the rail at mid-height (poor feet) then pull up. It creates a longer route but adds very little else.
FA. T.Daniells 1970s

3 The Purvee 7a *6b*
The centre of the wall has a difficult start.
FA. G.Wickham 15.7.1990

4 Lady of the Light Bulb .. 6b+ *5c*
The right arete on spaced holds.
FA. D.Reid 16.2.1992

5 Orion Chimney 3c *3c*
A dirty green chimney climb. Not everyone's cup of tea.
FA. R.Mazinke 14.12.1997

6 Orion Arete .... 6b+ *5c*
The vague arete becomes more defined the higher you go.
FA. T.G.DeLacy 8.2.1976

7 Orion Crack 5a *4c*
Climb the shallow crack to a platform and finish up the groove.

8 Brian Arete .... 6a+ *5b*
Climb the fat green arete to finish rightwards up the slab.
FA. C.Arnold 1998

Orion **High Rocks** 281

9 Scimitar . . . . 6c+ *6a*
The Ghostbusters are required to get rid of the oozing ectoplasm from within the green crack. Once they have cleaned up, it is apparently "not too bad" (rumour has it).
FA. M.Boysen 1960s

10 Tubby Hayes is a Fats Waller . . 7a *6b*
Mossy wall climbing. Give yourself the tick for just thinking about it.
FA. D.Turner 12.8.1990

11 The First Crack . . . . 7a+ *6b*
A fierce jamming testpiece for masochists in search of esoteria.
FA. R.Thomas, N.Cordery, G.Clarke, Aided the crack using a variety of Pitons, tent pegs and other wooden instruments. Graded at A2 and originally the line headed right along the upper break to exit.
FFA. (with a direct finish) M.Fowler 9.7.1978

12 Clown's Pocket f7B
A large dyno from side-pulls to a jug.
FA. C.George 2005

High Rocks — Missing Link

1 Missing Link 7b *6b*
Climb the arete to the break and traverse left to where those with long arms can pull onto the upper face and tiptoe to victory.
FA. M.Boysen (aid) 1982. FFA. G.Wickham 1990

2 Anaconda Chimney 5a *4c*
Shimmy your way up, working further inside the higher you go.

3 Bolt Route .... f6B+
Follow the series of bolt holds to the first break.

4 Wonder Boy ...... 7c+ *6c*
A left-hand start to *Fungal Smear* up a series of monos. Traditionally done as a boulder problem to the first break *f7B*, but better if continued.
FA. I.Stronghill 2008

5 Fungal Smear 7b *6b*
Dust off your best dirty clothes and shimmy that chimney, breaking left at half height to finish carefully up the slab.
FA. G.Wickham

6 Rattlesnake 2 .... 7a *6b*
Start as for *Fungal Smear* and move left at half-height to layback the arete. *Photo opposite.*
FA. I.Mailer 26.7.1986

7 Boa-Constrictor Chimney ... 5c *5a*
Continue the chimney squeezing all the way to the top.

8 Boa by the Back 4b *4b*
Shimmy up the very back of the chimney.

Missing Link

The first of the northwest-facing sections of the crag has some pretty difficult routes. It only sees the sun in the late afternoon/evening. The tree clearance of 2004/2005 by the SVG has dramatically improved the condition of this area.

Approach (see map page 277 and overview page 278) - Make your way leftwards from the main entrance for approximately 220m to the bulging arete just before the northeast boundary fence.
Set-up and Descent - Left of Orion - p.280.

The facial expression of many an off-width climber crawling their way up one of the chimneys and cracks on Southern Sandstone. Here Robin Mazinke battles his way up and onto *Rattlesnake 2* (7a *6b*) - *opposite* - at the Missing Link area of High Rocks.

High Rocks — The Second Generation

The Second Generation
Back in the early 1990s this area was centre stage for a major evolution in hard sandstone climbing. A good breeze is required to put these lines into good condition.
Approach (see map page 277 and overview page 278) - Make your way left from the main entrance for approximately 200m. The area is past the steps leading from the alcove of Chimaera.
Set-up and Descent - Go up the steps left of Chimaera - page 287.

❶ Bone Machine 7c 6c
A brutal climb up the steep overhanging wall, trending left at the break and finishing up the crack on the left side of the wall. The direct start is **Venom** which is yet to be freed.
FA.. G.Wickham 25.7.1993. FA. (Venom - aid) 1950's

❷ Adder .... 6c+ 6a
The first of the more popular routes at High Rocks (when the conditions are good enough to climb it). Head up the thin crack and finish past the tree stump.
FA. G.DeLacy 1976

❸ The Second Generation 8a 6c
A contender for the hardest route on sandstone (despite the grade), especially with the wearing of a crucial hold. Follow the series of pockets past multiple desperate moves. Then consider the figure of four move on the upper face which may or may not enable you to gain the upper pockets and arete. Climb this on its left side to finish.
FA. T.Tullis (aid) 1970s. FFA. J.Sharpe. 24.6.1990. This line even caught the eye of northern climbing legend Ben Moon at the time who, after Dave Turner's second ascent, quickly grabbed the third.

❹ Pammy f7C
A problem up the blunt arete. Reachy moves to small holds.
FA. C.George 2002

❺ Cobra Chimney 6a 5a
An ultra-wide chimney that requires effort and flexibility.

❻ Resurrection Traverse .. f7C
The extended start to *Resurrection*. Only for the ultra strong.

Boa-Constrictor Chimney - p.282

The Second Generation — High Rocks

⑦ Renascence .... 7b+ *6b*
An icon of hard sandstone climbing. Climb the centre of the lower face to the break (often bouldered at **f6B+** to here). Move right to combat the rounded arete above with a series of sustained hard moves. The most difficult move is the very last.
FA. D.Turner 14.7.1990

⑧ Resurrection *f7C*
A hard direct problem start to *Renascence* with a few (sadly) chipped holds (purists avoid these). Linking into *Renascence* has yet to be achieved, but it won't be long.
FA. I.Stronghill 2005

Right of *Resurrection*, and left of the steps, are three short routes which are awkward to protect with a top-rope.

⑨ Sorrow 6a *5b*
Climb the front side of the face on positive but sandy holds.
FA. T.Daniells 1979

⑩ Sorrow Right-Hand 4c *4c*
The face just right of the arete.

⑪ Lunatick 6c *6a*
Climb the short wall above the widest step.
FA. T.Skinner 17.7.2005

Belinda Be Fuller attempting *Chimaera* (8a+ *7a*) - *opposite* - hoping to become a member of the elite group of climbers to have climbed this cutting-edge route.

Chimaera High Rocks 287

Chimaera
The location of the mythical iconic wall that has currently one of the hardest routes on sandstone. The wall is generally clean and dry despite the lack of sun in this area but top-outs can often be green.
Approach (see map page 277 and overview page 278) - Make your way left from the main entrance for 180m to reach a small alcove area and some steps. The wall is to the right of the steps.
Set-up and Descent - Use the conveniently placed steps to the left.

❶ Arab Spring 7c 6b
Climb the round rib left of *Step Crack*.
FA. J.Dawes 2013

❷ Steps Crack 6b 5b
An excellent slim crack which can be finished direct at 6c 6a.
FA. J.Morin 1926

❸ Cornerstone . . . . f7B+
A direct start to *Chimaera* finishing at the break. Originally done as just a boulder problem.
FA. T.Gore 2013

❹ Chimaera . . . . . Top 50   8a+ 7a
The first to be awarded the grade of UK **7a** on sandstone and still, more than 25 years later, has only seen a handful of ascents, including one incredible solo ascent. Climb the bulging wall to the break and traverse left under the sharp arete and slim groove. Climb this deploying power, precise footwork and finesse to arise victorious above. Take care on the final few moves as they can often be greasy. *Photo opposite.*
FA. D.Turner 14.7.1990. After a number of repeats the line was remarkably soloed by Matt Cousins on 21.7.2013.

❺ Moving Staircase . . . 7a 6b
Start as for *Chimaera* and move right onto the rightward-trending ramp-line, which increases in difficulty the higher you go. Finish delicately up the final slab.
FA. M.Boysen 1986

❻ Very Steep Moving Staircase
. . . . 7a+ 6b
A direct start to *Moving Staircase*, tackling the right side of the cave and joining the main route at the base of the upper ramp-line.

❼ Slopertrocity f6C
From two jugs in the lower break, span up to the next break using an undercut side-pull. Traverse right on slopers and finish at the shallow scoop just before the rail runs out.
FA. I.Bull 2013

High Rocks — Judy

Judy

This wall mainly features hard and conditions-dependent problems and routes with plenty of potential for future development.

Approach (see map page 277 and overview page 278) - Make your way left from the main entrance for 160m to reach the walls just right of the alcove area of Chimaera.

Set-up and Descent - Go up the steps left of Chimaera - p.287.

1 Pegasus 7a *6b*
Climb the crack to the row of small pockets and stalactites in the break. Traverse right along these and climb the left side of the arete.
FA. P.Widdowson 27.5.1990

2 Twinkle Toes .... f7A+
A delicate problem starting over the nose. Gain the slab and finish at the break.
FA. B.Ventham 2013

3 Chockstone Chimney 4a *4a*
Climb the chimney, passing the aforementioned chockstones. Climbing the left arete avoiding contact with the right wall to the first break is **Gethsemane**, *f7A*.
FA. (Gethsemane) T.Gore 2013

4 Vandal .... f7A+
A highball problem up the left nose which is usually finished at the small ledge, although it does go to the next break.
FA. J.Wardle 2003

5 Superman f7A
A poor direct start to *Judy* which is usually just done as a crimpy boulder problem to the pocket. The first move requires a jump to catch the rail.
FA. I.Stronghill 2005

Judy High Rocks

6 Judy .... 7b+ *6b*
Above a steep and powerful start, traverse left along a stalactite rail and up to the left side of the roof. Follow the rail back right over the bulge, laybacking the flared crack to gain the headwall and finish up the slab above.
FA. G.McLelland 1982

7 Punch 7c *6c*
A more direct line to *Judy* up the flared crack.
FA. L.Percival 6.8.1995

8 Shadow of the Wind .... f7B+
A good left-hand boulder problem start to *Telegram Sam*, finishing at the break.

9 Telegram Sam .... 7a+ *6b*
Climb the nose with an awkward start to the break and finish direct up the slab. Pulling on rhododendrons is allowed.
FA. P.Widdowson 24.7.1990

10 Monolithic Man f6A
Climb the shallow groove to the break.

11 Rag Trade 7a *6b*
A nicely positioned climb up the arete with a difficult start.
FA. M.Fowler 1980

High Rocks — Designer Label

Designer Label

A neglected area right of Judy. Many of the routes are either hard or have become overgrown at the top.

Approach (see map page 277 and overview page 278) - From the main entrance, make your way left for approximately 140m, passing the left-hand entrance to Bell Rock Passage and the Salad Days wall to its left. This area is to the left in a square-cut area of rock.

Set-up and Descent - Go up the steps left of Chimaera area - p.287.

① **Designer Label** 7a 6b
Climb the arete on its left side, moving right to finish.
FA. I.Mailer 23.4.1987

② **Morpho** 7b 6b
Climb the scooped ramp with difficulty.
FA. C.George 2005

③ **Recess Wall** 3c 3c
Climb the chimney and make a long traverse back left to finish.

④ **Onions** f5A
A poor green problem up the arete.
FA. I.Hufton 7.6.2005

⑤ **Sunzilla** .... 6b+ 5c
The arete right of the chimney with an overgrown top-out.
FA. I.Hufton 7.6.2005

⑥ **Too Crimpy for Chris.** 7a 6b
A long and fingery traverse, leaving *Sunzilla* at the break and, without pumping out, finishing on the final moves of *Salad Days*.
FA. T.Daniells 2008

Oscar Krumlinde making the slappy move on *Darth Vader* (**f7A+**) - *page 312* - at the Kinda Lingers area of High Rocks.

High Rocks — Salad Days

Salad Days

A great wall with mainly hard lines (and one adventurous one) to seek out. Also the entrance to the left side of Bell Rock Passage. The main wall stays in good condition throughout the summer. The northeast face struggles to stay clean, except in dry weather.

Approach (see map page 277 and overview page 278) - Make your way left from the main entrance for approximately 130m, passing the left-hand entrance to Bell Rock Passage and the Salad Days wall.

Set-up and Descent - Go up the steps left of Chimaera area - p.287.

❶ Salad Days 7b *6b*
A great line. Start up the difficult lower arete and swing right to tackle the distinct thin flake at mid-height. Move back left to finish up the arete.
FA. G.McLelland 21.7.1982

❷ Dogtown *f7C*
This powerful problem up the centre of the face has now sadly lost a crucial undercut.
FA. I.Stronghill 2005

❸ Pet Cemetery . . . . 7c+ *6c*
The right-hand start to *Salad Days* is often bouldered to the break at *f7B*. Link into *Salad Days* for the full original experience.
FA. L.Percival 28.8.1995

❹ Leglock . . . . 7a+ *6b*
Start up the lower unappealing crack (which can be avoided by starting up *Cut Steps Crack* and traversing left along the first break to join the route - **6c** *6a*). Head upwards following the crack/corner and finish by stepping left and climbing the wide crack at the top.
FA. W.Maxwell 14.9.1954

❺ The Real Slim Shady *f7A*
A complex problem with a number of solutions. Head out over the bulges and finish at the break.
FA. I.Stronghill 2005

❻ Crossing the Rubicon 7a *6b*
From the circular hold, head for the break and move left up the face and over the bulge above, avoiding contact with *Leglock*.
FA. M.Vetterlein 19.7.1990

Not much sun | 2 min | Green

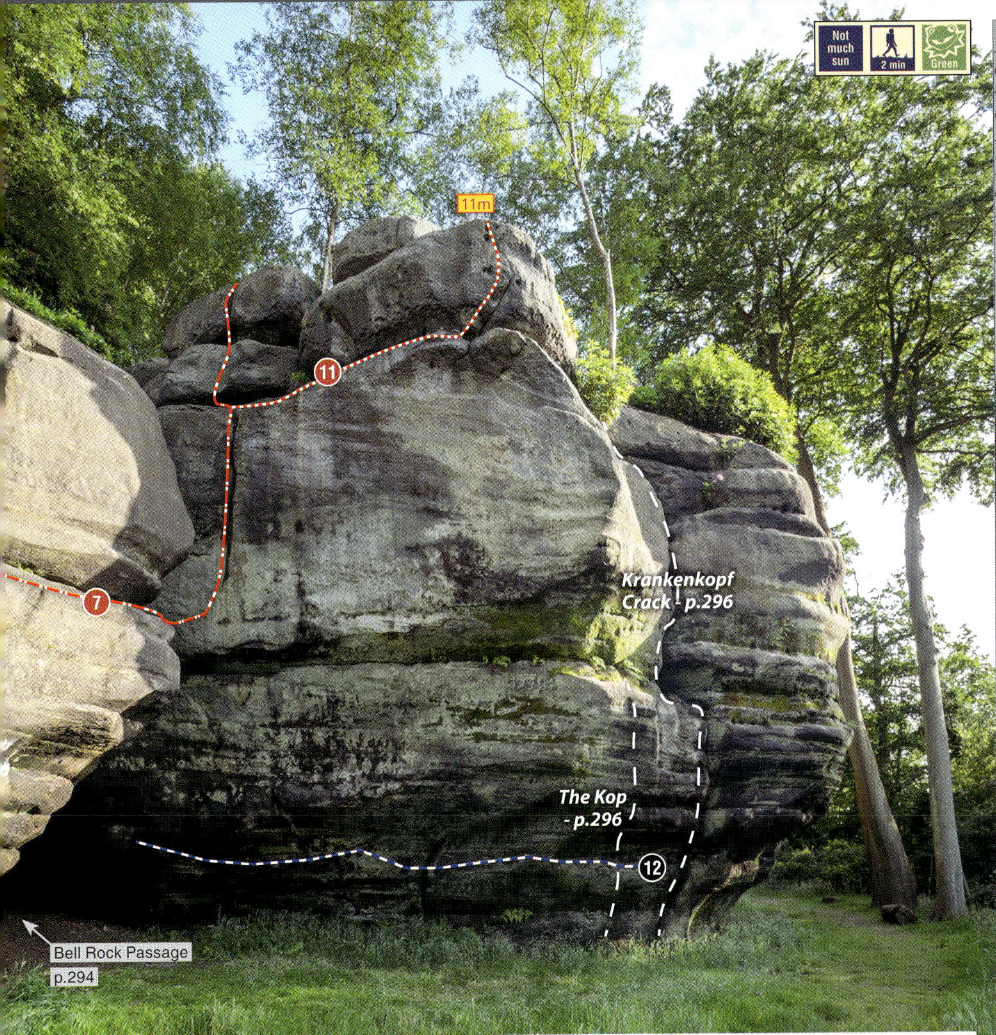

11m
11
7
Krankenkopf Crack - p.296
The Kop - p.296
12
Bell Rock Passage
p.294

7 Cut Steps Crack 2 6c *6a*
A complex line. Climb the cut-out holds (slopers) to the break and traverse right to the passageway. Reach across and climb the crack on the opposite wall (often a bit green) without bridging. Bridging the last section reduces the grade. The *Fresh Air Finish* gives a longer outing.
FA. T.G.DeLacy 1970s

8 Too Tall for Tim 1 7a *6a*
Start as for *Cut Steps Crack* and continue direct to the second break via a long reach, to finish more easily above.
FA. C.Arnold 1984

9 Atomic Mushroom . . . . . 1 *f7A+*
From decent holds, reach out for the sloping feature up and left, then shimmy your way to finish at the break.
FA. G.Taylor 2005

10 Too Hard for Dave . . . . . 1 7a+ *6b*
Make a dynamic move on the overhanging nose to reach the break (a popular problem on its own at ***f6A+***). Finish up the left side of the arete.
FA. P.Widdowson 14.7.1990

11 Fresh Air Finish . . . . 2 6c+ *6a*
The exciting finish to *Cut Steps Crack*. Traverse right along the top break and finish on the nose. A creative top-rope set-up, (often with two top-ropes), is required to avoid a big crashing swing if you come off at the start.
FA. R.Mazinke 10.7.2005

12 A Path Seldom Taken 2 *f7B*
A good low-level traverse starting up *Spanked* (page 296) and finishing at the large flat hold at the entrance to the Bell Rock Passage. Make sure you keep your bum off the ground near the end.
FA. T.Gore 4.9.2013

Bowles Rocks
Eridge Rocks
Harrison's Rocks
High Rocks
High Rocks Annexe
Happy Valley
Bull's Hollow
Toad Rocks
Mount Edgcumbe
Bassett's Farm
Under Rockes
Stone Farm

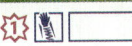

High Rocks — Bell Rock Passage

Bell Rock Passage

An entertaining maze of passages which offers some surprisingly good climbing when in condition, though it can be pretty green and slimy otherwise. Many of the routes are standard 'back and foot' chimney climbs which are difficult to grade. They can be easier or harder depending on how tall (and wide) you are, which way you face, which precise section you climb and how green they are. If you do find these routes in condition, then they make an excellent cooling off spot in hot weather.

Approach (see map page 277 and overview page 278) - Make your way left from the main entrance for approximately 80m, passing the passageway of the Grand Canyon and reaching the Infidel Area. From here you can either enter the passage to the right of the Infidel Area or walk left for 40m and enter to the right of Salad Days.

Set-up and Descent - Use the steps at the end of the Grand Canyon - p.304.

1 Strangler 5c *5a*
The wall starting up the crack and move right to finish up *Deadwood Chimney*. Finishing direct up a thin crack and the wall above is 7a *6b*.
FA. T.Daniells 1977. FA. (Direct) P.Widdowson 1992

2 Deadwood Chimney 3c *3c*
Choose your own adventure by starting approximately 3m into the chimney and heading skywards.

3 Outer Limits 6b *5c*
Bridge the passageway just before the narrowing and the bridge. The difficulty depends on how tall you are.

4 Bell Rock Transverse Passage Route 1
.... 5b *5a*
Chimney the section just beyond the bridge and finish on it.

5 Bell Rock Passage 4a *4a*
Chimney up the dark side passage towards the light.

6 Bell Rock Transverse Passage Route 2
.... 4c *4c*
More chimneying just beyond the crossroads in the passage.
FA. F.K.Elliot 18.4.1943

7 Spider's Chimney....... 3c *3c*
A second narrow chimney leading off the main passage.

8 Crown of Thorns 4a *4a*
An extension to *Spider's Chimney*. Stop a few metres short of the top and traverse inwards for approximately 5m. Exit through a hole in the ground.
FA. M.Eden 1997

9 Bell Rock Transverse Passage Route 3
.... 4c *4c*
Climb the passageway right of *Spider's Chimney*.

10 Giant's Stride 3c *3c*
Climb the chimney and stride across onto a ledge on the south face. Move right to finish up the slab.

11 Another One up the Back Passage
.... 6c+ *6a*
The arete right of *Giant's Stride* finishing up the slab.
FA. C.Arnold 2005

12 The Chute 5b *5a*
Climb the wide niche, then reach across the passage and chimney the rest of the way.

13 Senile Walk 7a *6b*
The arete to the rear of the balcony. Exit left under the block.
FA. M.Boysen 25.7.1992

14 Warning Rock Chimney.. 3c *3c*
Chimney/scramble under the chockstones to exit on the balcony.

15 Mish Bell 8a *7a*
The narrow wall gives a hard route. The aretes are in but no chimneying allowed, obviously!
FA. C.George 3.10.2007

16 One of Our Chimneys Is Missing
.... 3c *3c*
Chimney up the passageway.
FA. R.Mazinke 19.6.1994

17 Insinuation Crack...... 3c *3c*
A bit of a squeeze.

18 Hidden Arete.......... 6a+ *5b*
The arete to the right of *Insinuation Crack*. No chimneying.
FA. M.Vetterlein 19.6.1994

The next four routes are best approached from Krankenkopf Crack area - p.297.

19 Exe Chimney .... 6a+ *5a*
Close to the entrance, climb until it is possible to bridge the chimney. Finish outside the block.
FA. R.Mazinke 12.6.2004

20 Wye Chimney 4a *4a*
An easy alternative 3m further into the passageway, before it splits.

21 Slab Chimney 3c *3c*
The left chimney/passageway is very narrow.

22 Smooth Chimney 4a *4a*
The right passageway.

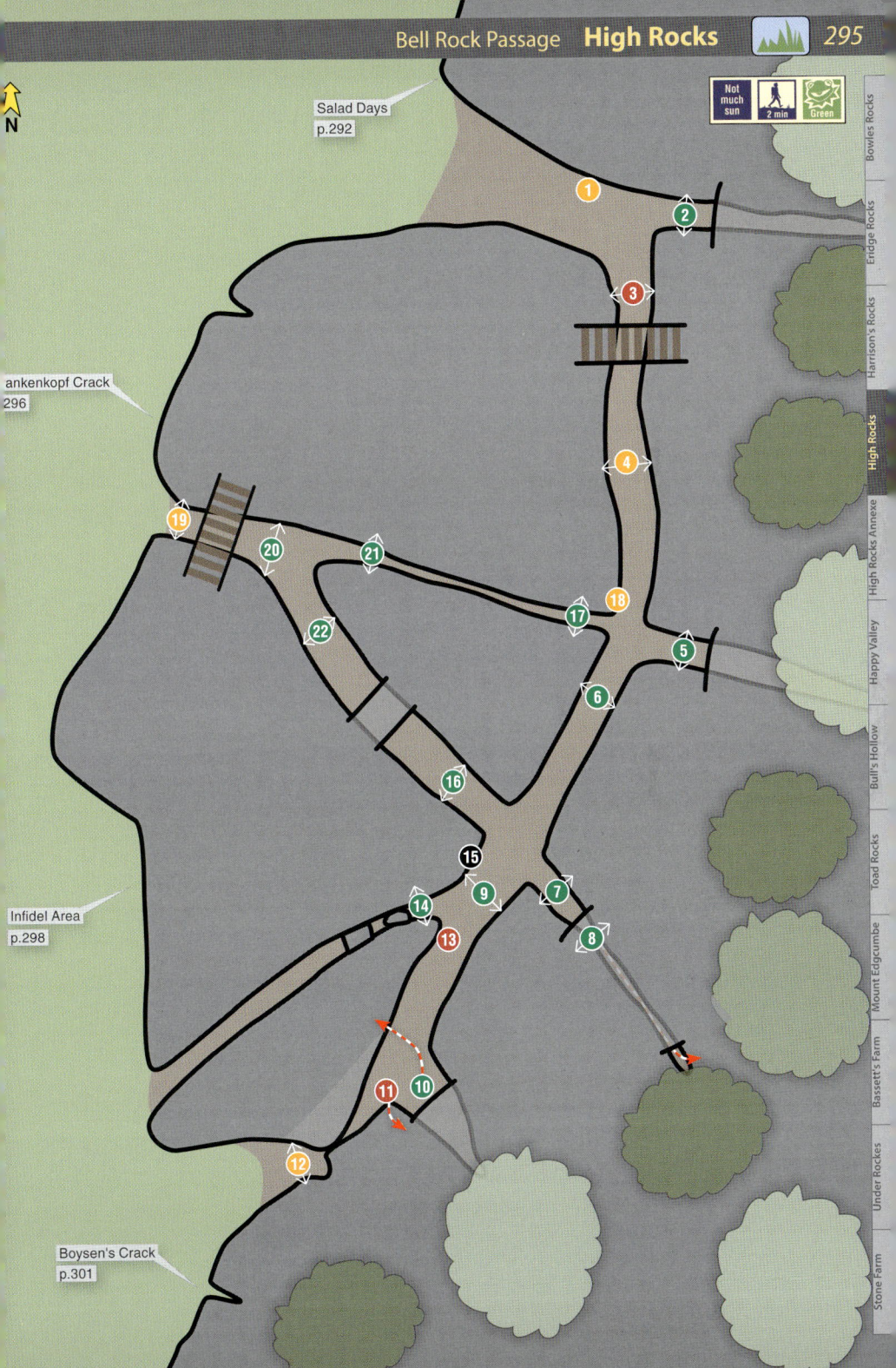

High Rocks — Krankenkopf Crack

1 The Kop f6B
Start on good holds and finish at the lip. Often green.

2 Krankenkopf Crack .... 6b+ 5c
Jam your way up the crack, which eases the higher you get. If you are no good at jamming, you will find this hard!
FA. W.Maxwell 18.7.1954

3 Spanked f6C
Long moves between reasonable holds, finishing at the jug.
FA. I.Stronghill 12.7.2005

4 Superfly f7A
A popular testpiece here. Start as for *Spanked* and head up and right to finish at the break. Purists will avoid using the large ledge out right for your heel. It can be done from a standing start at **f6C+** and used as a direct start to *Kraken* - **Kranked, 7b 6b.**
FA. I.Hufton 12.7.2005

Krankenkopf Crack — High Rocks

❺ Kraken .... 7a+ *6b*
Dyno for the ledge (difficult start for the short) and climb the blunt arete above *Superfly*.
FA. P.Widdowson 7.4.1990

❻ The Dragon .... 6c+ *6a*
Perhaps the most popular route on this wall. Follow the overhanging crack to the ledge and move diagonally left to reach an upside-down scoop. Things ease after this.
FA. J.Smoker, aid 6.9.1959. First free ascent went unrecorded.

❼ Robin's Route .... 6c+ *6a*
After a steep bulging start, head for the off-width at the top.
FA. R.Harper 1960s

❽ So What? .... 7a+ *6b*
Climb the bulge on spaced holds to some poor slopers at the halfway mark. An undercut helps you gain the ledge above. Climb the rest with care - popping off at this point is just plain annoying!
FA. P.Hayes 15.7.1990

❾ The Rip *f6C*
A good low-level traverse finishing at the higher starting holds on *Superfly*.

Krankenkopf Crack

An often overlooked area to the left of the impressive Infidel Area. It is often green and mossy, but a heat wave and northwest winds can bring this wall back to life. Once things dry up there is something of interest though mainly in the higher grades.

Approach (see map page 277 and overview page 278) - From the main entrance, head left for approximately 100m, passing the Infidel Area, until you reach the bulging wall close to the fence.

Set-up and Descent - Use the steps at the end of the Grand Canyon - p.304.

❿ Snowdrop 8a *7a*
A direct line, avoiding the crack on *Dysentery*, to just over the bulge. Continue direct over the lip and finish technically above.
FA. J.Dawes 3.4.1997

⓫ Dysentery .... 6b+ *5c*
A thin and often greasy crack with a winding top section that wanders up *Exe Chimney* for 3m before moving back right to finish.
FA. N.S.Head 1973

⓬ Poppet's Persistence 8a *7a*
An extension to an established boulder problem (**The Gangster, f6B+**) which continues up the face, eventually into an off-width crack.
FA. J.Pearson 8.4.2006

⓭ The Prangster 7a *6b*
A left-hand start to *The Prang* - page 298.
FA. S.Quinton 26.5.1992

High Rocks — Infidel Area

① The Prang — 7a *6a*
Start as for *Magnetic* (standing start) and use a slanting flake to reach for a jug at the break. Grasp the row of stalactites in the break above and traverse left around the arete. Make some sketchy moves on small holds to reach the upper break and finish as for *The Prangster* - page 297.
FA. N.S.Head 1970s

② Magnetic — f7A
A popular sit-start to *The Prang*, encompassing a series of long moves between good but sloping holds. Finish at the row of stalactites. *Photo on page 276.*

③ Lobster — 7a *6a*
A super line up the centre of the wall with a hard move to reach the dirty break. Finish up and right behind the tree or, better still, up the crack in the top block. *Photo opposite.*
FA. P Smoker 1959

④ Infidel — 7a *6a*
A sandstone classic, more for its picturesque and atmospheric nature than the climbing itself. Make some awkward moves low down on wearing pockets to the break. Establish yourself on this with difficulty, and reach for the next break. Traverse right under the roof to make a careful exit around the side-wall.
FA. M.Fowler 13.3.1977

⑤ Henry the Ninth — 6b+ *5c*
A wonderous and seemingly impossible layback up the left side of the arete, which is easier once you know how. Finish as for *Infidel*. *Photo on page 300.*
FA. T.Mayes 1950s

Infidel Area

A stunning wall (also known as Warning Rock) which is easily identified by the Infidel Poem engraving from 1831 on the right-hand wall. There are surprisingly few routes here, mainly due to the steep and featureless nature of the upper faces. Some of the holds are becoming worn, so please take care especially when damp.

Approach (see map page 277 and overview page 278) - From the main entrance, head left for approximately 80m (passing the entrance to the Grand Canyon) until your reach the face.

Set-up and Descent - Use the steps at the end of the Grand Canyon - p.304.

Special Considerations - Unique and protected rock formations are to be found above the routes *Infidel* and *Henry the Ninth*. Please take extra care protecting the rock when setting up ropes and also when climbing. Please also avoid contact with the engravings of the Infidel Poem.

Robin Mazinke powering his way up *Lobster* (7a 6a) - *opposite* - at the Infidel Area of High Rocks.

Emma Harrington on the classic *Henry the Ninth* (6b+ 5c) - *page 298* - at the Infidel Area of High Rocks.

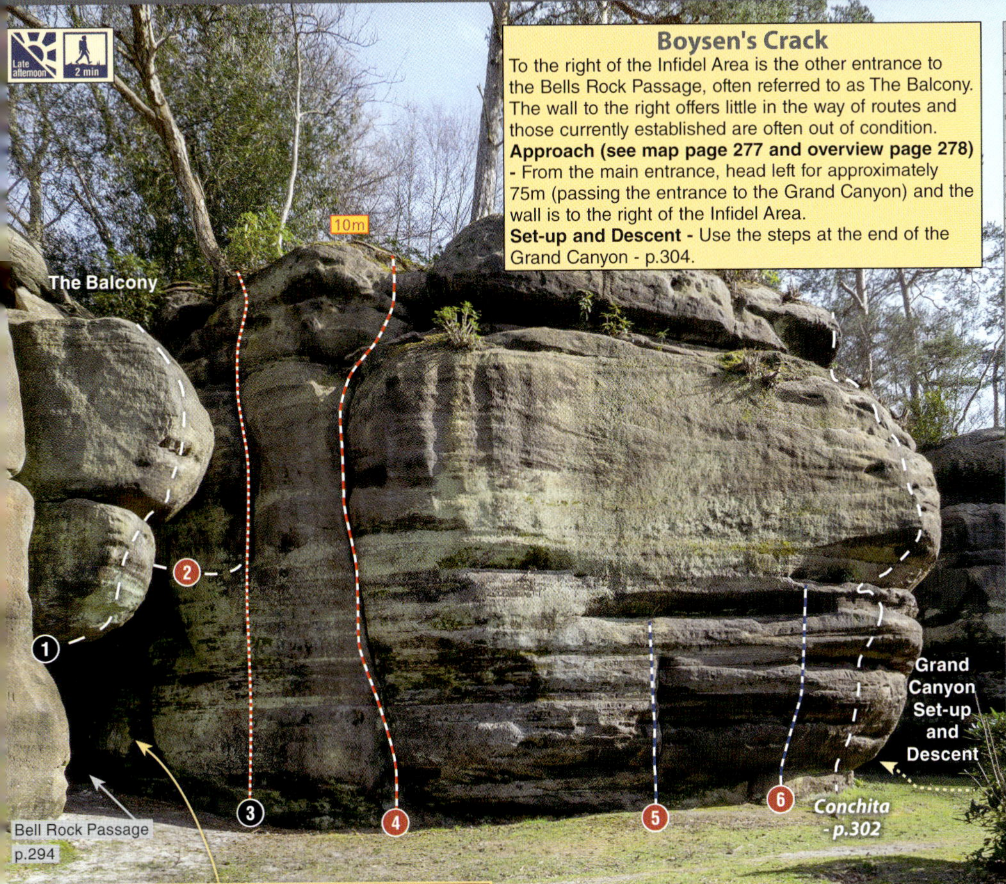

Boysen's Crack — High Rocks

Boysen's Crack

To the right of the Infidel Area is the other entrance to the Bells Rock Passage, often referred to as The Balcony. The wall to the right offers little in the way of routes and those currently established are often out of condition.

Approach (see map page 277 and overview page 278) - From the main entrance, head left for approximately 75m (passing the entrance to the Grand Canyon) and the wall is to the right of the Infidel Area.

Set-up and Descent - Use the steps at the end of the Grand Canyon - p.304.

① Slowhand 7b *6b*
A powerful route up the overhanging nose.
FA. P.Widdowson 5.5.1990

② Jaws 6c *5c*
Start by climbing the left wall and, where possible, bridge out and work your way out of the chimney towards the crack on the opposite wall. Finish by climbing this. Continuing up the left wall from the start without bridging is **Orca, 6b+** *5c*. With bridging and a bit deeper in is **Balcony Direct 4b** *4b*. Both variations finish on The Balcony.
FA. T.Daniells 1970s

③ Fat Start 7c *6c*
A hard direct start to *Jaws*.
FA. J.Dawes 1997

④ Boysen's Crack 6c *6a*
The greasy jamming crack which is good when in condition.

⑤ Boysen's Sack *f4*
Climb the crack from a standing start.

⑥ Boysen's Back *f6A*
Follow positive holds all the way to the break.

High Rocks — Outer Canyon

Outer Canyon

The outer section of the Grand Canyon has a few nice jamming excursions to get stuck into. The top halves of the routes can get dirty and overgrown at times.

Approach (see map page 277 and overview page 278) - From the main entrance, head left for approximately 60m to a large alcove area with the Grand Canyon located at its centre.

Set-up and Descent - Use the steps at the end of the Grand Canyon - p.304.

1 Conchita — 6c+ *6a*
A hard route up the rounded nose. It can be done with a traverse in from the top of *Boysen's Sack* to make things a little easier.
FA. J.Smoker 14.6.1958

2 Havasupai — f5+
Climb the break on big holds throughout.

3 Arizona — f5+
Climb the face to the break avoiding the crack out right.

4 Marquita — 6c *5c*
Tape up those hands and jam your way up the crack. The top section can get muddy at times.
FA. J.Smoker 14.6.1958

5 Lucita — 6c *6a*
Either take the hard direct start, or traverse in more easily from the right (original line). Finish with some off-width action at the top. The top section can get dirty.
FA. J.Smoker 28.6.1958

6 Slant Eyes — 6b+ *5c*
Follow the series of pockets up and right to join *The Gibbet* at the tree.
FA. M.Fowler 12.8.1978

7 Mocasyn — 7b+ *6c*
A hard variation with a tiny mono and some reachy moves. Keep things pure by avoiding the break out right at two thirds height.
FA. L.Percival 5.8.1995

8 The Gibbet — 6a+ *5b*
A grotty crack. Exit beyond the tree.
FA. J.Smoker 24.11.1956

David Collom mid-flight on *Chez's Dyno* (**f7B**) - *page 316* - on Mulligan's Wall at High Rocks.

High Rocks — Grand Canyon

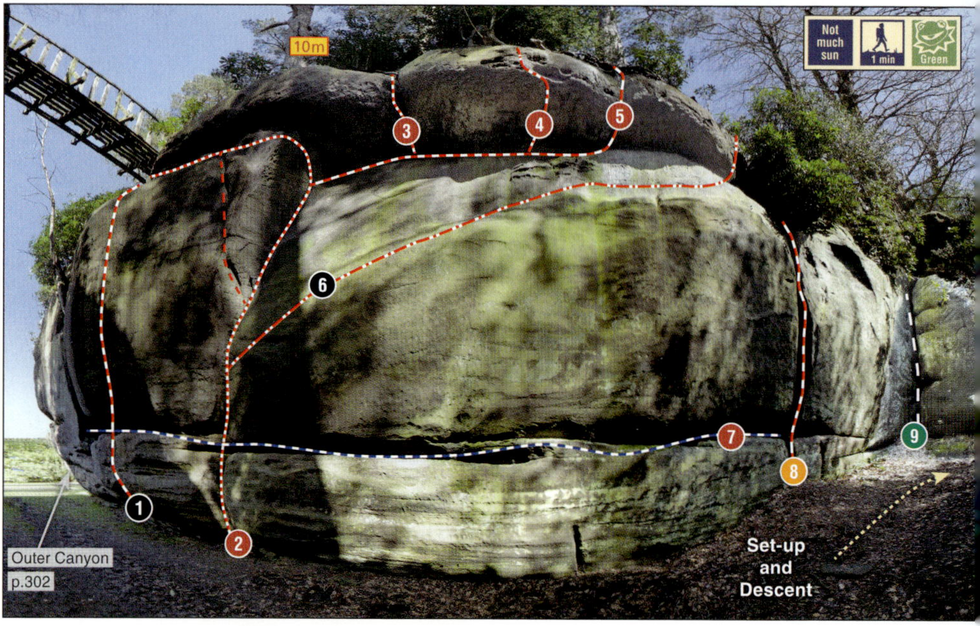

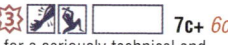

Grand Canyon
Cut deep into the rocks is the Grand Canyon, with its green and shady walls. The further in you get, the more esoteric the routes become. Good conditions are rare.
Approach (see map page 277 and overview page 278) - From the main entrance, head left for approximately 60m to a large alcove area with the Grand Canyon at its centre.
Set-up and Descent - This is easily done via the steps at the end of the passage.

❶ Cool Bananas . . . . . **7c+** *6c*
Take the rounded arete and face for a seriously technical and sustained outing with an uncomfortable top-out.
FA. D.Turner 20.8.1987

❷ Effie **6b** *5b*
Climb the crack to the roof and traverse left to finish at the bridge. Taking the left fork at just over half height is **6c** *6a*.
FA. G.Clarke 1.11.1956

❸ Effie Right-hand Finish . . **6c** *5c*
The first in a trilogy of right-hand exits to *Effie*, this one tackling the first crack in the roof.
FA. M.Fowler 1976

❹ PMA . . . . **6c+** *6a*
Tackle the bulge at its centre just below the tree stump.
FA. P.Hayes 1987

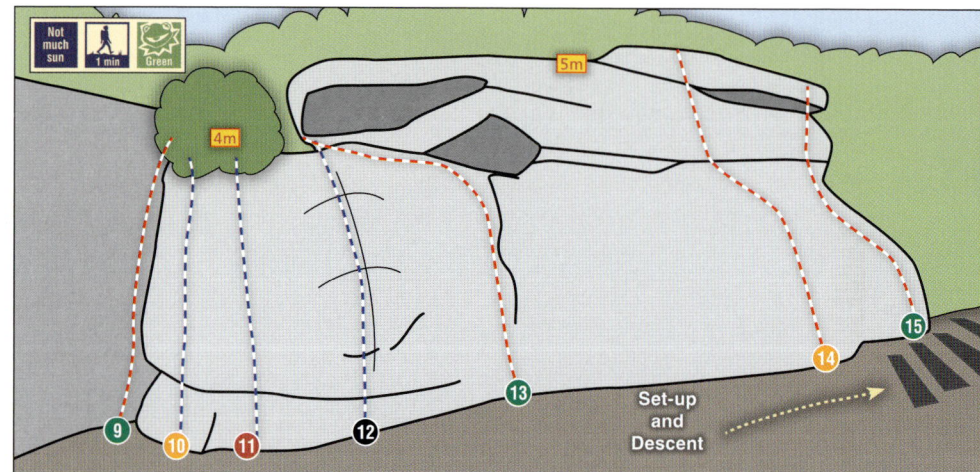

Grand Canyon High Rocks

5 Canyon Crack .... 6b+ *5c*
A thinner but slightly easier crack climb through the bulge.
FA. M.Fowler 1976

6 Indian Railways .... 7a+ *6b*
Move right out of *Effie* onto the slab and make a desperate rising traverse across the vague rib.
FA. J.Dawes 2011

7 Grand Canyon f6C
A sustained low-level traverse on slopers for the most part, finishing at the start of *The Gibbet* - page 302.

8 Mamba Crack .... 6a+ *5b*
A short and unpleasant crack climb.

9 Colorado Crack 3c *3c*
A poor crack climb finishing on the ledge.

10 Harold Hill Arete f5
The face and arete right of *Colorado Crack*.
FA. M.Vetterlein 30.1.2005

11 Ockendon Slab f6A
A short problem up the arete, moving onto the slab to finish.
FA. S.Allen 16.7.1989

12 Orcanyon f7A
A hard, green slab problem up centre of the face.
FA. C.George

13 Rattlesnake 4c *4c*
An esoteric corner-crack.

14 Bright Eyes .... 6a+ *5b*
Climb diagonally left to finish at the tree stumps. Never in condition.
FA. T.Daniells 1970s

15 Short Chimney 2 .... 3a *3a*
The grotty crack is like something out of an Indiana Jones movie.

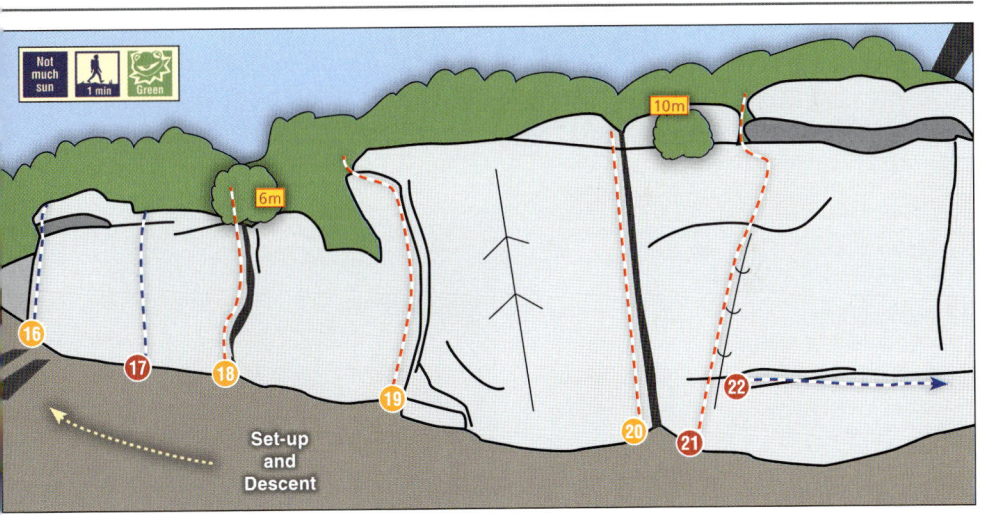

The other side of the Grand Canyon gets no sunlight and is always green. The routes listed have been climbed but you will need exceptional conditions to do them.

16 The Carcass .... f5+
A short mossy arete problem.
FA. I.Stronghill 2005

17 Growing Pains .... f6C+
A reachy problem up the face. The grade depends on your height and the conditions.
FA. C.George 2005

18 Issingdown .... 6a+ *5b*
Layback the crack, top out and take a shower after.

19 Python Crack 5c *5a*
The flake/crack, traversing left to finish.
FA. F.K.Elliot 18.4.1943

20 Beanstalk .... 6a+ *5b*
An awkward off-width crack.
FA. J.Smoker 24.11.1956

21 Peapod 7a *6b*
Climb the vague and difficult groove diagonally rightwards. Exit left up the top crack.
FA. M.Boyson 1986

22 Pea Cheetah f6B
Traverse the break finishing on the jugs at the top of *Ben's a Woofter*.

High Rocks — Krait Arete

1 Ben's a Woofter f6C
Follow the crack-line finishing at jugs.

2 The Green Mile f6A
Traverse right finishing at the break.

3 Cheetah .... 7a+ *6b*
The arete on its right side with a hard move over the lower mossy bulge. Exit left at the top.
FA. T.G.DeLacy 1973

4 Coronation Crack .... 6b+ *5c*
Serious jamming technique is required for this true High Rocks classic.
FA. W.Maxwell 18.7.1954

5 All Hale f6C
A series of undercut holds lead to the thin break.

6 Hale Bopp 8a *7a*
An outstanding project which awaits completion. The left-hand start is the same grade. Can you finish it?
FA. (to current high point) J.Dawes 1997

7 Krait Arete 7b *6b*
A true classic and perhaps the best of its grade in the southeast. The move onto the arete is very tricky, but after this the holds improve the higher you go. *Photo opposite.*
The direct start is **Krait Direct, 7b+** *6b*.
FA. M.Boysen 1980s. FA. (Krait Direct) J.Dawes 2007

Krait Arete — High Rocks

8 Bad Blood 7c *6c*
Start up *Krait Arete* but finish up the wall out left avoiding the arete at the top.
FA. J.Sharpe 19.8.1991

9 Shelter Arete .... 6b+ *5c*
An eliminate launching from the top of the air-raid shelter to tackle the upper arete without touching the right-hand wall (which is near impossible). Finish on the left wall inside the passage.

10 Chimney Routes 3c *3c*
The chimney from the air-raid shelter is **3c** *3c*. **Shelter Passage, 4b** *4b* starts halfway up the passage and has several variations to it. **Moria, 7a** *6a* takes the crack on the right-hand wall avoiding the back wall and not stepping back at the top. This can also be done as a chimney route.
FA. (Moria) R.Mazinke. 12.6.2014
FA. (Moria Chimney Variation) D.Beail 26.6.1998

11 The Oligarchy 6c *6a*
Start on soft rock and finish using the right-hand arete.
FA. M.Vetterlein 19.5.1991

The master of movement and levitation - Johnny Dawes who has in the past made reference to the futuristic possibilities at High Rocks. Here Johnny is climbing one of the star prizes at High Rocks - *Krait Arete* (7b *6b*) - *opposite*. Photo: Tim Skinner

Krait Arete
To the right of the Grand Canyon is a wall with two classic sandstone routes and an old air-raid shelter.
Approach (see map page 277 and overview page 278) - From the main entrance, head left for approximately 50m to a large alcove area with the Grand Canyon at its centre. This wall is to the right of the entrance.
Set-up and Descent - Use the steps at the end of the Grand Canyon, or squeeze your way up or down the air-raid shelter passage.

High Rocks — Advertisement Wall

Advertisement Wall

A popular wall with some great lines, which are easily identified by the series of square cut-out holds across the upper face. The holds were originally created for attaching an advertisement board.

Approach (see map page 277 and overview page 278) - From the main entrance, head left for 30m and follow the path to emerge in this area.

Set-up and Descent - Use the steps at the end of the Grand Canyon - p.304 - or squeeze your way up or down one of the passages.

❶ Advertisement Wall Direct 6b *5c*
Climb the arete and the left side of the wall, which is quite worn in places.

❷ Engagement Wall. . . . . . Top 50 6c *6a*
Fantastic climbing throughout. Start delicately up the centre of the lower slab, then transfer onto the upper wall using the cut-out pockets to gain the break above. Negotiating the last section is much easier once you know how.
Photo opposite and page 7.
FA. J.Smoker 19.7.1958

❸ Advertisement Wall . . . . Top 50 6a *5b*
Another great route, with an adventurous section crossing the slab to gain the square pockets on the left side of the wall. Finish more steeply up the headwall. *Photo on page 270.*
FA. P.Smoker 11.3.1956

❹ Dyno-Sore. . . . . 2 7a+ *6b*
More square pocket pulling, this time with a big dyno required to gain the second break.
FA. D.Turner 16.8.1987

❺ Quirkus. 5a *4c*
Start up the crack and traverse right onto the side face. Exit above using the tree.

❻ Genevieve. . . . . 1 6c+ *6a*
A tricky and awkward arete problem avoiding use of the tree.
FA. P.Widdowson 18.3.1990

Zara Bloomfield on *Engagement Wall* (6c *6a*) - *opposite* - on the Advertisement Wall at High Rocks.

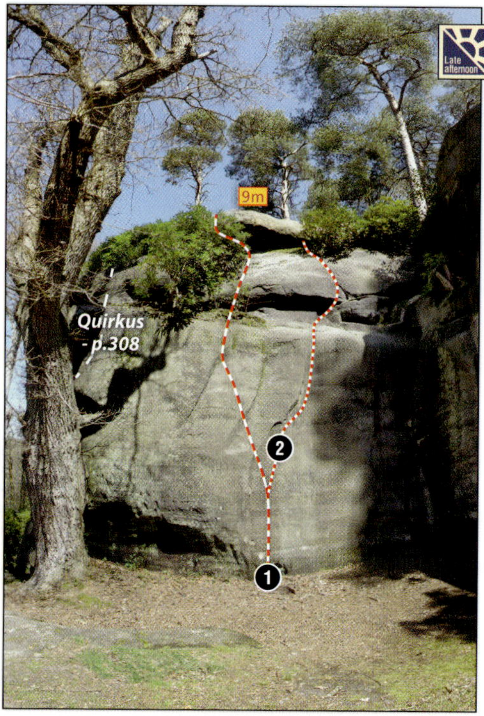

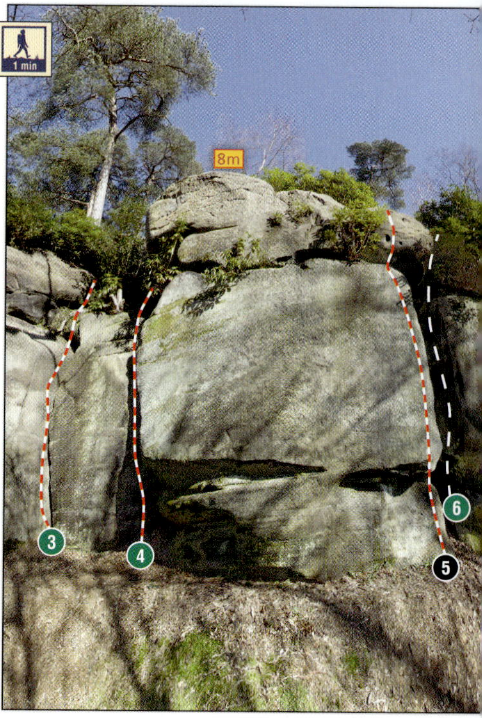

High Rocks — Crypt Crack Area

Crypt Crack Area
An interesting area with a mixture of easy and hard routes incorporating a variety of climbing styles.
Approach (see map page 277) - Head left from the main entrance for 30m to emerge approximately in this location. This area is just right of Advertisement Wall.
Set-up and Descent - Head around the Yoda boulder, and for a bit more fun on the descent, squeeze down the *Short Chimney* passage.

❶ The Continuing Adventures of Porg .... 7c+ *6c*
Powerful terrain up the face using layaways.
FA. L.Percival 26.8.1995

❷ Porg's Progress 7c *6c*
The right-hand version has a difficult mantel onto the first ledge.
FA. P.Widdowson 17.5.1992

❸ Dirty Dick 4c *4c*
The short thin corner crack is a good laybacking problem.

❹ Crypt Crack 4b *4b*
An awkward off-width which is harder higher up.

❺ Look Sharp .... 7a+ *6b*
Layback the arete avoiding the temptation to slip into *Short Chimney*.
FA. G.McLelland 1.9.1984

❻ Short Chimney 4a *4a*
Squirm up the front entrance of the passage.
Starting further inside the passage gives **Jalapeno, 3c** *3c*.
Broadwood, 3c *3c* is a few metres in from the far end.
Sharp Arete, f6B tackles the short arete, from a sit-start, at the entrance to the far side.
FA. G.McLelland 1.9.1984. FA. (Jalapeno) M.Eden 25.4.1999. FA. (Broadwood) R.Mazinke 25.4.1999
FA. (Sharp Arete) R.Mazinke 19.4.1999

❼ Natterjack 7a *6b*
The leftmost set of square pockets gives a very fingery climb.
FA. M.Vetterlein 1.4.1990

❽ Death Cap 7a *6b*
Pocket pulling up the centre of the wall.
FA. M.Vetterlein 13.5.1991

❾ Mervin Direct 7a *6b*
Keep firmly to the right-hand set of pockets, avoiding all contact with the arete and flake of *Crack and Wall Front* at the top.
FA. G.Wickham 1986

❿ Crack and Wall Front ... 6b *5c*
Tackle the lower crack to gain the arete and make some delicate moves to gain the equally delicate flake above.

Crypt Crack Area — High Rocks

11 Yoda Assis f7C
An eliminate problem (avoiding contact with the wall out left) with a nasty mantel finish.
FA. I.Stronghill 2006

12 Yoda .... f7A+
The standing start variation of *Yoda Assis*, starting slightly to the right.
FA. C.George 2005

13 Tarkin Slab f5
A short slab climb to the left of the face.

14 Dagobah f6B
The face to the right of the slab.

15 Dagobah Scoop f6A
The vague nose and scoop.

16 Re-emergence .... f6A+
From a crouch start, tackle the bulging nose and perform a difficult mantel to finish. Using the dirty crack on the right reduces the grade significantly.

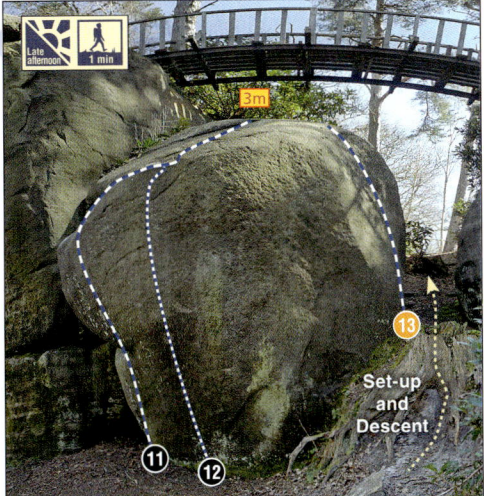

High Rocks — Kinda Lingers

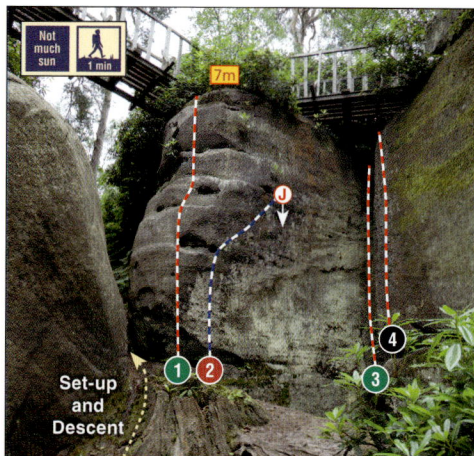

Kinda Lingers

To the right of the passage and wrapping back down to the main path from Crypt Crack Area is a monolith of rock which has found a new lease of life, primarily with boulderers.

Approach (see map page 277) - Head right from the main entrance and up the steps for about 30m. Turn left on the path running under the rocks and walk for 10m to reach the wall with its large roof on its right side.

Set-up and Descent - Go up the gully to the left.

No climbing is permitted when weddings are taking place - see page 274.

❶ Hut Transverse Arete 4c *4c*
The arete is often overgrown at the top.

❷ Outspan .... f6C+
A short problem leaping from pocket to pocket.
FA. I.Stronghill 2005

❸ Hut Transverse Passage Ordinary Route
.... 3c *3c*
Back and foot up the passage, closest to the entrance.

❹ I'll Be Back .... 7b+ *6c*
The arete on its right side, finishing around the bridge above.
FA. J.Sharpe 26.8.1991

❺ Educating Airlie 7a *6b*
A green outing, up the right side of the face. The small crack higher up gives much needed assistance.
FA. M.Vetterlein 10.8.1991

❻ Deva Loka f7C
A left-hand start into the *Kinda Lingers* boulder problem. Good heel action and powerful moves are required on the arete to reach the first break where this problem ends.

❼ Kinda Lingers 7c *6c*
Climbing the arete to the first break from a standing start, is a popular boulder problem at *f7A+*. Continue up the remainder of the arete for the full experience and a damn fine finish!
FA. J.Sharpe, G.Wickham 13.5.1990

❽ Kinda Lingers Original Start ... 7b+ *6c*
The original start is pretty hard as well. Make a series of impossible moves to gain the line of pockets. Traverse back left onto the arete and finish up it.
FA. G.Wickham 28.7.1986

❾ Kinda Wanders .... f7A+
A hard traverse along the break line, finishing with some long moves between pockets ending at the vague break. Link into *Kinda Lingers* for a king tick!

❿ Darth Vader .... f7A+
An excellent arete problem with a stopper move just before the upper break. The break out left is often used. From standing it is only slightly easier at *f7A*. *Photo on page 291.*
FA. C.George 2005

⓫ Roobarb 7a *6b*
Climb the centre of the wall and traverse right to exit up the chimney.
FA. M.Fowler 8.7.1979

⓬ All That Meat but Only Two Veg
.... 6c+ *6a*
Start as for *Roobarb*, but then bridge out to the tree and proceed upwards moving between rock and tree. Desperate!
FA. M.Saunders 1980s

⓭ Roobarb Arete .... f5+
A short problem up the right arete to the break. Can also be done as a direct start to *Roobarb*.

High Rocks — Boonoonoonoos

Boonoonoonoos

Approach (see map page 277) - The first area you come to when turning right at the entrance and following the path for 30m.

Set-up and Descent - Go past the Yoda boulder, left of the Kinda Lingers area - p.312.

🚫 **No climbing is permitted when weddings are taking place - see page 274.**

❶ Brushwood Chimney 3c *3c*
The wide green chimney has an unfortunate mossy finish.

❷ Amnesia Variations 6b *5c*
An alternative and easier start to *Unforgettable*. Traverse right under the roof from *Brushwood Chimney* and join *Unforgettable* at the top of the arete.
FA. M.Gallagher 1992

❸ Miracle . . . . f6A+
The arete, mainly on its right side, to the break.

❹ Unforgettable . . . . . 7c+ *6c*
An impressive route with a tough lower section followed by a magnificent and taxing arete. Thankfully it eases above.
FA. P.Hayes 1989

❺ Crackless . . . . f5+
A short problem up the crack without actually using it.

❻ Boonoonoonoos . . . . 7a+ *6b*
A classic steep route that can soon zap your energy, especially if you can't easily dispatch the reachy moves on the upper wall. Avoid all use of the tempting tree to your right.
Photo opposite and page 51.
FA. D.Turner 1980s

Tim Skinner making the reachy moves on *Boonoonoonoos* (7a+ 6b) - *opposite* - at the Boonoonoonoos area of High Rocks.

High Rocks — Mulligan's Wall

Mulligan's Wall

One of High Rocks' most picturesque and popular climbing areas. The route *Celebration* stands out as a fine example of what High Rocks has to offer. The routes starting above the steps can be started with or without them.

Approach (see map page 277) - Turn right at the entrance and continue for approximately 40m to the steps past Boonoonoonoos.

Set-up and Descent - Head left and walk up and around the Yoda boulder in the Kinda Lingers Area - p.312.

⛔ No climbing is permitted when weddings are taking place - see page 274.

Hut Transverse Passage Rufrock Route - p.318

Tilley Lamp Crack - p.31

1 Firebird .... 6c+ *6a*
Climb the wall left of (and avoiding contact with) *Mulligan's Wall*. It has good holds throughout, but never as good as you want them to be.
FA. T.Daniells 1978

2 Mulligan's Wall 6c *5c*
Launch from the steps and follow the crack, jamming as you go, to the break. Either finish direct at 7a *6a*, or make an unusual traverse left to finish with the help of the tree.
FA. D.Ingray 3.5.1959

3 Bludgeon 6c *5c*
A link from *Mulligan's Wall* into the final moves up the open crack on *Firefly*.
FA. M.Boysen 1959

4 Smoke .... 7b+ *6b*
From the steps, climb the series of bulges direct to finish left of *Firefly* via some slightly sloping holds.
FA. A.Grigg 11.9.1992

5 Firefly 7b *6b*
Gain the poor crack above the first break - sandy holds. Head diagonally leftwards to finish up the wide and difficult crack.
FA. M.Fowler 13.7.1977

6 Chez's Dyno f7B
An impressive dyno between breaks. Using additional holds between drops the grade to **f6B+**. Photo on page 303.
FA. C.George 2002

7 Celebration 6b *5c*
A High Rocks classic. Start up the honeycomb wall to the break and head left to the rounded arete. Climb this, moving slightly right to finish. Use of the rhododendron stump is allowed at the top.
FA. P.Smoker 10.4.1959

8 Champagne Celebration . 6c+ *6a*
A hard direct finish to *Celebration*, using a series of slots and crimps to the same exit as the original.
FA. G.McLelland 1981

Laurence Ellis digging his fingers into the crimpy *Nemesis* (7a+ *6b*) - *page 318* - at the Nemesis area of High Rocks. Photo: Tim Skinner.

High Rocks — Nemesis

Nemesis

The pockety main wall of Nemesis is both inspiring and intimidating. Tape up before trying anything here unless your fingers are made of steel!

Approach (see map page 277) - Turn right at the entrance and continue for approximately 50m up the steps past Mulligan's Wall. The wall runs behind the Hut Boulder.

Set-up and Descent - Head left and walk up and around the Yoda boulder in the Kinda Lingers area - p.312.

⛔ **No climbing is permitted when weddings are taking place - see page 274.**

4 Tilley Lamp Crack .. 7a *6a*
Attack the crack then make some fingery moves to gain the break. Save a bit for the final groove at the top.
FA. G.Clarke 1960s

5 Lord .... f6A+
A nice traverse along the break with a tricky finish.
FA. D.Atchison-Jones 1982

1 Hut Transverse Passage Rufrock Route
.... 4c *4c*
A chimney climb.

2 Bletchley Park ..... 7c+ *6c*
An eliminate up the arete without bridging, and avoiding the routes to the right.
FA. J.Dawes 2011

3 Lamp Light .... 7a+ *6b*
A tight eliminate up the centre of the face - no crack allowed.
FA. B.Knight 1996

6 Much Too Much 7a *6b*
Fingery face climbing which is not entirely independent of its neighbour *Nemesis*.
FA. S.Thomas 7.8.1998

7 Nemesis ...... Top 50 7a+ *6b*
A fingery and powerful testpiece with some fierce pocket pulling to gain the break. Finish up and right with whatever forearm strength you have left. *Photo on page 317.*
FA. G.Wickham 3.7.1986

Nemesis — High Rocks

8 Nemesis Inferno ... 7c *6c*
A squeezed-in eliminate using pockets which slowly deteriorate the higher you go. Make a very hard move to gain the break. Step left to finish.
FA. J.Thornton 28.7.2014

9 A Touch Too Much 7a *6b*
More pocket pulling with a difficult move to reach the break.
FA. M.Saunders 14.10.1985

10 Viper Crack .... 6a+ *5b*
Layback, bridge and jam the corner-crack. *Photo on page 275.*

11 Shattered 7a *6b*
Much harder than it looks and often highballed.
FA. D.Atchison-Jones 1982

12 Ponytail Pearson (and His Shorts of Doom)
.... 7c *6b*
A blank and technical problem up the face.
FA. J.Sharpe 28.4.1991

13 Jug of Flowers. .... 7b+ *6b*
Using undercuts to get started, climb the right side of the wall past a square-cut pocket.
FA. G.McLelland 1980s

14 Easy Crack 3c *3c*
A straightforward jamming crack.

15 Mike's Left Knee .... 6c+ *6a*
Aim for the square-cut pocket and finish above.
FA. P.Widdowson 7.4.1990

16 Bald Finish 6a *5a*
A good arete climb with a ...... guess!

17 Unfinished Business. .... *f6A+*
A short problem with a crouching start from a crimp using the left arete to slap up to the top. Finish with a bushy mantel or jump off and call it quits.
FA. I.Stronghill 21.7.2005

High Rocks — Hut Boulder

Hut Boulder

The Hut Boulder is named after a tiny hut which was built into the rocks in Victorian times. The boulder is popular, with routes all the way round at reasonable grades.

Approach (see map page 277) - From the main entrance, take the right-hand fork after approximately 55m and go up the steps to the boulder opposite Nemesis.

Set-up - Carefully solo either *Crack Route* or *Long Stretch*. For a protected ascent, locate the bolts opposite the boulder on the mainland side (using the steps which run to the left side of Rhododendron Routes - page 322). Attach an extended top rope anchor that will reach over the far side of Hut Boulder above *Crack Route*. Top rope to the top of the boulder and then set up a new anchor using the bolts there.

Descent - Down-climb *Crack Route* - please do not lower off or abseil!

⛔ No climbing is permitted when weddings are taking place - see page 274.

❶ Cough Drop . . . . 6a+ *5b*
Head up the open crack and move left to climb the thin flakes finishing by the small tree.
FA. D.R.Stone 16.5.1953

❷ Rhino's Eyebrow 6a *5a*
A dirty climb with which rarely sees sunlight.
FA. V.Hayden 16.8.1953

❸ Corsican Proposal 7a *6b*
The arete and mossy face above. Often avoided.
FA. C.Arnold 1996

❹ Roofus 7a *6b*
A impressive route on good holds up the overhanging nose to a horrific top-out. The original line of Id, 6c *6a*, finishes up and right of the nose.
FA. G.McLelland 19.8.1983. FA. (Id) G.Hughes 1962

❺ Long Stretch 6c *6a*
Difficult moves to gain the crack. Things ease off there-after.
FA. J.Smoker 17.5.1958

❻ Bludnok Wall 6b *5c*
A reachy proposition to gain the thin break above. Either traverse left to finish, or make things hard for yourself by topping out direct - **7a** *6b*.
FA. J.Smoker 24.8.1957. FA. (Direct Finish) R.Mazinke 7.5.2005

❼ Crack Route 4c *4c*
The easiest way up and down the block, but ensure you know where the jugs are, especially if soloing.
FA. A.R.Serraillier 1930s

Hut Boulder — High Rocks   321

12 Roof Route 6a *5b*
The main artery crossing the back side of the boulder, which is also used to start two other routes. For the full outing, follow the crack all the way right to finish left of the tree stump.

13 Birthday Arete 6a *5b*
A lovely outing up the right arete on nicely spaced in-cut holds. It is also a potential down-climb if you have something left in the tank, but keep that rope slack!
FA. D.R.Stone 15.8.1953

14 Sequins of Cosmic Turbulence
. . . . 6b *5c*
The face right of *Birthday Arete*. Eliminate in places, but enjoyable nevertheless.
FA. D.Atchinson-Jones 1992

15 Diamonds in Orion . . . . . 6b+ *5c*
After a series of moves over the bulge on some plastery and burnt-out square pockets from the remains of the hut, continue direct up the face above more easily (ish).

16 Rockney 6c *5c*
Manoeuvre over the remains of the old hut past a large square-cut hold. Make a difficult move past this to easier climbing beyond. It is easier to start further right over the bricks if desired.
FA. B.Franklin 1980s

8 Pinchgrip 6b *5c*
Delicate face climbing to the right of the crack.
FA. W.Maxwell 1.4.1956

9 Pussyfoot 6a *5b*
A nice line up the arete past a series of rounded ledges.
FA. J.R.Lees 14.5.1949

10 Swing Face Direct . . 6b+ *5c*
The direct start to *Swing Face*. Often done as a boulder problem from a sit-start to where it joins *Swing Face* - **Unfinished Business** *f6A*.

11 Swing Face . . . . 6a+ *5b*
A great route up the centre of the face after an awkward initial traverse. Missing the good holds between the breaks can make things very pumpy indeed. *Photo on page 322.*
FA. F.K.Elliot 18.4.1943

Sarah Goodman on *Swing Face* (6a+ *5b*) - page 321 - on the Hut Boulder at High Rocks.

High Rocks — Rhododendron Routes

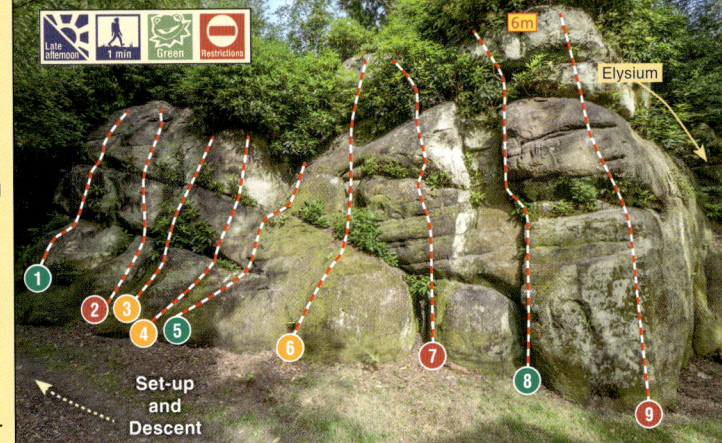

Rhododendron Routes

A selection of short routes which are quickly overrun with rhododendrons if not maintained. Very green.

Approach (see map page 277) - Take the right-hand fork at the main entrance and follow the path up the steps and onto the flat concreted path that runs past the Hut Boulder. The wall is beyond this up on the left.

Set-up and Descent - Stairs to the left lead to the top of the crag.

⛔ No climbing is permitted when weddings are taking place - see page 274.

❶ Bush Arete 4b *4b*
The left arete.

❷ Hornet 6b *5c*
The nose left of the groove.
FA. T.Skinner 7.5.2005

❸ Open Groove 6a *5b*
The groove, making good use of the breaks where possible.

❹ Spoon 5b *5a*
The nose right of *Open Groove*.
FA. R.Mazinke 7.5.2005

❺ Green Ernie 3a *3a*
Easy mossy gully climbing for true adventure fiends.
FA. G.Adcock 7.5.2005

❻ Helyotosis 5b *5a*
Mossy slab climbing and nothing much else.
FA. H.Boylan 7.5.2005

❼ Hull Motors 6c *6a*
Much like the name, pretty uninspiring.
FA. B.Kavanagh 17.4.2006

❽ Rhododendron Route 4a *4a*
Climb the groove and do battle with the plant life.
FA. JMCS 1942

❾ Seaman's Wall . . . . 6b+ *5c*
An impossibly green lower wall which improves higher up.

Elysium

A green wall which is only climbable after prolonged dry spells.

❿ Elysium . . . . f6B+
A short-lived and frustrating slab climb.
FA. G.Taylor 2005

⓫ Sinbad f7B
The centre of the slab with a difficult mantel.
FA. G.Taylor 2009

⓬ Step On f6A
Technical and mossy.
FA. R.Mazinke 7.5.2005

⓭ Silly Corner f3
The dirty corner-crack finishing left of the bridge.
FA. C.Boylan 7.5.2005

⓮ Amelia's Little Problem . . . f4
A short problem up the nose.
FA. A.Randall 17.4.2005

Bowles Rocks
Eridge Rocks
Harrison's Rocks
High Rocks
High Rocks Annexe
Happy Valley
Bull's Hollow
Toad Rocks
Mount Edgcumbe
Bassett's Farm
Under Rockes
Stone Farm

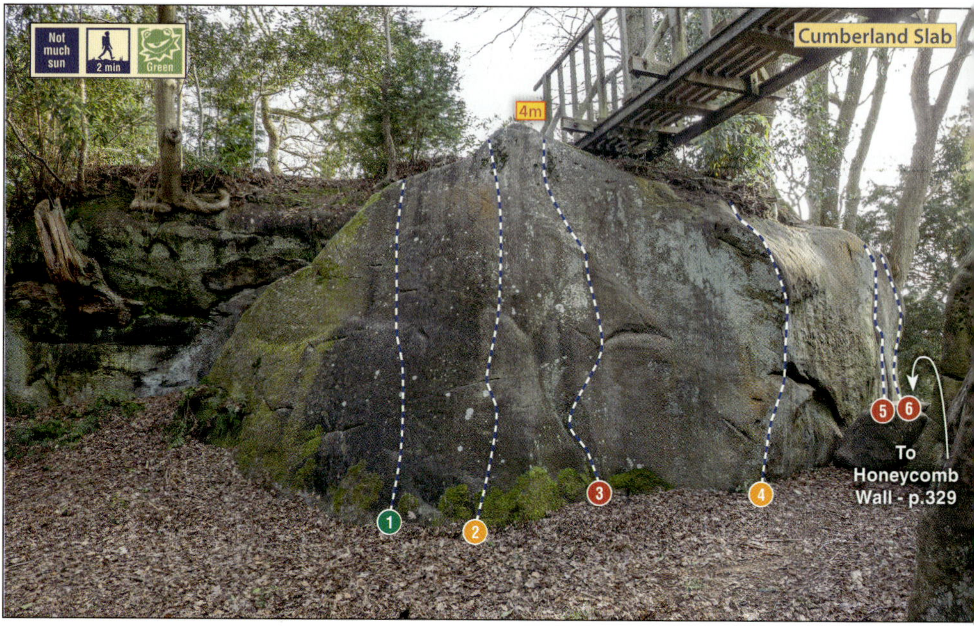

Secret Garden

A pleasant little area for boulderers.

Approach (see map page 277) - Take the right-hand fork at the main entrance and follow the path up the steps and onto the flat concreted path that runs past the Hut Boulder. Continue rightwards up the gully to the left of Odin's Wall, to the area around to the right behind the main walls.

Please take note of any bouldering restrictions that may be in place. See page 276 for further information.

Cumberland Slab

A nice slab to the left of the bay.

1 Yellimo . . . . 1★ f3
A nice problem manteling past a shallow ledge.

2 Cumberland . . . . 1★ f5
Technical moves to the finish just left of the pinnacle.

3 Extender . . . . 2★ f6B+
Harder than its cousin *Cumberland* and certainly more engaging. It is possible to finish with a dyno to the bridge from the sloping ledge - **A Bridge Too Far**, *f6B*.

4 Tricky Dicky . . . . f4+
Finish just right of the bridge. The top-out is a little dirty.

5 Barbed Wire Kiss . . . 1★ f6C
Climb the flakes with difficulty.

6 Quality Control . . . . f6C+
The face just left of the arete is safer to top rope.
FA. I.Hufton 2005

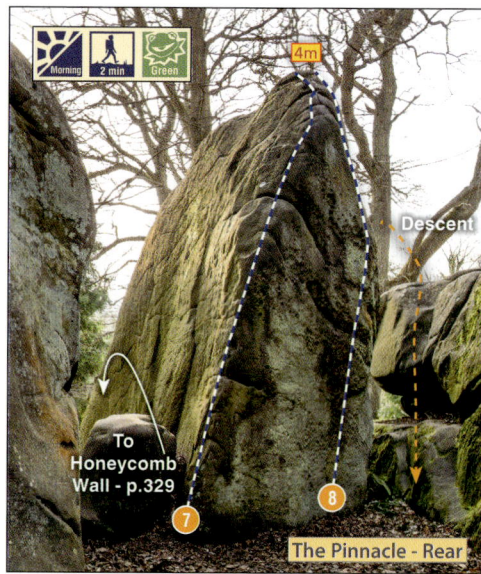

The Pinnacle - Rear

The pinnacle has various names given to it. The descent is slightly awkward, first to the platform to the right, and then back down into the gully. Also see 'The Pinnacle - Front' on page 328.

7 Testimony . . . . 2★ f4+
A fine and popular problem up the arete on good holds.

8 Delirium . . . . 1★ f5
The wall right of *Testimony*.

Secret Garden — High Rocks

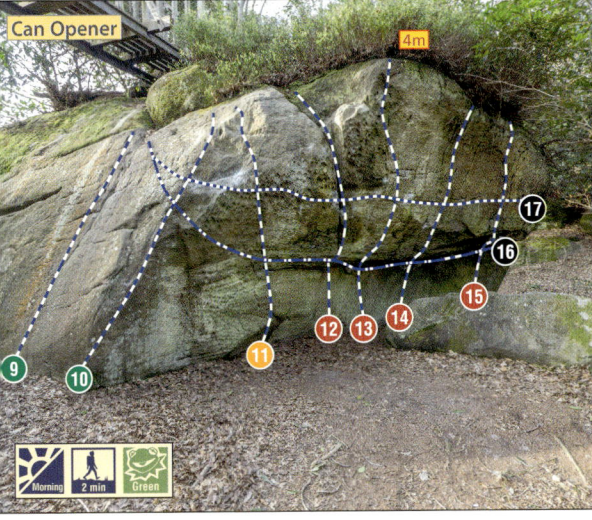
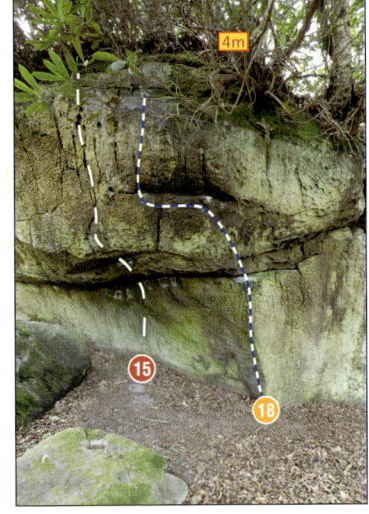

Can Opener
The top-outs on this wall are dirty and awkward. They can all be done without topping out, but expect to give yourself a full grade harder if you do.

⑨ Holly Slab .... ☐ f3
A short slab climb. Topping out is not essential.

⑩ Slappy Arete .... ☐ f4
The arete has a few variations.

⑪ Slap Happy .... ☐ f5+
A good problem to try before tackling the harder ones to the right. Climb the face past the positive curving pocket.

⑫ Can Opener .... ☐ f6C+
An eliminate up the crack using nothing else around it.

⑬ Carbon Fibre ...... ☐ f6C
Powerful moves on pockets and crimps. A two-hand finish at the top, or a battle through the bushes!

⑭ Going Going ...... ☐ f6C+
A good but incredibly fingery undertaking up the featured face.
FA. P.Zeigenfuss 2003

⑮ Moss Side Story ...... ☐ f6B
An easier problem than *Going Going*, but still very fingery!
FA. P.Zeigenfuss 2003

⑯ Bum Dragon .... ☐ f7C
A sustained and powerful traverse starting on *Scrap Arete* and traversing the lower break. Low to the ground in places.
FA. P.Zeigenfuss 2003

⑰ Crosstown Traffic ... ☐ f7C
An intensely crimpy traverse across the featured face. Finishing just before *Can Opener* is f7B.
FA. I.Stronghill 2003

⑱ Scrap Arete .... ☐ f5
From a crouching start with both hands on the lower break, slap up to the good pocket and move up and left to finish.
FA. R.Mazinke 10.5.2005

Around the corner is a short green wall with difficult top-outs. Boulderers only need to grab a rhododendron to finish.

⑲ Solo .... ☐ f6A
The crack up the centre of the face was originally done from a standing start at **5b** *5a*.

⑳ Han .... ☐ f6A
Pull on using the flake and crimp up the green face above this. Topping out is not essential.

High Rocks — Odin's Wall

Odin's Wall

A good little wall when dry, with one particular star attraction.

Approach (see map page 277) - Take the right-hand fork at the main entrance and follow the path up the steps and onto the flat concreted path that runs past the Hut Boulder. Continue up and right of the gully.

Set-up and Descent - Use the steps past Rhododendron Routes - p.323 - or navigate either left or right around the back of the Secret Garden area - p.324.

Conditions - The walls see little sunlight and tend to stay in a green state for most of the year, but most of the routes are climbable when dry.

🚫 **No climbing is permitted when weddings are taking place - see page 274.**

① Awkward Corner .... 6a+ *5b*
The arete and face to a rounded finish.

② Bow Crack .... 6a+ *5a*
The crack has a hard finish.

③ The Ghost 6c *6a*
An eliminate avoiding holds on adjacent routes. The top-out is problematic.

④ Orrer Crack 6b *5c*
The best on this wall. Claw carefully up the short crack.

⑤ Rum, Bum & Biscuits .... 6c+ *6a*
The face on sharp holds to the break. A dirty top-out follows.
FA. C.Arnold 1980s

⑥ Navy Way 6c *5c*
Climb the wall, keeping away from the arete, using a series of good crimpy holds to the break. Awkward moves above can be even harder in the wrong conditions.

Odin's Wall — High Rocks

7 Bow Spirit .... 6c+ *6a*
This awkward arete has a difficult top section to gain the ledge.

8 Climbers Behaving Badly ... 6b+ *5c*
An eliminate up the face avoiding use of the arete. The top section rejoins *Odin's Wall*, so don't worry about what holds are in or not for the finish.
FA. M.Randall 2000

9 Odin's Wall 6b *5c*
A great route using some incredible honeycomb features to reach the upper break. Take a shake-out before attempting the finish. *Photo on page 334.*
FA. M.Boysen 23.5.1959

10 Something Crack 6c *6a*
Climb the crack which gets thinner the higher you go. Do not underestimate this one!

11 Whiff Whaff .... 7a+ *6b*
A very mossy slab that makes use of the two crack-lines in its upper half.
FA. P.Hayes 1989

At the right-hand side of the slab, up a few short steps, is a curved nose with a few awkward problems on it.

12 Village Life .... f6A+
A basic mantelshelf problem and nothing more.

13 Slick City f7A
A slappy problem on slopers with a mean mantel to finish.

14 Thrust f6A
The shortest of the three and yet another mantelshelf move to scream at.

High Rocks — The Pinnacle - Front

The Pinnacle - Front

The front side of the Pinnacle has a few worthwhile routes.

Approach (see map page 277) - Take the right-hand fork at the main entrance and follow the path up the steps and onto the flat concreted path that runs past the Hut Boulder. Continue up and right to follow the path up a further set of steps. The Pinnacle is at the top of this.

Set-up and Descent - Use the steps to the right of The Diver Roof - p.332 - or climb up behind The Pinnacle-Rear - p.334 - by going around the right side of The Pinnacle into the Secret Garden.

1 Vingt-et-un .... 6c+ 6a
The steep left-hand arete, climbed mostly on its left side. Often underestimated
FA. M.Vetterlein 15.8.1994

2 Profiterole 6b 5c
Keep to the centre of the face, avoiding holds on adjacent routes.
FA. G.McLelland 24.8.1983

3 Degenerate 6a 5a
The nose on good but occasionally rounded holds.

4 Pinnacle Gully .... f6A+
The centre of the wall taking care of the landing.

Honeycomb Wall — High Rocks

Honeycomb Wall

The famous honeycombed wall is one of the many star attractions at High Rocks. It must be treated with care as the holds are delicate and will break if too much pressure is applied.

Approach (see map page 277) - Take the right-hand fork at the main entrance and follow the path up the steps and onto the flat concreted path that runs past the Hut Boulder. Continue up and right to follow the path up a further set of steps. The wall is just right of The Pinnacle.

Set-up and Descent - Use the steps to the right of The Diver Roof - p.332.

5 The Gob 7c *6c*
Start on the left-hand slab and transfer onto the right-hand face higher up to finish. Usually too green.
FA. L.Percival 1994

6 Honeycomb Variant .... 7b+ *6b*
The face to the left of *Honeycomb*. Friable holds throughout so take extra care. Look out for some chipped holds at the top.
FA. D.Turner 1986

7 Honeycomb .... Top 50 7a *6b*
A classic fingery excursion up the honeycomb wall, with the crux requiring you to unlock your preferred sequence of pockets since there are many to choose from. The last move is particularly frustrating and is a little worn. *Photo on page 330.*
FA. M.Fowler 1970s

8 Honeycomb Direct ..... 7a+ *6b*
A direct and slightly harder variation on *Honeycomb*. Also known as **Barracuda**.
FA. D.Atchinson-Jones 1981

9 Craig-y-blanco ..... Top 50 6c+ *6a*
A golden route up the arete which is commonly done by moving left and back right onto the arete. The original direct version is now much harder after the loss of a hold.
FA. P.Maher 18.7.1960

Catherine Gallagher on *Honeycomb* (7a *6b*) - *page 329* - on the magical Honeycomb Wall at High Rocks.

Wishful Thinking — High Rocks

Wishful Thinking

A short wall which is more suited to bouldering than top-roping these days. It can be green.

Approach (see map page 277) - Take the right-hand fork at the main entrance and follow the path up the steps and onto the flat concreted path that runs past the Hut Boulder. Continue up and right to follow the path up a further set of steps. The wall is just right of Honeycomb Wall.

Set-up and Descent - Use the steps to the right of The Diver Roof - p.332.

⛔ **Please take note of any bouldering restrictions that may be in place - see page 276.**

1 Dagger Crack 6c *6a*
After a good start to the left-trending break (**f5+** to here) things soon get slimy and dirty as you near the top.
FA. M.Fowler 14.5.1980

2 Greasy Crack 5a *5a*
As the name implies ....

3 Wishful Thinking .... f6A+
Climb delicately using the engraved scripture to reach the (often dirty) break. Finish up and left, finally pulling on some rhododendron roots to exit.
FA. G.McLelland 1981

4 Woofus Wejects f6A
Always green and always wet.
FA. C.Arnold 20.8.1983

5 Ides of March .... f6A+
The left face with mossy holds at the top.
FA. G.McLelland 26.3.1983

6 Final Destination f7C
An impressive dyno from pockets is needed to latch the poor holds at the top. An awkward mantel follows.
FA. I.Hufton 2004

7 Lunge'n'Shelf .... f6A+
A much shorter and easier dyno than its neighbour.
FA. G.McLelland 23.10.1983

8 Puzzle Corner f4
Climb the arete and finish using the bridge.

High Rocks — The Diver Roof

The Diver Roof

A decent roof, but the landings and holds over the lip leave something to be desired.

Approach (see map page 277) - Take the right-hand fork at the main entrance and continue right to enter the open grassy lawn area. Cross this diagonally up and left into the trees and pass the Slab Boulder (on your right) then head up the steep banking to the left of the Isolated Boulder which is situated behind the Slab Boulder. It is just right of the Wishful Thinking area.

Set-up and Descent - The steps to the right provide easy access to and from the top of the crag.

> Please take note of any bouldering restrictions that may be in place - see page 276.

1 Sideshow .... f5+
A tricky side wall climb up the vague ramp.
FA. R.Mazinke 11.5.2005

2 Marathon Man f6A
The left side of the nose keeping a close eye on that tree.
FA. D.Atchinson-Jones 1982

3 Beer Gut Shuffle f6B
Roof climbing with a poor sloping top-out.
FA. B.Knight 1983

4 The Diver Roof .... f6A+
Use the rail to latch the holds on the lip and make an awkward top-out.

5 The Diver f6B
The final roof climb.
FA. A.Grigg 13.9.1992

Hidden Boulders — High Rocks

Hidden Boulders

A few short boulder problems located below The Diver Roof up behind the Isolated Boulder.

Approach (see map page 277) - Take the right-hand fork at the main entrance and continue right to enter the open grassy lawn area. Cross this diagonally up and left into the trees and pass the Slab Boulder (on your right) and then the Isolated Boulder which is situated behind it. The Hidden Boulders are tucked up behind Isolated Boulder on the left.

🚫 **Please take note of any bouldering restrictions that may be in place - see page 276.**

6 Ephidrina .... f2+
A slabby nose situated down to the left below The Diver Roof.

A few metres to the right on the path leading up to the right side of The Diver Roof is a short wall comprising mainly of soft rock.

7 Endoparasitoid f4
A poor mossy problem.

8 Priapus .... f3+
Similar to its neighbour but with slightly better holds.

9 Substance f4
Slightly better climbing up the nose.

10 Proteus .... 💥 f3
The best of the four here, with good holds and less moss.

Tim Daniells, a long standing sandstone climber with numerous first ascents under his belt, climbing *Odin's Wall* (6b *5c*) - *page 327* - on Odin's Wall at High Rocks.

Isolated Boulder — High Rocks 335

Isolated Boulder

Isolated Boulder has many excellent climbs, but unfortunately there is no easy way to get to the top to set up a rope. It is recommended that anyone hoping to climb here should gain some sandstone climbing experience before setting out. The boulder stays in relatively good condition all year round.

Approach (see map page 277) - Take the right-hand fork at the main entrance and continue right to enter the open grassy lawn area. Cross this diagonally up and left into the trees and pass the Slab Boulder to reach the Isolated Boulder immediately behind it.

Set-up and Descent - Climb *Ordinary Route* to reach the top for rigging a top-rope. To descend, either down climb *Ordinary Route* or use the branch on the large tree on the west side of the boulder to rig an abseil which enables you to descend without touching the rock.

① Ordinary Route — 4a *4a*
The easiest way on and off Isolated Boulder. It's better to know where the holds are as those at the top are not as good as you want them to be, so take extra care.

② Oven Ready Freddy — 6c *6a*
The upper wall out left is pretty awkward and short lived.
FA. G.Wickham 1989

③ Return of the Mojo — f6B+
Climb *Plantagenet* from a sit-start using undercuts, then slap around the nose to finish on the ledge above. Exit by hand traversing left onto the block.
FA. C.George 2002

④ Plantagenet — 7a+ *6b*
Climb the blunt nose with difficulty to the ledge and tackle the roof above. Practice your pull-ups first.
FA. P.Widdowson 11.4.1992

High Rocks — Isolated Boulder

The area between *Ordinary Route* and the tree is appealing to boulderers due to the steep bulging starts.

❺ Children of the Bong f7B
Start as for *Return of the Mojo* (page 335) and traverse right along the sloping break to finish up *Optic Eye*.

❻ Mysteries of the Orgasm .... 7a+ 6b
Tackle the lower bulges with difficulty, finishing more easily up and right of *Ordinary Route* - page 335.
FA. A.Grigg 11.9.1992

❼ The Mojo f7B
Slap out over the bulge on slopers and continue slapping until you reach the shallow break midway.
FA. C.George 2003

❽ Optic Eye .... f6B+
From crimps and a side-pull, use all holds going to the same finishing point as *Mojo*. An eliminate only using slopers over the lip goes at *f7A*.

❾ Devastator .... 6c+ 6a
Tackle the groove above the bulge, which can also be reached by traversing in from the right. Finish direct past the small tree growing out of the rock.

❿ Graveyard Groove .. 6b+ 5c
Start awkwardly, avoiding all contact with the tree. Finish up the groove at the top.
FA. J.Smoker 27.9.1958

Isolated Boulder — High Rocks

These climbs are some of the more popular routes on the boulder, and all with exciting names!

11 Tool Wall .... 6c+ *6a*
A very tight eliminate up the narrow strip of rock to the bulging finale. Avoid the tree and the crack on *Fork*.
FA. A.Grigg 11.9.1992

12 Fork 6b *5c*
Attack the fine crack.

13 Toothpick .... 6c+ *6a*
Another eliminate up the face avoiding routes either side. The temptation to use the cracks can be overwhelming at times. Don't get too obsessed with what's in or out.
FA. M.Eden 25.4.1999

14 Knife 6b *5c*
A fine crack climb moving left to finish.

15 Two Fine Jugs .... 6c+ *6a*
The direct variation of *Dinner Plate*. Once on the line, avoid the crack of *Knife* and the remainder of *Dinner Plate* and finish over the upper bulge. It can also be done by climbing up the first part of *Dinner Plate* and moving back left above the lower bulge - slightly easier at 6b *5c*.
FA. T.Markham 1998

16 Dinner Plate 6b *5c*
Follow the crack and groove making good use of the surrounding holds. The upper part is much easier, hence some experienced climbers use this to access the top.

High Rocks — Isolated Boulder

17 The Full Monty .... 7a+ *6b*
The powerful start over the bulging nose.
FA. M.Lewis 1989

18 Early Breakfast .... 7a+ *6b*
A powerful direct start to *Breakfast*. The final roof is often avoided by moving left into *The Full Monty* at no overall change in grade.
FA. D.Atchinson-Jones 1980

19 Breakfast 6c *5c*
Negotiate the open crack low down. Swing left onto the face on juggy holds and finish over the roof. Many sneak off left and exit more easily, as for *The Full Monty*. Continuing direct up the initial crack makes a good direct to *Simian Progress* at 6a+ *5b*.
FA. M.Boysen 23.5.1959

20 Happy Days f7A
From a crouching start, make some hard moves over the bulge to jugs. Doing it as a two-handed dyno gives you **The Fonz**, *f7A*.
FA. C.George 2000. FA. (The Fonz) J.Wardle 2005

21 Simian Face Direct 6b *5c*
A direct start to *Simian Face*. Done from a sit-start to the break is **Happy Days Variation**, *f6C*.

22 Simian Progress .... 6a+ *5a*
The classic of the boulder. The incredibly awkward start is done from either the small boulder in front of it, or using a good reach and a jump to the break. Traverse left on good holds into the crack and finish up this.
FA. A.R.Serraillier 1930s

23 Simian Face .... 6a+ *5b*
After completing the burly start of *Simian Progress*, continue straight up the centre of the face, slowly watching those forearms run out of juice.
FA. D.Salter 4.9.1954

24 Monkey Nut 6b *5b*
A great route up the steep prow on big holds. Start on the right of the nose. From a sit-start to the break is *f6A+*.
FA. H.Barnes 19.6.1955

Isolated Boulder — High Rocks — 339

This steep face contains some great compact sandstone features and large ironstone holds.

25 Monkey's Sphincter .... 6c+ *6a*
Follow the series of ironstone holds across the upper face, heading up just before reaching the arete. Continuing left to finish up the arete gives **Monkey Business, 6c** *6a*.
FA. I.Mailer 23.4.1987. FA. (Monkey Business) D.Atchinson-Jones 1981

26 The Sphinx .... 6c+ *6a*
After a slightly bouldery start, continue from the flake and climb direct, using ironstone holds, to a taxing finish.
FA. J.Smoker 1.5.1959

27 Simian Mistake .... 6b+ *5c*
A fantastic and pumpy line with a frustrating finish that can often be a bit slimy.
FA. M.Midgley 23.5.1971

28 Simian Crimp .... 7a+ *6b*
A squeezed-in eliminate with its own independent hard start - done to the break it is *f6B*.
FA. (Start only) D.Wazjner 1981

29 Sputnik .... 6c+ *6a*
The sharp arete, either started from the boulder, or the ground.
FA. J.Smoker 2.11.1957

30 North Wall 5b *5a*
Layback the corner-crack and traverse left to finish.
FA. A.R.Serraillier 1930s

31 Apollo 11 .... *f7A+*
A dynamic problem up the blank face using crimps.

Marcin Franiak making an ascent of *The Wish* (**f7C+**) - *page 342* - on the Slab Boulder at High Rocks. The Slab Boulder is an iconic boulder with some of the hardest problems on Southern Sandstone. Photo: Szymon Dziukiewicz

High Rocks — Slab Boulder

Slab Boulder

The deceptively-named Slab Boulder is often referred to as the Matterhorn, as most of the problems are situated on its steep northeast-facing side. It is home to some of the hardest boulder problems on sandstone.

Approach (see map page 277) - Take the right-hand fork at the main entrance and continue right to the open grassy area. Cross this diagonally up and left into the trees to the Slab Boulder which is just north of the Isolated Boulder.

⛔ Please take note of any bouldering restrictions that may be in place - see page 376. Keep chalk use to a minimum.

1 John Player Special f6A
The right side of the arete with at lovely big flake. It can also be done from a sit-start at **f6A+**.
FA. B.Franklin 1980s

2 Tom's Mantel f6B
An awkward mantel onto the top slab.
FA. I.Butler 1999

3 Miss Embassy f6A
Making use of the flake to top out is not all that easy.
FA. B.Franklin 1980s

4 Z'Mutt f5
A popular juggy problem.

5 Old Kent Road ... f7A
A classic hand-traverse avoiding the large flake at the end (**f6B** with). Finish up the remainder of *John Player Special*.
FA. G.McLelland

6 Without Acid .... f6B+
A crimpy and technical undertaking up the lower face.

7 The Wish .... f7C+
Negotiate the two distinctive crimps and make a wish!
Photo on page 340.
FA. M.Migdal

8 Don't Pierdol ... f8A+
The sit-start to *The Wish* is one of the hardest boulder problems on sandstone. Reversing *Old Kent Road* from the far left arete into *Don't Pierdol* gives **Font Blues**, *f8B*.
FA. P.Wycislik. FA. (Font Blues) B.Ventham 2014

9 The Slow Pull ... f7C+
A hard low-level traverse across the entire face starting as for *Brenva Assis* and finishing up *John Player Special*, avoiding the large flake.
FA. P.Zeigenfuss

10 Brenva f6A
A classic highball up the arete with a frustrating start for the short. Lots of good holds higher up, so commit!
Photo on page 347.
FA. J.Smoker 24.8.1957

11 Brenva Assis ... f7A
The hard sit-start to *Brenva*.
FA. P.Ziegenfuss

Slab Boulder **High Rocks** 343

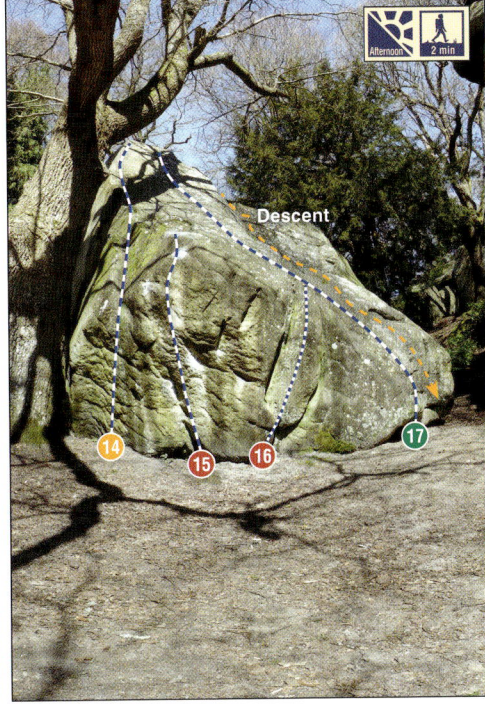

12 Mean Goblin .... f7B+
Brenva Assis then a hard traverse right finishing on the slab.

13 Green Goblin f6B
A technical wall up and right, next to the tree.
FA. B.Knight

14 Gattaca f5
A fairly straightforward way up using the rail but not the tree.

15 Jabberwocky f6A
Uncurl yourself from the starting moves and finish with a mantel onto the slab.

16 Crucible .... f6B+
A short and awkward problem to a mantel finish.
FA. C.George

17 Central Route f2A
Straight up the sandy slab.

18 Guy's Problem .... f6B+
A hard to start and balancy problem.

19 Guy's Link f7A
Traverse right into the top half of *Neil's Eliminate*.

20 Neil's Eliminate f7A
The left side of the arete has a rounded top-out. It has a sit-start at this grade but many choose to try the standing version at *f6B*. The face without using the arete from a sit-start is *f7B*.

High Rocks — Bowling Green Boulders

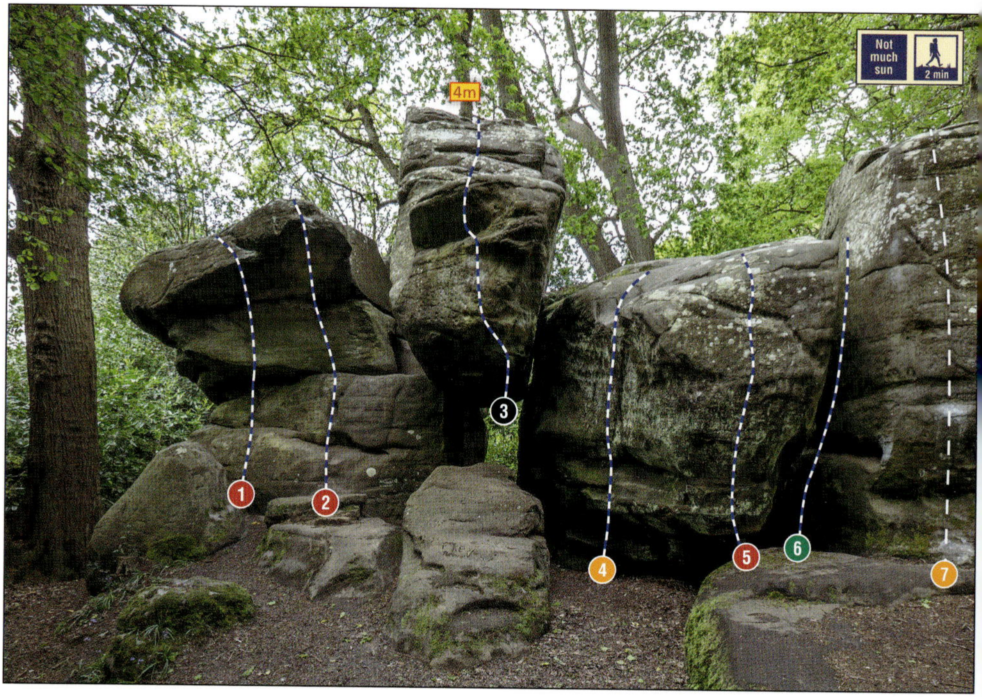

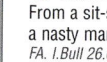

Bowling Green Boulders

A less busy collection of boulders with some worthwhile problems to explore. The best problems are on the south side, but there are some more esoteric green offerings on the north side.

Approach (see map page 277) - Take the right-hand fork at the main entrance and continue right to enter the open grassy lawn area. Head rightwards across the lawn in a southeast direction to reach the Boulders. This wall is around the back of the block.

Descent - Shuffle down between the tree and the rock just right of *Epstein*.

⛔ Please take note of any bouldering restrictions that may be in place - see page 276.

❶ Picasso *f6A*
A short mantelshelf problem over the roof.

❷ Dali .... *f6B+*
Wrestle with the roof and make a desperate mantel to finish.

❸ The Lemur .... *f7B+*
A brutal problem up the hanging block avoiding the walls on either side of the passage.
FA. P.Zeigenfuss 2003

❹ Barbizon .... *f4+*
A balancy problem with a mantel finish.

❺ Lichen Prow .... *f6B+*
From a sit-start on the stone block, slap your way up the arete to a nasty mantel finish.
FA. I.Bull 26.6.2013

❻ Reine Sofia .... *f2+*
A quick squeeze up between the two blocks.

❼ Sandman .... *f5+*
The short left arete using whatever you feel is appropriate without reaching too far right for holds on the next problem.
FA. I.Stronghill 2002

❽ Rodin .... *f5+*
The centre of the face is a delicate undertaking and much more fun for the short.

❾ Bowling Ramp .... *f5+*
Climb the face about a metre left of the arete, reaching for a good side-pull for the right hand higher up.

❿ Bowling Green Arete .... *f3+*
The arete mainly on its left side.

⓫ Fiorentino *f4*
Climb the face to a sandy top-out. Avoid contact with the arete out left.

⓬ Buonarroti *f5*
Challenging moves up the face with some small pockets to contend with.

⓭ Epstein *f4*
The right side of the face, avoiding the tree.

Bowling Green Boulders — High Rocks

High Rocks — Bowling Green Boulders

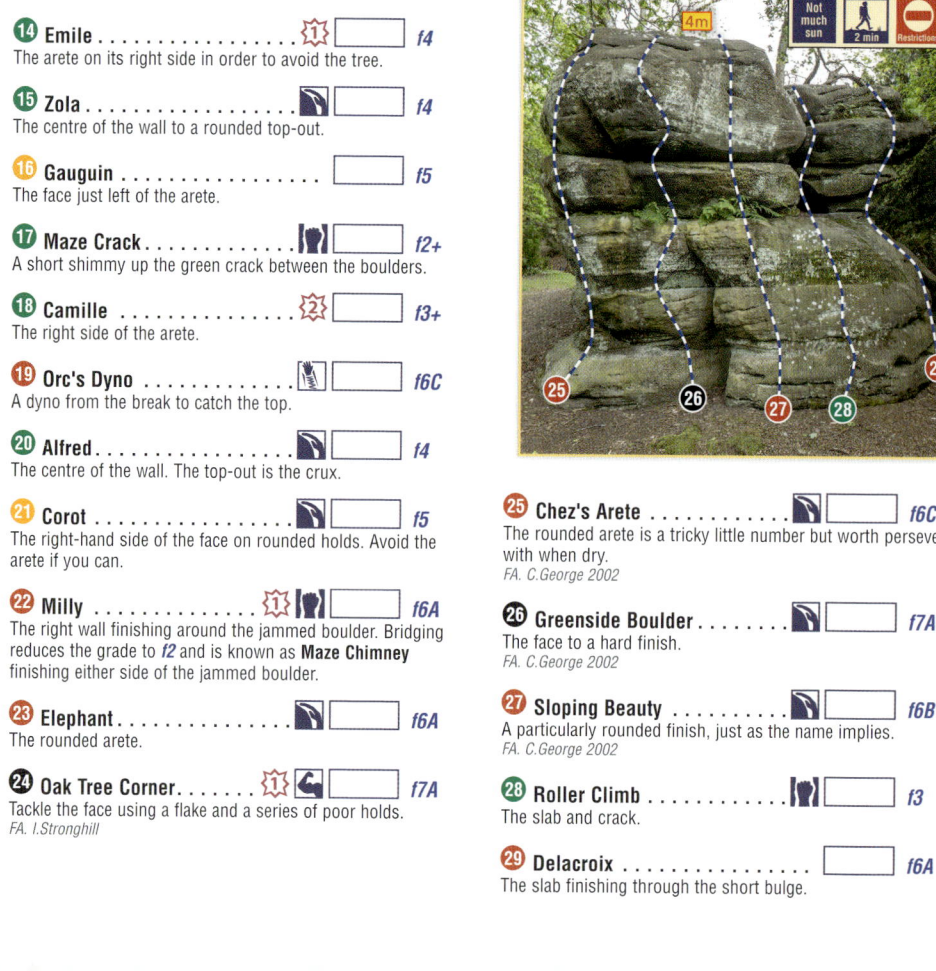

14 Emile f4
The arete on its right side in order to avoid the tree.

15 Zola f4
The centre of the wall to a rounded top-out.

16 Gauguin f5
The face just left of the arete.

17 Maze Crack .... f2+
A short shimmy up the green crack between the boulders.

18 Camille .... f3+
The right side of the arete.

19 Orc's Dyno f6C
A dyno from the break to catch the top.

20 Alfred f4
The centre of the wall. The top-out is the crux.

21 Corot f5
The right-hand side of the face on rounded holds. Avoid the arete if you can.

22 Milly f6A
The right wall finishing around the jammed boulder. Bridging reduces the grade to f2 and is known as **Maze Chimney** finishing either side of the jammed boulder.

23 Elephant f6A
The rounded arete.

24 Oak Tree Corner f7A
Tackle the face using a flake and a series of poor holds.
FA. I.Stronghill

25 Chez's Arete f6C
The rounded arete is a tricky little number but worth persevering with when dry.
FA. C.George 2002

26 Greenside Boulder .... f7A+
The face to a hard finish.
FA. C.George 2002

27 Sloping Beauty f6B
A particularly rounded finish, just as the name implies.
FA. C.George 2002

28 Roller Climb f3
The slab and crack.

29 Delacroix f6A
The slab finishing through the short bulge.

Natalie Tanzer on *Brenva* (**f6A**) - *page 342* - on the Slab Boulder at High Rocks.

High Rocks Annexe

Roland O'Leary making a leap of faith on the highball boulder problem, *Southern Softie* (**f7A**) - *page 352* - on the foreboding Left Walls at High Rocks Annexe.

High Rocks Annexe

	No star	★	★★	★★★
2a to 4c/f2 to f4	15	6	2	-
5a to 6a+/f4+ to f5+	6	9	7	1
6b to 7a/f6A to f6C+	3	3	5	1
7a+ up/f7A up	-	-	2	1

High Rocks Annexe is a dark and foreboding place hidden in the trees. The rocks are covered with green and there is lots of seepage throughout the year. However, appearances can be deceiving and the rock is climbable when dry becoming a decent bouldering destination with some good highball problems and short routes, including one or two classics. Most of the routes have been graded as boulder problems, but top-roping is not frowned upon.

Approach   Also see map on page 18

The Annexe is close to High Rocks which is relatively easy to find with plenty of brown tourist signs showing you the way. If leaving Tunbridge Wells on the A26 then High Rocks is signed to the right across Tunbridge Wells Common, with a left turn onto High Rocks Lane. If on the A264, turn left down Tea Garden Lane just after leaving the town. Both ways lead you to High Rocks lane by the railway. The Annexe is situated to the east of the triangular junction by the railway, in the woods. Parking is difficult - there is a small lay-by just beyond the railway bridge on the left. The High Rocks carpark is not to be used for this venue. At the left bend just before the small bridge on your right is the main entrance, which currently has no fence in place. A vague fence does run along the road but is in a state of disrepair. Shrubbery has been put in place to create wildlife habitats and boundary markers, so only enter the woodland from the west (left) side as described. Make your way diagonally rightwards up a vague path and into a more densely wooded area, then join the main strip of clear land in front of the rocks.

Access

The rocks are situated on open access land and access has never been an issue. As a common courtesy it is requested that you seek permission from the landowner at Rusthall Farm Bungalow on the corner of Tea Garden Lane. If no one is in then please leave a note.

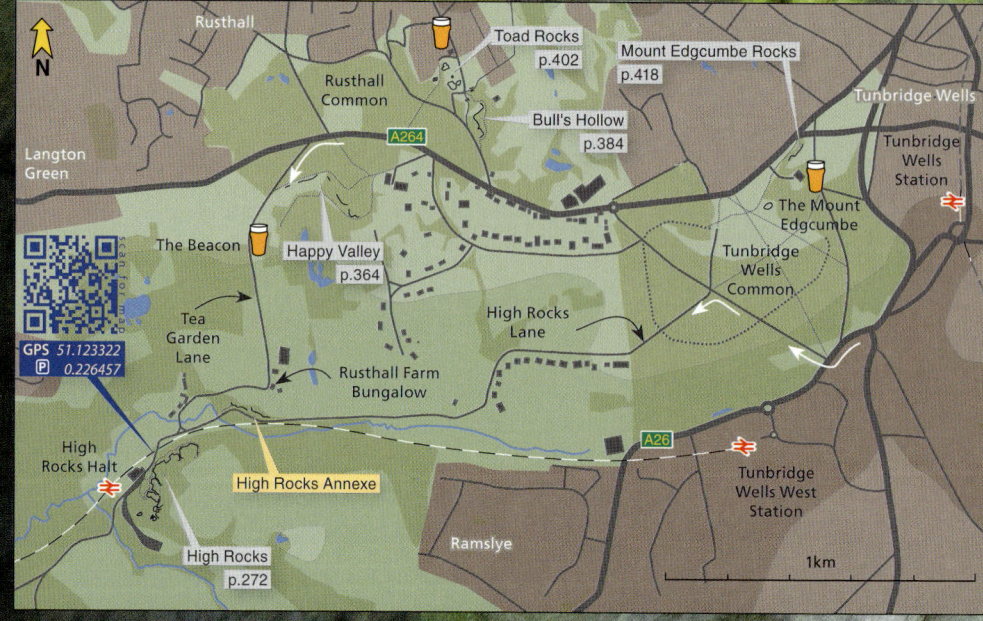

High Rocks Annexe

Conditions
The rocks see little light and are usually very green. There is also significant seepage after wet weather. Decent conditions can be found in dry spells from spring to autumn, if there is a good breeze. In hot weather the rock can get greasy due to humidity build up from all the foliage. The rocks face southwest which allows light to penetrate through the trees in early spring and, at times, can create a magical atmosphere.

Equipment
Top-ropes need to be set up using the trees as anchors - some trees are situated away from the edge (see page 38 for further info). There are no bolt anchors here.

Roland O'Leary climbing *Middle Stump* (6a *5b*) - *page 357* - on the Cricket Pitch Wall at High Rocks Annexe.

High Rocks Annexe — Left Walls

Left Walls
A series of walls giving some highball boulder problems.
Approach - Easily approached from the road at the left side of the wood via a vague path.
Conditions - Much of the rock here appears green all year round; this is because it has become impregnated into the stone. A majority of the lines are surprisingly climbable in the late summer months, although the rock does take longer to dry after long periods of bad weather.

Southern Softie
The first wall here suffers some what from the dreaded green monster, but has a few interesting outings when dry.

1 Yew Tree Wall *f3*
A short climb just left of the crack.

2 Yew Tree Crack . . . . *f3+*
Thrutch and jam the dark and green off-width.

3 It's Only Natural *f6A*
Use the right side of the crack to establish yourself on the break. Reach for large pockets and finish direct.
FA. T.Skinner 8.7.1999

4 Southern Softie *f7A*
A difficult blank slab which feels highball. Much harder for the short. *Photo on page 348.*
FA. J.Dawes 25.3.1997

5 Shidid . . . . *f6A+*
Climb the rounded arete.

6 Annexe Slab *f5*
Climb the slab and trend rightwards to finish on tree roots.
FA. J.R.Lees, J.S.Brownsort 13.8.1949

Twitch
An almost isolated block with some sloping landings.

7 Titch Arete . . . . *f6A+*
A short technical climb up the arete.
FA. C.Morley 1.9.1957

8 Meander . . . . *f5+*
Begin as for *Titch Arete* and quickly move right to a mantel finish. Can be started independently just to the right.
FA. P.L.Bars, C.Morley 1.9.1957

9 Twitch . . . . *f6B+*
Climb the blunt arete after a difficult start with a short dynamic move in the centre. Finish more easily.

10 Arnold Thesanigger . *f6B*
A short and powerful problem up the rounded arete.
FA. M.Smith 1990

Left Walls High Rocks Annexe

Nose One

11 Boogie Woogie Walk — f7B
The dark and green groove requires a long reach and very strong fingers. Finish left of the tree and watch the landing.
FA. L.Percival 8.8.1998

12 Double Top — f6B+
Climb the line of shallow pockets to finish just right of the tree.
FA. N.S.Head 1982

13 Rupert and His Chums — f6A
A delicate slab climb just left of the nose.
FA. M.Vetterlein 29.2.1992

14 Nose One — f5
Stick to the nose using sandy holds and be prepared for a spicy finish.

15 Chimney Wall — f3+
Often used as a cop-out finish to Nose One (but no tick).

16 Chimney One — f2+
The dirty chimney requires a lot of thrutchy moves... and probably a change of clothes.

Spleen Slab
Just right of the chimney is a fine wall.

17 Spleen Slab — f4+
Climb delicately up the slightly rounded nose, with more holds for your hands than your feet. Finish on the tree roots.

18 Change in the Weather — f7A
A classic problem. Climb the steep slabby face on spaced holds to a finish right of the tree. Direct is slightly harder.
FA. L.Percival 9.8.1998

19 Gea — f6B
Better holds than its left-hand neighbour.

20 Brain's Missing — f5
Climb the thin crack with difficulty.
FA. D.Atchinson-Jones 6.1981

21 Nose Two — f3
The short face left of the arete.

High Rocks Annexe — Left Walls

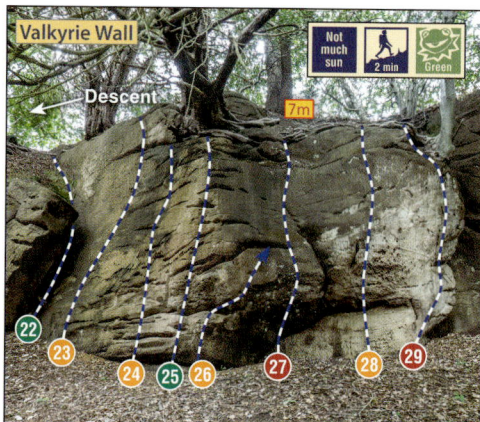

Valkyrie Wall
A wall of a more acceptable height for bouldering.

22 Chimney Two .... f2+
An easy chimney or a difficult way down.

23 Fahrenheit .... f5+
Precarious face climbing on shallow pockets and holds.
FA. P.Widdowson, M.Vetterlein 1.3.1992

24 Thinner. .... f4+
Climb the face direct to finish left of the tree.
FA. M.Sullivan 9.6.1957

25 Nose Three .... f2+
Climb the nose and finish on tree roots.

26 Green Pesto .... f5+
A short problem that finishes up *Thug*.

27 Thug f6A
Pass the bulge with difficulty and finish up the groove.
FA. P.Widdowson 8.3.1992

28 Valkyrie Wall. .... f5+
Climb the short technical bulge and finish more easily.
FA. N.Cordery 17.5.1953

29 Valkyrie Arete f6A
Climb the right side of the face eliminating the ramp to the right at the start.

Gorilla Wall
A wall with three more problems and an unfortunately placed green slab in front of it.

30 Chute and Chimney ...... f2+
Similar to *Valkyrie Arete*, but this time feet are allowed on the ramp and side-wall. Rather dirty and green.

31 Didshi .... f5+
Short and crimpy climbing on sandy holds.

32 Gorilla Wall .... f4+
Step off the block and zig-zag up the short wall above.

Purgatory
Down the slope is a blank-looking slab with only two problems on the far right-hand side.

33 Purgatory f5
A good route despite the sandy finish. Climb the vague flutings and honeycombed lower wall to two large pockets. Finish up and slightly to the left.
FA. J.R.Lees 1950

34 Augustus. f5
Climb the arete trying to avoid holds on *Purgatory*.
FA. N.S.Head 10.2.1974

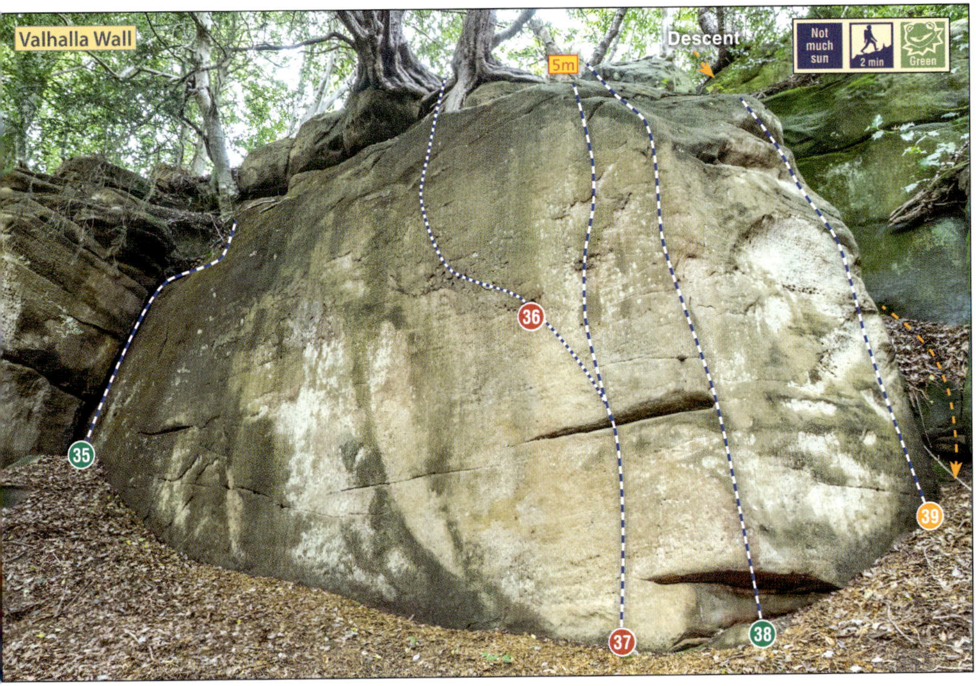

High Rocks Annexe — Left Walls

Valhalla Wall
A nice little face.

35 Corner Crack . . . . **f2+**
The dirty crack tucked in the corner is often gooey and green.

36 The Entertainer . . . . **f6B+**
A heart-stopping dance on small holds, moving leftwards from *Billy the Bong* to a difficult finish.
FA. D.Atchinson-Jones 1980

37 Billy the Bong **f6A**
Climb the wall direct without using the arete.
FA. M.Smith 1990

38 Valhalla Wall **f4**
Climb the arete avoiding the holds on *Billy the Bong*.

39 Fig Roll . . . . **f4+**
Climb the slab left of the gully, also using the arete.
FA. T.Skinner 8.7.1995

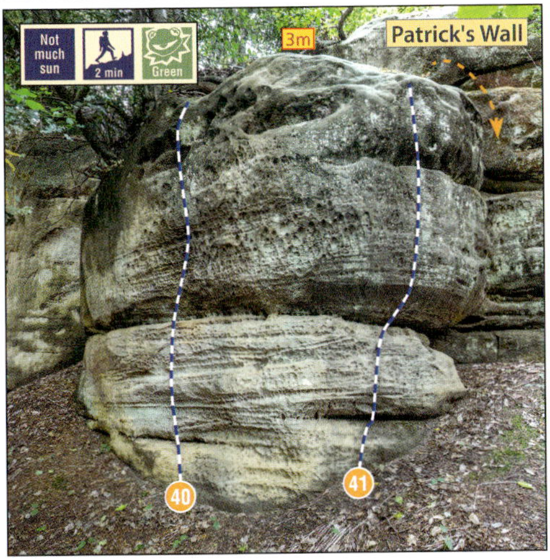

Patrick's Wall
Just right of Valhalla Wall is an isolated block with two short (but often green) problems on them.

40 Patrick's Wall . . . . **f5+**
Climb the steep front face with a poor top-out.

41 Dumpy **f5**
The nose with a dirty top-out.

High Rocks Annexe — Horizon Wall and Monolith Buttress

Horizon Wall
This wall sees little attention and usually glows with green, but is climbable in mid-to-late summer.
Approach - Clamber up the gully/slope to the right of Patrick's Wall to a small green block on the right.

1 Horizon Wall Crack .... 　 f2+
Climb steadily up the short flake/crack.

2 Horizon Wall 1. .... 　 f2+
Climb the short left side nose of the block. A good variation up the bulge to the left goes at the same grade.

3 Horizon Wall 2. .... 　 f2+
A short stepped problem with a number of variations to the left and right.

Monolith Buttress
Continuing rightwards and down from Patrick's Wall is a short buttress with an off-width crack up its centre. It is less green but a tiny bit fragile in places.

4 Wonderwall. .... 　 3a *3a*
A short route starting with a step across the gully. Take care, it can be slippy.

5 Wonderwall Ramp ..... 　 6a+ *5a*
Climb the wall to the right of the gully. Finish any way you like.

6 Monolith Left Buttress .. 　 5c *5c*
Climb the nose direct. It is possible to exit left at **4a** *4a*.

7 Monolith Crack .... 　 3c *3c*
The crack can be climbed a number of ways.

8 Monolith Right Buttress . 　 4a *4a*
Climb the front of the buttress to a slightly awkward finish.

Cricket Pitch Wall — High Rocks Annexe

Cricket Pitch Wall

Continuing on further right from Monolith Buttress is the Cricket Pitch Wall, which has few good micro routes. This tends to be the driest of the lot and a bit high for a bouldering mat.

9 Leg Break 5b *5a*
A short climb up to the right side of the tree.

10 Nob Nose 6a *5b*
Climb direct up the nose. Also know as 'Wicked Maiden'.
FA. D.Atchison-Jones 6.1982

11 The Yorker 4b *4b*
The direct start to *The Googly*.

12 The Googly 4b *4b*
Climb the small crack and move left to an easier finish.

13 Off Stump 4c *4c*
A direct right-hand finish to *The Googly*.

14 Middle and Off 5b *5a*
The centre of the wall finishing just right of the tree.
FA. M.Sullivan 26.5.1957

15 Middle Stump 6a *5b*
Climb direct on small holds. *Photo on page 351.*

16 Leg Stump 5b *5a*
Climb the crack and face above. One of the best on the wall.

17 Out 4b *4b*
Climb the right-hand face past a difficult move.

18 Boundary Gully 3c *3c*
An esoteric gully climb. Not for your average climber.

There is a very overgrown wall to the right with a few unclimbable routes which are omitted for obvious reasons.

Continuing further right from Cricket Pitch Wall for about 30m is one last piece of rock close to the road. Please respect the fencing and do not be tempted to enter or exit here.

19 Green Groove .... f2+
An easy short climb up the left side of the rock. Has been known to dry out.

20 Seat Climb .... f2+
Slightly cleaner and more likely to be dry.

Rusthall and Tunbridge Wells Commons

Laura Benn enjoying one of the problems found at Happy Valley - *The Short Sharp C* (*f2+*) - *page 376* - on the Masters of Muck wall. Happy Valley has increased in popularity since many of the climbs which used to be considered micro routes not worthy of attention are now bouldered above big juicy crash pads.

Rusthall and Tunbridge Wells Commons

The various lumps and blocks spread across Rusthall and Tunbridge Wells Commons were once left as esoterica for the local connoisseur to discover. Times have changed and the increasing popularity of bouldering means that many of the rocks now have something to offer modern climbers armed with a decent pad.

The 'Commons' have four venues, each with their own character.

Happy Valley has a large selection of boulder problems and micro routes that run along the valley edge overlooking the surrounding countryside.

Bull's Hollow has quarried walls and some hidden gems. Sadly it is sheltered in the trees and suffers from poor conditions and lots of green rock. Find it in good nick though, and you will be rewarded.

Toad Rocks has an iconic toad-shaped rock situated at its centre and is surrounded by the Southeast's very own mini Fontainebleau. It is very accessible with plenty of problems to keep anyone happy, although some can be a bit sandy in places.

Mount Edgcumbe Rocks has a good number of boulder problems and a few highballs, although the rock can be a bit soft here. It is a good venue for a quick evening session followed by a refreshing drink in the bar overlooking the rocks. Close by is the children's playground maze of Wellington Rocks, which is a little small for bouldering but worth a look, especially if you have children.

All four of these venues are managed by the Tunbridge Wells Commons Conservators who do their best to keep the area attractive and accessible. They rely on volunteers to help where possible, so if you wish to get involved with clearing and conservation then please visit **twcommons.org** for more information. The Sandstone Volunteers Group (SVG) also help in this area especially at Bull's Hollow (see page 54).

Rusthall and Tunbridge Wells Commons

Amanda Webster on *Chalybeate* (6b+ *5c*) - *page 381* - on the Cheeswring Rock at Happy Valley. This photo was taken before the removal of the tree that leaned against the block, which now makes protecting the routes here more problematic. This will hopefully change in the near future.

Happy Valley

	No star	★	★★	★★★
2a to 4c/f2 to f4	25	13	4	-
5a to 6a+/f4+ to f5+	10	5	3	1
6b to 7a/f6A to f6C+	16	6	3	-
7a+ up/f7A up	3	1	2	-

Happy Valley is a great venue which is gradually gaining interest, especially amongst the bouldering community. Development was helped by a significant deforestation campaign in 2013 which uncovered a number of forgotten walls and boulders.
The valley is split into three areas, with the first being the West Valley Boulders covering the rocks to the west of the 'Historic 101 Steps' and the Deforestation Boulder. The Main Cliff is best known for its low-level walls sitting clearly on the southeastern edge of the valley. Most of the routes here were originally done on top-rope, but nowadays ascents above mats are more common. Take care though, some are quite high and the landings not always straightforward. Furthest to the east is the unusual isolated block of the Cheeswring Rock above the lower path, which has some longer outings.

Equipment
No bolts are installed at the time of writing so all top-ropes need to be set up using trees as anchors; some of these are set back from the rocks (see page 38 for more on setting up top-ropes).

Approach   Also see map on page 362
Take the A264 along the north side of Tunbridge Wells Common to the mini roundabout at its northwest corner. Continue along the A264 towards Groombridge, passing the Rusthall Road turn-off (Toad Rocks) on your right and continue for another 160m until a blue sign is visible on your left to 'St.Paul's Parish Church'. Turn left here and drive down the tree-lined road and park. Please do not block the turning circle in front of the entrance to the church. Follow the path that continues in the same direction into the woodland and head straight until you reach the upper valley path that runs parallel with the top of the rocks. Details of the approaches to the individual areas are included in their relevant sections.

Conditions
The rocks face in a southerly direction and are exposed to lots of sunshine making it a quick-drying venue. Unfortunately, some of the rock is soft and sandy so take extra care. The area can quickly get overgrown in spring and summer, making autumn and late winter ideal times to visit.

West Valley Boulders — Happy Valley

Reach for the Dead — 3m

West Valley Boulders
An ideal area to indulge in a bit of bouldering away from the crowds. Although most of the problems are friendly enough, some get a bit high and the landings aren't always perfect. Most problems can be a little sandy, but stay in good condition throughout the year. Some areas can become overgrown in the spring.

Approach (see overview on page 366) Turn right (northwest) when emerging from the woodland and continue to the 'Historic 101 Steps'. Below and to the left is the Deforestation Boulder. Continuing for another 20m another set of stairs that run rightwards down the hill. Just below the top of these stairs is West Valley Wall. Continuing down the stairs/path is the main area of the West Valley Boulders. *Reach for the Dead* is best reached by continuing along the top path and dropping down towards the dead tree trunks.

Reach for the Dead
An isolated problem at the far left-hand side of the crag.

1 Reach for the Dead . . . . f3+
Find the ironstone ledge to the left of the face, and match with your hands, in order to get your feet on and throw for the top.
FA. D.Beail 16.5.2015

Reach for the Dead | Hidden Gem p.368 | The Back Wall p.370 | Sweeps Cave Area p.371 | West Valley Wall p.371 | Bane's Boulder p.370

Happy Valley

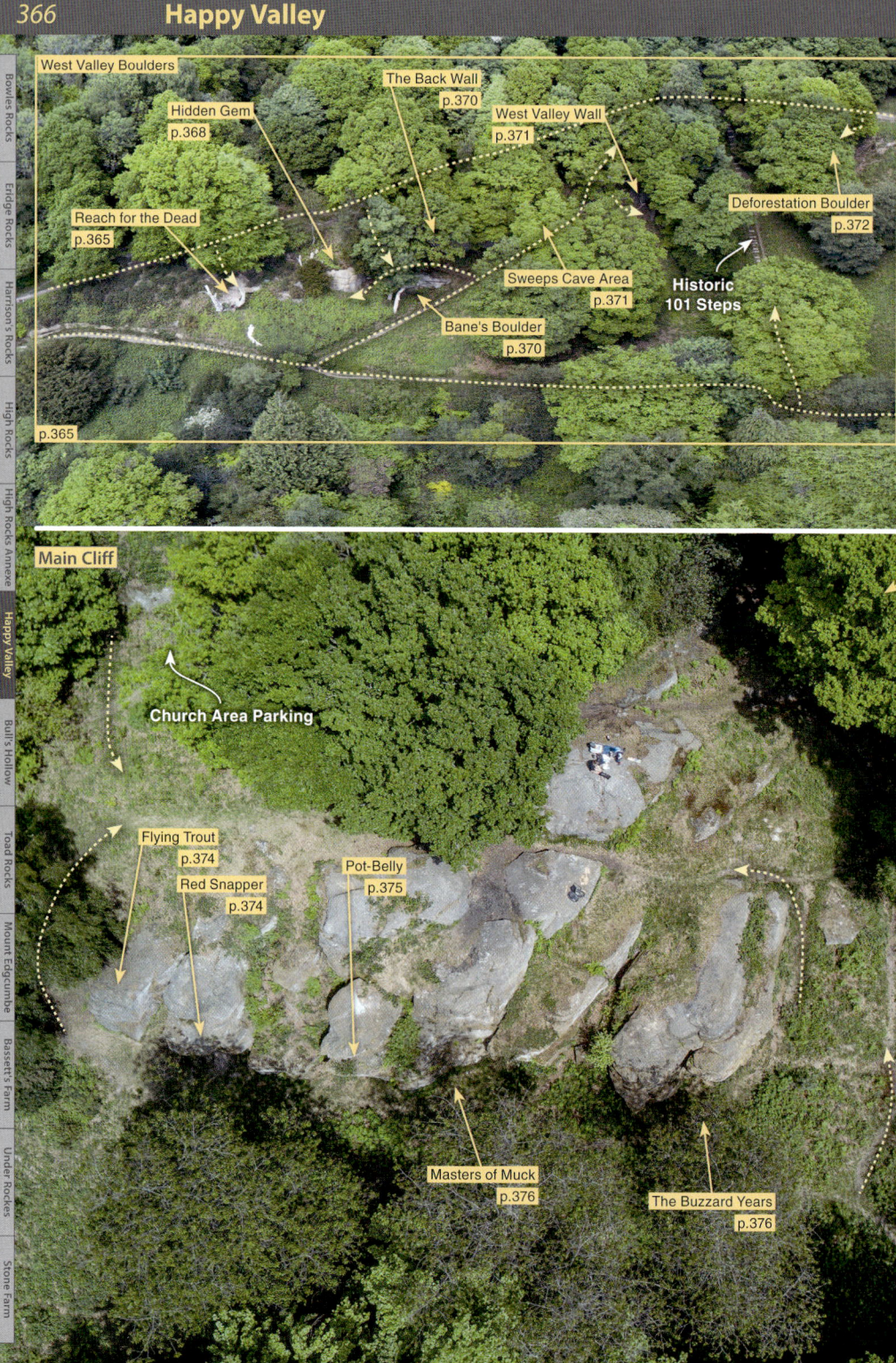

Happy Valley — West Valley Boulders

Hidden Gem
A great piece of rock just up and left of Bane's Boulder (page 370) with a few good lines which are best bouldered.

1 Beacon Wall f4
The centre of the wall, trending left to finish up the narrow groove at the top. A spicy top-out for the untrained sandstone climber.
FA. T.Skinner 1994

2 Magic Fountain f4
Starting just left of the flake, climb easily up the centre of the wall to an exciting finish. Much easier once you know how. *Photo on page 379.*
FA. D.Beail 16.5.2015

3 Hidden Gem f4
Probably the best route on this wall. Climb the flakes to the 'I wish I had a few more holds' finish. *Photo opposite.*
FA. D.Reid 1994

4 Doug's Come-uppance .. f4+
Locate undercuts and pockets and climb directly via good side-pulls to the upper break. Move left to finish up the final moves of *Hidden Gem*. A direct line finishes over the top at a much tricker f6A.
FA. I.Stronghill 1994

Daimon Beail on the route of *Hidden Gem* (*f4*) - *opposite* - which is part of the West Valley Boulders at Happy Valley. Photo: Emma Harrington.

Happy Valley — West Valley Boulders

The Back Wall
A small hidden wall behind Bane's Boulder.

1 The Happening .... f6A+
The line of pockets to the tree root (which is very much in!)
FA. C.Murray, A.Vallintine 1.2009

2 It Is What It Is f7A
An incredibly thin problem up the centre of the wall. Not entirely independent as it uses a pocket out left which is also used on *The Happening*. The sit-start is **Genesis** and goes at *f7B+*.
FA. N.Hart, C.'Orc'Searle 5.2009. FA. (Genesis) T.Gore 27.11.2011

3 Winter Blues .... f6B+
Climb the face, eliminating the arete except for the flat hold near the top.
FA. A.Vallintine 1.2009

4 1000 Moomins f5
A fine problem up the right side of the arete with a tricky finish.

Bane's Boulder
The large boulder situated by the lower path offers a few lower grade problems.

5 Born in a Barn f4
The smooth face past the slanting break. Tricky landing.

6 Budgy Smugglers f4
Climb rightwards towards the top of *Bane Rabbit*.

7 Bane Rabbit .... f3+
A bit tricker than it first appears.

8 Bane Cat f3
The easiest of the lines on this block has a super undercut. Traverse slightly right at the top for a better finish.

West Valley Boulders — Happy Valley

Sweeps Cave Area
A set of man-made caves situated near to the top steps and a short wall to the left.

9 The Deer Hunter .... f5+
A tricky problem with a long reach to hidden holds.

10 Bambi's Mother f4
A nice short problem on less-than-perfect holds.

11 Kate Moss f5
Start next to (but avoiding) the block to the left of the face and unearth hidden holds and snappy crimps. Move up and right to a large ironstone hold and a very mossy finish.
FA. D.Beall 16.5.2015

12 Sooty .... f6A+
Bridge your way up to a tricky mantel to finish.

13 Inglenook Left-hand f6B
Locate two pockets on the left side of the back wall and, eliminating the left wall and ledge, reach out to gain the lip. Now powerfully mantel your way out.

14 Inglenook .... f5+
For the original problem, mantel over the centre of the cave from a standing start.
FA. D.Potts 14.7.2005

15 Inglenook Right-hand .... f6B+
Locate the pockets on the right side of the back wall and, eliminating the right wall and ledge, reach for the lip and power over to finish.

West Valley Wall
Set just below the top path, and few metres to the right of the steps, is a short wall with some micro problems.

16 West Wall f5
A slopey top-out.

17 Mash Potatoes .... f3+
The line of layaway holds.

18 West Valley Wall Traverse f5
Starting as for *Mash Potatoes*, traverse the sloping break rightwards to finish up *Stag Arete*.

19 Stag f4
The short scooped wall.

20 Stag Doo f6A
Start by reaching the break and, without much for the feet, go for the top. Tricky.

21 Stag Arete .... f2+
A short problem that only just qualifies as an arete.

Happy Valley — West Valley Boulders

5 Slopey Goodness *f5*
Start 1m left of *Iron Arete* and climb through the roof to finish on a rounded top-out.
FA. I.Bull 13.3.2014

6 Iron Arete .... *f6A+*
Start with your feet on the ledge and attack the arete.
FA. I.Bull 13.3.2014

Deforestation Boulder

Situated below the top path by an open seating area and left of the 'Historic 101 Steps' (heading down). The problems are short and the quality of the rock is good, although most of those on the front face are quite difficult. The boulder suffers from the encroaching plantation in the spring.

1 A Day in the Park *f2*
A short but worthwhile mini problem up the back bum crack of the boulder.

2 Scooped Out *f2*
The scooped out step.

3 Herne the Hunter *f2*
The micro problem up the back of the boulder.

On the overhanging left face are three lines.

4 Underverse .... *f5+*
Start on the left and move up to traverse right across the lower and then upper lip to reach the crack and surrounding pockets. Finish on the ledge above. **Oververse**, *f6A* - a direct variation that mantels over the lip from a sit-start.
FA. E.Harrington 16.5.2015. FA. (Oververse) H.Trewhitt 23.4.2017

The following problems are on the front face of the boulder.

7 Warm Up .... *f6A+*
Probably not the best name for this one. From the break, make a long reach for the flake and top out rapidly. Hard for the short. *Photo opposite.*
FA. T.Gore 19.5.2013

8 The Road to Salvation .... *f6C+*
Start at the base of *Warm Up* and traverse the break, ensuring your feet do not touch the ground! Finish up *Pentecost*.
FA. T.Gore 19.5.2013

9 The Groove *f6B*
An eliminate up the groove sharing some holds with *Warm Up*.
FA. T.Gore 19.5.2013

10 The Face .... *f6B+*
From the break, climb the smooth face via some sloping holds. The holds out left on *The Groove* are allowed.
FA. T.Gore 19.5.2013

11 Pentecost *f6C*
From good holds in the break, make a powerful move up and right to a vertical crack before reaching back left to top out on the bulge. Topping out further right is easier.
FA. T.Gore 19.5.2013

12 Zacchaeus .... *f6B+*
The arete, climbed on its left-hand side, has a hard start.
FA. T.Gore 19.5.2013

Emma Harrington on the inaccurately named problem, *Warm Up* (**f6A+**) - *opposite* - on the Deforestation Boulder at Happy Valley. Although the problems are short, they certainly pack a punch.

Happy Valley — Main Cliff

Main Cliff

The Main Cliff has the best climbing at Happy Valley. The lines are graded here as boulder problems, but they do get quite high so use a top-rope if unsure. If setting up a top-rope, make sure you bring a long static line as the trees are set quite far back from the crag. The cliff has improved with age and, although some sections are still dirty in places, most of the popular lines remain in good condition. The cliff faces in a southerly direction so dries quickly.

Approach (see overview on page 366) - The cliff is easily reached by following the main path to the cliff edge path. Turn left towards the rocks and, almost immediately, follow the zig-zag path to the left of the crag (looking in).

Descent - It is easy to descend at either end of the crag since the cliff is so short here.

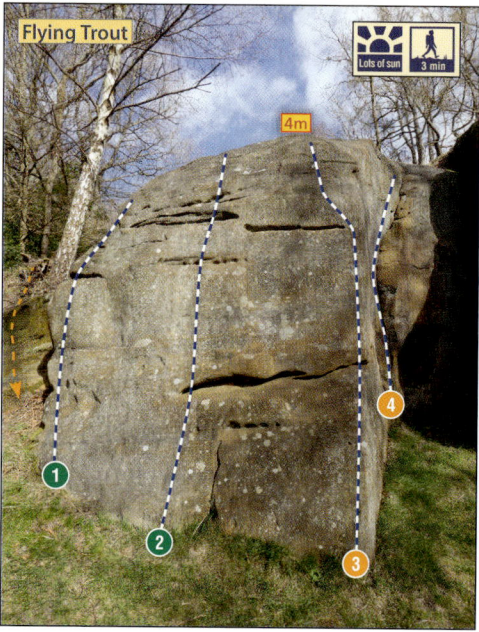

Flying Trout
A popular area for starting out that also provides a few challenging problems.

1 Starting Block .... f2+
The left arete is nice and friendly.

2 Ever So Minnow Minnow.... f2+
The centre of the face.

3 Flying Trout.......... f5
Climb the right side of the arete, then move left onto the slab. It is tricky to protect this with pads, so have an active spotter.

4 Minnow .... f4+
The flake has some good holds, but some may find it trickier than they would like.

Red Snapper
To the right of the chockstone gully are some of the most popular problems in the valley. Take care when climbing the lines from Sushi to Going Turbot, as rain water has significantly eroded the ground below. The hollows created can be smoothed out with an extra mat or two.

5 Sushi f5
A green and dirty wall starting just right of the chockstone gully. Use the bulging right-hand flake to start and make some rounded and dirty moves to the top.
FA. R.Mazinke 12.6.1999

6 Stonefish f4
A great little problem up the ironstone wall. Keep an eye out for the gully below.
FA. T.Skinner 1994

7 Moray. . . . . f3+
A great little problem. Start by climbing the left-hand arete and quickly tackle the short roof to finish on the ledge to the left of the main overhang. It requires a bit of commitment for those final moves, but all the holds are there.

Main Cliff Happy Valley

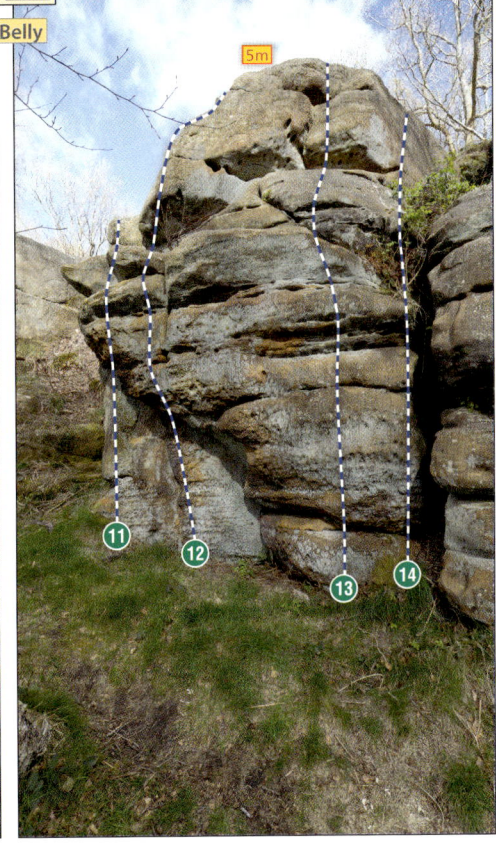

8 Red Snapper — f5
Climb the centre of the honeycomb wall and follow the vague crack-line through a series of overlapping roofs. Taking on the last overhang is not as easy as one would like - watch that landing.
FA. T.Skinner 1994

9 Going Turbot — f5
The least popular of the three roof climbs. Climb the lower roof and finish up the leftward-trending groove. Traversing the lower lip into and finishing up *Moray* is **Mullet Over,** *f5*.
FA. T.Skinner 1994. FA. (Mullet Over) H.Trewhitt 17.4.2017

10 Kippers — f3
The short crack/narrow gully is often overgrown especially in spring. If clear then climb it to the upper slabby face on the left.

Pot-Belly
5m to the right of Red Snapper is a odd-shaped wall that has a number of lower-grade problems.

11 Cleft — f2
The short left-hand arete.

12 Cornucopia — f4
Start under the overlap and climb the thin crack and wall above.
FA. R.Mazinke 12.6.1999

13 Pot-Belly — f4
Climb the right side of the face moving leftwards slightly near the top to use the holds in the crack.
FA. T.Skinner 1994

14 Mist — f2+
Bridge the gully and finish up the wall to the left. Often overgrown.
FA. T.Skinner 1994

Happy Valley — Main Cliff

Masters of Muck
Slightly longer outings that are often top roped, but can be bouldered with a good mat.

1 Festive .... f2+
Climb the short blunt arete and the slab above.
FA. R.Mazinke 28.12.1995

2 Just-In .... f2+
Climb the short wall to join the final part of *Festive*.
FA. R.Mazinke 20.9.2003

3 The Short Sharp C .... f2+
A nice line up a series of flakes, pockets and in-cut holds to finish up the thin crack. *Photo on page 358.*

4 Master of Muck f5
The centre of the wall requires some 'Tai Chi' moves. The top-out force many to finish right, which reduces the grade somewhat.
FA. D.Reid 1994

5 November Rain .... f2+
The tricky and green off-width crack is finished by climbing the arete above.
FA. R.Mazinke 1.8.1996

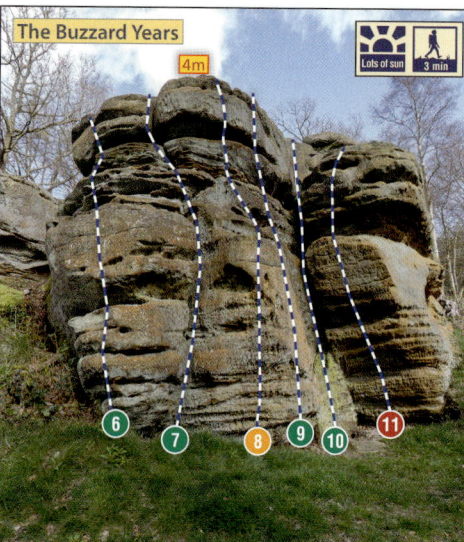

The Buzzard Years
The final section on this level also curves around to the side. Take care with landings on the upper slope.

6 Home to Roost. .... f3+
The left-hand side of the bulging arete to a rounded top-out.
FA. R.Mazinke 1.8.1996

Main Cliff **Happy Valley** 377

⑨ And Tigger Too *f4*
Locate the skull engraved into the rock and follow the sloping crack and wall direct.
FA. R.Mazinke 1.8.1996

⑩ Corner Crack *f3*
It does what it says on the tin.

⑪ Pooh's Route *f6A*
A pretty hard line up the centre of the overhanging wall just right of *Corner Crack*. A popular sit-start is **Shhh I'm Taking a Little Pooh**, *f6B*.
FA. P.Church 18.7.1996

⑫ Rotpunkt .... *f4+*
Climb the right-hand side of the carved out slab on the arete.
FA. T.Skinner 1994

⑬ The Deadly Lampshade ...... *f2+*
The short S-shaped crack.

⑭ Malcolm McPherson's a Very Strange Person
.... *f2+*
The very short crack-line slightly further up the banking.
FA. I.Stronghill 1994

⑦ The Buzzard Years *f3*
The crack using good holds either side.

⑧ By A Narrow Margin .... *f4+*
A squeezed-in line with good holds - avoiding the crack is tricky.

Foxtrot Area
This area is approximately 18m to the right of The Buzzard Years. It's esoteric, but dedicated sandstoners will cope. Due to the steep slope below, the lines are difficult to protect with pads and a solo mentality needs to be applied at all times.

⑮ Foxtrot .... *f3+*
The bulging nose. Care is required due to the protruding ledge.
FA. R.Mazinke 1.8.1996

⑯ Meeny .... *f2+*
A short line up the side-wall, using cut-out holds.
FA. A.Evans 17.7.1999

⑰ Tango *f4*
The short arete a few metres down the slope from *Foxtrot*. Mats and a good spotter are advised.
FA. G.West 20.9.2003

⑱ Pogo .... *f5+*
The left side of the concave wall and finishing up the groove above.
FA. R.Mazinke 20.9.2003

⑲ Two Step .... *f5+*
Starting at the far right of the wall, climb the mossy lower arete to a ledge and finish on the upper slab. More of a solo than a boulder problem.
FA. T.Skinner 1994

Happy Valley — Welcome to the Jungle

Welcome to the Jungle
This wall was dramatically transformed by clearance work back in December 2016. Despite this, the wall has a reputation for being overgrown and green. The top-outs are earthy and can be significantly overgrown in summer, making exiting difficult.
Approach (see overview on page 366) - Located below the Foxtrot Area, and left of the lower Cheeswring Rock.

1 Welcome to the Jungle ..   *f6C*
Mount the lip right of the nose with difficulty and finish above.
FA. R.Mazinke 19.5.1996

2 Single Life *f6C*
The central crack has a difficult start past the lip to gain the niche. Moving left at the top of the first crack provides a slightly better finish.
FA. R.Mazinke 19.5.1996

3 The Cross *f7A*
From *Good Friday* traverse the lower lip leftwards until forced to yard out and heel hook round to gain pockets under the lip. Finish up the final section of *Welcome to the Jungle*.
FA. T.Gore 14.4.2017

4 Good Friday *f7A*
Start as for *The Cross* and climb the steep bulging wall above, moving slightly right midway. Finish through the undergrowth.
FA. T.Gore 14.4.2017

5 NS (Not Skinnered) ....   *6b+ 5c*
A meaty off-width crack climb up the often gooey overhanging corner. Move right at the top of the crack onto the right wall and climb the vague arete to finish.
FA. D.Reid 1994

Daimon Beail on the committing final move of *Magic Fountain* (*14*) - *page 368* - on the Hidden Gem Block which is part of the West Valley Boulders at Happy Valley. Photo: Emma Harrington

Happy Valley — Cheeswring Rock

Cheeswring Rock

Happy Valley's biggest attraction (size wise) is the isolated block on the lower footpath at the far southeastern side of the valley. A man-made plinth encompasses and protects the lower section of the block.

Approach (see overview on page 366) - From the upper path, walk southeast to a point were the path curves down to become the lower path. The block is on the right.

Set-up and Descent - It's relatively easy (with care) to step onto and off the boulder from the top. A fallen tree used to lean onto the top and provide an excellent anchor. This was removed in December 2016 and, at time of writing, there are no anchors for top-roping. This may change in the future. Routes in and nearby the narrow passageway suffer from green, and one or two of the routes are slightly friable.

❶ **The Chimney** 3a *3a*
Bridge the passageway at the midway point between Cheeswring Rock and the back wall.
FA. T.Skinner 1994

❷ **Harveys** 7b *6b*
The left arete on the west face is tricky, especially at the start. Finnish with a reachy move.
FA. R.Mazinke 20.6.1999

❸ **Thoroughly Kentish** .... 6b+ *5c*
Start at the crack-line and climb the centre of the face.

❹ **Colour of the Sun** ... 7a+ *6b*
Difficult climbing up the right-hand arete using very small holds.
FA. I.Stronghill 19.5.1996

❺ **Eckpfeiler** .... 6c+ *6a*
The small thin crack. Start by climbing the lower plinth.
FA. M.Fowler, M.Morrison 28.8.76

Cheeswring Rock **Happy Valley** 381

6 Brouillard .... 6c+ *6a*
The large left-hand crack is steep to start.
FA. M.Boysen 1958

7 Nightrain .... 7a+ *6b*
The centre of the bulging wall between the two main cracks.
FA. R.Mazinke 8.6.1996

8 Freney 6c *6a*
Climb the right-hand crack on soft and friable rock.
FA. M.Boysen 19.9.1958

9 Sandstone Safari ... 6c+ *6a*
The steep face on the far right-hand side of the wall provides the best route on this block.
FA. T.Skinner 3.8.1991

10 Chalybeate .... 6b+ *5c*
Climb the right-hand arete up and onto the east face.
Photo on page 361 and 383.

11 From Behind 6b *5b*
From the wedged block at the far east side of the chimney, climb the scooped wall to the upper break. Here the route moves left onto the east face and finishes up a wide crack.
FA. T.Skinner 6.8.1994

Happy Valley — Route Minor Wall

Route Minor Wall

The small buttress to the right of the Cheeswring Rock is often green, but if you catch it after a dry spell the routes are worthy of your attention. Just check the conditions at the top of the routes before you try them. To the right is another short wall with a couple of problems.

Approach (see overview on page 366) - From the upper path, walk southeast to a point were the path curves down to become the lower path. Cheeswring Rock is on the right and this is next to it.

① Rhody-O .... 6b+ *5c*
The left side of the face past the everlasting rhododendron.
FA. T.Skinner 6.8.1994

② Route Minor 4c *4c*
The centre of the wall via some cut-out holds (naughty), to finish up the short crack above.

③ Undercut Rib 4b *4b*
The rib on the far right-hand side of the wall.
FA. T.Skinner 6.8.1994

④ Grimace 4b *4b*
The short face left of the tree stump.

⑤ The Race Home 4c *4c*
The slabby nose right of the tree stump.

Amanda Webster on *Chalybeate* (6b+ *5c*) - *page 381* - on Cheeswring Rock at Happy Valley.

Bull's Hollow

	No star	👤	👤👤	👤👤👤
2a to 4c/f2 to f4	23	6	4	-
5a to 6a+/f4+ to f5+	6	2	2	-
6b to 7a/f6A to f6C+	15	8	5	2
7a+ up/f7A up	-	1	1	-

Close to Toad Rocks is a hidden quarry that dates back to 1890 known as Bull's Hollow. Averaging between 8 and 10 metres in height, this quarry gives a unique and alternative sandstone experience. The rocks surround a murky swamp, which grows significantly with rainfall.

Access
Bull's Hollow is owned by the Lord of the Manor of Rusthall and managed by Tunbridge Wells Commons Conservators who help maintain the quarry for public access in conjunction with the Sandstone Volunteering Group. The rocks are an SSSI (Site of Special Scientific Interest) - see page 50 for more information.

Approach   Also see map on page 362
Take the A264 along the north side of Tunbridge Wells Common to the mini roundabout at its northwest corner. Continue along the A264 towards Groombridge and, after around 300m, turn right onto Rusthall Road. 250m down, turn right onto Harmony Street and snake your way down to park opposite the sandpit by Toad Rocks. Head back up the road to the corner and a tarmac footpath.

The Northern Approach - Drop down the steep path to your left into the woods. Stephens Rock is almost immediately on your right at the bottom of the slope. Follow the path through the trees and veer leftwards (at the foot of the hill) just before the path heads rightwards into what appears to be a fox or badger set. Shortly after is Toad Wall, where a steep descent drops into the north side of the quarry.

The Top Path Approach - Follow the tarmac path, passing Sleepy Hollow (page 406), for approximately 100m to reach Rusthall Road. Turn left past the bus stop and, after the second lamp post, descend down a path to emerge at the south side of the quarry.

Bull's Hollow

Equipment
Setting up a top-rope is relatively easy here, with plenty of trees to anchor to and a good number of bolts which can be hidden under the moss and leaves.

Conditions
The quarry is usually in best condition in the summer and autumn months. The best climbing is found in the south-facing quarried section where the tree coverage is less dense. Away from this wall the rocks tend to be very green and only come into condition after extended periods of dry weather.

Daimon Beail taking advantage of some dry conditions at Bull's Hollow by climbing *The Wall* (6c *5c*) - *page 394* - which is situated on the sunnier south-facing side. Photo: Emma Harrington

Bull's Hollow

Main Quarry

- Waistline p.388
- Ferne p.388
- Yew Wall p.389
- Taurus Wall p.390
- Possibility Wall p.390
- From Rusthall Road and the Top Path Approach

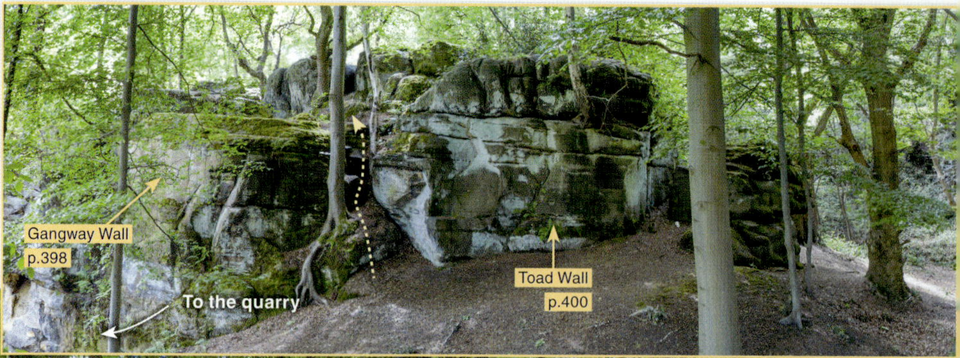

- Gangway Wall p.398
- To the quarry
- Toad Wall p.400

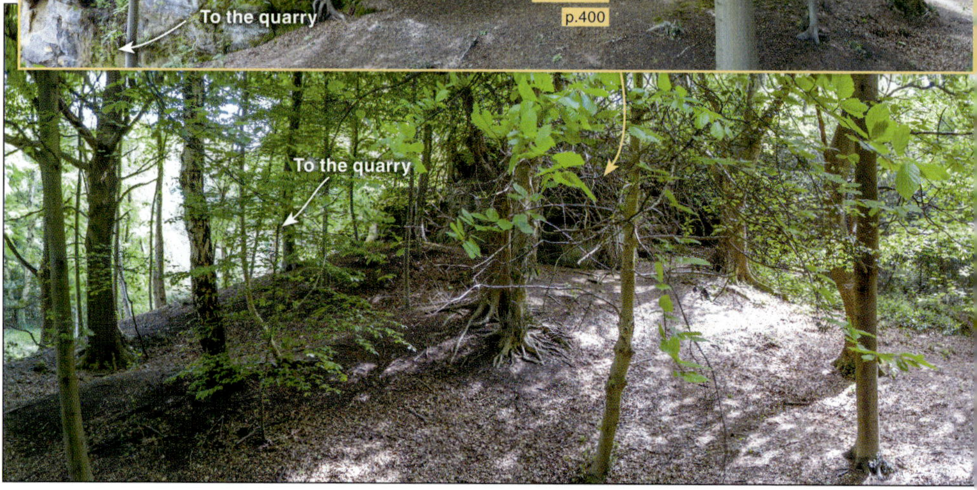

- To the quarry

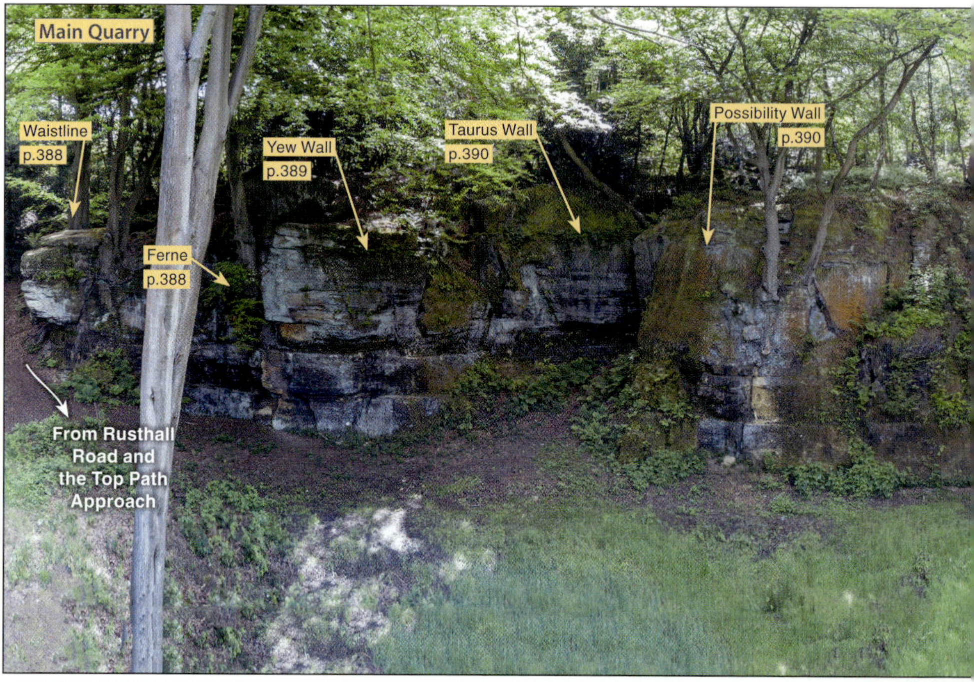

Bull's Hollow

Bull's Hollow — Waistline to Yew Wall

Waistline to Yew Wall

The esoteric wonderland at the far left-hand side of the crag will begin or end your adventures at Bull's Hollow. **Approach (see overview on page 386) -** Use the Top Path Approach from Rusthall Road. Near the end of the path, drop down another steep path which leads to the south side of the quarry. Waistline is the prominent prow.

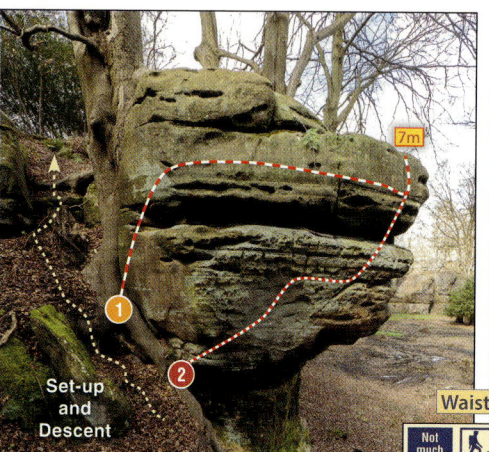

Waistline
This bulging green prow is found at the far left of the crag.

1 Waistline 5a *5a*
Starting from the tree, climb direct to stand on the break and traverse rightwards to finish up the arete.

2 Bulging Waistline 6c *6a*
The direct and much harder version of *Waistline*.
FA. R.Mazinke 19.10.2005

3 Callum .... 6c+ *6a*
Climb the dirty lower wall into the green scoop and finish as directly as possible, avoiding the tree stump.
FA. M.Brewster 2005

4 Broken Crack 3a *3a*
The right-trending crack is more a tree climb than anything else.

Ferne
The next set of 'enticing' routes are situated to the right of Broken Crack. They are all rather green low down.

5 The Chasm 3b *3b*
A disjointed and dirty climb passing a shallow cave.

6 Ferne .... 6a+ *5b*
Try to levitate over the lower wall and proceed up the cleaner and steeper arete above.
FA. M.Brewster 2005

7 Uncertainty 6b *5c*
An esoteric challenge enjoyed by masochists.
FA. M.Fowler 1975

8 Tree Climb 3a *3a*
It is all in the name. Probably best left alone unless this is your thing.

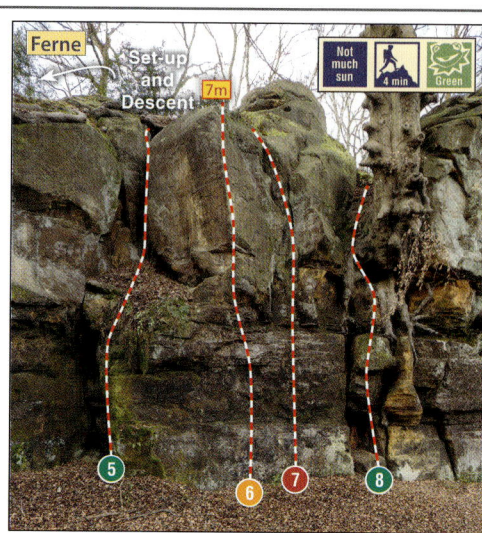

Bull's Hollow

Waistline to Yew Wall

Yew Wall
As you move right there is a slight improvement in quality, though it is still far from ideal.

9 Sandcastle .... 6b+ *5c*
Climb the right-hand side of the nose. Soft and sandy.
FA. J.Harwood 1966

10 Yew Wall 6b *5c*
Climb the short crack to the ledge and make reachy moves to establish yourself on the upper face. Head leftwards towards the yew stump to finish.
FA. N.S.Head 27.2.1972

11 Poltergeist .... 6b+ *5c*
Climb to the ledge and attack the crack above. Probably the best route on this wall, though seldom in condition.
FA. N.S.Head 1975

12 Yellowstone Wall 3b *3b*
A dirty and sandy outing up the crack.

Bull's Hollow — Taurus Wall to Apis

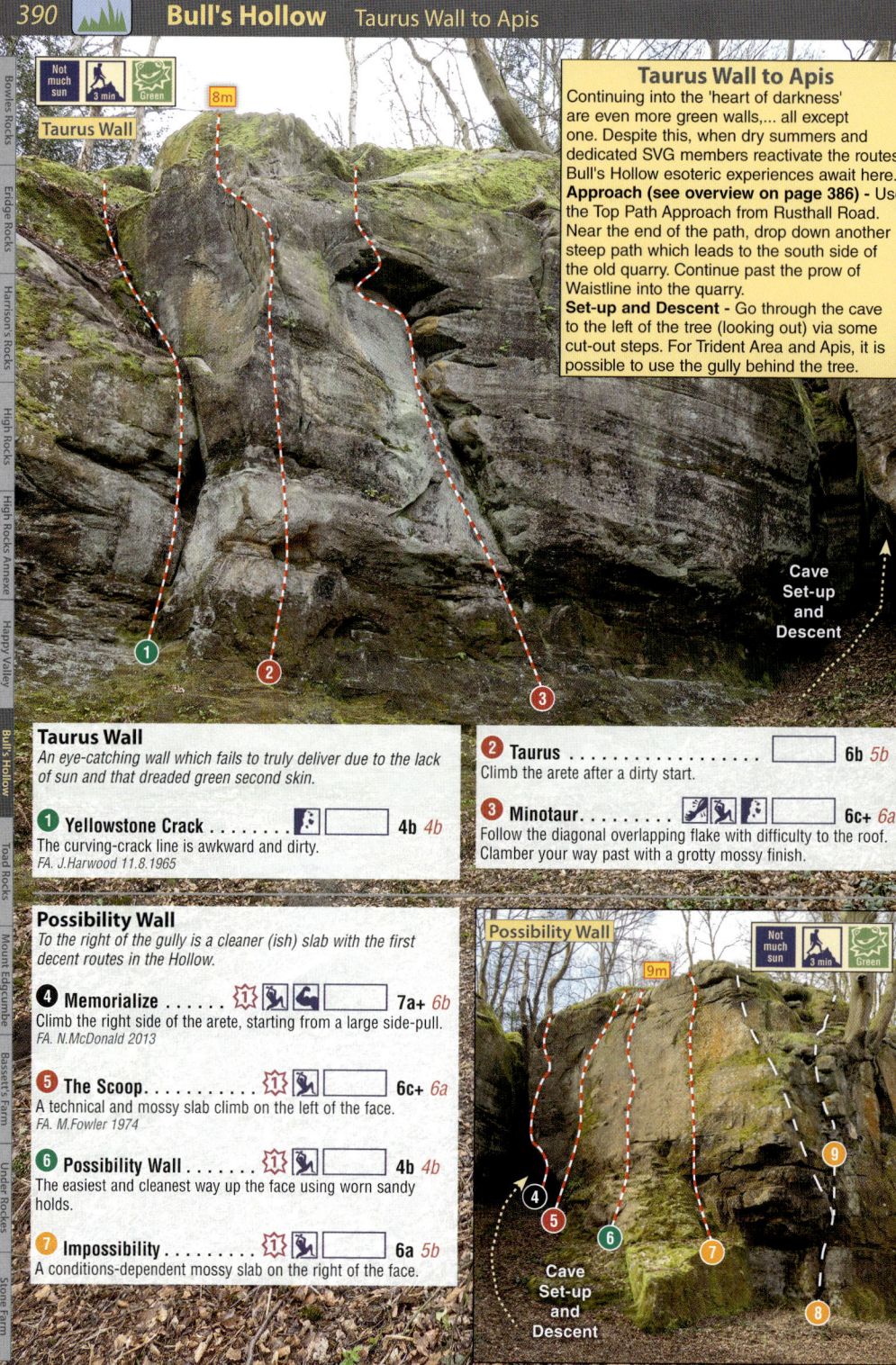

Taurus Wall

Taurus Wall to Apis
Continuing into the 'heart of darkness' are even more green walls,... all except one. Despite this, when dry summers and dedicated SVG members reactivate the routes, Bull's Hollow esoteric experiences await here.
Approach (see overview on page 386) - Use the Top Path Approach from Rusthall Road. Near the end of the path, drop down another steep path which leads to the south side of the old quarry. Continue past the prow of Waistline into the quarry.
Set-up and Descent - Go through the cave to the left of the tree (looking out) via some cut-out steps. For Trident Area and Apis, it is possible to use the gully behind the tree.

Taurus Wall
An eye-catching wall which fails to truly deliver due to the lack of sun and that dreaded green second skin.

① Yellowstone Crack 4b *4b*
The curving-crack line is awkward and dirty.
FA. J.Harwood 11.8.1965

② Taurus 6b *5b*
Climb the arete after a dirty start.

③ Minotaur .... 6c+ *6a*
Follow the diagonal overlapping flake with difficulty to the roof. Clamber your way past with a grotty mossy finish.

Possibility Wall
To the right of the gully is a cleaner (ish) slab with the first decent routes in the Hollow.

④ Memorialize .... 7a+ *6b*
Climb the right side of the arete, starting from a large side-pull.
FA. N.McDonald 2013

⑤ The Scoop .... 6c+ *6a*
A technical and mossy slab climb on the left of the face.
FA. M.Fowler 1974

⑥ Possibility Wall 4b *4b*
The easiest and cleanest way up the face using worn sandy holds.

⑦ Impossibility 6a *5b*
A conditions-dependent mossy slab on the right of the face.

Possibility Wall

Taurus Wall to Apis — Bull's Hollow

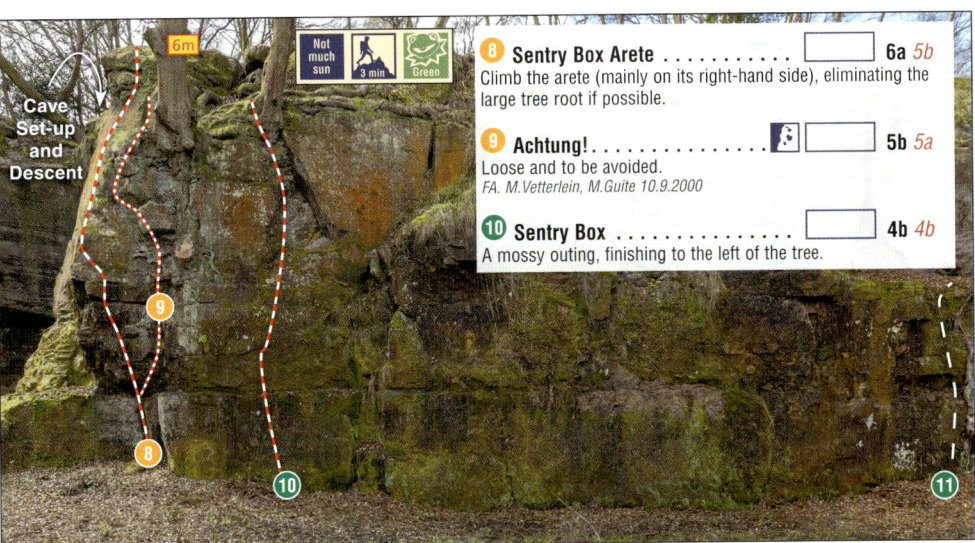

8 Sentry Box Arete 6a *5b*
Climb the arete (mainly on its right-hand side), eliminating the large tree root if possible.

9 Achtung! 5b *5a*
Loose and to be avoided.
FA. M.Vetterlein, M.Guite 10.9.2000

10 Sentry Box 4b *4b*
A mossy outing, finishing to the left of the tree.

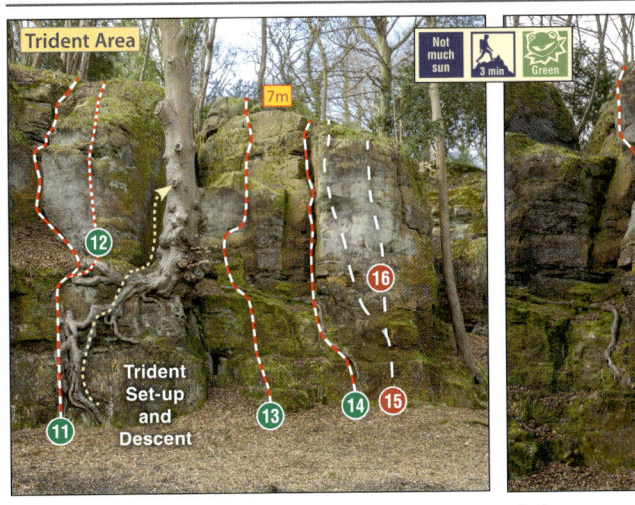

Trident Area
After a section of unclimbable rock (don't you believe it!) the wall splits into two levels. The next routes are left of the tree.

11 Trident Left 3a *3a*
A disjointed route. Start on the tree roots to gain the ledge, and finish up the crack beyond.

12 Neptune Arete 4a *4a*
From the ledge on *Trident Left*, climb the arete to a tricky finish.
FA. F.K.Elliot 1943

13 Trident Arete 3a *3a*
A disjointed, esoteric outing up the series of ledges.

14 Trident Chimney 3a *3a*
Climb the scrappy chimney.

Apis
Another wall which is usually green.

15 Apis Poor Variation .... 6b+ *5c*
A difficult undertaking up the left side of the arete.
FA. R.Mazinke 8.8.1996

16 Apis Variation 6b *5c*
A slightly better route than its neighbour. Climb direct up the blunt arete.
FA. N.S.Head 1960s

17 Apis 4b *4b*
Aim for the short crack higher up.

18 Moss .... 6a+ *5b*
Slippy, slopey, mossy and not much fun.
FA. N.S.Head 1.5.1976

Bull's Hollow — Conway's Buttress

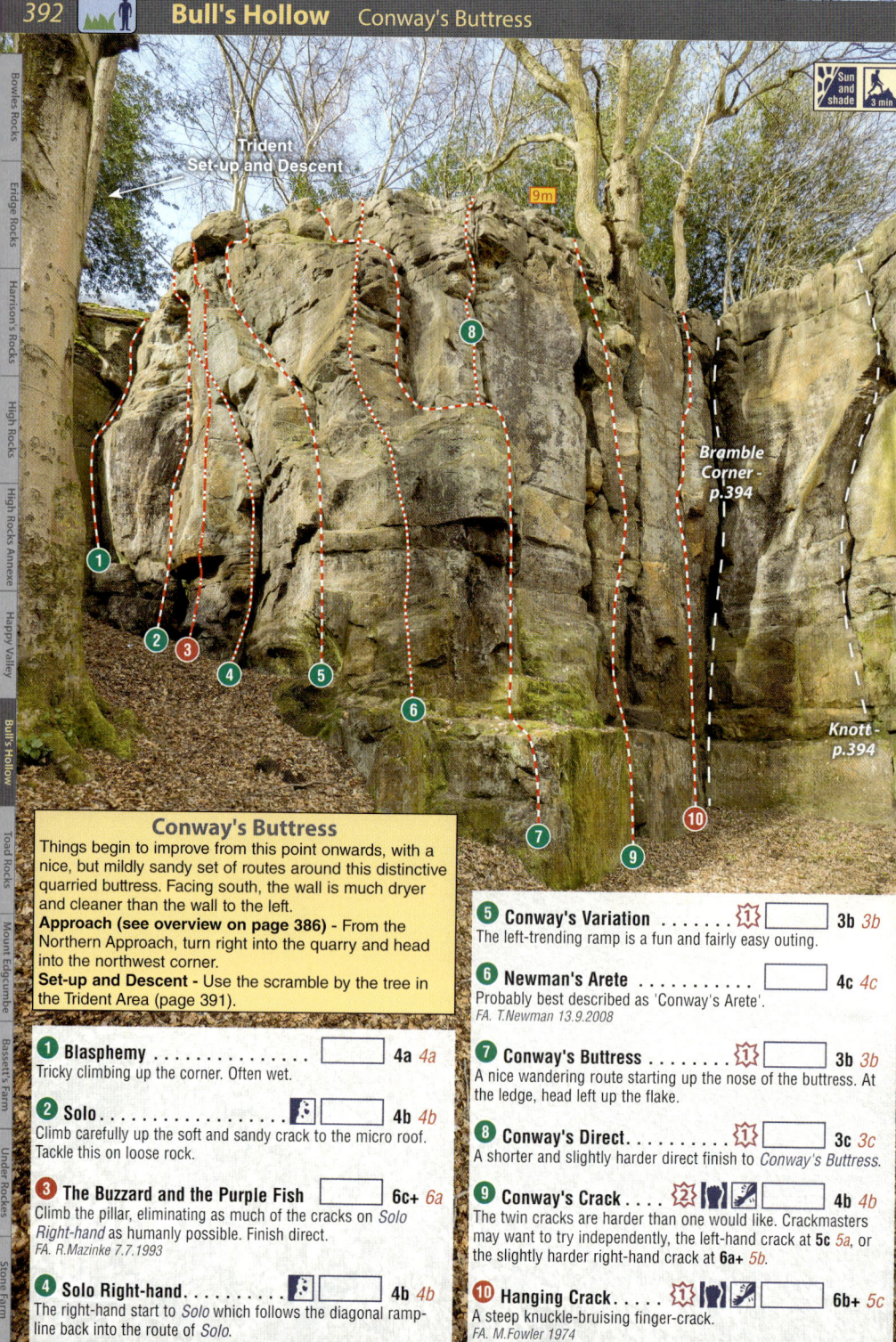

Conway's Buttress

Things begin to improve from this point onwards, with a nice, but mildly sandy set of routes around this distinctive quarried buttress. Facing south, the wall is much dryer and cleaner than the wall to the left.

Approach (see overview on page 386) - From the Northern Approach, turn right into the quarry and head into the northwest corner.

Set-up and Descent - Use the scramble by the tree in the Trident Area (page 391).

1 Blasphemy 4a *4a*
Tricky climbing up the corner. Often wet.

2 Solo 4b *4b*
Climb carefully up the soft and sandy crack to the micro roof. Tackle this on loose rock.

3 The Buzzard and the Purple Fish 6c+ *6a*
Climb the pillar, eliminating as much of the cracks on *Solo Right-hand* as humanly possible. Finish direct.
FA. R.Mazinke 7.7.1993

4 Solo Right-hand 4b *4b*
The right-hand start to *Solo* which follows the diagonal ramp-line back into the route of *Solo*.

5 Conway's Variation 3b *3b*
The left-trending ramp is a fun and fairly easy outing.

6 Newman's Arete 4c *4c*
Probably best described as 'Conway's Arete'.
FA. T.Newman 13.9.2008

7 Conway's Buttress 3b *3b*
A nice wandering route starting up the nose of the buttress. At the ledge, head left up the flake.

8 Conway's Direct 3c *3c*
A shorter and slightly harder direct finish to *Conway's Buttress*.

9 Conway's Crack 4b *4b*
The twin cracks are harder than one would like. Crackmasters may want to try independently, the left-hand crack at 5c *5a*, or the slightly harder right-hand crack at 6a+ *5b*.

10 Hanging Crack .... 6b+ *5c*
A steep knuckle-bruising finger-crack.
FA. M.Fowler 1974

American climber Alex Armitage on the arete of *Broken Nose* (6b+ *5c*) - *page 395* - on The Wall, Bull's Hollow.

Bull's Hollow — The Wall

❸ The Shield .... 6c+ 6a
One of Bull's Hollows better routes. A technical and sustained outing that is conditions dependent - a hot summer and a breeze will do the trick. Finishing direct is harder at 7a+ 6b.
FA. M.Fowler 6.4.1975

❹ The Wall 6c 5c
The best route at the Hollow curves its way around the slightly bulging and featureless wall after a tricky mantelshelf start.
Photo on page 385.

❶ Bramble Corner 4c 4c
The corner-crack gives a good route when dry.

❷ Knott .... 6b+ 5c
Climb the thin crack to the left of the smooth wall. Things ease off in the upper half.

The Wall   Bull's Hollow

The Wall
This is the best it gets at the Hollow and most visits here will be rewarded. The wall faces south and receives plenty of sun in the summer, which keeps 'most' of the green at bay. After long spells of rain, the boggy area just in front of the wall swells, cutting off access to the left side, and seepage from the lower break makes the starts of some of the routes much more difficult.

Approach (see overview on page 386) - From the Northern Approach, turn right into the quarry and head across to the central bay.

Set-up and Descent - Use the scramble by the tree in the Trident Area (page 391) or to the right of Gangway Wall (page 398).

5 Caesar 6c *5c*
From the ledge on *Centurion's Groove*, climb the left arete.
FA. N.S.Head 3.2.1974

6 Centurion's Groove 4c *4c*
An enjoyable route up the slabby corner-crack. The bottom half can be dirty.
FA. F.K.Elliot 1942

7 Squeak Ya Heel Cups ... 7a *6b*
A difficult and steep face climb that breaks out left from *Centurion's Groove*.
FA. J.Dunlop 8.7.1993

8 Pseudonym .... 6c+ *6a*
Follow the thin crack to the slab. Technical face climbing follows.
FA. J.Harwood 1966

9 Pseudonym Right-hand ..... 6c+ *6a*
An easier right-hand finish, but it still packs a punch.
FA. J.Harwood 1966

10 Broken Nose .... 6b+ *5c*
Climb the left side of the nose. The rock is a little on the soft side. *Photo on page 393.*

Bull's Hollow — Slab Chimney

Slab Chimney

Not quite as good as the 'The Wall', this section still provides some playful and powerful routes including the current hardest on the crag. Some of the slabs are mossy, but a dry spell helps dry slimy holds.

Approach (see overview on page 386) - From the Northern Approach, turn right into the quarry and head across to the central bay.

Set-up and Descent - Use the scramble by the tree in the Trident Area (page 391) or to the right of Gangway Wall (page 398).

❶ Cauliflower Ear 6c *5c*
Climb the corner to a sloping ledge as for *Slab Chimney* and make some crimpy moves to gain the face. Follow the holds diagonally leftwards to a thin break (eliminating the arete), and move back right to finish up the centre of the face.
FA. G.Adcock 15.5.2005

❷ Slab Chimney 4a *4a*
Climb the corner to a sloping ledge and step right to gain a sloping green ledge. Climb the thin chimney.

❸ Slab Variant 5a *4c*
Climb the slab using the thin crack. Finish up and right across the top block with a tricky mantel at the end.

❹ Time Waits for No One .. 7b+ *6b*
From the easy-angled slab on *Slab Variant*, step out right onto the face and perform some thin and powerful moves up the face.
FA. D.Atchinson-Jones 1982

❺ Full Moon .... 6a+ *5a*
A good crack climb (with plenty of good holds) and a large tree stump at its centre. *Photo opposite.*

❻ Eyewash 6b *5b*
A dirty and green route up the centre of the face.
FA. N.S.Head 1.5.1976

❼ Triangle Arete 6a *5b*
The arete/nose of this buttress is often damp and very greasy.

Sarah Taylor climbing the unusual route *Full Moon* (6a+ 5a) - *opposite* - on the Slab Chimney area of Bull's Hollow.

Bull's Hollow — Gangway Wall

Gangway Wall

A fine sandstone wall with a proud and inspiring arete. The rock is a bit sandy and broken in places but generally okay.

Approach (see overview on page 386) - From the Northern Approach, this area sits on the northeastern point as you enter the main quarry.

Set-up and Descent - Use the scramble to the right of Gangway Wall.

1 Triangle Climb 3a *3a*
A dirty clamber up the chimney.

2 Too Hot to Handle .... 6c+ *6a*
A direct start to *Handle with Care*.
FA. David Atchinson-Jones 1982

3 Handle With Care 6c *6a*
Climb the centre of the wall to the ledge and traverse left to a niche. Climb the crack to a tricky finish.

4 Crossply 6b *5b*
From the start of *Handle With Care*, move right across the bulging face using a slanting crack. Finish direct.
FA. T.G.DeLacy 1974

5 The Bitch and the Meal Ticket .. 6b *5c*
A direct start to *Crossply*.
FA. C.Tullis 1994

6 Gangway Wall 3a *3a*
Make your way up the dirty and disjointed start and climb diagonally leftwards up the shallow flake. *Photo on page 401.*

7 Square Cut .... 6b+ *5c*
A striking line up the arete.
FA. J.Stevenson 1975

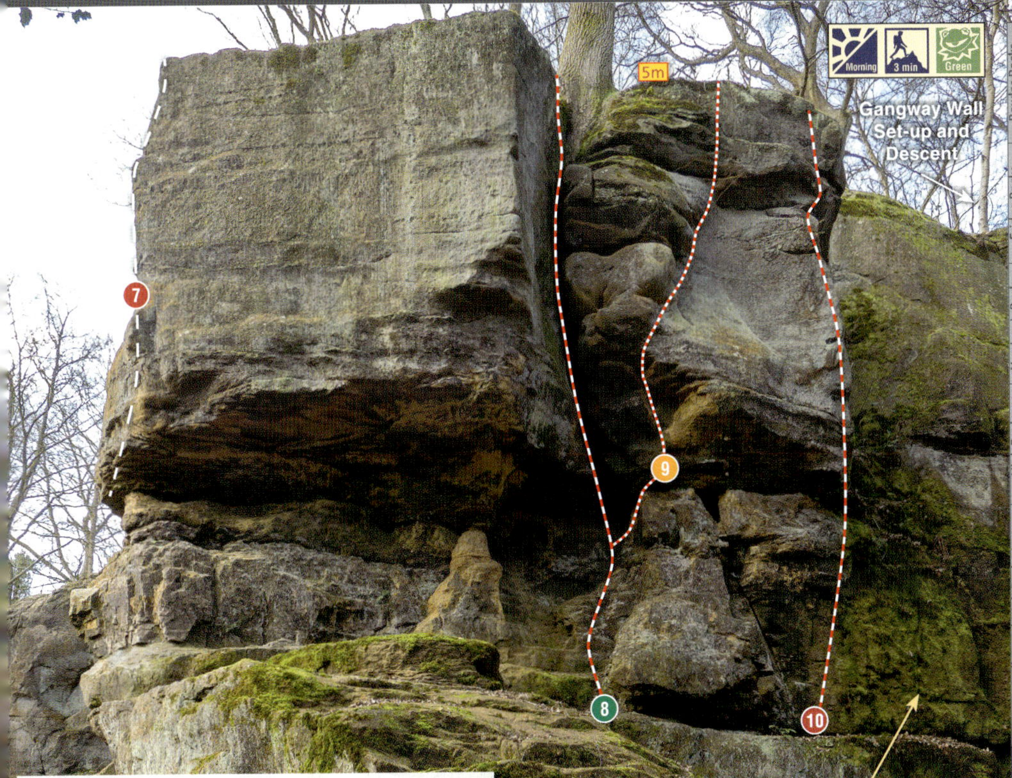

Gangway Wall — Bull's Hollow

8	**Overhanging Crack**	4c *4c*
Jam your way up the damp overhanging crack.
FA. J.Harwood 11.8.1965

9	**Sandy Wall**	6a+ *5b*
Difficult moves lower down lead to easier and better territory higher up.

10	**Avalanche Arete**	6c *6a*
Make some tricky and powerful moves to gain the arete.

11	**Fortuitous**	6b+ *5c*
The green face is rarely climbed.
FA. J.Stevenson 1975

12	**Avalanche Route**	3a *3a*
The dirty green corner which sees few ascents.

13	**The Burglar and the Carving Knife**	6a+ *5b*
A green and mossy face. The true story behind the name is of more interest than the route itself.
FA. T.Skinner 12.5.2005

14	**Birch Tree Wall**	3b *3b*
Climb the green and mossy groove. Probably a 3 star route if you're into this kind of thing!

15	**Birch Tree Buttress**	3b *3b*
The last of the greenys, and another groove.

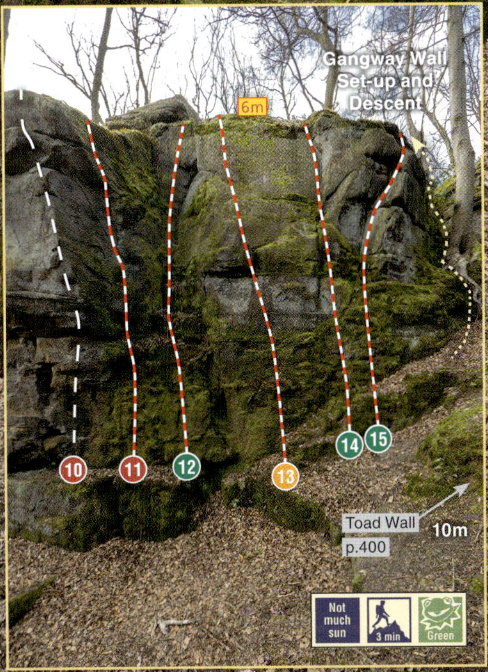

Bull's Hollow — Toad Wall and Stephen's Rock

Toad Wall and Stephen's Rock

These two rocks are close cousins of the neighbouring Toad Rocks. They are mainly sandy and green, but maybe worth check out if you're bouldering in the vicinity.
Approach (see overview on page 386) - These rocks are passed when approaching the Hollow on the Northern Approach.

① Toad Wall Left-Hand .... f2+
Trend rightwards to finish just left of the original.

② Toad Wall .... f2+
A sandy but strangely worthwhile problem up the centre of the wall. Wait for a hot summer though!

③ Toad Arete f4
The arete right of the tree has little for your feet at the start.

④ Turkey Breast and Gravy ..... f2+
Easy climbing around the side of the block. It gets quickly overgrown in the spring.
FA. D.Beail 2015

⑤ Stephen Goes to McDonald's in the Batmobile
.... f4+
Climb just left of the tree on small crimps (no touching the tree). When dry, the rock is good. The upper wall is often too green to finish on, so down climb the tree.
FA. D.Beail 2015

Sarah Taylor enjoying *Gangway Wall* (3a *3a*) - page 398 - on Gangway Wall, Bull's Hollow.

Toad Rocks

	No star	⭐	⭐⭐	⭐⭐⭐
2a to 4c/*f2 to f4*	28	13	3	-
5a to 6a+/*f4+ to f5+*	4	4	6	-
6b to 7a/*f6A to f6C+*	1	3	-	-
7a+ up/*f7A up*	1	1	-	-

This cluster of rocks on the outskirts of Tunbridge Wells is commonly known as Toad Rocks (also referred to as Denny Bottom Rocks). It is southern sandstone's own mini Fontainebleau - a small maze of rocks around the protected Toad Rock sandstone formation - offering a good number of small and relatively easy boulder problems. Some problems have been omitted due to their soft and fragile nature. A few routes have been recorded here, but these have also been omitted due to the difficulty in setting up a top-rope. Being close to the pub, children are often set free to run around while their parents enjoy a Sunday lunch.

Conditions

Many of the problems face north and can get mossy. Some are a little soft and sandy, so take great care to protect the rock by avoiding sketchy footwork and not using inappropriate brushes. The grades given tend to change depending on conditions and the degree of sand and moss. Old chipped holds are common but please never chip your own!

Access

The rocks are classified as a Site of Special Scientific Interest (SSSI) mainly focused around the famous Toad Rock itself.
There have never been any access issues although people should be mindful when bouldering on Rusthall Park which is a private road.

Approach   Also see map on page 362

Take the A264 along the north side of Tunbridge Wells Common to the mini roundabout at its northwest corner. Continue along the A264 towards Groombridge and, after around 300m, turn right onto Rusthall Road. 250m down, turn right onto Harmony Street and snake your way down to park opposite the sandpit by Toad Rocks.

Toad Rocks

Adrian Scadding on *1908* (*12*) - *page 411* - at the connoisseurs venue of Toad Rocks. A good alternative for boulderers looking for something a little different in the area, despite the much softer and sandier nature of some of the rock found here.

Gemma Trickey climbing one of Toad Rocks' surprisingly good problems, (once you master the softer nature of the stone here that is). *Ratty* (*f3*) - *page 416* - on the Bishop's Head at Toad Rocks.

Toad Rocks — Sleepy Hollow

Sleepy Hollow

A small number of boulders situated on the tarmac footpath to the east of Bull's Hollow.

Approach (see overview on page 404) - From the sandpit parking area, head back up the road to the corner with a tarmac footpath and left turn into Rusthall Park private road. Follow the footpath for 50m to the Sleepy Hollow boulders.

Just below the path are three unearthed problems which nature desperately wants back.

1 Micro Machine Left .... f2+
The left side of the nose.

2 Micro Machine Right .... f2+
The arete on its right is often damp.

3 Shoe People .... f2+
Climb the left side of the nose and find those hidden holds.

4 Battleship Traverse f3
A right-to-left traverse using the top of the boulder for hands.

5 Sleepy Hollow f5
Climb the arete, then make a precarious step to the left to finish on the face. Topping out is tricky.

Parson's Nose — Toad Rocks

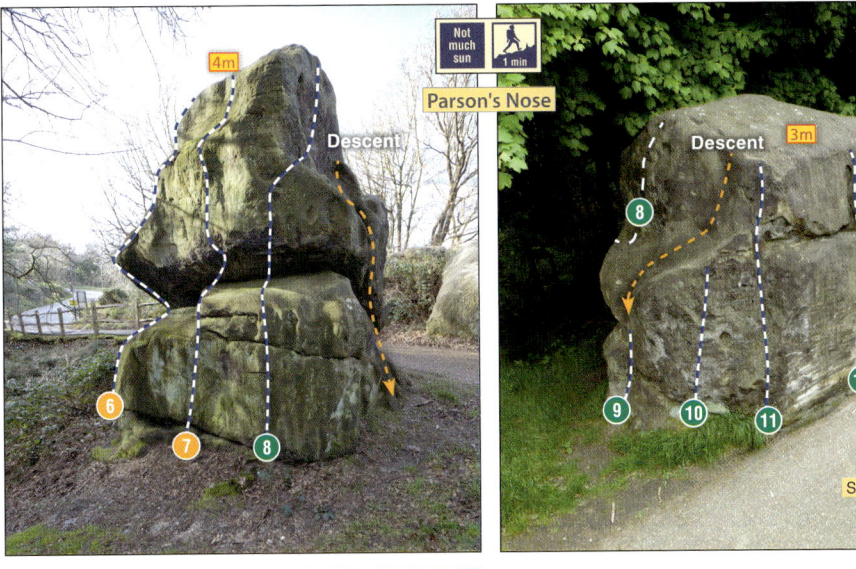

Parson's Nose
Two great little boulders close to the beginning of the private Rusthall Park road.
Approach (see overview on page 404) - From the sandpit parking area, head back up the road to the corner with a tarmac footpath and turn left into Rusthall Park private road; Parson's Nose is to the right and Spotters Block to the left.
Access - The road is private for cars but no access issues have been reported for climbers. Ensure you climb with a spotter so they can whisk mats away and wave politely to drivers.

Parson's Nose
The first boulder on the south side of the road, easily identified by the car scrape marks.

6 Bogey .... f5+
An awkward arete with a bulging nose. Bad landing.

7 I Love Me f5
The centre of the face.

8 Fred .... f3+
Start from two good jugs and pull right onto the platform. The last move is thought provoking.

9 Rusthall Wall f2
The worn scooped steps are used for the descent.

10 Spray .... f2+
A short problem on the rounded cut holds.

11 Paint Job f4
The sandy arete is not entirely independent.

12 Scrape Wall f4
An easy line up the right side of the wall, above the car scrapes.

Spotters Block
Immediately opposite Parson's Nose.

13 Spotter f4
A nice line up the face using cut-out holds.

14 Slap My Boy Up .... f5+
The arete lacks footholds lower down.

A number of other boulder problems have been claimed on the back of the block, but the rock is extremely soft and it is strongly advised that they are left well alone.

Toad Rocks — The Basins

The Basins
An overlooked area which provides a number of fun little problems.
Approach - Head back up the road from the sandpit parking and turn right down the grassy banking just before the road curves sharply right. The first problems described are just beyond this, through the narrow passage past the tree.

Baby J
This block is on the left, just after you pass through the narrow passage.

1 Baby J .... f3+
A nice slab, with a step rightwards at the top.

2 Ramp-line .... f2+
Climb the short ramp-line to a tricky mantel finish.

Lemonade
Located at the northeast side of the bay.

3 Lemonade f4
Reach for the lip and mantel to finish.

Leftism
To the right of Lemonade past a narrow gully.

4 Leftism f3
The short arete on its right-hand side.

5 Sporty .... f2+
The face and crack.

6 Planted f4
Start on two big side-pulls and move up and left eliminating the crack out left.

7 Flutings f3
Climb the short but tricky wall just right of the arete.

Jaba's Little Helper
A sandy boulder on the north side of the connecting passage.

8 Jaba's Little Helper .... f3+
Climb the sandy slab just right of centre on cut-out holds.

The Basins Toad Rocks

Books with Batteries
Just to the west of the connecting passage in the lower basin.

9 Books with Batteries. . . . . f2+
A nice outing just left of the way down.

10 You Make Toast f4
A thin mini problem on the nose.

11 I Make Art! f4
The arete, eliminating the crack out right.

Fish and Chips
Three little problems right of Books with Batteries.

12 Walk in the Park . . . . f2+
Climb the face on the cut-out holds.

13 Chicken in the Basket. . . . . f3+
The arete, moving onto the left face near the top.

14 Fish and Chips. . . . . f3+
The centre of the wall is a nice little problem.

Toad Rocks — Saltbox

Saltbox
The isolated roadside boulder is often green and conditions dependent requiring traffic and some tender loving care.

Approach (see overview on page 404) - Head south up the hill from the sandpit parking area and the boulder is on your left just off the road.

① Saltbox .... **f4+**
Climb the right corner of the block and claw your way up to good holds on the top.

Sandpit Area
The sandpit is what most people associate with Toad Rocks. It has a number of good problems.
Approach - This area is opposite the parking area.

The Retreat

Bench Wall
Behind the bench, hence the name.

② Bench Mark .... **f5+**
Start as for *Bench Wall* and break left to reach for the lip. Continue to traverse left to finish up the arete.

③ Bench Wall .... **f2+**
The centre of the wall.

The Retreat
A few metres to the right of Bench Wall.

④ The View **f2**
The slab eliminating the arete.

⑤ The Retreat .... **f2+**
The line of in-cut holds is a little balancy.

Sandpit Area — Toad Rocks

Snakebite Block
A distinctive isolated block above the sandpit.

6 Snakebite f6A
Climb the short ramp to reach a pocketed wall. Mantel to finish.

7 Snake Charmer .... f6A+
Make reachy moves to a sandy hole, then a long move to the top.

8 Sidre .... f5+
The nose on rounded holds - needs a good spotter in place.
Photo on page 413.

9 Dizzy f3
The centre of the wall.

10 Scoop f4
Start on two big jugs and climb the short concave wall to a juggy top-out.

Grumpy Face
20m right of the Snakebite Block. Clamber up onto some rocks.

11 Grumpy Face .... f3+
A short but spicy problem above a poor landing.

1908
10m right of Grumpy Face.

12 1908 .... f2
Very short with a mantel finish. *Photo on page 402.*

Toad Rocks — The Lion

The Lion

The Lion is situated beyond Toad Rock and on the upper levels. The problems are conditions-dependent, giving good climbing when dry.

Approach (see overview on page 404) - Cross the sandpit and make your way up behind the Toad Rock. Continue for another 10m and the rocks are on your left.

1 The Lion's Crack f4
Climb the dirty crack, unless it's been cleaned by now!

2 Forever Green f5
Climb the groove any way you can. Climb with care and be as static as possible otherwise it will spit you out.

3 Marry Poppins .... f4+
Climb the bulging wall on good holds and move slightly left at the top. Nice although often damp due to the overhanging tree.

4 The Lion's Head f7B
Climb the steep nose using the ramp for feet and good holds for the hands with a stopper move to reach the top.

5 The Lion's Face f7B
Using crimpy side-pulls and poor foot holds, and reach for the sky!

Unfortunately the wall from the Lions Face to The Sleeping Lion never dries out and is best avoided.

6 The Sleeping Lion .... f3+
A nice little line to finish off the day. Climb the small rib at the far right side of the wall.

Guy Atkinson on *Sidre* (**f5+**) - *page 411* - on the Snakebite Block at Toad Rocks.

Toad Rocks — Little Toad and The Ship

Little Toad and The Ship

These two little sandstone gems are tucked away just outside the main area of Toads Rocks, and are well worth seeking out.

Approach (see overview on page 404) - From the sandpit parking area, continue down the road and turn left past the pub. Follow the road round, passing a row of terraced houses, until a tarmac footpath appears. Follow this a short way to the rocks.

The left-hand boulder does actually look like a toad from the correct angle.

1 The Mantel .... f6A+
Start below the roof using undercuts to grab the fat lip and mantel away.
FA. G.Atkinson 12.4.2015

2 The Reach of Faith f4
Climb the arete and make a reach of faith for the top.
FA. D.Beail 12.4.2015

3 Diamond White f4
Reach for the big holds and climb the nose without anything for your feet.

4 White Lightning f6A
A fine problem with a difficult top-out.

5 Happy Slappy .... f5+
Reach for a crimp and slap your way over the top.
Photo opposite.
FA. A.Paisey 12.4.2015

The right-hand Ship boulder still has room for further developments.

6 Childs Play f5
Start in the niche and climb up and left to reach the edge of the break. Slap for a shallow crimp and the rest is up to you.
FA. D.Beail 12.4.2015

7 Resurrection .... f5+
Start with your right hand in the slot and make thin moves to grab for the top.
FA. D.Beail 12.4.2015

8 Strongbow f4
Climb the nose on big holds! Keep a cool head for the top.

Not much sun — 2 min

Adrian Paisey making the first ascent of *Happy Slappy* (*15+*) - *opposite* - on the Little Toad at Toad Rocks, an area that benefitted from a voluntary clean up back in 2015.

Toad Rocks — The Bishop's Head

The Bishop's Head
The Bishop's Head is a cluster of rocks surrounding a small inlet. This area gets a lot of sun, so dries quickly. The trees and bushes quickly shoot up in front of the wall hindering access.

Approach (see overview on page 404) - Head past the right-hand (north) edge of the sandpit to the rocks.

The Dog's Head
There is a line on the left side of this block that almost always has chalk on it. Unfortunately the rock is poor and best avoided.

1 The Dog's Head f5
The powerful nose climb is not as hard as it appears. Unfortunately this is due to a conveniently placed, chipped hold.

2 Mole's Wall . . . . f3+
A short one-move wonder up the side-wall, avoiding the wall behind you.

3 The Willows . . . . f3+
An easy but dirty line up the left side of the face. Lots of nice big holds await at the top though.

4 Ratty f3
A fun and easy problem just left of centre. *Photo on page 405.*

5 Otter V Portly f3
A cheeky mantelshelf problem eliminating the crack out right.

The Inlet
The next problems are in the circular inlet reached either by walking round, or squeezing through, the small passageway either side of The Dog's Head. The first problem is on the left side of the back entrance.

6 The Weasels f2
The right side of the shallow crack has a nice mantel to finish. Tricky for those unfamiliar with sandstone top-outs.

The Bishop's Head Toad Rocks

7 Magic Mike .... f2+
A straightforward problem, though a bit committing at the top.

8 Hook .... f4+
Climb the centre of the wall past a break at half-height. Good fun with more than one way to do it.

9 Pan .... f3+
Climb the smooth ramp-line, eliminating the back wall, and balance right to a mantel finish.

10 Lid f4
Pop for the top above some carved out and now faded foot holds. Very height dependent.

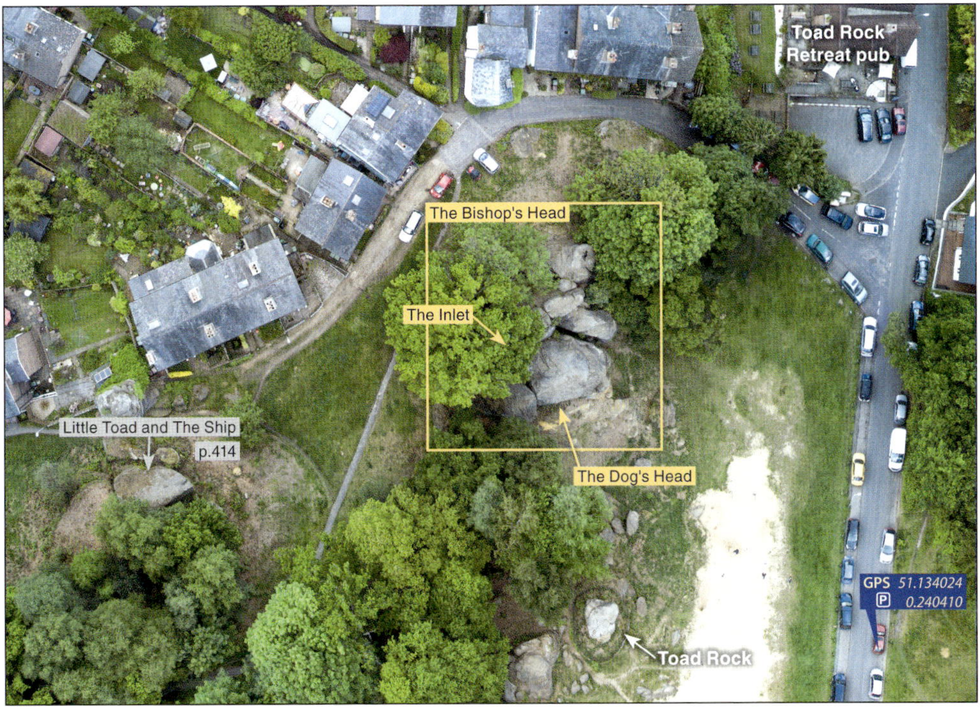

Mount Edgcumbe Rocks

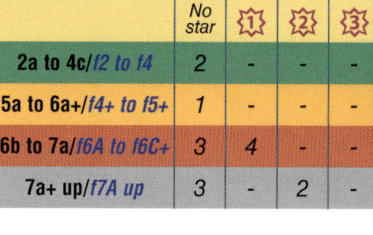

	No star	★	★★	★★★
2a to 4c/f2 to f4	2	-	-	-
5a to 6a+/f4+ to f5+	1	-	-	-
6b to 7a/f6A to f6C+	3	4	-	-
7a+ up/f7A up	3	-	2	-

Tunbridge Wells Common is not the first place that comes to mind when thinking about southern sandstone but, thanks to Tom Gore's developments, Mount Edgcumbe Rocks has now appeared on the climbers' map. Close by is Wellington Rocks which is a favourite with children. It is of limited interest to climbers, though worth a look to marvel at the rock formation.

Approach Also see map on page 362

Mount Edgcumbe Rocks is situated on the north side of Tunbridge Wells Common, south of the A264 near the junction of Mount Ephraim Road and Church Road. There is parking (Mon to Sat, 8am to 6pm, 2 hours max, Sun, free all day) at the side of the road close to a small road leading to the Mount Edgcumbe Restaurant. From the parking, follow the road towards the restaurant for 45m and turn left before the tree line down a path to the rocks on your left. For Wellington Rocks, head down the same road, but turn right after 20m and follow the path through the woodland for 100m.

The much loved and unique playground of Wellington Rocks.

Conditions

The rock is soft and sandy in this area and you must climb with care and precision. Some problems remain dirty and mossy due to the lack of traffic. Glass left by inconsiderate individuals can be a problem at times, so check your top-outs and landings. The best time to visit is in early spring and autumn as the plant life can be quite overpowering when untamed, especially at Mount Edgcumbe.

Mount Edgcumbe Rocks

Tom Gore on *Mustard Seed* (**f5+**) - *page 421* - at Mount Edgcumbe Rocks. Tom has been an active sandstone climber in recent years and, with Ben Read and others, began to explore the further possibilities of bouldering and hard route climbing on sandstone back in the late 2000s. Mount Edgcumbe is a testament to Tom's efforts, having turned a neglected and overlooked area into a challenging bouldering venue.

Mount Edgcumbe Rocks — Lower Left Walls to Upper Tier

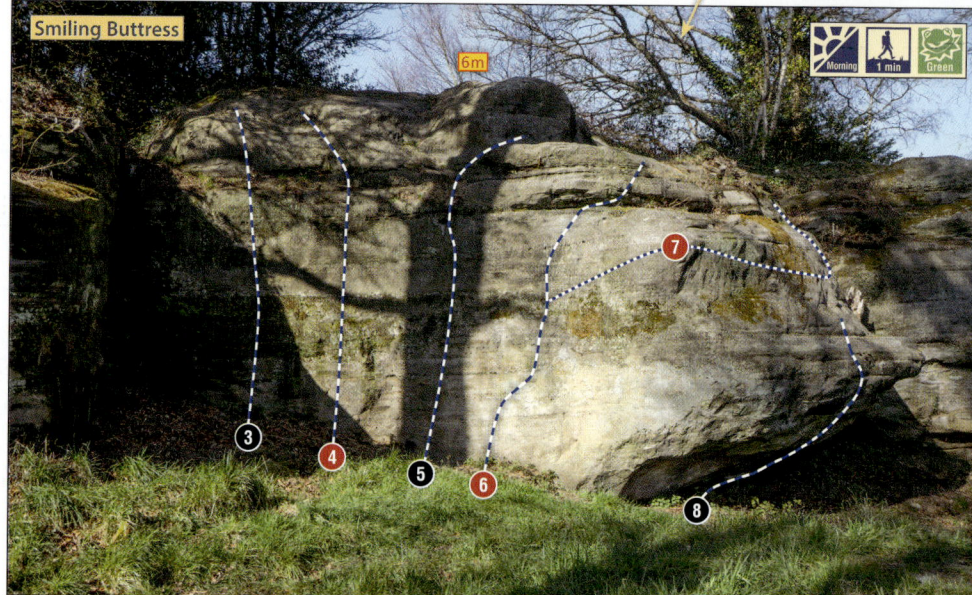

Lower Left Walls to Upper Tier

A connoisseurs choice with some hard problems. The rock is soft so take care. As this is an urban crag, broken glass can at times be found on some of the top-outs.

Lower Left Walls

1 Candy Crush .... `f3`
The arete on its right-hand side.
FA. Emma Harrington 20.3.2016

2 Bejeweled .... `f2+`
A short problem past the square cut-out holds.
FA. Emma Harrington 20.3.2016

Smiling Buttress

3 The Smile .... `f7A+`
Reach for the sloping rail and use a good foot hold to assist with a slap to the ledge. Mantel to finish.
FA. T.Gore 1.6.2014

4 The Diaconate ..... `f6B+`
Climb the shallow groove using shallow pockets and eliminating holds out left on *The Smile*.
FA. T.Gore 1.6.2014

5 Covenant .... `f7A`
Starting from two monos, make a crimpy move to reach the pocket. Finish more easily above.
FA. T.Gore 14.3.2015

6 New Jerusalem .... `f6C+`
Climb diagonally to reach a shallow dish before making a snatchy inelegant move to finish.
FA. T.Gore 5.4.2014

7 New Jerusalem Right-hand .. `f6C+`
An extension traverse finishing on the ledge out right.
FA. T.Gore 10.4.2014

8 Fruit of the Spirit ... `f7B`
A crouch start from side-pulls to a jug and an awkward top-out.
FA. T.Gore 1.5.2016

Mount Edgcumbe Rocks

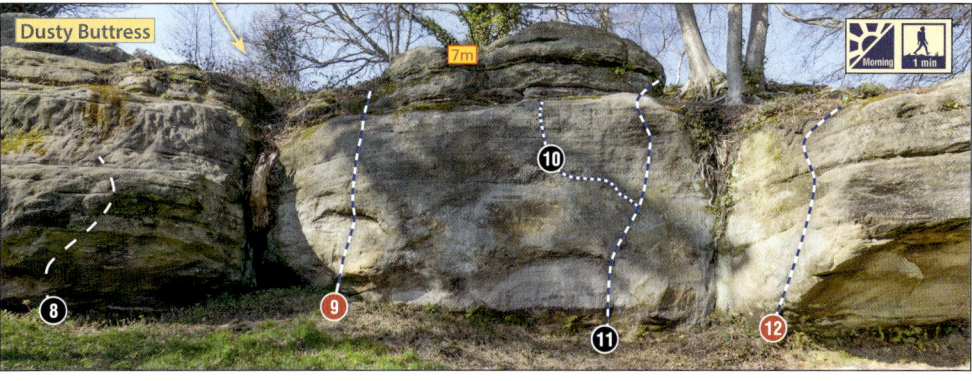

Dusty Buttress

9 Through the Dust f6C
Start from the undercut below the overlap. Reach up to the pockety seam above in order to line up for the slappy finish.
FA. T.Gore 1.6.2014

10 Grace f7C
Follow a series of monos, pockets and slopers across and up - Mount Edgcumbe's hardest problem.
FA. T.Gore 22.7.2014

11 Faith f7B
A fine, technical line up the right side of the wall.
FA. T.Gore 22.7.2014

12 Meekness Not Weakness
.... f6C
A highball problem with a reachy start above a poor landing.
FA. T.Gore 1.5.2016

Upper Tier

13 Curb Rash f6C
A technical and bunched traverse across the wall, finishing as for *Mustard Seed*. The top of the boulder is obviously out.
FA. T.Gore 7.6.2015

14 Mustard Seed .... f5+
A micro line starting from undercuts. *Photo on page 419.*
FA. T.Gore 19.2.2015

15 Over the Hill .... f6C+
From the sloping ledge, use two poor holds to slap for the top.
FA. T.Gore 7.3.2015

Bassett's Farm Rocks

Away from the hustle and bustle of the busier crags, Richard Barlow enjoys the challenges of *Excavator* (6b+/5c) - *page 431* - on Ken's Wall at Bassett's Farm Rocks.

Bassett's Farm Rocks

	No star	☆	☆☆	☆☆☆
2a to 4c/*f2 to f4*	7	2	-	-
5a to 6a+/*f4+ to f5+*	6	3	1	-
6b to 7a/*f6A to f6C+*	7	6	2	3
7a+ up/*f7A up*	-	2	-	-

The most northerly sandstone crag is hidden away in some of southwest Kent's most stunning countryside. The main attractions here are the clean-cut red-streaked Ken's Wall and its neighbour Hypothesis Wall, with their vertical testpieces and finger intensive traverses. Across the field are some smaller rocks which are best avoided as the rock is very soft.

Conditions
The crag is north facing and sees no sun, which makes for an excellent shady venue in the summer months. The downside is that it takes longer to dry after periods of bad weather and the more overgrown areas are prone to be green. The main wall (Ken's Wall) is open and benefits from a good northerly breeze in winter, which helps keep things in relatively good condition for the spring.

Approach   Also see map on page 18
From Royal Tunbridge Wells, head west along the A264 towards Groombridge for approximately 3 miles. On entering open countryside, take a sharp right onto the A264 signed 'East Grinstead', and then almost immediately fork right again onto the B2188 signed 'Fordcombe'. Drive for just under 3 miles and turn left, just after Fordcombe's cricket green, signed 'Walters Green'. Drive for another mile passing over the narrow Hedge Barton bridge, and continue until you can turn left at the small triangular traffic island down a narrow lane. At another triangular island, turn right up the hill and follow this for just over half a mile to a sharp left turn signed 'Bassetts and Cowden', just before the T-junction. Drive for another mile until you begin to descend steeply down a hill, and cross a miniature bridge under trees at its base. Immediately to the right is a grassy area where there is parking for two possibly three cars. Continue up the hill on foot (passing the actual Bassett's Farm on your left) to where the road bends to the left and a public footpath and metal gate with stile are in front of you. Cross this and walk along the path for 170m to reach the first section on your left - 100m after that is Ken's Wall.

Bassett's Farm Rocks

Equipment
There are no bolts at Bassett's Farm Rocks so all top-ropes need to be set up using trees as anchors. Make sure you bring a good range of set-up gear including rock and equipment protectors (see page 38 for more).

Access
The rocks are on private land (with a public footpath running right next to them). The owners have never been successfully identified and there have not been any reported issues. Accessing the top is tricky and it is advisable to approach most areas from the path at the far right-hand side of the crag.

Howard Peters on *Dan's Wall* (6c+ *6a*) - *page 431* - on Ken's Wall at Bassett's Farm Rocks.

426 Bassett's Farm Rocks

Bassett's Farm Rocks

Bassett's Farm Rocks
A Snip in Time to Nice But Dim

A Snip in Time to Nice But Dim
About 170m after the metal gate is the first of a small selection of spaced outcrops, which have a limited number of routes and problems. Many of them being a bit grim and rarely climbed.

① A Snip in Time . . . . 6a+ *5b*
Climb the arete and slab on the left side. It is seldom in condition, being wet sometimes and overgrown at others.
FA. R.Mazinke 9.6.2005

② St Patrick's Chimney 4c *4c*
One of the more unusual routes on sandstone. Enter the cave and bridge, squeeze and heave your way to the top and out of a small hole. Bring a change of clothes. It has been aided on rope ladders in the past.
FA. Paul and Rosie 16.3.2008

Nice But Dim
The rock improves about 70m beyond *A Snip in Time* and to the right of *St Patrick's Chimney*. The lower wall is hard to top out and the stone is a little soft in places.

③ Tim Nice But Dim Esquire . . . 4b *4b*
Climb the face, finishing left of the tree.
FA. M.Vetterlein 3.8.1994

④ Sleeping with Allsorts f4
A horrific top-out. Best practice is to touch the top and retreat.
FA. C.Gibson 15.7.2006

⑤ Bertie . . . . f4+
Best finished by touching the tree and retreating.
FA. T.Skinner 31.1.1993

Chossy Arete and Holly Tree Wall — Bassett's Farm Rocks

Chossy Arete and Holly Tree Wall

Things begin to improve here, but not before you encounter the green and often damp Chossy Arete area which is best left for serious heat waves. Adjacent to this is Holly Tree Wall, which is the first decent wall at Bassett's Farm.

Set-up and Descent - The right side of the crag is the best option if not overgrown, otherwise use the steep gully to the right of *Silly Arete*.

9 Keep the Faith .... 6b+ *5c*
A tricky climb starting on the left side of the shallow cave. Curve left slightly for an unpleasant top-out.
FA. A.Serrecchia 13.8.1995

10 Tree Route 5a *4c*
The sandy right side of the cave finishing to the right of the tree.
FA. K.Wallis 1987

11 Silly Arete 5b *5a*
The short arete. Less spectacular than its Welsh namesake!
FA. K.Wallis 1987

12 Holly Tree Wall .... 6a+ *5b*
A short route finishing just left of the tree.
FA. M.Vetterlein 2.12.1989

13 The Indian Face .... 6b+ *5c*
A climb made difficult by an abundance of sandy holds. Finish right of the tree.
FA. M.Vetterlein 2.12.1989

14 Get Orf Moi Land .... 6a+ *5a*
The longest route on the wall has a tricky start.
FA. M.Smith 2.5.1990

15 Carpet Slab 4a *4a*
Climb the slabby right-hand arete, which can be greasy at times.
FA. M.Vetterlein 2.12.1989

6 Really Chossy Flake 3a *3a*
Climb the flake at the centre of the face. Dirty!

7 Liquorice Wood 6a *5a*
A fairly dirty route direct to the tree.
FA. C.Gibson 15.7.2006

8 Chossy Arete 6b *5c*
A green and greasy arete climb.
FA. I.Mailer 1987

Bassett's Farm Rocks — Ken's Wall

Ken's Wall

The showpiece wall at Bassett's Farm Rocks is home to a good number of quality routes, but is not somewhere to take a beginner. The wall generally dries quickly and is more open to the elements than the other walls here.

Approach (see overview on page 426) - This wall is the first major section of rock reached on the approach, about 250m after the gate.

Set-up and Descent - Use the right of the crag if clear, or use the steep gully to the left.

① Beyond Our Ken .... 6a+ *5b*
Climb the arete on its left, moving right close to the top.
FA. M.Vetterlein 3.8.1994

② Ken's Wall 6b *5c*
Start by climbing the thin crack, moving rightwards at half-height. Head up past a series of breaks to a difficult finish.
FA. I.Mailer 1987

③ Hound Dog 6b *5c*
Thin face climbing low down leads to the niche. Finish up the arete.
FA. D.Riley 1996

④ Kenian Crack 4b *4b*
A pleasant (ish) outing up the crack, which is the easiest way up the wall.
FA. K.Wallis 1987

The next three lines are boulder traverses.

⑤ Good Boy .... f6B+
The lowest level traverse in either direction has good holds but nothing much for your feet.
FA. D.Potts 2.4.2004

⑥ Pirelli .... f7A+
The hardest of the traverses crosses the thin centre rail from left to right. Right to left is slightly harder at *f7B*.
FA. M.Diaz 2004

⑦ Bad Boy .... f6A+
The easiest of the three traverses uses a combination of the top two rails and has relatively decent holds for both hands and feet. Can be done in either direction at the same grade.

Ken's Wall — Bassett's Farm Rocks

⑧ Harvester 6c *6a*
Climb the face just right of the crack and finish using the arete out left.
FA. R.Mazinke 26.8.2003

⑨ Dislocator 7a *6a*
A knuckle-busting series of moves using some very old bolt holes. Either finish direct or more easily to the left.
FA. I.Mailer 1987

⑩ Karate Liz 7b *6b*
Climb the wall direct to the left side of the shallow scoop close to the top. Make a long reach, or dyno, to finish. Hard for the short.
FA. I.Mailer 1987

⑪ Dan's Wall ...... 6c+ *6a*
Climb direct to the right side of the scoop, and again, make reachy moves at the top. *Photo on page 425.*
FA. D.Lewis 1987

⑫ Excavator .... 6b+ *5c*
Climb the arete and finish on the face with a tricky top-out. *Photo on page 422.*
FA. I.Mailer 1987

⑬ Charming Chimney 4b *4b*
A slightly contrived route. Bridge the gully without touching the ground and finish on the right wall just left of *Pearl Necklace*.
FA. P.Highams 14.7.2006

Hypothesis Wall — Bassett's Farm Rocks

10 Das Vaterland 4a *4a*
A dirty esoteric crack climb. Best left alone.
FA. R.Mazinke 20.9.2003

11 Docker's Armpit 4b *4b*
Climb the green bulge to the right of the crack.
FA. T.Skinner 31.1.1993

Mark Elwell on the excellent *Conclusion* (6b *5b*) - *opposite* - Hypothesis Wall, Bassett's Farm Rocks.

Lucy Groen on the classic *Uganda Wall* (6b+ *5c*) - *page 438* - on the wall with the same name at Under Rockes.

Under Rockes

Under Rockes

	No star	☆	☆☆	☆☆☆
2a to 4c/f2 to f4	8	1	-	-
5a to 6a+/f4+ to f5+	1	5	2	-
6b to 7a/f6A to f6C+	8	8	4	4
7a+ up/f7A up	1	2	-	-

Under Rockes is the southernmost climbable venue. It is tucked away on the north edge of a wood and comprises a number of walls including the impressive Uganda Wall. This fine clean-cut wall has some large square-cut holds which once upon a time held wooden posts to support a lean-to building. These holds now make key features of several of the better routes on the wall. Further right the quality drops a little, although there are a few decent routes. The overall setting is very pleasant and it becomes especially beautiful in spring when the bluebells arrive!

Approach   Also see map on page 18

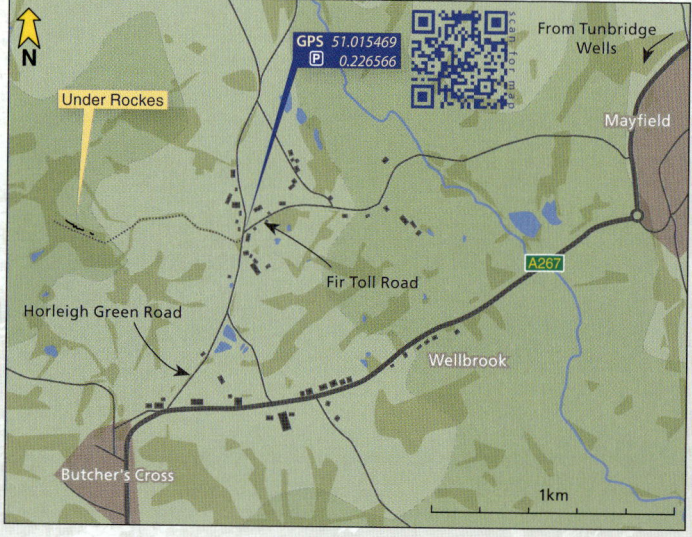

The crag is situated in woods to the west of the historic village of Mayfield. Head south from Tunbridge Wells on the A267 for 10 miles until you reach a large roundabout directly west of Mayfield. Take the second exit (signed 'Eastbourne') and continue for 1.5 miles to a sharp right into Horleigh Green Road (signed 'Rotherfield'). Drive for half a mile to Fir Toll Road on your right (signed 'Mayfield') and a red letter box on the corner. Park on the roadside somewhere here **but not in front of the long wooden fence bordering the house** on the right as you enter Fir Toll Road.

Walk a little way back down Horleigh Green Road and, opposite the large house, is a narrow footpath heading into the trees. Follow this to a track (muddy after rain) that runs through a narrow strip of woodland. Follow this for approximately 500m to a stile/fence on the right. Cross this and head diagonally left down into the lower field, gradually following the vague path down towards another stile on the edge of the wood. Continue on the path through the wood and the rocks appear on the right.

Equipment

There are no bolts here so all top-ropes need to be set up using trees as anchors, some of which are set back from the rocks. Be sure to bring the correct set-up equipment (see page 38 for more).

Access

The approach to the rocks is on private land. The owners of the rocks have never been formally identified and access has never been an issue. Check the BMC RAD for up-to-date access information and if asked to leave, please do so politely.

Under Rockes 437

Conditions
The walls are tucked away under a shady tree canopy making them slow to dry and susceptible to green. However, it faces southwest allowing the sun through, especially when the leaves have gone making early spring, with its amazing bluebells, and autumn the prime times to visit. Summer can be vegetated and humid, so pick a cooler breezy day. Some of the rock is soft, especially on the less travelled routes.

Lucy Groen climbing *Lionheart* (6c+ *6a*) - *page 438* - on the Uganda Wall at Under Rockes.

Under Rockes — Uganda Wall

Uganda Wall

This showpiece wall at Under Rockes has all the best routes. Many of the routes are close together creating a few eliminates. For the original routes, don't be afraid to grab a hold if you think it's in, as it probably is! There are some overgrown routes to the left of this wall which have not been included. The wall stays in remarkably good condition despite the tree cover. Some of the holds can be sandy, but the top-outs are flat and generally clear of any foliage.

Set-up and Descent - Go up a steep gully to the left of the wall.

① Wide Crack 2a *2a*
A dirty crack with an even dirtier finish.
FA. J.C.Scola 2.11.1963

② Birthday Buttress 6c *6a*
Climb the wall just right of the arete and avoid the large pot-holes on *The Thirteenth Light*. Eliminate.
FA. R.Mazinke 6.8.1995. Also claimed by D.Standridge.

③ The Thirteenth Light 6c *6a*
The first of the pot-hole climbs is not an easy one.

④ Lionheart .... 6c+ *6a*
Climb through the line of pot-holes past a difficult section midway. Finish left or right of the tree. *Photo on page 437.*
FA. T.Daniells 1970s

⑤ Over the Hill 6c *6a*
Tackle the overlap and continue direct, avoiding the large pot-holes, with some thin moves at half-height. Eliminate.
FA. W.O.R.Hill 11.2.1989

⑥ Uganda Wall .... 6b+ *5c*
A great route up the centre of the wall using the large pot-holes. Tricker than it first appears. *Photo on page 434.*
FA. P.J.Watson 3.11.1963

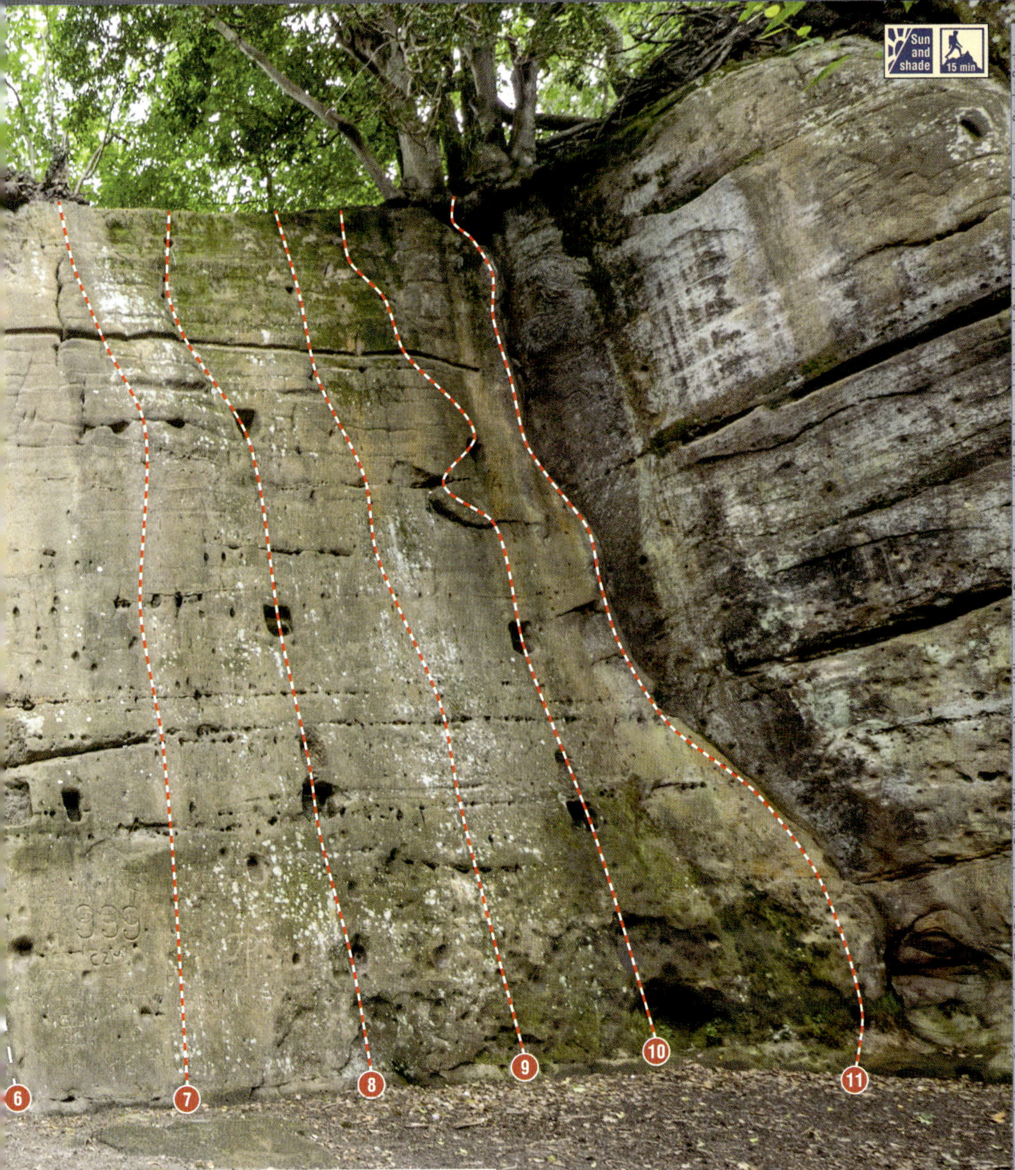

Bowles Rocks
Eridge Rocks
Harrison's Rocks
High Rocks
High Rocks Annexe
Happy Valley
Bull's Hollow
Toad Rocks
Mount Edgcumbe
Bassett's Farm
Under Rockes
Stone Farm

7 Magic Pebble 1 6c *5c*
Climb the fingery pocketed wall. Eliminate.
FA. W.O.R.Hill 11.2.1989

8 Fireball . . . . 3 6b+ *5c*
Climb direct through the series of pot-holes. Slightly harder than *Uganda Wall*.
FA. M.Boysen 1960

9 Dogs of War 1 6c *6a*
Thin face climbing avoiding the big pot-holes. It is a bit mossy at the top. Eliminate.
FA. W.O.R.Hill 11.2.1989

10 In One Hole 2 6c *6a*
The last line of pot-holes on this wall, some of which are shared with the next route, *Central Crack*. The top can be green.
FA. D.Wajzner 7.1981

11 Central Crack . . . . . Top 50 6b *5c*
The best route at Under Rockes and much harder than it looks. Attempt to climb the crack-line which can be started in an number of ways. Continue up the cleaner wall using some of the pot-holes out left but sticking primarily to the crack. Exit steeply on large tree roots. *Photo on page 445.*
FA. M.Boysen 1960

Under Rockes — Evening Arete

Evening Arete
The clean side-wall right of Uganda Wall has two routes, both finishing on the arete. The slabby front face has a number of easier routes, although many of them are covered in moss.
Set-up and Descent - Go up a steep gully to the left of Uganda Wall or to the right of Dark Crack Buttress.

❶ The Touch 6b *5c*
A good climb up the centre of the face. Finish up the rounded arete.
FA. B.Knight 8.1982

❷ The Alien Succumbs to the Macho Intergalactic Funkativity of the Funkblasters
.... 6b+ *5c*
A slight eliminate up the face, avoiding use of the lower arete.
FA. D.Atchinson-Jones 8.1982

❸ Evening Arete 6a *5b*
Climb the slabby right side of the arete. Either finish direct or traverse more easily off to the right.
FA. M.Boysen 1960

❹ Hear No Evil 5b *5a*
The first of the mossy outings has a long reach to start.
FA. R.Maher 9.8.1972

❺ Speak No Evil 5b *5a*
A squeezed-in eliminate.
FA. G.W.Jennings 10.11.1963

❻ See No Evil 4c *4c*
The climbing is almost entirely on moss.
FA. N.S.Head 8.1972

❼ Channelsea Crack 3a *3a*
A dirty crack climb with a lot of loose foliage at the top.
FA. M.Vetterlein 6.1993

Dark Crack Buttress — Under Rockes

Dark Crack Buttress
To the right of the mossy wall of *Channelsea Crack* are two large and rounded buttresses, split by a long dark crack at their centre. The rock is soft so take care. A number of the routes are green and seepage can also be a problem. Wait for a dry season for this one.
Set-up and Descent - To the right of this buttress.

8 Outfall Crack **6c** *6a*
A very awkward route indeed. Climb the sandy off-width crack with no bridging back onto *Channelsea Crack*. Exiting this route makes you feel like David Bellamy.
FA. T.Skinner 6.1993

9 What the Buck **6c** *6a*
Climb the wall direct (with difficulty) to the oak tree.
FA. T.Gerard 3.1990

10 Anything Goes . . . . **6c+** *6a*
Climb the arete and tackle the bulging nose just above half-height. Often green.
FA. R.Mazinke 27.6.1996

Under Rockes — Dark Crack Buttress

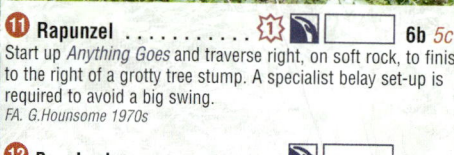

⑪ **Rapunzel** 6b *5c*
Start up *Anything Goes* and traverse right, on soft rock, to finish to the right of a grotty tree stump. A specialist belay set-up is required to avoid a big swing.
FA. G.Hounsome 1970s

⑫ **Bow Locks** .... 6b+ *5c*
Climb the steep wall direct via a short crack to a dirty finish.
FA. M.Vetterlein 28.8.1994

⑬ **Mastercard** .... 7a+ *6b*
Locate the horseshoe carving on the rock. From here, climb steeply to the left side of the tree stump. An awkward finish.
FA. P.Widdowson 19.5.1990

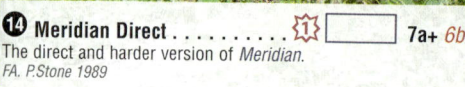

⑭ **Meridian Direct** .... 7a+ *6b*
The direct and harder version of *Meridian*.
FA. P.Stone 1989

⑮ **Meridian** 7a *6b*
Start left of *Dark Crack* and climb leftwards using a series of breaks to pull onto the nose. Finish to the right of the stump.
FA. D.Atchinson-Jones 8.1982

⑯ **Funnel Web** 7b *6b*
Start as for *Meridian* and climb the wall direct. Unfortunately the rock is very soft in places.
FA. P.Stone 2.1990

⑰ **Dark Crack** 6c *5c*
A pretty hard overhanging crack climb.
FA. R.Maher / T.Daniells 1970

Dark Crack Buttress — Under Rockes 443

18 One Up All Up, Except Mat ⭐ 7a *6a*
Climb the nose to a large stalactite/thread and power over the bulge to finish by the small tree. Often wet at the top.
FA. P.Stone 10.10.1992

19 Peregrine ⭐⭐ 6a *5b*
Start as for *One Up*... and, at half-height, traverse right and finish right of the holly tree. Creative belay set-up required.

20 Kestrel 6b+ *5c*
Climb direct to a large thread/stalactite and finish up the upper face, which is often wet, to a mossy top-out.
FA. M.Vetterlein 28.8.1994

21 Merlin 4a *4a*
An easy (but usually dirty) climb up the face.
FA. M.Vetterlein 28.8.1994

Further right and up a steep slope behind the rope swing (if in place) is a densely vegetated slab and buttress. This has a number of recorded routes, but is best avoided.

Under Rockes — Departure Slab

Departure Slab

The final rock of interest is 30m right of Dark Crack Buttress and up on the banking (beyond the rope swing). It is an overgrown crag which can give a few worthwhile climbs if cleaned. The wall is not very high so you can boulder the routes, but with poor landings and the dirty nature of the rock, a top-rope is advised.

Set-up and Descent - You can use *Easter Crack* or to the right of *Baggins* if not too vegetated.

1 The Waltzing Buzzard 6b *5c*
A short slab finishing on the right side of the arete.
FA. R.Mazinke 23.2.1992

2 Trouble with Rubble 6a *5b*
Climb the short slab.
FA. A.Hughes 1988

3 Hardcore 4b *4b*
A slab climb with a good pocket higher up.
FA. M.Vetterlein 1990

4 Down the Hatch 5b *5a*
An awkward route out of the niche which often has a sapling sticking out to make things less fun.
FA. M.Vetterlein 1990

5 Departure Slab 4a *4a*
A short slab climb departing from the right side of the niche.
FA. J.C.Scola 3.11.1963

6 Manteloid 6b *5c*
Climb out of the small cave to a mantel finish.
FA. M.Smith 3.1990

7 Easter Crack 2b *2b*
A straightforward crack which can also be used as a way down.
FA. R.Maher 1960s

8 Lamplight 6a *5b*
Climb the left nose of the slab - mossy near the top at times.
FA. N.S.Head 18.8.1972

9 Roger's Wall 6a *5b*
A nice pocketed wall up the centre of the slab.
FA. T.G.DeLacy 18.8.1972

10 Wind and Wuthering 6b *5c*
A short squeezed-in eliminate. Avoid holds out left and right if you can, and finish with a mossy top-out.
FA. M.Spencer 3.1990

11 Bilbo 3a *3a*
A very short climb up the crack.
FA. T.G.DeLacy 9.8.1972

12 Baggins 3a *3a*
Barely a route. Climb the short slab and finish as for *Bilbo*.
FA. R.Maher 9.8.1972

Sara Ortiz jamming her way up *Central Crack* (6b 5c) - *page 439* - on Uganda Wall at Under Rockes.

James Nicholson on *SW Corner Scoop* (6a+ *5a*) - *page 475* - on the picturesque Inaccessible Boulder at Stone Farm.

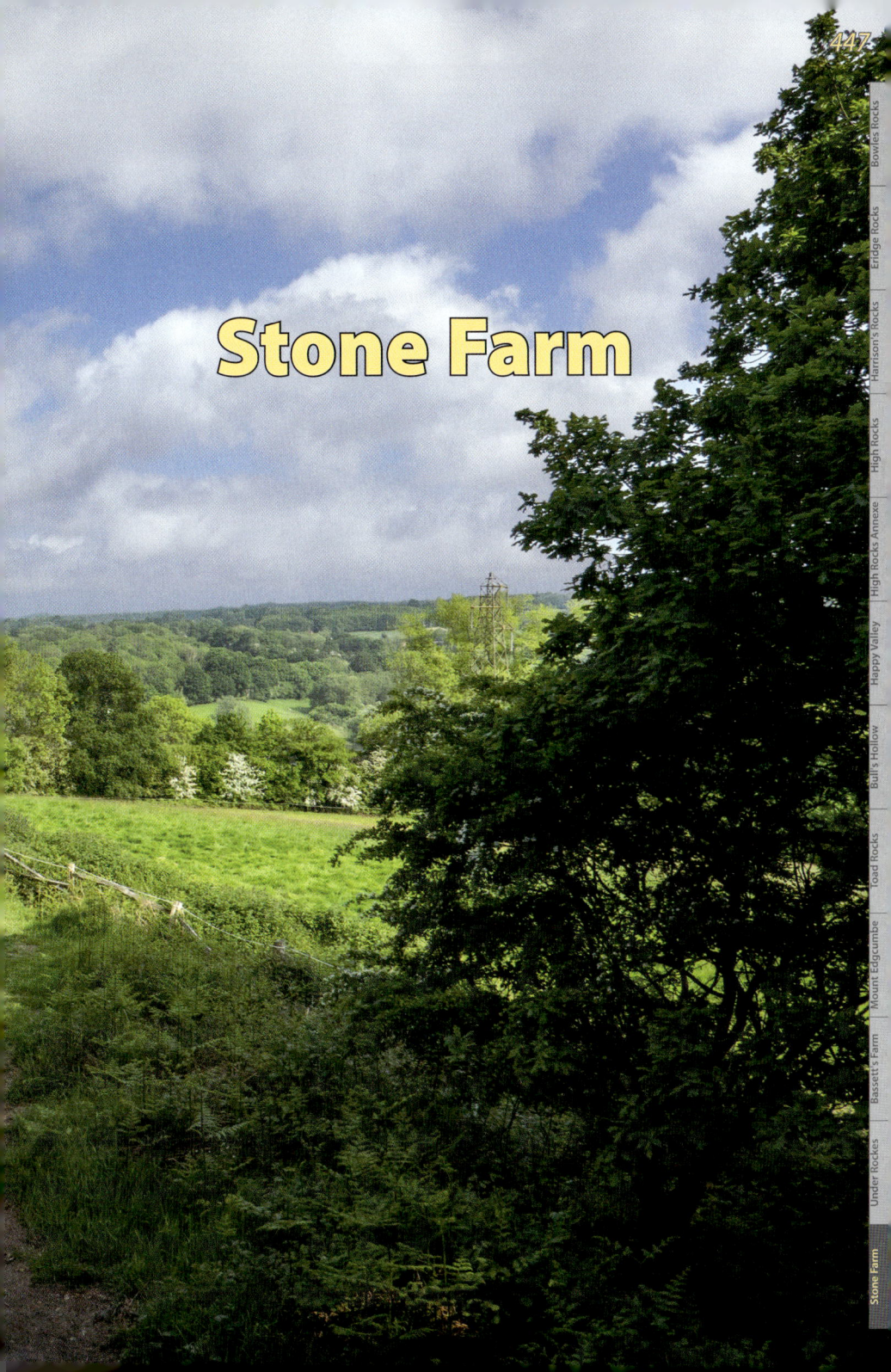
Stone Farm

Stone Farm

	No star	☼	☼☼	☼☼☼
2a to 4c/f2 to f4	38	16	6	-
5a to 6a+/f4+ to f5+	13	7	8	3
6b to 7a/f6A to f6C+	22	20	13	1
7a+ up/f7A up	3	-	4	2

Just south of East Grinstead (West Sussex) is the picturesque outcrop of Stone Farm which sits proudly on the hillside overlooking the Weir Wood Reservoir. Although a bit of an outlier from the main sandstone crags, it is very popular and the closet venue to south London - spring and summer weekends can be crowded, especially if groups are also present.

Stone Farm stretches for around 200m and has a number of great routes mostly in the mid-to-low grades. At a height of around 6m to 8m, it has something to offer boulderers albeit mostly highball problems. Whether going for routes or bouldering, a pad is a good addition to your kit to help reduce ground erosion and protect tricky starts.

Conditions and Equipment

Stone Farm is south-facing and dries quickly, except for the sections heavily shaded by trees. Years of use has made the rock quite soft and many of the holds have a light sandy feel to them, so please take extra care and protect the rock by only cleaning holds delicately. Many of the routes have bolt anchors at the top, but some require longer non-stretch belays to set up off trees.

Access

The rocks are on open access land owned and managed by the BMC (see page 52). Problems are caused here by people lighting fires for barbeques and by children vandalising the rock with charcoal and chalk. Stone Farm is a Site of Special Scientific Interest (see page 50) and anyone intentionally damaging the rocks or lighting fires could be liable to a significant fine! Check the Code of Conduct - page 32.

A busy weekend at Stone Farm Central.

Stone Farm

Approach

Also see map on page 18
From East Grinstead, navigate around the one-way system and head southwest on the B2110.
At the roundabout on the edge of the town, take the third exit on the B2110 signed 'Turners Hill'. Follow this for just short of a mile to a crossroad and branch left signed 'West Hoathly'. Drive down here to a large triangular traffic island and keep right. After just over half a mile, follow the road downhill past a large house to a junction from where the reservoir is visible ahead. Turn left here and park immediately on your right if room allows (space for 3 or 4 cars).
There is more parking approximately 300m further down this road, on the left. This parking is unofficial, but it is regularly used by walkers and sightseers.
Back at the junction by the house, head up the hill a little way and then left onto a bridleway (no parking here). After approximately 100m, turn left to reach the Inaccessible Boulder.
Further limited parking can be found further down the main road, just before a small bridge. A path leads through the woods direct to the crag from here, but it is not a right of way.

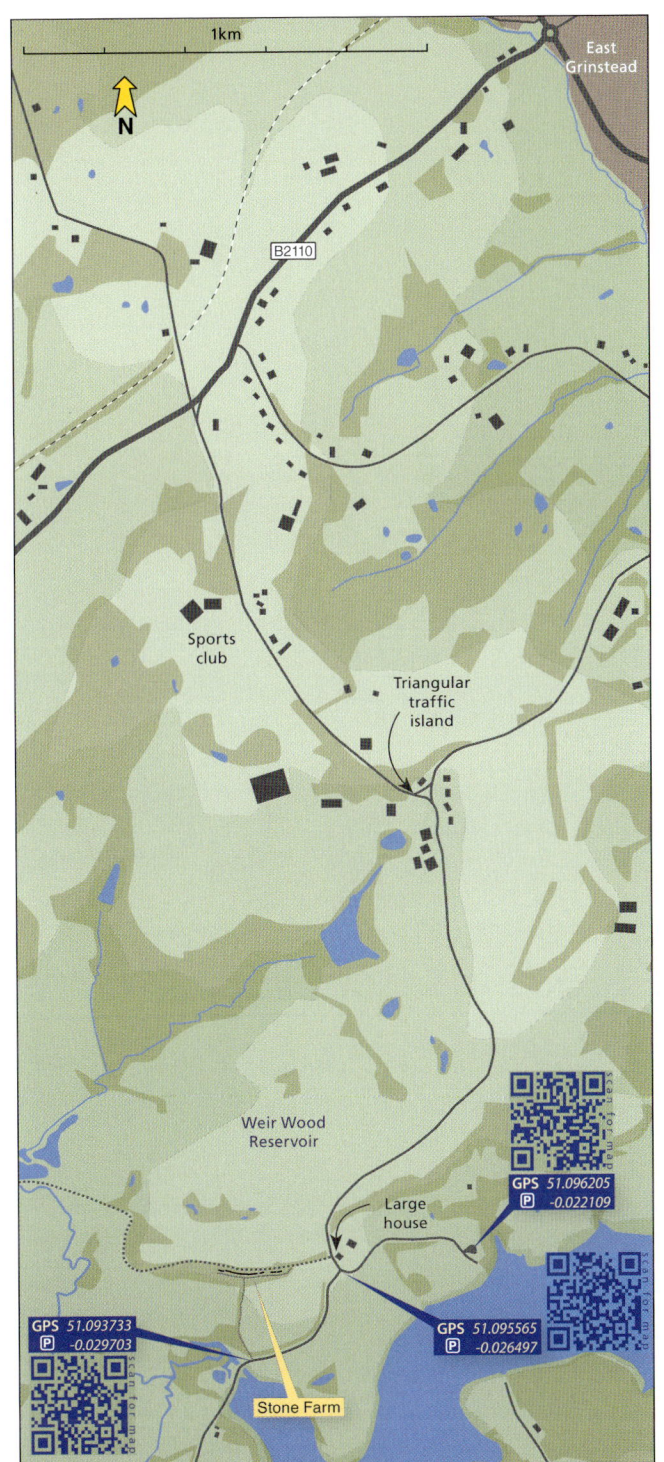

Stone Farm

Stone Farm — Moss Wall

Moss Wall
A trio of slabby buttresses at the far end of the crag which can be a little green at times.

Approach (see overview on page 450) - Follow the path along the bottom of the crag to its end. Moss Wall is hidden a few metres further on from the Kneeling Boulder. Alternatively, you can just walk along the top track to it.

1 Moss Wall Left Block - Left .... f3+
The left side of the block to a slightly uneasy finish.

2 Moss Wall Left Block - Centre .. f3
A short delicate slab climb.

3 Moss Wall Left Block - Right ... f4
The right side of the slab.

4 Moss Wall Centre Block f3
A green slab climb.

5 Moss Wall Right Block - Left ... f4
The difficult and sandy arete.

6 Moss Wall Right Block - Centre . f3
A rounded short problem up the sandy centre of the face.

Kneeling Boulder — Stone Farm

Kneeling Boulder
A nice little wall at the far left of the main crag with a number of short problems, some giving heart pounding finishes on the top block.

Approach (see overview on page 450) - Approach from the top track or the main path below the crag.

7 Pyramid Route .... f3+
Climb the arete to the ledge and exit left.

8 Kneeling Boulder .... f5+
A link problem from the start of *Pyramid Route*, avoiding the hard mantel move on *Giza the Geezer*, to finish over the top block on some good holds.

9 Pharaoh's Curse f5
Climb the face using the shallow flake to finish more sketchily on the front side of the block.
FA. G.West 13.3.2000

10 Giza the Geezer f6A
The direct of *Kneeling Boulder*, on slopers with a hard mantel. Good holds are used to gain the top block to finish.
Photo on page 454.

11 Bisquee f5
Climb the face just right of the sloping ledge, using the same layaway pocket as *Kheops Progress*.

12 Kheops Progress f5
A good problem on layaway pockets, with a tricky finish over the top block.

13 One Hold Route f3
A short wall to a slightly awkward finish onto the ledge.

14 Obscene Gesture f3
The right arete with an undercut that give the route its name.

Jack Gardner climbing *Giza the Geezer* (**f6A**) - page 453 - on the Kneeling Boulder at Stone Farm.

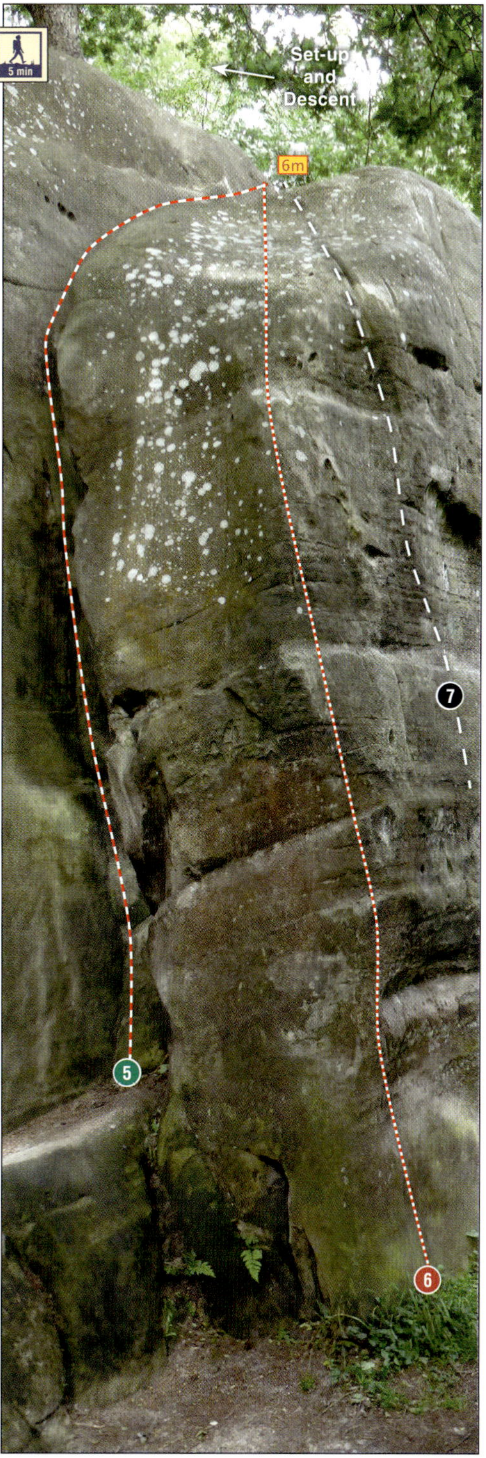

Cat Wall Area **Stone Farm** 455

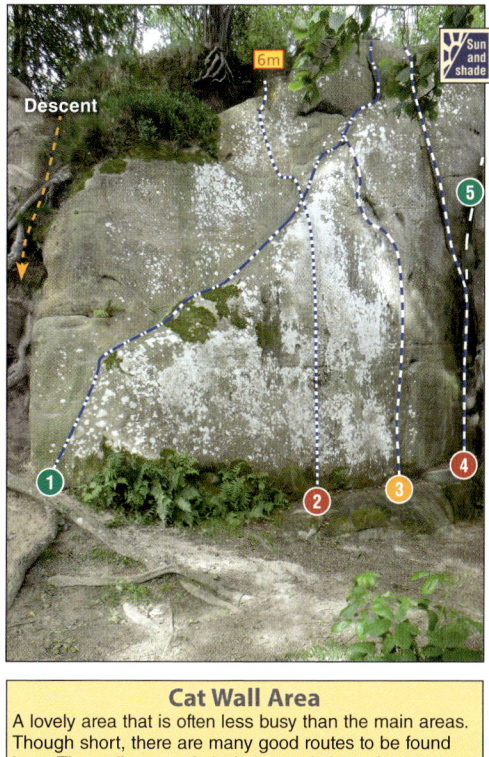

Cat Wall Area
A lovely area that is often less busy than the main areas. Though short, there are many good routes to be found here. The walls stay relatively dry and clear of green, except for the far right which is shadowed by trees.
Approach (see overview on page 450) - Approach from the top track or the main path below the crag.
Set-up and Descent - To the left or right of the wall.

The short back wall to the left has a poor landing.

❶ Medway Slab *f3*
Walk/work your way up the narrow ramp.

❷ Grave Digger......... *f6A+*
Thin moves above a poor landing. Finish nicely on jugs.

❸ Footie. .... *f5+*
A chipped problem, but if you ignore this blemish you are left with a testing piece of climbing on undercuts and flakes.

❹ More Footie Fun ... *f6B+*
Start up *Stone Farm Chimney* and move left to tackle the thin crack.
FA. I.Bull 24.7.2008

❺ Stone Farm Chimney 4a *4a*
A nice chimney climb with an awkward upper section.
FA. B.N.Simmonds Pre 1940s

❻ Chalk 'n' Cheese ... 7a *6a*
The arete on mainly rounded holds which is much harder than it looks.
FA. G.McLelland, B.Knight 4.6.1983

Stone Farm — Cat Wall Area

Cat Wall
The main face of Cat Wall has some good testpieces which are tricky to start. They can be done as highballs.

⑦ Kathmandu .... 7a+ *6b*
Climb the face without using the arete out left, on some poor holds and a distinct undercut. Finish carefully on the slab above.
FA. D.Atchinson-Jones 1982

⑧ Top Cat .... 6c+ *6a*
After a difficult start, climb direct to the bend on *Cat Wall* and finish direct.

⑨ Cat Wall .... 6b+ *5c*
A great route with a slightly smooth and awkward start. Climb the overlapping flake on good holds and dart back right to finish.
FA. F.K.Elliot pre 1950s

⑩ FooFoo 7a *6a*
A hard eliminate joining the finish of *Cat Wall*. Originally done as a highball problem at *f6B*.

⑪ Sweet Carol 6c *6a*
An eliminate just left of (and avoiding) *Stone Farm Crack*, on good but hidden holds. Starting the route from *Stone Farm Crack* reduces the grade to around **6b** *5c*.
FA. D.Atchinson-Jones 13.6.1982

Cat Wall Area — Stone Farm

Pine Buttress

Pine Buttress
The walls to the right of Cat Wall offer a few more short routes - the two cracks are the most popular.

12 Stone Farm Crack 4b *4b*
A short and popular route up the crack.

13 Pine Buttress 6b *5c*
A good technical outing up the slab. Traverse right to finish.

14 Pine Buttress Direct ..... 6b+ *5c*
A sustained, direct finish to *Pine Buttress*.

15 Biometric Slab 7a *6b*
A slight eliminate direct up the face, avoiding the holds out right in and around *Pine Crack*. Finishing as for *Pine Buttress*.
FA. C.Gibson 21.7.2007

16 Pine Crack 4c *4c*
Climb the short crack with a tricky mantel finish.

17 The Ramp 3c *3c*
Tiptoe rightwards up the ramp-line and exit just left of *Root Chimney*, on a green and unsatisfying face. Using the tree roots makes the finish more feasible.

18 The Face 4b *4b*
Start as for *The Ramp* and proceed direct up the carved face. Finish to the left (easier, but avoid venturing over to the crack), or direct (slightly harder at 5a *4c*).

19 Root Chimney 2b *2b*
A dirty corner climb, finishing on tree roots.

Stone Farm — Yew Wall Area

Slab Buttress

Yew Wall Area

Just to the right of *Root Chimney* is a large yew tree which spreads itself dramatically over this section of the crag. There are a number of short green routes and boulder problems below. It stays green for most of the year, but is definitely climbable when dry.

Approach (see overview on page 450) - Approach from the top track or the main path below the crag.

Set-up and Descent

Approach to Yew Wall

Diamond Sl

Slab Buttress
Left of the yew tree are a few micro routes.

1 A Barely Independent Problem . . . . 6a+ *5a*
After a hard start low down on soft rock, climb the centre of the wall. Can be bouldered at f5 but the landing is poor.

2 Slab Buttress 4b *4b*
A tricky problem. Delicately manoeuvre onto the slab and continue moving slightly rightwards to easier climbing above.

3 Slab Buttress Centre 4a *4a*
A short slab climb up the centre of the face.

Diamond Slab

On the main path below Yew Wall is a small green diamond-shaped slab with three easy problems.

4 Slab Left .... f2+
The shortest of the three, and keeping as left as possible.

5 Slab Direct f3
The centre of the slab on worn holds.

6 Slab Arete .... f2+
The right side of the slab using the arete. Eliminating the arete gives a slightly harder *f4+*.

Yew Wall

Back on the upper level and past the yew tree to the right of Slab Buttress is another wall.

7 Yew Just Crimp 6c *6a*
A short crimpy problem, often bouldered at *f6A+* with a not so good landing, hence the top-roping.
FA. A.Rowland 14.3.1999

8 Yew Arete 6b *5b*
Climb the arete with difficulty.

9 Yew Wall 7a *6b*
A fine (but hard) line up the otherwise blank slab. Unfortunately it suffers from the dreaded green.
FA. B.Ventham 20.8.2009

Stone Farm — Stone Farm Central

Stone Farm Central

The central walls are some of the most popular at Stone Farm, and understandably so. They are fairly short and mostly slabby with a good selection of low-to-mid grade routes. The routes can be bouldered, but some poor landings means top-roping is more common. Facing south and open to the elements, this wall dries quickly. Some of the rock is soft and sand particles tend to stick to the walls and pockets after rain making things less than ideal.

Approach (see overview on page 450) - Either walk along the top path (making your way down the numerous descents) or take the bottom path for approximately 200m until you reach the canopy free area. Garden Wall is at the far end of this before the giant yew tree.

Set-up and Descent - There are numerous ways to and from the top scattered along this section.

Garden Wall
The first of the central walls is short and offers a few easy routes.

1 Garden Wall Crack 3b *3b*
Climb the short smooth wide crack.

2 Remote 4c *4c*
Climb the short slab with just one tricky move. Check for bees at the top before you climb.

3 Control 6c *5c*
Climb the steep slab to undercuts and use some chipped holds. Make sure you keep faith in your footwork!
FA. B.Franklin 15.9.1985

4 Control Freak .... 6c+ *6a*
From the undercuts on *Control*, move out right to a taxing finish.

5 Holly Leaf Crack 2a *2a*
A short crack climb behind the boulder.

6 Garden Wall Traverse .... *f2+*
A little traverse crossing the wall from the base of *Holly Leaf Crack* to the ledge below *Garden Wall Crack*.

The routes on the lean-to boulder are rather soft and sandy and usually done as boulder problems.

7 Sahara *f6B*
The left side of the boulder on slopers.

8 Arabian *f6A*
The central line (with a soft and sandy start for your feet) to a rounded finish.

9 Gobi .... *f6A+*
The right side of the boulder to a rounded finish.

Stone Farm Central **Stone Farm**

Mark De Backer on *Chipperydoodah* (7a *6a*) - *page 462* - on the Curling Crack Area of Stone Farm.

Stone Farm — Stone Farm Central

Curling Crack Area
The middle buttress of Stone Farm Central is a good, short wall with a selection of popular first-class routes.

⑩ Very Very Fat 6b *5b*
A good (but slightly eliminate) route to the left of the rounded nose. Avoid using the tempting footholds in the gully.

⑪ Thin .... 6b+ *5c*
Start on the rounded nose and manoeuvre right to gain the slab. Finish delicately to the right of the top lip.

⑫ Chipperydoodah 7a *6a*
After a heavily chipped start, continue up the technical blank slab before trending back left to join the final moves on *Thin*.
Photo on page 461.

⑬ Chipperydoodah Direct Finish .. 7a+ *6b*
The hard and direct finish to *Chipperydoodah*.

⑭ Curling Crack 4a *4a*
A short crack, ideal for practicing those jamming skills.
FA. F.K.Elliot 1943

⑮ Illusion 7a *6a*
A thin balancy and technical slab climb which is (unfortunately) chipped.
FA. B.Franklin 19.9.1985

⑯ Disillusion 6c *5c*
The right-hand arete, avoiding the boulder in the gully.
FA. B.Franklin 29.9.1985

Stone Farm Central — **Stone Farm**

17 Inside Out 3a *3a*
Tackle the jammed boulder and gully above.

18 Gus the Dog .... 6b+ *5c*
A squeezed-in route up the left of the face avoiding the jammed boulder to the left.
FA. R.Hitchcock 2001

19 Front Face .... 6a+ *5b*
Start at the left-hand edge of the face then move right to finish with a tricky top-out.

20 Excalibur 7a *6a*
The centre of the wall has some reachy moves midway and unavoidably shares some of the last moves with *Front Face*.
FA. D.Atchinson-Jones 1981

Around the right side of the wall from *Excalibur*.

21 Mania 6c *6a*
Steep climbing over the nose with a reachy move to a vertical slot. Continue mostly on the left side of the nose to finish.
FA. P.Hayes 1984

22 Undercut Wall 4b *4b*
Pull steeply over the small lip and finish on nice big holds.
Photo this page.

23 Undercut Wall Arete 4a *4a*
The right-hand variation of *Undercut Wall*.

Coriolan Rat on Undercut Wall *(4b 4b) - this page - at the popular Curling Crack Area of Stone Farm.*

Stone Farm — Stone Farm Central

Pinnacle Buttress

Pinnacle Buttress
To the right of the wide gully is another short wall. It has a few slabby routes which are tightly packed together.

24 A Cheeky Little Number 6a *5b*
Climb the wall direct (avoiding the gully and holds out right on the arete) to the ledge and the top.
FA. G.West 16.5.2002

25 Pinnacle Buttress Arete ..... ⭐2 6b *5b*
The left side of the arete, stepping right onto the front face at just over half-height.
FA. 1950s

26 Barn Door Experience .... ⭐1 6c *6a*
The right-hand side of *Pinnacle Buttress Arete* with some rather on/off moves, as you might expect from the name.

27 Pinnacle Buttress Direct ..... ⭐2 6a+ *5b*
Climb direct to the scoop and exit more easily.

28 Praying Mantels .... ⭐1 6a+ *5b*
An eliminate that gives a fun outing.

29 Pinnacle Buttress Original ... ⭐1 4b *4b*
The original line. Start just left of the crack and cross the wall to finish up the scoop.

Stone Farm Central — Stone Farm

Bare Necessities

30 Pinnacle's Progress f5
A short boulder problem to a tricky mantel finish.

31 Easy Crack 2a *2a*
The crack is popular with kids who have not even learnt to walk yet!

Bare Necessities
To the left of Key Wall has some very nice routes which can also be done as highball boulder problems.

32 Bare Necessities 6c *5c*
A good route up the right side of the rounded arete.
FA. P.Hayes 1984

33 Bare Essentials . . . . 6b+ *5c*
Climb direct up the centre of the face and move left on cut-out holds to finish.

34 Bare Essentials Direct . . 7a *6a*
The direct finish to *Bare Essentials* to a rounded top-out.

35 Belly Up 7a *6a*
The right-hand arete, finishing artificially on rope grooves.
FA. T.Skinner 1995

36 Pinnacle Chimney 3a *3a*
A thrutchy squeeze upwards between the two walls.

Stone Farm — Key Wall

Key Wall
The isolated buttress at the far right of the central area has a number of good routes and an outstanding project that is likely to be Stone Farm's hardest line. The south and west-facing walls dry quickly, but the back wall retains dampness for much longer.

Approach (see overview on page 450) - Either walk along the top path (making your way down the numerous descents) or take the bottom path.

Set-up and Descent - Use the route *Central Jordan* - a thought-provoking step onto or off the back side of the buttress.

The blank wall between *Belle Vue Terrace Direct* and *Quoi Faire* is home to a renowned Stone Farm project.

❶ Key Wall .... 6a+ *5a*
A popular route up the disjointed crack to a taxing finish. It can also be finished out right at the same grade. *Photo on page 468*.

❷ Belle Vue Terrace 6c *6a*
A great route up the arete with a distinct layback move to reach a slot on the southern face. Finish up the slabby rounded arete.

❸ Belle Vue Terrace Direct .... 7a+ *6b*
The steep direct version of *Belle Vue Terrace* requires a hard pull thought the overlap.

❹ Quoi Faire 7c *6c*
A hard route up the right-hand side of the face with a powerful move onto the upper face. Move slightly left to finish.
FA. G.McLelland 10.4.1983

❺ L'ottimista .... 7b+ *6b*
Gain the upper arete with difficulty and attack it mainly on its left-hand side, before making a reachy move to a sloping finish.
FA. J.O'Neil 2009

❻ Key Wall Lower Traverse ... *f5*
A right-to-left traverse of the lower break.

❼ Key Wall Upper Traverse .... *f6A+*
A more powerful right-to-left traverse of the upper break.

Key Wall Stone Farm

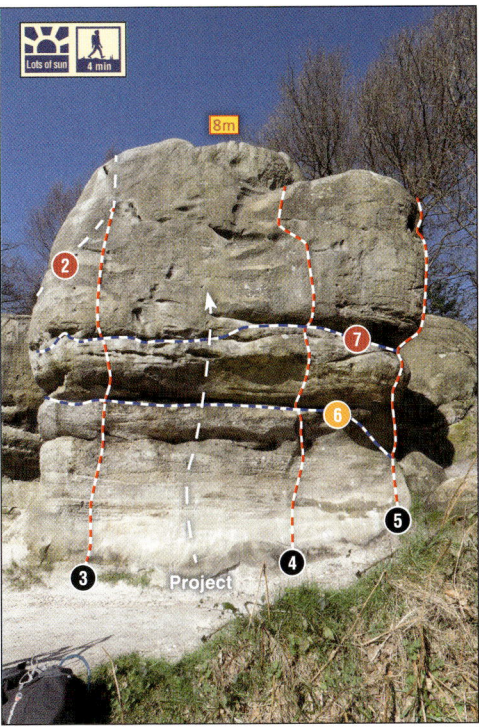

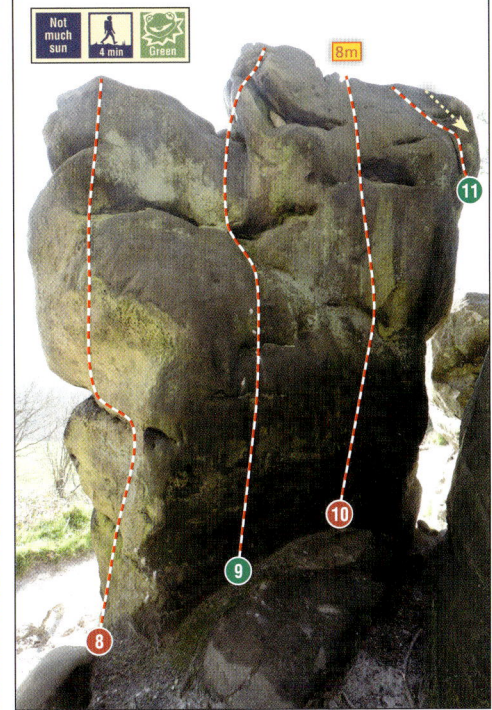

The green back wall offers less pleasant outings, but can be of interest on blistering hot summer days.

8 Nose Direct 6c *5c*
Climb the face starting on the right and moving slightly left to finish with an awkward mantel.

9 East Jordan Route 4a *4a*
A green outing up some large holds. Often bridged at the start.

10 Leisure Line .... 6b+ *5c*
A sandy and green outing which is conditions dependent. Bridging is unavoidable at the start.

11 Central Jordan 2a *2a*
Make a short, thought-provoking step onto the block.

Arthur's Boulder

Immediately behind the back wall of Key Wall is a small dirty boulder which has some soft rock.

12 Absent Friends f6B
The dirty, rounded, left arete.

13 Arthur's Little Problem .... f6B+
Dirty, with an annoying start on a mossy sloper.
FA. P.Hayes / J.Sharratt 5.8.1987

14 King Arthur f6B
The short right-hand arete, starting from a mossy sloper.

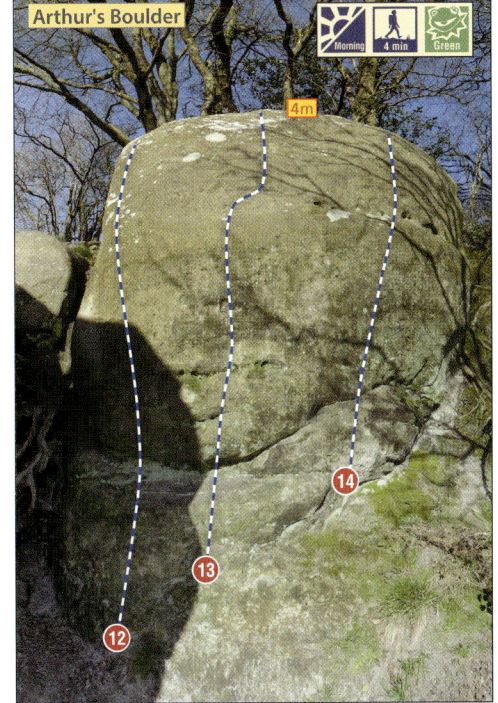

Stone Farm — Key Wall

Key Wall (6a+ *5a*) - *page 466* - on the Key Wall at Stone Farm, beautifully illuminated by the light of Neal Grundy's head torch, as he makes a self-photographed night time ascent. Photo: Neal Grundy - **nealgrundy.co.uk**

Stone Farm Boulders

A small selection of boulders between Stone Farm Central and The Inaccessible Boulder. The Milestone Boulder has a mixture of low-grade and brutal problems. Beyond this is The Pleasure Dome - a short wall with a good selection of low-grade problems. There are also some smaller boulder problems in this area which will appeal to children. Beyond this are Ashdown Wall and Tiger Wall, which give a number of problems/micro routes.

Conditions - Milestone Boulder stays in good condition year round, but can get a little green at times. The Pleasure Dome does not see much sun and can be green. Ashdown Wall suffers from green on its western face, but improves on the south face.

Approach (see overview on page 450) - The Milestone Boulder is 10m right of Key Wall, just above the path. For Pleasure Dome, continue into the wooded area for another 10m along the main path. Ashdown Wall and Tiger Wall are another 5m right of this.

Josh Leigh on *Milestone Stride* (f3+) - page 470 - on the Milestone Boulder at Stone Farm.

Stone Farm — Stone Farm Boulders

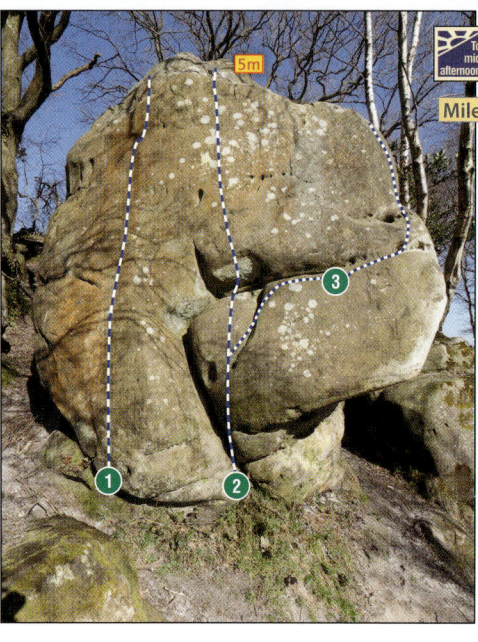

Milestone Boulder
10m right of the Key Wall Buttress.

1 Milestone Arete f3
A delicate slab.

2 Milestone Stride .... f3+
The crack and upper face on good holds throughout.
Photo on page 469.

3 Milestone Right f4
Hand traverse the rail and finish up the face.

4 Milestone Mantel .... f6B+
Use a few pads to reach the starting hold (which is becoming harder) due to ground erosion. Pull hard into an unbelievable mantel and finish above. Much harder for the short.

5 The Painkiller .... f7B+
A slopey, slappy sit-start to *Milestone Mantel*. It could well be f7C, only time will tell.

6 Concentration Cut .... f6A+
From the large chipped pocket, make some difficult moves to establish yourself on the face.
FA. P.Hayes 1.7.1982

Magic Numbers
10m right into the wooded area, and up and left of The Pleasure Dome, is a small lone boulder.

7 Magic Numbers f3
A short problem up the blunt arete.

Stone Farm

The Pleasure Dome
Short problems on a green face, 10m into the woodland from Milestone. It is good when dry.

8 Jump Start . . . . f2+
The slab on the back of the boulder.

9 Pleasure Dome . . . . f2+
The right-hand ramp-line.

10 Nobbly Knee . . . . f4+
A short and awkward mantel.

11 Backhander . . . . f5+
An awkward finish.

12 Hairy Scary . . . . f4+
A good problem on the left with a tricky finish.

13 Grooving Away f5
The central crack. The wall just right is an eliminate at f7A.

14 Font Blue f5
The holds are where you need them, just...

15 Step Up . . . . f3+
Easy climbing up the face.

16 Bin the Trainers f4
The face left of the rounded arete.

17 Christ Will Return Slab . . . . . f3+
The slab with the words 'Christ Will Return'.

The Baby Slab
The short slab up and to the right of Pleasure Dome has some short problems.

18 Baby's Slab f2
The short left side of the face, without hands!

19 Baby's Nose f2
The central nose.

20 Baby's Wall f2
The short bulging wall.

Stone Farm — Stone Farm Boulders

Ashdown Wall

A popular wall with boulderers. The top-outs are a little highball, but the top holds are generally good. The left wall is usually green.

㉑ Thomas the Tank f3
A short climb up the pocketed green wall.

㉒ Tiny Wall f3
Climb the wall on good pockets.

㉓ Open Chimney f3
The main indentation in the left face on good holds - not quite a chimney.

㉔ Transparent Accelerating Banana . . . . f5+
A tricky line just right of *Bulging Corner*.
FA. D.Atchison-Jones 1982

㉕ Bulging Corner . . . . f4+
A good wandering line. Finish by moving right.

㉖ Poohped f6A
A hand-traverse of the lower break, starting from the base of *Bulging Corner* and finishing up *Prelude*.

Ashdown Wall

Stone Farm Boulders — Stone Farm

㉗ Euro Rail f6B
Start on the front face and traverse right - with difficulty - along the sloping break, to finish more easily up *Epitaph*.

㉘ Bulging Wall f6A
A sit-start problem off undercuts. Climb the left side of the wall on good holds throughout. The standing start is *f5+*.

㉙ Ashdown Wall .... Top 50 f4+
A demanding problem with some taxing moves off some large sloping holds.
FA. F.K.Elliot 1940s

㉚ Gap Traverse f3
It can be started all the way round on *Zog the Dog* but it is more commonly done as a continuation to *Introductory Climb*. Traverse the wall left on the higher line of holds onto the left face and finish down *Thomas the Tank*.

㉛ Prelude f3
The direct start to the final crack of *Introductory Climb*.

㉜ Epitaph .... f2+
Difficult to start. It can also be used as an alternative start to *Introductory Climb*.

㉝ Introductory Slab .... f2+
A squeezed-in line up the slab.

㉞ Introductory Climb .... f2+
The main problem on this wall, crossing the ramp into the crack in the centre of the wall.

㉟ Dinosaurs Don't Dyno f2
An easy slab. The arete is in, but many forgo hands altogether.

Tiger Wall
Immediately right of the gap are three short problems.

㊱ Marmelade .... f2+
A simple problem up the left of the face.

㊲ Tiger the Tiger f3
Climb the thin overlap/crack up the centre of the wall.

㊳ Zog the Dog .... f2+
The right side of the face. Also used as the original start of *Gap Traverse*.

Tiger Wall

Descent

Stone Farm — Inaccessible Boulder

Inaccessible Boulder

The spectacular Inaccessible Boulder, which overlooks the nearby Weir Wood Reservoir, is the iconic symbol of Stone Farm. It is popular amongst boulderers, but is a bit too high for most, hence the route grades. The open and south-facing rock dries quickly. The back side of the boulder is green and sees little attention.

Approach (see overview on page 450) - This is the first area you reach when entering Stone Farm from the east side.

Set-up and Descent - Bolts are situated on top but are difficult to reach. The brave mainly access these via *SE Corner Crack* (page 476) but it can also be approached from *NE Corner*. Descent is down climbing *SE Corner Crack* - do not abseil or lower off.

❶ **Guy's Route** 7c *6c*
Climb the centre of the overhanging face, keeping clear of the block behind you. The crux is low down and can be avoided by stepping off the top of the rear block to reduce the grade.
FA. G.McLelland 1980s

❷ **Hungry Heart** 6c *6a*
Start up the lower face of *Leaning Crack* and trend left into the top moves of *Guy's Route*.
FA. D.Atchinson-Jones 1980

❸ **Leaning Crack** ..... 6a+ *5b*
A hard appealing way to the top, and also the original. Climb the face to the triangular scoop and finish by lay-backing the smooth crack to the top.

❹ **Leaning Crack Right-hand** 5c *5a*
Often (and understandably) confused for the original. This right-hand start is slightly more awkward despite the grade.

❺ **Ducking Fesperate** 6c *6a*
Climb the pocketed lower wall and make delicate moves to the ledge at mid-height. Finish carefully up the slab.
Bouldering to the first break is *f5+*. *Photo opposite and page 44.*

Inaccessible Boulder **Stone Farm** 475

Emily Smith bouldering the starting moves on *Ducking Fesperate* (*f5+*) - *opposite* - on the Inaccessible Boulder at Stone Farm.

6 SW Corner Scoop . . . . . . Top 50 **6a+** *5a*
Pocketed climbing leads to a nice finish on the right side of the scooped slab. *Photo on page 446.*

7 SW Corner **6b** *5b*
Start on the rounded arete on shallow side-pulls and mantel onto the ledge. Finish up the nose to the left of *Primitive Groove*. Not entirely independent in its upper half.
FA. R.Mazinke 10.3.1996

8 Wind Me Up **f6A**
A good short problem up the right side of the bulge. It can be continued into the finishing moves of *SW Corner* at **6c** *6a*.

Stone Farm — Inaccessible Boulder

9 Primitive Groove 4b *4b*
After a tricky start, head left to finish up the wide crack.

10 Mad as a Hatter .... 6b+ *5c*
A squeezed-in roof climb between the top crack of *Primitive Groove* and the bulging *Boulder Wall*.

11 Boulder Wall .... 6c+ *6a*
The original hard roof climb on this bulge.

12 Time Warp 6b *5b*
A slightly easier steep roof climb to the right of *Boulder Wall*.

13 SE Corner Crack 4b *4b*
Head up and right from the start of *Primitive Groove* and finish up the crack on the east face.

14 Sticky Fingers .... *f5+*
A short problem from the break moving up to catch the poor sloper. Pull, and hopefully stick the finish on the ledge above.

15 Peter Pan *f6B*
A sit-start from the large pocket, finishing on the ledge.

16 Stinging Nettle Variation *f7A*
A popular and better version of the original, which is often climbed by mistake. Hug and slap your way up the nose from a sit-start. Exit on the left side of the nose.

17 Stinging Nettle ..... *f7A+*
The original 'Stinging Nettle'. Start to the right of the nose and move left onto it to finish.
FA. I.Stronghill 2002

18 Southern Chimes .... *f4+*
A short and relatively easy problem.

19 Balham Boot Boys 7a *6b*
Make a hard mantel onto the shelf and finish over the bulge above. The first section can be done bouldered from a crouching start at *f6A*.

20 Southern Chimes Traverse .. *f6B*
A hard crimpy traverse across the wall. Start right of *Balham Boot Boys* and finish as for *Southern Chimes*.

Inaccessible Boulder — Stone Farm

21 NE Corner — 5c / 5a
Start from the ledge at the rear of the boulder and climb the arete to another ledge. Move leftwards to finish up the crack and bulge above.

22 Diagonal Route — 6a+ / 5b
One for a dry summer only. Start up *NE Corner* and make a rising traverse to the top of the northwest arete (*Birdie Num-Nums*).

23 Simpering Savage — 6a+ / 5b
The green and damp bulging wall has some in-cut holds.

24 Green Wall — 6a / 5a
Climb the artificial in-cut holds on the centre of the face and finish either left or right.

25 Green Wall Direct — 6a+ / 5a
The steep direct finish to *Green Wall*.

26 Birdie Num-Nums — 7c / 6c
Reach for the pocket and make powerful moves to establish yourself on the arete, where things ease. Starting from the back block behind reduces the grade to around **6c** *6a*.
FA. E.Stone 13.10.1986

Route Index

Stars	Grade	Route	Photo	Page
*	f5	1000 Moomins		370
	f2	1908	402	411
	6c	5.11 Crack		129
	f4	6:00 a.m Route		125
	6c	991.8 Days		72
***	6b	Abracadabra		88
	f6B	Absent Friends		467
	7a	Achilles' Last Stand		146
	5b	Achtung!		391
	4a	Acromantula		97
**	6c+	Adder		284
4	6a	Advertisement Wall	270	308
	6b	Advertisement Wall Direct		308
	6c+	Afterburner		135
	6a+	Agent Orange		243
	7a	Alexander Beetle		248
	f4	Alfred		346
	6b+	Alien Succumbs to the Macho vIntergalactic Funkativity...		440
**	5a	Alka		98
*	f6C	All Hale		306
*	6c+	All That Meat but Only Two Veg		312
	f6B	Alligator Snatch		167
	f4	Amelia's Little Problem		323
	6b	Amnesia Variations		314
*	5a	Anaconda Chimney		282
**	f3	Analord		117
*	f4	And Tigger Too		377
	f6B+	Animal Friends		177
	f5	Annexe Slab		352
	6c+	Another One up the Back Passage		294
	f5+	Another Wet Bank Holiday		153
*	6b	Antoninus		144
	6c+	Anything Goes		441
*	6c	Aphrodite		75
	4b	Apis		391
	6b+	Apis Poor Variation		391
	6b	Apis Variation		391
	f7A+	Apollo 11		339
*	6c	Appetite for Destruction		147
*	6a+	Apple Crumble		247
	7c	Arab Spring		287
	f6A	Arabian		460
*	6c	Arachnophobia		254
	6b+	Araldite Wall		258
*	6b	Archer's Wall	30, 203	202
**	6c	Archer's Wall Direct		204
	f6A	Arco		218
	f5+	Arizona		302
*	f6B	Arnold Thesanigger		352
	3a	Arrow Crack		201
	f6B+	Arthur's Little Problem		467
	3a	Artist's Conk		171
	6b+	Arustu		243
	3a	AS Peck		101
4	f4+	Ashdown Wall		473
*	f6B	Ashes and Dust		117
***	6b	Asterix		144
**	6c	Asterix Direct	104	144
*	f7A+	Atomic Mushroom		293
**	6b+	August Variation		96
**	f5	Augustus		354
	6c	Avalanche Arete		399
	3a	Avalanche Route		399
	6a+	Awkward Corner		326
*	6c	Awkward Crack		185
**	f7A	Azazel	145	143
*	4c	Baby Boulder		99
*	f3+	Baby J		408
	f2	Baby's Nose		471
	f2	Baby's Slab		471
	f2	Baby's Wall		471
	5a	Babylon		77
	f6B+	Back Breaker		168
	f5+	Backhander		471
	f2+	Backwards in Time		112
	5a	Backyard		140
**	7c	Bad Blood		307
***	f6A+	Bad Boy		430
*	f3+	Badger's Head		68
	f2	Badgering the Badger		68
	3a	Baggins		444
*	6a	Bald Finish		319
*	6a	Baldrick's Balderdash		254
	7a	Balham Boot Boys		476
*	4b	Ballerina		99
**	f4	Bambi's Mother		371
	f4+	Bamboo		173
***	6c	Banana		77
	f6C	Banana Hammock		77
	7b+	Banana Republic		229
	f3	Bane Cat		370
	f3+	Bane Rabbit		370
	f6C	Barbed Wire Kiss		324
**	4c	Barbican Buttress		156
	f4+	Barbizon		344
**	6b+	Bare Essentials		465
*	7a	Bare Essentials Direct		465
*	6c	Bare Necessities		465
	6a+	Barely Independent Problem, A		458
*	4b	Barham Boulder		99
*	6c	Barn Door Experience		464
	4b	Basilisk		97
*	6c	Baskerville		266
*	6c+	Battle of the Bulge		250
***	6a+	Battlements Crack		156
*	f3	Battleship Traverse		406
*	f4	Beacon Wall		368
	6a+	Beanstalk		305
*	f2+	Beaten to It		112
	3a	Beech Corner		189
	5b	Beech Crack		189
	f6B	Beer Gut Shuffle		332
**	7a+	Beguiled, The		128
	f2+	Bejeweled		420
*	4a	Bell Rock Passage		294
*	5b	Bell Rock Transverse Passage Route 1		294
*	4c	Bell Rock Transverse Passage Route 2		294
*	4c	Bell Rock Transverse Passage Route 3		294
4	6c	Belle Vue Terrace		466
	7a+	Belle Vue Terrace Direct		466
*	7a	Belly Up		465
**	6a	Belts and Braces		231
	f4+	Ben		101
	f6C	Ben's a Woofter		306
**	f5+	Bench Mark		410
	f2+	Bench Wall		410
	f4+	Bertie		428
*	6a+	Beyond Our Ken		430
*	6b+	Biceps Buttress		258
	f5+	Biceps Mantel		258
*	7a	Big Boss		136
**	3b	Big Cave Route 1		253
*	4a	Big Cave Route 2		253
	4c	Big Crack		198
**	6b	Big Fat Tart		119
	6c+	Big Stretch, The		88
	4c	Big Toe Wall		206
	3a	Bilbo		444
	5b	Bile Duct		250
	5a	Billy Bong		218
*	f6A	Billy the Bong		355
*	f4	Bin the Trainers		471
*	7a	Biometric Slab		457
	f6A+	Bioplastic		179
*	3c	Birch Crack		94
	6a	Birch Nose		234
	3b	Birch Tree Buttress		399
**	4c	Birch Tree Crack		260
	6c	Birch Tree Variations		262
	3b	Birch Tree Wall (Bull's H)		399
*	4c	Birch Tree Wall (Harrison's)		262
	4b	Birch Tree Wall Variation		262
***	6b	Birchden Corner		248
4	6b	Birchden Wall		248
	7c	Birdie Num-Nums		477
***	6a	Birthday Arete		321
	6c	Birthday Buttress		438
*	f5	Bisquee		453
	6b	Bitch and the Meal Ticket, The		398
	f3	Bivouac Chimney		124
**	f6C	Black Cadillac		152
*	f3	Black Knight		236
**	6b	Blackeye Wall	183	182
**	6b+	Blackeye Wall Direct		182
	4a	Blasphemy		392
	f4+	Blaster		116
	f6A	Blenjeel		149
	7c+	Bletchley Park		318
*	6c+	Bloody Fingers		249
	7a	Bloody Staircase		249
*	6b	Bloody Sunday		212
	6c	Bludgeon		316
*	6b	Bludnok Wall		320
*	7a	Blue Moon		72
*	7a+	Blue Murder		191
*	6b+	Blue Peter		189
	4b	Boa by the Back		282
	5c	Boa-Constrictor Chimney		282
	f5+	Bogey		407
*	7a+	Boiling Point		87
	f6B+	Bolt Route		282
*	7a	Bolts, The		213
*	6b	Bonanza		228
*	7a+	Bonanza Direct		228
*	7c	Bone Machine		284
**	f7B	Boogie Woogie Walk		353
	f2+	Books with Batteries		409
4	7a+	Boonoonoonoos	51, 315	314
	f4	Born in a Barn		370
	6c	Bostic		224

Route Index 479

Stars	Grade	Route	Photo	Page
	f5	Boulancourt		152
***	3a	Boulder Bridge Route		249
	5a	Boulder Chimney		119
	6c+	Boulder Wall		476
	3c	Boundary Gully		357
*	5a	Bovril		100
	6a+	Bovril - Left-Hand		100
*	6a+	Bow Crack		326
	6b+	Bow Locks		442
*	6c+	Bow Spirit		327
4	4a	Bow Window		197
*	4a	Bow Window Flake		197
**	f3+	Bowling Green Arete		344
*	f5+	Bowling Ramp		344
**	6c	Boysen's Arete		249
	f6A	Boysen's Back		301
**	6c	Boysen's Crack		301
	f4	Boysen's Sack		301
*	f5	Brain's Missing		353
**	4c	Bramble Corner		394
*	4b	Breadknife Buttress		176
**	6c	Breakfast		338
4	f6A	Brenva	*347* .	342
**	f7A	Brenva Assis		342
	6a+	Brian Arete		280
	6b	Brian's Corner		132
	f2+	Bridge Corner		170
	f2+	Bridge Corner Left		170
	f3	Bridge Corner Right		170
	6a+	Bright Eyes		305
	f6B	Brighton Rock		153
*	f4+	British Bulldog		68
	3a	Broken Crack		388
	6b+	Broken Nose	*393* .	395
	f6B+	Broken Path		156
*	7a	Brookslight		223
*	6c+	Brouillard		381
	3c	Brushwood Chimney . . .		314
*	7a+	Bubble Wrap		87
	f4	Budgy Smugglers		370
**	f4+	Bulging Corner		472
*	6c	Bulging Waistline		388
**	6b+	Bulging Wall (Harrison's)*269*	267
*	f6A	Bulging Wall (Stone F) . . .		473
**	f4+	Bull's Nose		68
**	f7C	Bum Dragon		325
*	f5	Buonarroti		344
***	6a+	Burlap		84
*	6c	Burlap Eliminate		84
	4b	Bush Arete		323
	6c+	Buzzard and the Purple Fish, The	
		. . . .		392
*	f3	Buzzard Years, The		377
	f4+	By A Narrow Margin		377
*	6c	Caesar		395
	6c+	Callum		388
*	f6B+	Camel	*13* .	78
	f3+	Cameo		154
**	f3+	Camille		346
*	f6C+	Can Opener		325
	5a	Candlestick		223
	f3	Candy Crush		420
	f4	Candyland		69
	7a	Cannibals		222
	6b+	Canyon Crack		305
**	4a	Capstan Wall		148
*	f2+	Caramel Nibbles		117
***	7c	Carbide Finger		87
**	f6C	Carbon Fibre		325
	f5+	Carcass, The		305
**	7a+	Cardboard Box		87
	f4+	Carlo		71
	6a	Caroline		231
	4a	Carpet Slab		429
**	6b	Carrera		181
	6a+	Casement Wall		197
**	6b+	Cat Wall		456
**	6c	Cauliflower Ear		396
	f6A+	Cave Boulder Crack		252
	f4+	Cave Boulder Flake		252
	f3	Cave Boulder Front		252
**	f6A	Cave Boulder Roof		252
*	5a	Cave Crack		88
*	6b+	Cave Wall		254
	4 6b	Celebration		316
**	6c	Celestial's Reach		192
	6a+	Cenotaph Corner Two . .		76
	6a+	Centaurs		97
	4 6b	Central Crack . . . . . *445* .		439
	6b	Central Groove		174
	2a	Central Jordan		467
*	3a	Central Route (Harrison's) .		170
	f2A	Central Route (High R) . .		343
**	6c	Centre Finish, The		192
**	4c	Centurion's Groove		395
	f3	Chalet Slab - Chimney . . .		70
**	6b	Chalet Slab Direct		70
**	3c	Chalet Slab Left		70
**	4c	Chalet Slab Right		70
***	7a	Chalk 'n' Cheese		455
*	6b+	Chalybeate . . . . . *361*, *383* .		381
	6c+	Champagne Celebration .		316
4	f7A	Change in the Weather . .		353
	3a	Channelsea Crack		440
*	4a	Charlie's Chimney		90
	4b	Charming Chimney		431
**	3c	Charon's Chimney		265
	3b	Chasm, The		388
	6a	Cheeky Little Number, A .		464
*	7a+	Cheetah		306
	3a	Chelsea Chimney		75
	f6C	Chez's Arete		346
**	f7B	Chez's Dyno . . . . . *303* .		316
	f3+	Chicken in the Basket . . .		409
**	f7B	Children of the Bong		336
*	f5	Childs Play		414
	4 8a+	Chimaera . . . . *286* .		287
	f2+	Chimney One		353
*	3c	Chimney Routes		307
	f2+	Chimney Two		354
*	f3+	Chimney Wall		353
	3a	Chimney, The (Happy) . . .		380
***	4a	Chimney, The (Harrison's)*239*242
*	f5	Chinese Panda		154
*	7a	Chipperydoodah . . . *461* .		462
	7a+	Chipperydoodah Direct Finish . .	
				462
*	4a	Chockstone Chimney . . .		288
	f4	Chocolate Nibbles		117
	6b	Chossy Arete		429
*	6b	Chris		94
	f3+	Christ Will Return Slab . . .		471

	f2+	Chute and Chimney		354
	5b	Chute, The		294
*	3c	Claire		99
	6b	Clamp, The		234
	f2	Cleft		375
	6b+	Climbers Behaving Badly .		327
	6c+	Close to You		118
	f7B	Clown's Pocket		281
	7a	Coast to Coast		75
***	6b+	Coathanger		78
*	6a	Cobra Chimney		284
	f4+	Cobra Kai		149
	4c	Coffin Corner		213
	3c	Colorado Crack		305
	7a+	Colour of the Sun		380
*	4c	Columnar Buttress		114
*	6b	Communist		137
	f6B	Composition, The		127
*	f6A+	Concentration Cut		470
*	6c+	Conchita		302
***	6b	Conclusion . . . . . . *433* .		432
***	6a+	Concorde		148
*	f6A	Condom Corner		125
	6c+	Conjuror		88
*	7c+	Continuing Adventures of Porg,	
		. . . .		310
**	6c	Control		460
*	6c+	Control Freak		460
*	3b	Conway's Buttress		392
**	4b	Conway's Crack		392
*	3c	Conway's Direct		392
*	3b	Conway's Variation		392
***	7c+	Cool Bananas		304
*	6a+	Coolcaringer		95
**	4c	Corbett Slab		95
	6b	Corner		259
	f3	Corner Crack (Happy) . . .		377
	f2+	Corner Crack (HR Annexe) .		355
**	6a+	Corner Layback		74
*	f7B+	Cornerstone		287
	f4	Cornucopia		375
**	7a	Coronation Crack (Harrison's) . .
		. . . .		194
4	6b+	Coronation Crack (High R) .		306
	f5	Corot		346
	7a	Corridor of Uncertainty . .		185
	4a	Corridor Route		234
	7a	Corsican Proposal		320
*	7a+	Cosmo Irrazionale		131
*	6a	Cottonsocks Traverse . . .		181
	6a+	Cough Drop		320
*	6c	Counterfeit		182
	4c	Court's Climb		72
	f7A	Covenant		420
*	4a	Crack and Cave		256
	6b	Crack and Wall Front . . .		310
	4c	Crack Route		320
*	f5	Cracking Up (Eridge) . . .		124
	3c	Cracking Up (Harrison's) .		234
*	f5+	Crackless		314
	f3+	Crackpot		154
	f4+	Crackpot Arete		154
	f2+	Crackpot Crack		154
	f4	Crackpot Nose		154
4	6c+	Craig-y-blanco		329
**	f7A	Cross, The		378

Route Index

Stars	Grade	Route	Photo	Page
	7a	Crossing the Rubicon		292
**	6b	Crossply		398
**	f7C	Crosstown Traffic		325
	f3+	Crouching Badger		117
**	6b+	Crowborough Corner		249
*	4a	Crown of Thorns		294
	f6B+	Crucible		343
*	7a+	Crucifix		259
	7a+	Crunch - Original Start, The		127
***	7b	Crunch Direct, The		127
	4b	Crypt Crack		310
	6b	Cucumber Madness		184
*	f5	Cumberland		324
*	f6C	Curb Rash		421
**	4a	Curling Crack		462
**	6c	Cut Steps Crack		293
	6c	Dagger Crack		331
	f6B	Dagobah		311
	f6A	Dagobah Scoop		311
	f6B+	Dali		344
*	6c+	Dan's Wall	425	431
***	3b	Dark Chimney		196
*	6a	Dark Chimney Buttress		196
**	6c	Dark Crack		442
***	f7A+	Darth Vader	291	312
	4a	Das Vaterland		433
*	f2+	Dave		179
*	f2	Day in the Park, A		372
*	f6B	Daylight Throbbery		143
	f2+	Deadly Lampshade, The		377
*	3c	Deadwood Chimney		294
	5a	Deadwood Crack		232
*	f4	Deadwood Pocket		232
*	7a	Death Cap		310
	f5+	Deep Thought		179
*	f5+	Deer Hunter, The		371
**	6a	Degenerate		328
	f6A	Delacroix		346
*	f5	Delirium		324
*	7a	Demons of Death		264
**	f5	Deniability		252
	7c	Dennis the Menace		266
	4a	Departure Slab		444
*	7a	Designer Label		290
*	6c+	Desperate Dan		266
	f7C	Deva Loka		312
4	6a+	Devaluation	58	90
*	6c+	Devastator		336
**	f6B+	Devour		90
*	f6B+	Diaconate, The		420
*	7b	Diagonal		111
**	6a+	Diagonal Route		477
**	f4	Diamond White		414
*	6b+	Diamonds in Orion		321
	4a	Dib		94
	f5+	Didshi		354
***	6c+	Digitalis		82
**	6c	Dilemma		136
**	6b	Dinner Plate		337
*	f2	Dinosaurs Don't Dyno		473
	6a	Dinosaurus		188
	6c	Dinosaurus Direct		188
	6b	Directors		207
*	4c	Dirty Dick		310
*	6c	Disillusion		462
*	7a	Dislocator		431

Stars	Grade	Route	Photo	Page
*	6a	Dival's Diversion		95
*	f6A+	Diver Roof, The		332
*	f6B	Diver, The		332
*	6c	Diversion		248
	f3	Dizzy		411
*	6a+	DJ Face the Music		170
	4b	Docker's Armpit		433
**	f5	Dog's Head, The		416
*	6c	Dogs of War		439
	f7C	Dogtown		292
	f5+	Domodossola		218
*	f2+	Don		179
*	6b	Don Juander		260
***	f8A+	Don't Pierdol		342
*	f6B+	Double Top		353
**	f4+	Doug's Come-uppance		368
*	5b	Down the Hatch		444
	4b	Downfall		205
**	7a+	Dr Pepper		242
*	f6A+	Dr. Kemp's Cure		125
**	6c+	Dragon, The		297
***	6a+	Drosophila		77
	4b	Dubonnet		102
	6c	Ducking Fesperate	44, 475	474
	f5	Dumpy		355
*	4c	Dusk Crack		128
	f5+	Dyna Blade		177
*	6b+	Dynamo		175
**	7a+	Dyno-Sore		308
*	6b+	Dysentery		297
	6b	Ear-ring		250
*	7a+	Early Breakfast		338
**	6c+	Earthrise		131
*	f6A	Earthrise Suprise		131
	4a	East Jordan Route		467
	2b	Easter Crack		444
	3a	Easy Chimney		185
*	3c	Easy Cleft Left		264
*	3c	Easy Cleft Right		265
*	3c	Easy Crack (High R)		319
	2a	Easy Crack (Stone F)		465
	2a	Easy Gully (Bowles)		99
	3a	Easy Gully (Eridge)		129
	6c+	Eckpfeiler		380
**	7a	Educating Airlie		312
**	6c	Edwards Effort		248
**	6c+	Edwards Effort Direct		248
*	6b	Edwards Wall		248
**	f6	Effie		304
*	6c	Effie Right-hand Finish		304
	f4+	Eigerrrr		217
*	f4	Ejector		180
*	f4	El Cid		236
	6b	El Loco		224
*	f5	Elastic		179
	f5	Elastic Headbands		153
*	6b+	Elementary		266
	f6A	Elephant		346
*	6c	Elephant's Arse		110
*	f6B	Elephant's Chode		110
**	6b+	Elephant's Head		110
	3b	Elephant's Tail		110
*	6a	Elevator		98
	f6B+	Elysium		323
*	6c+	Emerald		129
*	f4	Emile		346

Stars	Grade	Route	Photo	Page
	f2	Emillio		71
	6c	Empty Vee		132
*	6b+	Encore (Bowles)		98
	f6B+	Encore (Eridge)		127
	f2	End of it All		69
	f4	Endoparasitoid		333
4	6c	Engagement Wall	7, 309	308
*	7a	Enigma		120
**	f6B+	Entertainer, The		355
	f2	Enzo		71
	f2+	Ephidrina		333
	f2+	Epitaph		473
	f4	Epstein		344
**	6b	Equilibrium Wall	123	119
	6a	Eric (Eridge)		149
*	7a	Eric (Harrison's)		243
	5b	Eridge Tower Route		157
**	6a+	ES Cadet Nose		90
	6a	Escalator		98
	f6B	Euro Rail		473
*	f6A	Even Shorter Mention		124
*	6a	Evening Arete		440
	f2+	Ever So Minnow Minnow		374
**	7b	Evolution	139	138
*	7a	Excalibur		463
4	6b+	Excavator	422	431
*	6a+	Exe Chimney		294
	4c	Exit Cracks, The		134
**	f6B+	Extender		324
4	4b	Eyelet		178
	6b	Eyewash		396
	f6B+	Face, The (Happy)		372
	4b	Face, The (Stone F)		457
*	f5+	Fahrenheit		354
**	f7B	Faith		421
**	7a	Fallen Angels		72
	6a	Fallen Block Eliminate		208
	4a	Fallen Block Mantelshelf		208
	5b	Fallen Block Wall		208
4	6c+	Fandango (Bowles)		79
**	6b+	Fandango (Eridge)		149
*	7a+	Fandango Central		79
***	6c+	Fandango Right-hand		79
	6c	Fang		184
*	6b+	Far Left		266
	6b+	Fat and Middle-Aged		238
	7c	Fat Start		301
	6c+	Fenchurch		114
	6a+	Ferne		388
	f5+	Fernkop Crack		152
	f2+	Festive		376
**	f4+	Fig Roll		355
**	f7C	Final Destination		331
	6b	Final Solution?		432
***	7a+	Finale		98
*	f7A	Finger Flow		168
*	7a	Finger Popper		259
**	6b+	Finger Stain	200	198
	3a	Fingernail Crack		185
*	f4	Fiorentino		344
***	6b+	Fireball		439
*	6c+	Firebird		316
*	7b	Firefly		316
	6b+	Firenze		97
	7a+	First Crack, The		281
	f3+	Fish and Chips		409

Route Index 481

Stars	Grade	Route	Photo	Page
	f3	Flake Crack		124
*	7a+	Flakes Direct		194
4	7a	Flakes, The	14	194
*	f6A+	Flatwoods		86
	3a	Flotsam		231
	6a+	Flower Power Jules		231
*	f6A	Fluted Fancy		152
*	f5+	Flutings (Eridge)		152
	f3	Flutings (Toad)		408
**	6c+	Fly by Knight		146
	4b	Flying Scotsman		208
*	f5	Flying Trout		374
	5c	Foam Dome		432
*	6b	Foam Dome Direct		432
*	f5	Font Bleu		471
**	f6A+	Fontainebleau		152
	3a	Fonz, The		207
*	7a	FooFoo		456
**	f5+	Footie		455
4	6b	Forester's Wall		228
	6c	Forester's Wall Direct		228
	6c+	Forester's Wall Super Direct		228
*	f5	Forever Green		412
*	6c	Forget-me-Knot		254
**	6b	Fork		337
	6b+	Fortuitous		399
	f4	Forward in Time		112
**	5c	Four-by-Two		88
	f3+	Foxtrot		377
*	5c	Fragile Arete		96
*	4a	Fragile Wall		98
*	6c+	Frank's Arete		248
*	f3+	Fred		407
	f2+	Fredo - Left		71
	f2+	Fredo - Right		71
*	3a	Free Willy		102
	6c	Freney		381
**	6c+	Fresh Air Finish		293
	f6C+	Fridge, The		83
*	6b	From Behind		381
**	6a+	Front Face		463
**	f7B	Fruit of the Spirit		420
	6b	Fruits		149
*	7a	Fugazi		182
*	7a+	Full Monty, The		338
**	6a+	Full Moon	397	396
*	f6B	Full on Fling		168
*	7b	Fungal Smear		282
**	4a	Funnel	65	95
*	7b	Funnel Web		442
*	6b	G Force		99
*	7a	Gall Stone		250
**	3a	Gangway Wall	401	398
*	f3	Gap Traverse		473
*	6a	Garden Slab Left		258
*	5b	Garden Slab Right		258
*	3b	Garden Wall Crack		460
	f2+	Garden Wall Traverse		460
	6c	Gardeners' Question Time		201
	f5	Gattaca		343
	f5	Gauguin		346
**	f6B	Gea		353
*	6c	Genesis		140
*	6c+	Genevieve		308
*	7a	Geoff's Route		72
	7a	Geoffrey Moon Esquire		72
*	f3	Geronimo		124
*	6a+	Get Orf Moi Land		429
	6c	Ghost, The		326
**	f6A+	Giant Panda		173
	5b	Giant's Ear		207
	6c+	Giant's Face		207
*	3a	Giant's Staircase		201
*	3c	Giant's Stride		294
	6a+	Gibbet, The		302
**	f4+	Gillbert's Gamble		180
**	f6A	Giza the Geezer	454	453
*	7a	Glendale Crack		210
***	f7C+	Goat Rage		142
**	f7B+	Goat Rage Extension		143
	f6A	Goats Do Roam		215
	7c	Gob, The		329
	f6A+	Gobi		460
**	f6A+	Godfrey's Arete		236
**	f6C+	Going Going		325
	f5	Going Turbot		375
	4b	Golden Graham's		171
	4b	Gollum		184
*	f6B+	Good Boy		430
*	f7A	Good Friday (Happy)		378
	6c	Good Friday (Harrison's)		212
	f5	Good Man Friday		236
**	6b	Good Route ... Good Line		147
*	6c	Good Route ... Poor Line		147
*	4b	Googly, The		357
	f5	Gore Brothers		102
	f4+	Gorilla Wall		354
	f7C	Grace		421
*	4a	Graham		171
**	f6C	Grand Canyon		305
**	6a+	Grant's Crack	257	256
*	6c	Grant's Groove		256
*	6c+	Grant's Wall		256
	f6A+	Grave Digger		455
**	6b+	Graveyard Groove		336
	4c	Greasy Crack (Harrison's)		207
	5a	Greasy Crack (High R.)		331
	6c	Greasy Eliminate Left		207
	7a	Greasy Eliminate Right		207
*	6b+	Great Bald Turkey Meets a Dwarf with a Problem, The		144
	4a	Green Bollard Chimney		144
	3c	Green Cleft, The		224
	3a	Green Ernie		323
**	6c	Green Fingers		249
	f6B	Green Goblin (Harrison's)		216
	f6B	Green Goblin (High R.)		343
	f2+	Green Groove		357
	f6A	Green Mile, The		306
	f5+	Green Pesto		354
	6a	Green Wall		477
	6a+	Green Wall Direct		477
*	f6C	Green Wall Girdle		174
	f7A+	Greenside Boulder		346
*	7a	Gretta		210
	4b	Grimace		382
	f5	Grimey Grimsel Left		217
	f5	Grimey Grimsel Right		217
*	6c	Grist		202
	f6B	Groove, The		372
*	f5	Grooving Away		471
**	f4+	Groovy Graeme		167
	4c	Grotto Chimney		80
	3c	Grotty Groove		74
	f2+	Grotty Slab		74
	f6C+	Growing Pains		305
*	f3+	Grumpy Face		411
*	6a+	Gully Wall		92
	6b+	Gus the Dog		463
*	f7A	Guy's Link		343
	6c	Guy's Problem (Harrison's)		188
*	f6B+	Guy's Problem (High R.)		343
**	7c	Guy's Route		474
4	6a+	Hadrian's Wall		144
	6c	Hadrian's Wall Direct		144
*	f4+	Hairy Scary		471
	8a	Hale Bopp		306
*	6a+	Half Crown Corner		260
*	6c	Halibut Giblets		248
	f6A	Han		325
*	6c	Handle With Care		398
	6c+	Handvice		233
*	6b+	Hanging Crack (Bull's H)		392
**	5b	Hanging Crack (Eridge)	121	120
*	6c+	Hangover 1		192
***	6c	Hangover 2		192
4	7a	Hangover 3		194
**	7a+	Hangover Right-hand		194
**	f6A+	Happening, The		370
	3b	Happy Days (Harrison's)		207
*	f7A	Happy Days (High R)		338
*	f5+	Happy Slappy	415	414
	f4	Hard Furka		217
	4b	Hardcore		444
	3a	Harden Gully		95
	3a	Hargreaves		101
	f2	Haribo		215
	f5	Harold Hill Arete		305
*	f4	Hartleys		152
*	6c	Harvester		431
	7b	Harveys		380
4	6c+	Hate	89	91
*	f5+	Havasupai		302
*	f5+	Hawkwood Side-pulls		236
*	f5+	Hazel		153
	f2+	Healy		101
*	5b	Hear No Evil		440
	f2	Heath		101
*	7a+	Hector's House		259
	f2+	Heffalump		110
	f3+	Heffalump - Right		110
	f4+	Heidi		68
**	5a	Hell Wall		265
*	f6A	Hellbender		86
	6c	Helter Skelter		70
	5b	Helyotosis		323
	3a	Hen of the Woods		171
***	6b	Hennessy Heights	97	96
4	6b+	Henry the Ninth	300	298
	f2	Herne the Hunter		372
**	5a	Hibiscus		70
*	6a+	Hidden Arete		294
**	f4	Hidden Gem	369	368
**	f6A	Hidrosis	73	87
*	5a	High Traverse		77
	2a	Hillary		101
*	6a	Hipposuction		147

Route Index

Stars	Grade	Route	Photo	Page
	6b+	Hitchcock's Horror		231
*	2a	Holly Leaf Crack		460
	f3	Holly Slab		325
*	6a+	Holly Tree Wall		429
*	f3+	Home to Roost		376
4	7a	Honeycomb	330	329
**	7a+	Honeycomb Direct		329
	7b+	Honeycomb Variant		329
*	f4+	Hook		417
	f2+	Horizon Wall 1		356
	f2+	Horizon Wall 2		356
*	f2+	Horizon Wall Crack		356
	3c	Horizontal Birch		205
	6b	Hornet		323
	f3+	Hot Stepper		117
*	7a	Hottie		119
*	7b+	Hottie Arete		119
	6b	Hound Dog		430
	6a	Hour Glass		128
	6c	Hull Motors		323
	6c	Hungry Heart		474
	f6C+	Hurricane		153
*	4c	Hut Transverse Arete		312
	3c	Hut Transverse Passage Ordinary Route		312
	4c	Hut Transverse Passage Rufrock Route		318
**	f7B	Hypersonic		132
*	f6B	Hyphenated Jones		153
**	6a+	Hypothesis		432
	f5	I Bet He Drinks at Kensington Palace		154
	f5	I Love Me		407
	f4	I Make Art!		409
*	f6B	I.B's Arete		149
	7b+	I'll Be Back		312
	f5+	I'm not Worried, I'm a Tractor		155
	6b+	Ian's Answer		432
	6c+	Icarus (Bowles)		79
	f6B+	Icarus (Harrison's)		196
	f6A+	Ides of March		331
**	7a	Illusion		462
	6b+	Impacted Stool		132
	f5+	Imperial Knight	235	236
*	6a	Impossibility		390
	f7B	Improbable Mantle, The		116
**	7c	In Crisis		204
	6c+	In Limbo		210
**	6c	In One Hole		439
*	7a+	In the Beginning		140
	6b+	Incisor		184
	f6A+	Inclination to Sin		82
	4b	Index		102
*	f6A	Index Direct		102
	6b+	Indian Face, The		429
	7a+	Indian Railways		305
*	6c	Indian Summer		228
	f7A	Indian Traverse		142
4	7a	Infidel		298
	f5+	Inglenook		371
	f6B	Inglenook Left-hand		371
	f6B+	Inglenook Right-hand		371
	6c	Inimitability		189
**	6a+	Inland Empire		117
*	7a	Innominate Buttress		118
**	6a	Innominate Crack	119	118
	3a	Inside Out		463
	3c	Insinuation Crack		294
4	6b+	Inspiration		83
**	f2+	Introductory Climb		473
	f2+	Introductory Slab		473
	f6A+	Iron Arete		372
*	6c+	Iron Man Tyson		137
	f4+	Ironbar		116
	f3	Isobel		172
4	4c	Isolated Buttress Climb	244	247
*	6a+	Isolated Buttress Direct		247
*	f2	Isolated Slab Centre		245
	f2	Isolated Slab Left		245
	f2	Isolated Slab Right		245
*	2a	Isometric Chimney		267
	6a+	Issingdown		305
**	f7A	It Is What It Is		370
*	f6A	It's Only Natural		352
*	f5+	It's Pub o'Clock		112
	f3+	Jaba's Little Helper		408
	f4+	Jabba		83
	f6A	Jabberwocky		343
	3a	Jack O'Lantern		171
**	6a+	Jackie		86
	f4+	Jackie Direct		86
*	6a+	Jagger		250
*	f5+	Jakku		149
**	6c	Jaws		301
	6b+	Jean Genie		72
	f2	Jelly Baby		215
	f2	Jelly Bean		215
	3b	Jetsam		231
*	7a	Jihad		140
	6b+	Jingowobbly		266
*	f6A	John Player Special		342
	f7B	Joshua		111
*	f4+	Jousting Arete		236
*	6c	Juanita		83
***	8a+	Judamondo		128
**	7c	Jude's Wall		140
**	7a	Judy		289
	7b+	Jug of Flowers		319
	f2+	Jump Start		471
	f4+	Jumper		264
	7a+	Jumping Jack Flash		205
	3a	Junend Arete		207
*	4b	Just Cause		140
*	6a	Just CIA		140
	6a	Just Ice		140
	f2+	Just-In		376
	f6A	Kara		88
*	7b	Karate Liz		431
	7a	Karen's Kondom		242
	f5+	Kate Moss		371
**	7a+	Kathmandu		456
	6b+	Keep the Faith		429
**	6c	Kemp's Delight	81	80
*	7a	Ken Clean Air System		136
**	6b	Ken's Wall		430
*	4b	Kenian Crack		430
	4a	Kennard's Climb	103	94
	6b+	Kestrel		443
4	6a+	Key Wall	468	466
	f5	Key Wall Lower Traverse		466
*	f6A+	Key Wall Upper Traverse		466
	f5	Keystone Cop		150
*	f2+	Keystone Crack		150
	f4	Keystone Face		150
	f3	Keystone Wall		150
*	f5	Kheops Progress		453
*	7a	Kicks		231
	f2	Kids Slab		206
*	7b+	Killiing Joke, A		212
***	7c	Kinda Lingers		312
	7b+	Kinda Lingers Original Start		312
**	f7A+	Kinda Wanders		312
*	7a	Kinetix		132
	f6B	King Arthur		467
	f6A	King Dedede		177
*	7a+	Kinnard		82
	f3	Kippers		375
*	f4	Kirby's Adventures		177
**	6c+	Knam, The		241
	f5+	Kneeling Boulder		453
***	6b	Knife		337
	6b	Knight's Gambit		238
*	6b+	Knight's Move		238
	f5	Knighthood		236
	f7B	Knitwall		74
**	6b+	Knott		394
*	7a+	Knucklebones		75
**	6c	Koffler		92
	f6B	Kop, The		296
*	f6C+	Krafty Undercutz		130
4	7b	Krait Arete	307	306
*	7a+	Kraken		297
*	6b+	Krankenkopf Crack		296
	7a+	Krypton Factor		249
*	3c	Kukri Wall		176
	5a	Kukri Wall Direct		176
	5a	Kukri Wall Tree		176
*	7b+	L'ottimista		466
	6c+	Lady in Mink, A		100
*	6b	Lady Jane		231
	6b+	Lady of the Light Bulb		280
*	7a+	Lager Shandy		192
	7a+	Lamp Light		318
*	6a	Lamplight		444
	6c	Land of Green Ginger, The		181
	6b	Laraletme		178
*	6a+	Larchant		96
*	7c	Larger Frenzy		192
**	6b+	Last Chance		254
*	6b+	Last of the Summer Wine		118
	6a	Layaway		147
	f5+	Layaway Cure		167
**	7a+	Lazy Chive		143
*	6a+	Leaning Crack		474
	5c	Leaning Crack Right-hand		474
	f4	Lecco		218
*	6a+	Lee Enfield		88
**	6c	Left Circle		212
	3c	Left Edge		206
	f3	Leftism		408
	5b	Leg Break		357
	5b	Leg Stump		357
*	7a+	Leglock		292
	6b+	Leisure Line		467
	f4	Lemonade		408
*	f7B+	Lemur, The		344
**	f5	Letterbox		167

Route Index 483

Stars	Grade	Route	Photo	Page
	f4+	Leukwarm		217
	f2	Liberty Cap		172
**	6b	Libra		120
	f6B+	Lichen Prow		344
*	f4	Lid		417
	6c	Life in the Old Dog Yet		149
**	7b	Limpet, The		195
	f4	Lino		101
	f4	Lion's Crack, The		412
	f7B	Lion's Face, The		412
*	f7B	Lion's Head, The		412
***	6c+	Lionheart	437	438
	6a	Liquorice Wood		429
	3b	Little Cave		208
*	6b+	Little Sagittarius		202
***	7a	Lobster	299	298
	f6A	Local Vigilantes		155
	f2	Lolly Pop		215
*	7b+	London Pride		80
**	4c	Long Crack		204
4	6a+	Long Layback	161	194
	f5	Long Reach		218
	6a	Long Stretch (Harrison's)		213
**	6c	Long Stretch (High R)		320
	3a	Longbow Chimney		201
**	7a+	Look Sharp		310
	f6A+	Lord		318
	f6B+	Lord of the Light		111
**	7a	Lou		138
*	7a	Love		91
**	f6B	Love Without Resistance		94
	f2+	Luca		71
**	6c	Lucita		302
	f4	Lugano		218
*	6c	Lunatick		285
*	6c	Luncheon Shelf		194
*	f6A+	Lunge'n'Shelf		331
*	7a	Ly'in, The		84
	6b+	Mad as a Hatter		276
**	f4	Magic Fountain	379	368
	f2+	Magic Mike		417
	f3	Magic Numbers		470
*	6c	Magic Pebble		439
**	f7A	Magnetic	276	298
*	f6B	Magolor		177
	f2+	Malcolm McPherson's a Very Strange Person		377
	6a+	Mamba Crack		305
	4b	Mamba's Come Home to Roost		138
*	6b	Mammoth Wall		111
*	6c	Mania		463
**	6b+	Manita		86
**	6c	Mank, The		241
	f6A+	Mantel, The		414
	6b	Manteloid		444
	6b	Mantelpiece		189
	f6A	Marathon Man		332
	6c	Marcus's Arete		205
	f2+	Marmelade		473
*	6c	Marquita		302
**	f4+	Marry Poppins		412
*	f3+	Mash Potatoes		371
*	f3+	Master		116
	f4	Master Exploder		117
*	f5	Master of Muck		376
	7a+	Mastercard		442
	6a	Matt's Fingertip		223
	6c+	Max		268
**	f6A+	Maximum Orr		82
	f7B	Maybe When You're Older		75
	f2+	Maze Crack		346
*	6b	Meager's Right-hand		84
	f7B+	Mean Goblin		343
**	f5+	Meander		352
	6c+	Meat Cleaver		268
*	7a+	Meaty Thighs		128
*	f3	Medway Slab		455
*	f6C	Meekness Not Weakness		421
	f2+	Meeny		377
**	6c+	Mein Herr		134
	6c+	Mellow Toot		136
*	7a+	Memorialize		390
*	6c	Mental Balance		76
**	4a	Mercator's Projection		101
**	7a	Meridian		442
*	7a+	Meridian Direct		442
	4a	Merlin		443
*	7a	Mervin Direct		310
*	f6B	Meta Knight		177
	3a	Mezzanine		172
	f2+	Michael		71
**	6b	Mick's Wall		80
**	6c+	Mick's Wall Arete	4	80
*	6c+	Mick's Wall Variation		80
	f2+	Micro Machine Left		406
	f2+	Micro Machine Right		406
*	f6C	Micro Second		252
**	5b	Middle and Off		357
*	6a	Middle Stump	351	357
	5a	Middleclass Ponce		130
	6b	Mighty Midge		208
*	6c+	Mike's Left Knee		319
*	f3	Milestone Arete		470
	f6B+	Milestone Mantel		470
	f4	Milestone Right		470
**	f3+	Milestone Stride	469	470
*	f6A	Milly		346
*	f6A	Milly-la-Foret		152
*	f5	Minimum Orr		82
	f4+	Minnow		374
	6c+	Minotaur		390
*	f6A+	Miracle		314
	7a+	Mischivas		259
	8a	Mish Bell		294
*	f6A	Miss Embassy		342
**	7b	Missing Link		282
	f2+	Mist		375
	6c	Mister Splodge		262
*	6a	Misty Wall		148
*	7b+	Mocasyn		302
**	6b+	Mohrenkop		70
*	f7B	Mojo, The		336
	f3+	Mole's Wall		416
	f2+	Monch		217
***	6b	Monkey Nut		338
*	7a	Monkey's Bow		223
**	6a+	Monkey's Necklace		222
*	6c+	Monkey's Sphincter		339
	3c	Monolith Crack		356
*	5c	Monolith Left Buttress		356
*	4a	Monolith Right Buttress		356
*	f6A	Monolithic Man		289
	f2+	Montana		217
****	5a	Moonlight Arete	3	223
**	f3+	Moray		374
***	7a	More Cake for Me		127
*	f6B+	More Footie Fun		455
	7a+	More Funkey than Monkey		131
	f4+	More Ticks for Tim		152
	6c+	Morpheus		98
*	7b	Morpho		290
	6a+	Moss		391
	f6B	Moss Side Story		325
	f3	Moss Wall Centre Block		452
	f3	Moss Wall Left Block - Centre		452
	f3+	Moss Wall Left Block - Left		452
	f4	Moss Wall Left Block - Right		452
	f3	Moss Wall Right Block - Centre		452
	f4	Moss Wall Right Block - Left		452
***	7a	Moving Staircase		287
	7a	Mr Spaceman		249
	7a	Much Too Much		318
**	6c	Mulligan's Wall		316
*	6b	Mumbo Jumbo		70
*	6a+	Murph's Mount		86
*	6c+	Muscle Crack		259
	3a	Mushrooms		171
	f5+	Mustard Seed	419	421
*	6c	My Dear Watson		266
	7a+	Mysteries of the Orgasm		336
	7a	Nail, The		135
*	7a	Natterjack		310
	f2	Naughty Sporty		68
*	6c	Navy Way		326
	5c	NE Corner		477
**	4c	Nealon's		100
	7a	Neighbours		198
**	f7A	Neil's Eliminate		343
*	5b	Nelson's Column		95
4	7a+	Nemesis	317	318
*	7c	Nemesis Inferno		319
	4a	Neptune Arete		391
**	6b+	Nero		86
*	4c	Netwall		74
	7a	Neutral		268
	6b+	Never Forget		432
	6c+	New Hat		174
	f6C+	New Jerusalem		420
	f6C+	New Jerusalem Right-hand		420
	4c	Newman's Arete		392
4	6b	Niblick	230	229
4	f7A	Nicotine Alley	79	79
**	7a	Nigel Mantel		134
**	7b+	Nightfall		137
**	6c+	Nightmare		87
	7a+	Nightrain		381
*	f6B+	Nipple Rash		112
	6c+	No Chance		254
*	6a	Nob Nose		357
	f4+	Nobbly Knee		471
	6c	Nododendron		129
	3a	Noisome Cleft No 2		224
	3a	Noisome Cleft No.1		224

Route Index

Stars	Grade	Route	Photo	Page
	6a+	Noisome Wall		224
	6c+	Noisome Wall Direct		224
*	7c	Nonpareil		122
**	5b	North Wall		339
**	6c	Northwest Corner		246
	6c	Nose Direct		467
*	f5	Nose One		353
**	f2+	Nose Three		354
	f3	Nose Two		353
*	3a	November		99
	f2+	November Rain		376
	6b+	NS (Not Skinnered)		378
	7a+	Nut Tree		196
*	7b	Nutella		82
	6b+	Nuthin' Fancy		120
*	6c+	Nuts, The		220
*	f7A	Oak Tree Corner		346
*	6c	Obelisk		134
	f3	Obscene Gesture		453
	f6A	Ockendon Slab		305
*	5a	October		96
4	6b	Odin's Wall	334	327
*	4c	Off Stump		357
	f2+	OK Corral		169
***	f7A	Old Kent Road		342
*	6c	Oligarchy, The		307
*	f6B+	Oliver and His Amazing Underpants		152
**	7a+	Oliver James		223
**	6b	Oliver's Twist		100
	f3	One Hold Route		453
	f2	One in the Pink		68
*	7c	One Nighter		83
	7a+	One of Our Buzzards is Missing		95
*	3c	One of Our Chimneys Is Missing		294
*	7a	One Up All Up, Except Mat		443
	f5A	Onions		290
	f5	Ooh-er Missus		155
**	4b	Open Chimney (Harrison's)		181
*	f3	Open Chimney (Stone F)		472
	6a	Open Groove		323
*	f6B+	Optic Eye		336
	6a	Optical Racer		156
**	6b+	Orangutang		222
	f6C	Orc's Dyno		346
	f7A	Orcanyon		305
*	4a	Ordinary Route		335
	3c	Original Route		206
	6b+	Orion Arete		280
	3c	Orion Chimney		280
	5a	Orion Crack		280
*	6b	Orr Traverse		80
**	6b	Orrer Crack		326
*	6b	Otra!		98
*	f3	Otter V Portly		416
	4b	Out		357
	6b+	Out Of The Blue		189
	6b	Outer Limits		294
*	6c	Outfall Crack		441
	f6C+	Outspan		312
	6b	Oven Ready Freddy		335
*	f6C+	Over the Hill (Mount Edgcumbe R)		421
**	6c	Over the Hill (U Rocks)		438
	4c	Overhanging Crack		399
*	6b	Pain Killers		253
**	f7B+	Painkiller, The		470
	f4	Paint Job		407
	f5	Paisley		152
*	f7C	Pammy		284
*	f3+	Pan		417
*	f3	Panda Car		173
	f4	Panda Cub		173
*	f5	Panda Pop		173
*	f5	Panda Style		173
**	6c	Panther's Wall		188
	6b+	Papa Heaz		238
*	f6B	Papillon		168
**	f6A+	Parisian Affair	36	124
	6c+	Pascale		220
	3a	Passage Chimney		228
	f3	Passage Direct		166
**	6c	Pastry		79
	4a	Pat's Progress		102
**	7a	Patella		82
**	f7B	Path Seldom Taken, A		293
**	f7A+	Patience		132
*	f5+	Patient Parmer		179
*	f5+	Patrick's Wall		355
	f6B	Pea Cheetah		305
	6b	Peace on Earth		280
	7a	Peapod		305
*	6c	Pearl Necklace		432
	f3	Pedestal Wall		153
*	7a	Pegasus		288
	f6a+	Pelmet	209	197
	5b	Penknife		176
	f6C	Pentecost		372
**	6a	Peregrine		443
*	3c	Perspiration		87
***	6c	Perspiration Direct		86
	7c+	Pet Cemetery		292
	6b	Pete's Reach		231
	f6B	Peter Pan		476
**	6a	Peter's Perseverance		87
	f5	Pharaoh's Curse		453
**	f7C	Phasis		79
***	6c+	Philippa		259
	f5	Philippe		236
	6c+	Photinia		174
**	f6B	Piano		167
	f6A	Picasso		344
	3c	Pickled Pogo Stick		234
*	6b+	Piecemeal Wall		242
***	6b+	Pig's Ear	93	91
4	5a	Pig's Nose	cover, 9	92
***	6b+	Pillar, The	133	132
*	7a	Pincenib		229
*	6b+	Pincenib Arete		229
	6b	Pinchgrip		321
*	6b	Pine Buttress		457
*	6b+	Pine Buttress Direct		457
*	4c	Pine Crack		457
	6a+	Pink Pengster, The		138
*	6b	Pinnacle Buttress Arete		464
*	6a+	Pinnacle Buttress Direct		464
*	4b	Pinnacle Buttress Original		464
	3a	Pinnacle Chimney		465
	f6A+	Pinnacle Gully		328
	f5	Pinnacle's Progress		465
	6a+	Pipe Cleaner		221
*	f7A+	Pirelli		430
	6c+	Plagiarism		224
	7a+	Plantagenet		335
	f4	Planted		408
	f2+	Pleasure Dome		471
	6c+	PMA		304
*	7a+	Poff Pastry		79
	f5+	Pogo		377
**	8a+	Pollet Vertus		247
	6b	Polly Ticks		137
*	6b+	Poltergeist		389
*	7c	Ponytail Pearson (and His Shorts of Doom)		319
*	6c+	Poofy Finger's Revenge		143
**	f6A	Pooh's Route		377
	f6A	Poohped		472
*	5a	Pop's Chimney		97
*	5a	Pop's Slab		97
*	8a	Poppet's Persistence		297
**	7c	Porg's Progress		310
***	6b+	Portcullis		156
*	4b	Possibility Wall		390
	f4	Pot-Belly		375
*	7a+	Powder Monkey		222
*	7a	Power Finger		249
*	f6C+	Powerband, The		268
**	7a	Prang, The		298
*	7a	Prangster, The		297
*	6a+	Praying Mantels		464
*	f6A+	Prelude (Eridge)		127
	f3	Prelude (Stone F)		473
	f6C	Pretentious ... Moi?		155
	f3+	Priapus		333
	7a+	Primate Shot		223
*	4b	Primitive Groove		476
**	5a	Primrose	115	114
	6c+	Proboscis		77
***	f6B	Process of Elimination		96
*	6b	Profiterole		328
	f6B	Projectile		180
*	f3	Proteus		333
***	7a+	Prowess		122
**	6c+	Pseudonym		395
*	6c+	Pseudonym Right-hand		395
	7a	Psycho		222
**	6a	Pull Through		88
**	6c	Pullover		264
	f6A	Pumpkins		216
	7c	Punch		289
	6a+	Pure Arete		280
*	f5	Purgatory		354
	7a	Purvee, The		280
*	6a	Pussyfoot		321
	f4	Puzzle Corner		331
	f3+	Pyramid Route		453
	5c	Python Crack		305
	f6C+	Quality Control		324
**	6a	Quarterdome		201
*	5a	Quirkus		308
**	6c	Quiver		202
**	7c	Quoi Faire		466
	4c	Race Home, The		382
	5c	Rad's Cliff		99
	5c	Rad's Cliff Direct		99
**	7a	Rag Trade		289

Route Index 485

Stars	Grade	Route	Photo	Page
*	f5+	Ragtime		169
	f2+	Ramp-line		408
	3a	Ramp, The (Harrison's)		170
	3c	Ramp, The (Stone F)		457
	4a	Rampette Direct		170
*	6b	Rapunzel		442
	4c	Rattlesnake		305
**	7a	Rattlesnake 2	283	282
*	f3	Ratty	405	416
	f6A+	Re-emergence		311
*	f3+	Reach for the Dead		365
	7a	Reach for the Sky		238
*	f4	Reach of Faith, The		378
**	f7C	Read Line, The		143
	f7A	Real Slim Shady, The		292
	3a	Really Chossy Flake		429
	3c	Recess Wall		290
	3a	Reclamation Gully		76
*	3c	Reclamation Slab Left		76
**	3a	Reclamation Slab Right		76
*	6b+	Reclamation Slap		76
	7b+	Recurring Nightmare		87
*	3a	Red Peg		99
**	f6B	Red River		167
4	f5	Red Snapper		375
	f3+	Redwood		69
	f4+	Referendum		68
	f2+	Reine Sofia		344
*	4c	Remote		460
**	4c	Remus		146
***	7b+	Renascence		285
*	4b	Renison Gully		98
***	7a+	Republic	225	229
*	6a	Reserved		213
	f5+	Resistance		82
**	f7C	Resurrection (High R)		285
**	f5+	Resurrection (Toad)		414
*	f7C	Resurrection Traverse		284
	f2+	Retreat, The		410
*	f6B+	Return of the Mojo		335
*	f6B	Reve		168
**	6c+	Revelations		143
*	6b	Reverse Traverse		242
	6a+	Rhapsody Inside a Satsuma		234
	6a	Rhino's Eyebrow		320
	4a	Rhododendron Route		323
	6b+	Rhody-O		382
	6b	Rib		94
**	5b	Ricochet		88
*	6b+	Rift		268
**	4a	Right Circle		212
**	6c+	Right Unclimbed		266
*	6b	Right Under Your Nose		253
*	5b	Right-hand Crack		182
*	6b	Ringlet		178
**	f6C	Rip, The		297
	6b	Riverdance		204
	f6C+	Road to Salvation, The		372
	6c+	Robin's Route		297
*	6c	Rockney		321
*	f5+	Rodin		344
**	7a	Roofus		320
*	6a	Roger's Wall		444
	f3	Roller Climb		346
	5a	Roman Nose (Bowles)		72
*	6a	Roman Nose (Eridge)		146
**	7a	Roman Nose Direct		146
	6a+	Romulus		147
*	7a	Roobarb		312
*	f5+	Roobarb Arete		312
*	6a	Roof Route		321
	2b	Root Chimney		457
4	4a	Root Route 1		181
	4b	Root Route 1 Direct		181
	6a+	Root Route 1.5		181
*	6c	Root Route 2		181
*	6a+	Root Route 2.5		181
**	6b+	Root Route 3		181
	f4+	Rotpunkt		377
	6c	Rotten Stump Arete		185
	6b+	Rotten Stump Wall		185
	6b	Rough Boy		253
	4c	Route Minor		382
	6c+	Rowan Tree Wall		220
*	f3	Royal Oak	113	112
	6c+	Rum, Bum & Biscuits		326
*	4a	Running Jump		74
*	f6A	Rupert and His Chums		353
	f2	Rusthall Wall		407
**	5a	Sabre Crack		231
	f6A	Safe Sex		125
**	5b	Sagittarius		202
	f6B	Sahara		460
**	6b	Saint's Wall		210
**	7b	Salad Days		292
**	6b+	Salamander Slab		86
	f4+	Saltbox		410
	f2	Salvatore		71
*	f5+	Sand Piper		180
	6c	Sandbag		240
	6b+	Sandcastle		389
**	7a+	Sandman (Bowles)		90
*	f5+	Sandman (High R)		344
*	6a	Sandpipe, The		221
	6b	Sandstone Hell		129
**	6c+	Sandstone Safari		381
***	6c+	Sandstorm		127
	6a+	Sandy Wall		399
**	f7A+	Sansara		124
	f7A	Sansara Right-Hand		124
*	5a	Santa's Claws		75
4	5b	Sapper	23, 62	83
*	4a	Sashcord Crack		198
	6c+	Scimitar		281
*	5a	Scirocco Slab		74
**	4b	Scirocco Wall		74
*	f4	Scoop		411
*	f5+	Scoop Arete		264
*	6c+	Scoop, The (Bull's H)		390
*	f5+	Scoop, The (Harrison's)		264
	f2	Scooped Out		372
**	6a	Scooped Slab		135
*	6b	Scooped Slab Direct		134
***	7a	Scorpion		142
*	4c	Scouter Direct, The		94
	f5	Scrap Arete		325
*	f4	Scrape Wall		407
	6a	Scraping the Barrel		250
	6c	Scrimps		147
**	4b	SE Corner Crack		476
	6b+	Seaman's Wall		323
	f2+	Seat Climb		357
*	6c	Second Chance	255	254
***	8a	Second Generation, The		284
*	4c	See No Evil		440
**	6b	Seltzer		98
*	5b	Senarra		265
*	5c	Senarra Left-hand		265
	7a	Senile Walk		294
	4b	Sentry Box		391
	6a	Sentry Box Arete		391
	6b	Sequins of Cosmic Turbulence		321
4	6c+	Serenade Arete	1, 85	82
	6b	Serendipity		182
**	6b	Set Square Arete		240
*	6b	Sewer Wall		222
	6a+	Sewer-Rowan Connection		221
**	6a+	Sewer, The		221
**	f7B+	Shadow of the Wind		289
	5b	Shanty Wall		148
	6c	Sharp Dressed Man		224
**	7a	Shattered		319
*	6b+	Shelter Arete		307
**	f6C	Sheriff, The		169
***	f6A+	Shidid		352
***	6c+	Shield, The		394
*	6b+	Shodan		259
	f2+	Shoe People		406
*	4a	Short Chimney		310
	3a	Short Chimney 2		305
*	f2+	Short Sharp C, The	258	376
*	f5+	Short Work		153
	f3	Shrooms		172
	f5+	Shytte		180
	f5+	Sideshow		332
**	f5+	Sidre	413	411
*	6a+	Siesta Wall	35	118
*	6b	Signalbox Arete		208
	5b	Silly Arete		429
	f3	Silly Corner		323
	f6A	Silver Star		169
	5a	Silvie's Slab		96
	7a+	Simian Crimp		339
*	6a+	Simian Face		338
*	6b	Simian Face Direct		338
**	6b+	Simian Mistake		339
4	6a+	Simian Progress		338
	6a+	Simpering Savage		477
*	f3+	Simplon Route		218
	2a	Simpson		101
	f7B	Sinbad		323
*	3c	Sing Sing		86
	f6C	Single Life		378
	6c	Singlet		178
	6a+	Sinners Slimebag		210
*	5a	Six Foot		96
	7b+	Skallagrigg		90
*	f6B	Skid Marx		264
*	4a	Skiffle		79
	7a	Skin Job		238
*	5c	Slab		191
*	f2+	Slab Arete		459
*	4b	Slab Buttress		458
	4a	Slab Buttress Centre		458
*	f2	Slab Centre		170
*	4a	Slab Chimney (Bull's H)		396

Route Index

Stars	Grade	Route	Photo	Page
	3c	Slab Chimney (High R)		294
	6a	Slab Crack		191
**	6a+	Slab Direct (Harrison's)		191
*	f3	Slab Direct (Stone F)		459
	f2	Slab Left (Harrison's)		170
	f2+	Slab Left (Stone F)		459
	f2	Slab Right		170
*	5a	Slab Variant		396
	6b+	Slant Eyes		302
*	4a	Slanting Crack (Eridge)		134
	6c	Slanting Crack (Harrison's)		182
*	f5+	Slap Happy		325
	f5+	Slap My Boy Up		407
	f4	Slappy Arete		325
*	f3+	Sleeping Lion, The		412
	f4	Sleeping with Allsorts		428
**	f5	Sleepy Hollow		406
*	f7A	Slick City		327
**	6b	Sliding Corner		185
4	6c	Slim Finger Crack	211	204
*	f6C	Slopertrocity		287
*	f5	Slopey Goodness		372
	f6B	Sloping Beauty		346
**	f7C+	Slow Pull, The		342
*	7b	Slowhand		301
	6c+	Slyme Cryme		77
	3a	Small Bit of Black, A		182
***	3c	Small Chimney	214	212
*	6b	Small Wall		212
*	6b	Smart		268
	6b	Smear Campaign		184
	f7A+	Smile, The		420
*	6b+	Smiliodon		188
*	7b+	Smoke		316
*	4a	Smooth Chimney		294
*	f6B	Snail Bail		128
**	7a	Snail Trail		129
*	f6A+	Snake Charmer		411
	3a	Snake's Crawl		208
*	f6A	Snakebite		411
	6c+	Snap,Crackle...POP!...Splat		135
	6a+	Snip in Time, A		428
*	6a+	Snout	190	188
*	3c	Snout Crack		188
	8a	Snowdrop		297
*	7a+	So What?		297
	6c	Sod, The		224
*	7b	Soft Rock		182
	6b	Soft Rock'er		243
	4b	Solo (Bull's H)		392
	f6A	Solo (High R)		325
	4b	Solo Right-hand		392
**	6b+	Solstice		267
*	6b	Solution		432
**	6c	Something Crack		327
**	f7B+	Sonic Blue		79
	f2	Sonny		71
*	f5	Sonny Dribble Chops		153
*	f6A+	Sooty		371
	6a	Sorrow		285
	4c	Sorrow Right-Hand		285
***	7a	Sossblitz		228
	f4+	Southern Chimes		476
	f6B	Southern Chimes Traverse		476
*	f7A	Southern Softie	348	352
*	6c+	Southwest Corner		247
	f6C	Spanked		296
	5b	Speak No Evil		440
	7a	Special Invitation		174
*	6c+	Sphinx, The		339
*	f2	Spice		68
**	6a+	Spider Wall		254
**	f6B+	Spider Wall Traverse		254
*	3c	Spider's Chimney		294
***	f4+	Spleen Slab		353
	6b	Splendeedo		129
	5b	Spoon		323
	f2+	Sporty		408
	6a+	Spot the Dog and the Breath of Death		130
**	f4	Spotter		407
*	6b+	Spout Buttress		196
**	6b	Spout Crossing		196
	f2+	Spray		407
*	6c+	Sputnik		339
	6a	Squank		224
**	6b+	Square Cut		398
	7a	Squeak Ya Heel Cups		395
	4c	St Patrick's Chimney		428
*	4b	St. Gotthard		218
	f4	Stag (Happy)		371
	6b+	Stag (Harrison's)		233
	f2+	Stag Arete		371
	f6A	Stag Doo		371
*	f6A	Stalactite		264
*	6c	Stardust		192
*	5a	Starlight	219	223
	f2+	Starting Block		374
*	7a+	Station to Station		79
*	6c	Steamroller	151	156
	2c	Steck		101
***	6c+	Steelmill		140
*	6c+	Stem Son		138
	f6A	Step of Faith		117
	f6A	Step On		323
	f3+	Step Up		471
	4a	Steph		184
	3b	Stepped Slab		172
***	6b	Steps Crack		287
	f5+	Sticky Fingers		476
	6b	Sticky Wicket		185
	f4+	Still, It Could Be Worse		155
*	6c	Sting, The		205
***	f7A+	Stinging Nettle		476
***	f7A	Stinging Nettle Variation		476
**	6c	Stirling Moss		134
*	4a	Stone Farm Chimney		455
*	4b	Stone Farm Crack		457
*	f4	Stonefish		374
	7b	Stoneman		90
	7a	Storming Up the Cuvier Remparts		246
	6b	Stranger than Friction		184
	5c	Strangler		294
*	f6C	Strong Struggle		168
**	f4	Strongbow		414
	7a+	Stubble		268
***	6b	Stupid Effort		204
	f3+	Sub-space Mushroom		172
	f2+	Substance		333
*	f6A	Sugarplum		79
	f6A+	Sullivan's Stake		180
	f6A+	Sullivan's Travels		180
	5c	Sun Ray		267
	6c	Sun Ray Eliminate		267
*	f5	Sunset Wall		167
**	5a	Sunshine Crack		241
	6b+	Sunzilla		290
*	f7A	Superfly		296
	f7A	Superman		288
***	7b+	Supernatural	195	195
**	f6B	Supraspinatus		195
	f5	Sushi		374
	6b	SW Corner		475
4	6a+	SW Corner Scoop	446	475
**	6b	Swastika		87
	6c	Sweet Carol		456
**	6a+	Swing Face	322	321
**	6b+	Swing Face Direct		321
	3a	Tab Chimney		243
	6c+	Take That 'effing Chalk Bag Off...		212
*	2a	Tame Corner		232
*	3a	Tame Variant		232
	f4	Tango		377
**	6c	Target		88
	f6B	Target Direct		88
*	f5	Tarkin Slab		311
	6b	Taurus		390
*	7a	Teddy Bear's Picnic		174
*	7a+	Telegram Sam		289
*	7c	Tempestivity		224
***	7c	Temptation		82
	6b	Ten Foot Pole		224
**	f4+	Testimony		324
	7a	That Man's an Animal		202
*	7c+	Them Monkey Things		87
*	6c+	Thieving Gypsies		87
**	6b+	Thin		462
*	7b	Thing, The		83
*	6a+	Thingamywobs		256
	4b	Thingy		256
*	f4+	Thinner		354
*	6c	Thirteenth Light, The		438
	f3	Thomas the Tank		472
*	6b+	Thoroughly Kentish		380
*	f6C	Through the Dust		421
	f6A	Thrust		327
*	6c	Thrutch		131
	f6A	Thug		354
	f3	Thunder Dome		116
	f3	Tiger the Tiger		473
*	f3	Tight Chimney		179
*	f5+	Tight Chimney Direct		180
**	7a	Tilley Lamp Crack		318
*	4b	Tim Nice But Dim Esquire		428
**	7b+	Time Waits for No One		396
*	6b	Time Warp		476
	f3	Tiny Wall		472
	7a	Tiptoe through the Lichen		256
	6a	Tiptoe through the Tulips		258
	f6A+	Titch Arete		352
*	6b	TNT		78
*	f5+	Toad		179
	f4	Toad Arete		400
*	f2+	Toad Wall		400
	f2+	Toad Wall Left-Hand		400
	4a	Toadstool Crack		140
***	f6B+	Tobacco Road		79
***	f6B+	Tobacco Road - Extension		79
*	5a	Toeing the Line		232

Route Index

Stars	Grade	Route	Photo	Page
*	6c	Toevice		233
	f2	Tom		71
*	f6B	Tom's Mantel		342
*	6b	Tomcat / Simon's Wall		188
**	7a	Too Crimpy for Chris		290
*	7a+	Too Hard for Dave		293
	6c+	Too Hot to Handle		398
*	f6A+	Too Short to Mention		124
**	7a	Too Tall for Tim		293
	6c+	Tool Wall		337
	6c+	Toothpick		337
*	6c+	Top Cat		456
	f4+	Toreador		68
**	f6A+	Torque Wrench		168
**	f6A+	Torque Wrench Left		168
***	7a	Tortoise on a Spin Out	17	130
*	7a	Touch Down		142
	7a	Touch Too Much, A		319
*	6b	Touch, The		440
*	6c	Toxophilite		202
*	6b+	Trainer Drainer		120
	f5+	Transparent Accelerating Banana		472
	3a	Tree Climb		388
	5a	Tree Route (Bassett's Farm)		429
	f4	Tree Route (Eridge)		155
	4a	Trees are Green		174
	3a	Trembling Merulius		291
	6a	Triangle Arete		396
	3a	Triangle Climb		398
*	6c+	Triceratops		132
	f4+	Tricky Dicky		324
	3a	Trident Arete		391
	3a	Trident Chimney		391
	3a	Trident Left		391
*	f5	Trigger		169
*	6c	Trip of the Psychedelic Tortoise		181
*	6a	Trouble with Rubble		444
*	f3	Truncate		124
**	6a+	TT		91
	7a	Tubby Hayes is a Fats Waller		281
	6a	Tubesnake Boogie		224
*	f2+	Tullis		101
	f2+	Turkey Breast and Gravy		400
**	f7A+	Turning the Leaf		131
	6a+	Tusk		111
	6b	Tusk Direct		111
*	f7B+	Tusky		137
	6a	Tweedle Dee		138
	6b	Tweedle Dum		138
*	7a	Twiglet		178
	f6B	Twilight Zone, The		86
**	f7A+	Twinkle Toes		288
**	f7B	Twisted Vegas		79
*	f6B+	Twitch		352
*	6c+	Two Fine Jugs		337
	6b+	Two Short		120
	6b	Two Step (Bowles)		70
	f5+	Two Step (Happy)		377
**	5a	Two-Toed Sloth		243
4	6b+	Uganda Wall	434	438
**	6c	Umbilicus		72
4	6b+	UN		95
	6b	Uncertainty		388
*	f6B	Unclimbed Traverse		266
4	6b	Unclimbed Wall	261, 263	266
*	6b+	Unclimbed Wall Direct		266
*	6b	Unclimbed Wall Variation		266
	4b	Undercut Rib		382
**	4b	Undercut Wall	463	463
	4a	Undercut Wall Arete		463
*	f5+	Underverse		372
	f6A+	Unfinished Business		319
**	7c+	Unforgettable		314
*	7a	Upside Downies		91
*	7a	Urban Jock		77
	3c	Urban Slab		172
	4a	Usurer		172
	6a	Usurper		175
**	f4	Valhalla Wall		355
	f6A	Valkyrie Arete		354
*	f5+	Valkyrie Wall		354
**	f7A+	Vandal		288
*	f6A	Vapour Trails		143
***	f6C	Velcro Arete		130
	f7B+	Velcro Wall		130
	6b+	Venison Burger		233
	f3	Venom		216
	f3	Verbier		217
**	7a+	Very Steep Moving Staircase		287
	6b	Very Very Fat		462
**	4c	Vice, The		233
	6b	Victoria		234
	f2	View, The		410
*	6b	Viking Line		148
	f6A+	Village Life		327
*	6c+	Vingt-et-un		328
	7a	Violent Sprat, The		175
**	6a+	Viper Crack	275	319
	f2	Vito		71
*	6b	Vulture Crack		205
*	7a	Waffer Thin		134
***	6c	Wailing Wall		249
	7a	Wailing Wall Eliminate		249
*	5a	Waistline		388
	f2+	Walk in the Park		409
	6b+	Wall E Mammoth		111
4	6c	Wall, The	385	394
	6c+	Wallow, The		253
*	5a	Wally		100
	6b	Waltzing Buzzard, The		444
	6a+	Wander at Leisure		260
**	5a	Wanderfall		260
	f3+	War Horse		236
*	f6A+	Warm Up	373	372
*	3c	Warning Rock Chimney		294
**	7c+	Watchmen, The		120
***	7c+	Watchtower, The		120
	f2	Weasels, The		416
	5b	Weeping Slab		184
	f6C	Welcome to the Jungle		378
	7a	Well Left!		114
*	7a	Wellington Boot		231
**	4a	Wellington's Nose		229
	3a	Wells's Reach		95
*	f5+	West Face Route	169	168
	f5	West Valley Wall Traverse		371
	f5	West Wall (Happy)		371
4	6a+	West Wall (Harrison's)	251	247
**	7b+	What Crisis?		204
*	6c	What the Buck		441
	7a+	What the Butler Saw		229
	6a+	Whatsaname		256
	7a+	Whiff Whaff		327
*	3a	Whimper		101
*	f6A	White Lightning		414
*	f6C	White Lincoln		152
*	7a+	White Verdict		84
	2a	Wide Crack		438
**	f5	Wildcat Wall		232
	f5	William Marshal's Sloppiness		236
	3a	William's Layback		102
*	f3+	Willows, The		416
	f2	Wilson		101
	6b	Wind and Wuthering		444
	f6A	Wind Me Up		475
	f2+	Window Smasher		68
*	3c	Windowside Spout		197
	f6B+	Winter Blues		370
	6c	Wisdom		184
***	f7C+	Wish, The	340	342
*	f6A+	Wishful Thinking		331
*	6b+	Witches Broomstick		268
*	f6B+	Without Acid		342
*	4a	Wizard		171
	3a	Wizard's Little Apprentice		171
	f5	Wobble		153
*	7c+	Wonder Boy		282
	3a	Wonderwall		356
*	6a+	Wonderwall Ramp		356
	f3+	Wooden Stump		166
	7a	Woodside Blossom		232
	f6A	Woofus Wejects		331
**	7b+	Woolly Bear		246
4	7a	Woolly Cub		246
*	7b+	Wrecker, The		95
*	4a	Wye Chimney		294
*	5a	Y Crack		110
*	f7A	Yankee Affair		124
*	f3	Yellimo		324
*	7a	Yellow Soot		136
	4b	Yellowstone Crack		390
	3b	Yellowstone Wall		389
*	3b	Yew Crack		130
*	f3+	Yew Tree Crack		352
	f3	Yew Tree Wall		352
*	6b	Yew Wall		389
	f6A+	Yin-Yarn		177
*	f7A+	Yoda		311
*	f7C	Yoda Assis		311
	4b	Yorker, The		357
	6c	Yosemite Big Wall Climb		201
	f4	You Make Toast		409
	f5	Young Frau		217
**	4c	Yoyo		84
***	f5	Z'Mutt		342
	f6B+	Zacchaeus		372
4	6a	Zig-Zag Wall		268
***	6a+	Zig-Zag Wall Direct		268
*	f6A	Ziggy		166
	f2+	Zog the Dog		473
	f4	Zola		346
*	7a	Zoom		75
*	7a	Zugabe		98
*	7b+	Zugzwang		129

General Index and Map

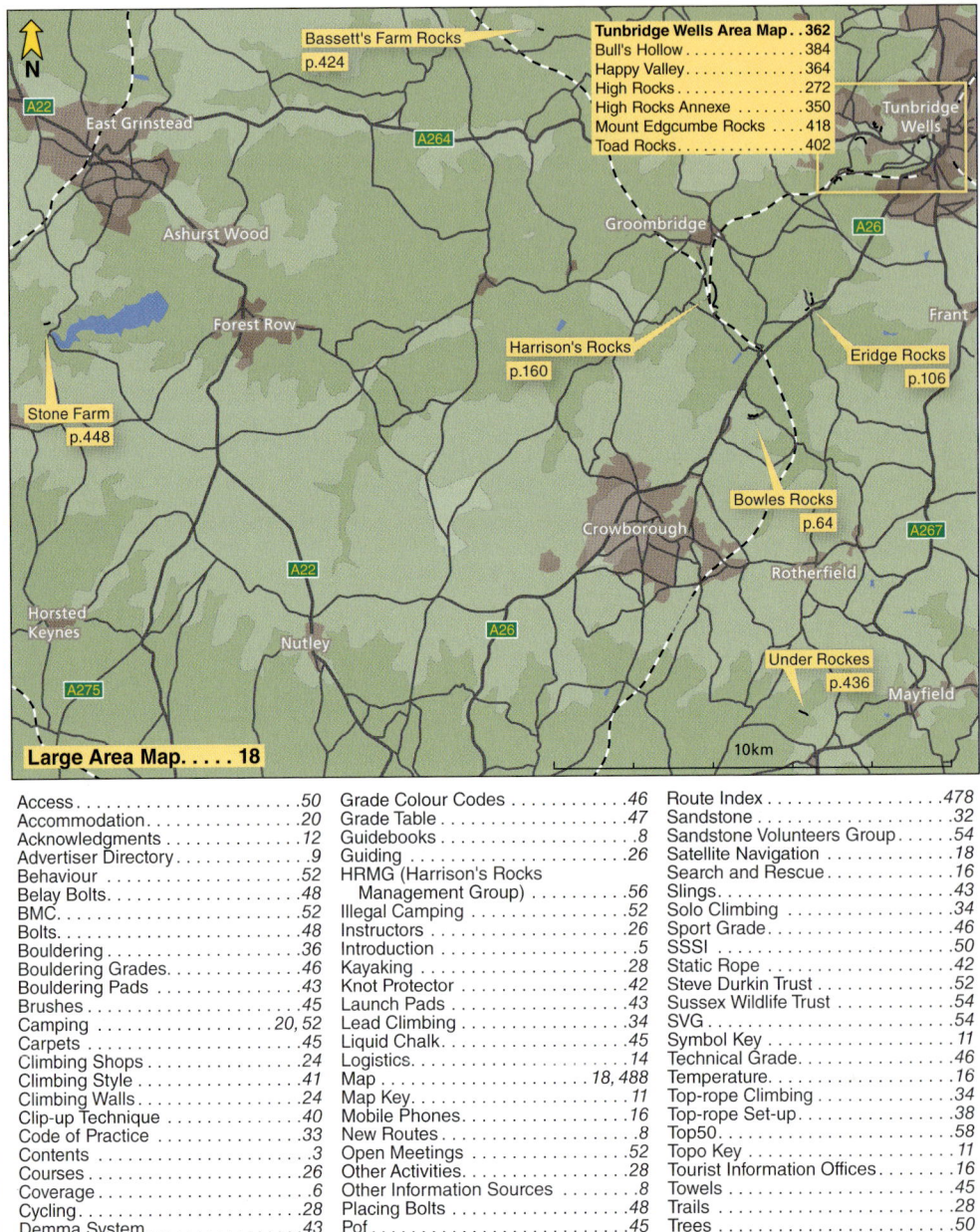

Access 50	Grade Colour Codes 46	Route Index 478
Accommodation 20	Grade Table 47	Sandstone 32
Acknowledgments 12	Guidebooks 8	Sandstone Volunteers Group 54
Advertiser Directory 9	Guiding 26	Satellite Navigation 18
Behaviour 52	HRMG (Harrison's Rocks	Search and Rescue 16
Belay Bolts 48	Management Group) 56	Slings 43
BMC 52	Illegal Camping 52	Solo Climbing 34
Bolts 48	Instructors 26	Sport Grade 46
Bouldering 36	Introduction 5	SSSI 50
Bouldering Grades 46	Kayaking 28	Static Rope 42
Bouldering Pads 43	Knot Protector 42	Steve Durkin Trust 52
Brushes 45	Launch Pads 43	Sussex Wildlife Trust 54
Camping 20, 52	Lead Climbing 34	SVG 54
Carpets 45	Liquid Chalk 45	Symbol Key 11
Climbing Shops 24	Logistics 14	Technical Grade 46
Climbing Style 41	Map 18, 488	Temperature 16
Climbing Walls 24	Map Key 11	Top-rope Climbing 34
Clip-up Technique 40	Mobile Phones 16	Top-rope Set-up 38
Code of Practice 33	New Routes 8	Top50 58
Contents 3	Open Meetings 52	Topo Key 11
Courses 26	Other Activities 28	Tourist Information Offices 16
Coverage 6	Other Information Sources 8	Towels 45
Cycling 28	Placing Bolts 48	Trails 28
Demma System 43	Pof 45	Trees 50
Descent Method 41	Previous Guidebooks 8	Tunbridge Wells Commons
Destination Planner 60	Public Transport 18	Conservators 54
Dogs 50	Pubs 22	UKClimbing Logbook 10
Eco Balls 45	PVC Braid Tubing 43	Vandalism 52
Emergencies 16	QR Codes 18	Volunteer Groups 54
Extended Top-rope Set-up 39	Rainfall 16	Walks 28
Fire 50	Rescue 16	Weather 16
Gear 42	Restrictions 50	Websites 8
Gear Shops 24	Rockfax App 10	When to Go 16
Getting Around 18	Rope Protector 43	Where to Stay 20
GPS Locations 18	Ropes 43	Working Routes 41